Weathering

Other Books by the Author

Cosmic Ray Origin Theories (Editor)

Future Facts: The Way Things Are Going to Work in the Future in Technology, Science, Medicine and Life

Weathering

*How the atmosphere conditions
your body, your mind,
your moods—and your health*

BY
Stephen Rosen

M. EVANS and Company, Inc. NEW YORK, NEW YORK

Library of Congress Cataloging in Publication Data

Rosen, Stephen, 1934–
    Weathering: how the atmosphere conditions your
body, your mind, your moods—and your health.

    Bibliography: p.
    Includes index.
    1. Weather—Mental and physiological effects.
I. Title.
QP82.2.C5R67   155.9'15   78-24560
ISBN 0-87131-267-0

M. Evans and Company, Inc.
216 East 49 Street
New York, New York 10017

Design by Robert Bull

Manufactured in the United States of America

9 8 7 6 5 4 3 2 1

Endpapers: Cosmographic Chart of Winds.
Prescientific peoples attributed personalities and human characteristics to
many weather elements to explain their workings and effects. Zeus is seen at
the top, left of center, astride his eagle and holding lightning in his right
hand. From *Cosmographie*, Petrus Apianus, Antwerp, 1581.

"Your father has been the sunshine of my life," my mother told me as she was dying. She loved sunshine, she loved life, and she radiated sunshine and life to everyone who knew her.

Weathering was one of the many things she did well. This book is for Emma Katzenelson Rosen (June 21, 1907–February 9, 1978), in loving tribute to the sweetness and light, the sunshine and life, she gave all of us.

Contents

Introduction: Why Everyone Talks About the Weather

The atmosphere energizes us. It has engineered the appearance, the development, the evolution, the racial differentiation of *Homo sapiens*—and perhaps even the creation of human genius.

Our ancestors probably knew better than we that weather and climate determine the range and direction of human competence, that weather and climate establish levels of our biological performance. Because 98 percent of our skin is in intimate contact with the ocean of air that engulfs us, at once our ancestral blanket, home, and master, the atmosphere *conditions* humanity. The weather, figuratively, *paraphrases* us.

The weather paraphrases us when the alpine foehn spills over the mountains into Munich or the Israeli sharav sweeps across the desert—leaving eye-popping hangovers, elevated blood pressures, coronaries, strokes, suicides, and traffic accidents in their wake. When London's "killer fog" of 1952 was responsible for 12,000 deaths, the weather matters.

The weather matters when the Luftwaffe could not penetrate the heavy fog that shrouded the Allied evacuation of Dunkirk or when the Japanese bombed Pearl Harbor under cover of rain. The weather matters on a Montana cattle ranch when the temperature is 45 degrees below zero and the livestock are starving because the snow is four feet deep and suddenly a warm wind of reprieve—the chinook, or snow-eater—in a life-giving rescue from disaster, melts the snow and sends the thermometer soaring in minutes.

The statement, "Everyone talks about the weather, but no one does anything about it," was never true. Merely consider the man who invented air conditioning. There are very few others—the ones who do something special about the weather. Scientists down through the ages (see Appendix A) have tried to understand how we are conditioned by weather, and contemporary scientists (virtually none American) still seek the connections between weather and people. These scientists call themselves biometeorologists.

Human biometeorology spans two vast territories of knowledge: the human body—its behavior, emotions, moods, illnesses, and health—and the atmospheric environment—the air, the weather, the climate. We may overreact to the atmosphere's majesty, yet we underreact to its subtleties. As the reader will see, human biometeorology *is* a majestic subject, unique for its minute phenomena yet massive scale, unique for the delicacy of our scientific observations and yet inferences that are touched with grandeur.

A classic fallacy in logic assumes that if one event occurs *after* another, it occurs *because* of the other (in Latin: *post hoc, ergo propter hoc*). It has been observed that in ancient times it almost always rained after battles. One could explain that those vast armies clashing on the battlefield raised vast amounts of dust which caused the downpour, that moisture condensing on the dust particles precipitated rainfall. One *could* explain it this way, and one would be *wrong*. In fact the generals of those ancient times invariably chose to enter battle on sunny, clear days—when they could see their adversaries—and rainfall almost always follows clear weather.

Human biometeorology is filled with similar cautionary tales. We are told to beware the loaded assumptions of cause and effect. Perhaps this explains why human biometeorology is forsaken in the United States. Virtually all of our physicians ignore or are unaware of the research reported here, particularly how the weather changes our body's response to medical drugs (see Appendix F). It is like throwing the baby out with the bathwater. American physicians discount or disregard the effect of weather on health probably because they were not taught otherwise, because human biometeorology is absent from medical school curricula. There are a few doctors who properly advise their patients to relocate in Arizona or Florida, but too often physicians are germ-killers when they should be physiologists; too often they have forgotten or never knew how we are inescapably yoked to and enslaved by the atmosphere. The penultimate chapter, various charts, the Appendix, and Chapter Notes are for those (skeptical physicians and meteorologists?) who may disbelieve results without scientific evidence.

A wide audience deserves to know these results for several reasons. The United States is behind, way behind, in biometeorology, and I would urge new research and encourage new interest. Normal weather injures more people than pollution of the air and water combined. In 1977, health costs ran to some $163 billion. A National Science Foundation report estimates that all kinds of "stress" erodes human performance and drains our economy of over $100 billion annually. And if a cold winter shaves off some $9 to $15 billion from our disposable income, weather-induced stress, which aggravates health problems, may cost the country perhaps $10 or $20 billion annually.

On the other side is perhaps half a billion dollars spent annually on weather forecasting and research, a pittance compared to the costs of weather ignorance. We need a joint effort—between med-men and met-men—to prevent or do something about weather-induced disorders. Europeans already provide medical–weather forecasts that tell physicians which of their patients will suffer what symptoms the next day or two. Because American scientific talent is abundant, because our forecasts of weather are increasingly better, because our health care is superlative, because our research capability is excellent, we can do it. And because perhaps 115 million Americans are weather-sensitive weather-addicts (see Chapter 2), we should do it.

Televised weather commentary enjoys consistently high ratings, but nine out of ten Americans want even more weather information (see Chapter 1). And our population shifts of the future will favor those age brackets—the very old, for example—who are most profoundly under the spell of weather.

In his novel Storm, George Stewart chronicled the evolution of a storm from its birth as a small low-pressure area southeast of Japan to its death over the United States twelve days later. The storm had a singular meaning to each character in the novel. To the farmers it meant relief from a serious drought. To the superintendent of a hydroelectric plant it was a close encounter with death. To the road maintenance crew on Route 40 it meant extra hard work removing snow from the road over Donner Pass. To the passengers on an airliner over Nevada it gave an unpleasant hour of airsickness and the joy of a safe landing. These singular experiences of the storm were matched by singular descriptions of it. Newspaper editors wrote human interest stories on the lives and crops lost. The pious quoted the psalmist: "Fire and hail, snow and vapours; stormy wind fulfilling his word." The mayor of New York, in an interview, calculated the cost of snow clearance. The meteorologist recorded the storm in terms of numbers representing air pressures, temperatures, cloud covers, winds, and precipitation in its path. Each personal experience or description, altered by the storm, exemplifies weathering.

In the universe of facts, only a very few are both true *and* interesting. Or, put differently, the trouble with what everyone knows is that no one knows it with enthusiasm and accuracy. I have sought to be accurate, enthusiastic, and interesting about a subject everyone talks about incessantly. Why does everyone talk about it? Because to each of us, the weather is a plural experience—with a singular feel.

One:
The Weather
Experience

Tell me what you think of the weather, and I shall know what to think of you.
—psychiatrist, to patient

Every stimulus is a second stimulus.
—Norbert Wiener

The climatic influence runs deep . . . at the deepest level of the subconscious mind of all those descended from ice age people, there swirls the genetic memory of an unending snowstorm.
—Loren Eisely

I remember the clean sparkling days, bright and cool, which come toward the end of summer, the sort of days my neighbor can't stand. He calls them "suicide days." Since I too have sometimes been saddened by the last days of August, I have tried to find out what it is about them that clutches at his vitals, but he can only say that he feels depressed, as though something were hanging over him. Those days provide perfect weather for hauling his traps, but that doesn't seem in any way to compensate for the melancholy which he receives, collect, from the white clouds in the perfect sky . . .
—E. B. White

Preceding Page: Wind Tower of Athens
The eight-sided tower was erected in the second or first century B.C. Each octagonal side faces a wind direction, and has its own sculpture. Each wind is named for a person, whose personal or physical attributes represent the wind.

Weathering

Weathering is what we do to get through life's weather—those stressful events and vicissitudes, those atmospheric turbulences and swirling vortexes, those "tides in the affairs of men."

Disintegrating under the action of weather is weathering. Exposure to the elements—wear and tear—is weathering. Being beaten by the weather, weather-beaten, is weathering. Aging and suffering, even dying, is weathering.

But weathering is also maturating and growing. Weathering is also riding out the storm of change. Weathering is also becoming weather-proof. Weathering is surviving, thriving. Defending oneself against repetitive environmental assaults—a sure sign of adaptability and good health—is weathering.

"Beat this weather!" Hesiod advised his brother twenty-eight centuries ago. "Get on homeward before the darkening cloud from the sky can gather about you." Clothe that thin layer of air that clings to you always, your air skin, or *micro*climate, and that is weathering. Heat or cool your *eco*climate, the building or shelter you inhabit, and that is weathering. Outside your door is an air mass, the *geo*climate, an ocean of atmosphere. You can change it by travel. Or, if you want a change in the weather, as they say in Vermont, "stand still a moment."

> Nothing is as consistently fascinating, variable, unpredictable and common to all as the day's weather and a hint of what will involve us tomorrow. . . . In a way, weather is about the only news that is totally new every twenty-four hours whether you're six or sixty.

We may resonate or reverberate to weather. Our mood response—from sad to mad to glad to bad—has vast variety. We may rejoice in our ponderous indifference or our exquisite sensitivity to weather. And these too are weathering.

No two people are alike, no weather situation is ever repeated, and no single individual is always the same. And yet there is a single explanation for our variety of weather response, as we shall see before this chapter ends. But first, your personal weather profile.

3

Your Weather-Sensitivity Risk-Factor Profile

Give yourself the indicated points if you answer "yes" to a question. Please answer each question.

Physique	points
Are you lean, slender, or lanky?	3
Are you muscular or of average build?	0
Are you broad, stocky, or stout?	1

Temperament
Do you tend to be amiable, extroverted, or jolly?	1
Are you often emotionally changeable, excitable?	3
Do you tend to be easily led or acquiescent?	3
Are you often irritable or moody?	1
Do you tend to be easily depressed or pessimistic?	2
Are you often shy, inhibited, or private?	3
Do you tend to be nervous?	4

Socioeconomic Status (approximate)
Are you a professional, executive, or upper-class person?	3
Are you a middle-management person or white-collar worker?	0
Are you a blue-collar, clerical, or factory worker?	3

Age
Are you 10–19 years old?	3
Are you 20–29 years old?	2
Are you 30–39 years old?	1
Are you 40–49 years old?	2
Are you 50–59 years old?	3
Are you older?	4

Sex
Are you female?	3

Add up the points you have checked to find your total. *The total is your weather-sensitivity risk score.*

- A score of 0 to 5 points indicates that you are relatively weather-*resistant*, or generally indifferent except for the seasonally dependent illnesses, or normal, weather-related diseases, and the daily, monthly, or yearly weather changes.
- From 6 to 10 points suggests that you are weather-*receptive*, or frequently aware of your reactions to weather changes.
- Between 11 and 15 points, you are weather-*sympathetic*, or never indifferent to weather conditions.
- If your score is 16 to 20 points, you are weather-*susceptible*, or always in touch with the weather and the symptoms it induces in you.
- From 21 to 25 points, you are weather-*responsive*; every passing front is felt in your body, your moods, and your behavior; they mirror the atmospheric conditions.
- Above 25 points is weather-*keenness*, the penultimate sensitivity to weather in which severe pain or pleasure tends to accompany each weather situation. In exceptional cases extraordinary feelings about the weather may be experienced by those rare individuals (often geniuses) who have a special "feel" for the weather, or who are weather-*intimate*.

(A lengthy and detailed self-discovery sensitivity questionnaire, enumerating a wide range of symptoms, will be found in Appendix C.)

"My psychiatrist asked what was bothering me one day," a friend tells me. "I told him the weather had me down. He said, 'Well, enough of that. Let's talk about what's *really* bothering you.' I lost confidence in him," she adds, "from that day forward. You see, it really was the *weather*."

"Lead off with the weather," the television news producer says, "when there's no exciting news breaking, give them the old grabber! You can tell from the phone calls, the ratings, and a survey that people really want *more* weather stories, not less."

"Darkening of the sky," a renowned meteorology professor tells me, "induces apprehension. So will a sudden gust of wind. But the first, new, clear snow induces smiles and friendliness between people passing on the street—at least that's the small-town response, the rural response. The first nice day after a week of rain or cold weather, or the common-plight-induced togetherness after a hurricane or severe thunderstorm, seems to be almost instinct."

The female rock star: "Sure, our audience is more fidgety in hot weather in a tent. They're sweating . . . and even *we* don't give our best then."

A twenty-eight-year-old flight attendant: "I *love* rainy days! It's the only time I stay home. I hibernate. It's comfy. City folks wouldn't know it, but even cows lie down when it's going to rain. But I don't like being in a plane when it's raining or bad weather. There's turbulence. It's very noticeable, the effect on the passengers. They're irritable and jumpy. All the freakiness comes out; the passengers want *everything!* They're outrageous and impolite."

She continues, "My mother is very emotional at the change of the seasons. We noticed that even as kids. She beat us up more, she was more worried, she got hysterical, you know, hyper.

"All airline attendants work in a controlled atmosphere. The cabin of a commercial airliner, like a DC-10, is kept at about one percent humidity. We feel our skin get dry. Because we travel, sometimes we feel several changes of weather in one day. But I like it. Any woman would, because you get to change clothes so often.

"My husband had a football injury and surgery on his knee. He just about dies in damp weather, either hot or cold. But no matter what kind it is, I *love* weather!"

The commercial airline pilot, forty-three years old, says: "I've had young, inexperienced copilots working for me who are *deathly afraid* of windy, gusty conditions. Maybe one-tenth of them are. Others get very uptight in thunderstorms. But I like that kind of weather to fly in. It's challenging.

"The bad weather bothers our flight attendants. There's a difference, over the intercom, in their voices: nervous, high pitched. Yet passengers are more friendly to me in bad weather. Maybe they're more dependent. When they enter the cabin, they'll say hello. It's like coming in out of a squall to a warm fireplace. Flying, to me, is a method of escape from the weather.

"I feel good when I wake up and see rain; I can be more active on paperwork and details. I'm a bachelor, so I do my laundry then.

"I wear different clothes. In New York, a sports jacket and button-down shirt and tie. In Miami, a sports shirt. I like to leave Miami when it's 80 degrees, get to New York at 35 degrees, and then go back to Miami. It's really just the change. It *stimulates* me!"

A forty-year-old mother of three says, "It's not the weather alone, but whatever else is happening. If everything is going well, I can enjoy the rain, because I'm a gardener. I feel really happy if rain is watering my garden, feeding my plants and the earth, and generating growth. Rain in the summer is wonderful—the smells are different even if it keeps you in. Other seasons I feel hemmed in, particularly when it rains for long periods.

"My mother has just had a heart attack and a stroke. She's in the intensive care unit at the local hospital. I feel scared about Mom in rainy weather. It's ominous. The lady in the bed next to hers died, maybe because the *weather* was so bad. I remember my father-in-law's funeral. Bad weather means tragedy.

"I like crispy, clear, coolish weather. Spring is a relief after the winter; a new beginning when the juices are flowing in the ground. I also like the summer. It means recreation. Less weight of clothing. Freshness."

Here is a seventy-two-year-old, retired car-wash operator: "Bright, clear, blue skies make me want to sing. Too much inclement weather and I revert back to the jungle. Lots of rain bothers me."

If one were to rank-order people and industrial groups in terms of the weather's overall influence on them (their health and its financial costs), the general public heads the list. Next in order of priority are the fishing and agricultural industries; lower down are the air, land, and water transportation industries; and at the bottom of the list, least effected, are industries such as communications, recreation, and finally manufacturing (see Appendix B).

Studies show that most people do want to know more about the weather, and feel that the weather where they live is unique and unpredictable. People also want to know more about their own seemingly unique and unpredictable response to weather conditions.

To find the spread in people's reactions to the weather, someone urged, "Speak to doormen, talk to cops, talk to bartenders." Here is the doorman at a large apartment building in a large eastern city: "The old folks here always ask me when they come outside, 'Should I take an umbrella? What's the forecast? Is it a nice day? Do you know will it rain today? Is the wind bad?'

"Elderly people are especially worried about winds. They don't want to be blown around. Then, when they go out, they sit on the 'gossip bench' and talk about the weather all the time. Oh, they talk about their grandchildren and their troubles, also. But the weather's really number one. It's important to them. Also if they're very lonely, they talk about the weather a lot . . . more than young people do. You know, old-timers don't have much to do to keep busy.

"A lot of them are afraid when the winter comes. The cold, the wind, the rain, the snow and ice. Old folks complain when the seasons change. Some of them go back upstairs to their apartments if it's really bad out. Some say they're going to move south. They gripe more if it's nasty out for several days straight.

"Young people, they're different. They *like* the weather. All kinds. Rain or shine. Some, they're just being polite. They say, 'It's a good morning' to me, even when it's raining. If I say that to old people when it's raining, they say, 'What's so good about it?' "

A bartender tells his customers: "After a few days of rain and overcast skies, I'm down. But when the weather clears up, finally, and the skies are blue again, I feel free."

I spoke to people—young and old, short and tall, rich and poor, male and female, healthy and sick, shy or aggressive, placid or active. I found differences and patterns. (You will find a way to explain the enormous individual differences shortly.)

People will tell you things about the weather they would never tell you about themselves. Yet that is precisely what they are doing—revealing their innermost thoughts. There are those who claim they are insensitive to the weather, yet reveal the same sensations and feelings about it that extremely weather-sensitive people experience. Weather touches the very fiber of our being. Catching us off guard, often unaware, our most intimate responses come from the very sky above and the air around us. Ignored and invisible by their very omnipresence, they are not less influential in our lives, but more.

Our blithe indifference to the weather's direct effect on us is nowhere more clearly demonstrated than in the fact that over the past one hundred years, no less than seventy-five scientific weather-classification schemes have been proposed. Meteorologists classify the climate or weather according to agriculture, or geography, or principles of physics, or the dynamics of air masses. Granted that such categories were invented by *human beings*, it is ironic that such weather-classification schemes ignore the subjective, human point of view of the man in the street. An exception is the human, weather phase system described in Chapter 9, "Objective" Weather-Sensitivity.

One wintry January afternoon, as I was walking home, icy winds were whipping and whistling and I noticed an elderly woman clinging to a tree for dear life. I asked, "May I help you? Is something wrong?" She said, "Yes. I'm frightened. The wind and the cold. I have a heart condition and I can't breathe in the cold wind." I placed my arms under hers and she clutched me like a drowning swimmer.

We struggled until she was safe. And when she thanked me she had tears in her eyes. They were not from the wind.

"I can't get out of bed on cold mornings," an attractive, single woman says. "I like to snuggle under the covers then. Particularly when I'm alone. I don't like to work when it's very cold, and I cannot work at all when it's very hot. When it rains, I like to be out-of-doors in the rain, feeling it."

Police see the weather as it affects their work. A young police sergeant puts it this way, "I've been on the force for ten years now. Either on foot patrol or car patrol. I've always maintained that during hot, sticky, humid days—*heavy* weather—there was always an increase in assaultive behavior: short tempers, stabbings, knifings, shootings. All crimes, really heavy crimes, too. Primarily I think it's because when more people are on the street, they're more likely to resort to violence. Cops always worry about those so-called, long, hot summers, since we know there are more rapes, aggravated assaults, murders, burglaries, cut-up bodies. Especially when people are unemployed.

"We have a saying on the force: '*Rainy weather is the policeman's best friend.*' It's true. Except for motor vehicle accidents, it's always a quiet tour of duty during rain. Less people are on the street.

"I know I always felt better in the winter getting out of the patrol car on a cold-weather tour. There are less people on the street, less chance for me to get physically hurt. It's an easier load. Usually deep winter we have the lowest crime rate. Except when the holiday season approaches; then we get robberies from people who need the money; we see more depressed people. Now these are mostly my own observations from meeting the public day to day all these years, but I hear that the statistics bear me out."

A short, overweight man in his early forties, a talent agent, says: "I'm from Idaho. We have the worst seasons there. The hot is hot. The cold is cold. And I've been around. I've lived in Washington, Hong Kong, and Chicago. When it was sultry we used to say, 'The weather is like the inside of a cow—hot, dark, and humid.' That's country talk. It's in the *Farmer's Almanac*, always *big* news when that's published.

Lecturing to his medical students, a professor of urology and surgery says: "When a group of old men gets together at a banquet in the winter and sings, 'In the Good Old Summer Time,' they know whereof they sing."

A slender psychiatric nurse, mid-thirties, tells me, "I'm a pessimist. And I guess you might call me a depressive. I *like* gloomy weather. It coincides with my mood most of the time. I can't stand the winter and the cold weather. I like rain and grey skies."

A twenty-five-year-old ballerina says: "I can be happy in sunny or cold weather or rain. Even though my joints ache in the rain, I generally like it then. I work better. I do my stretching exercises to limber up. My mood usually depends on whatever other things are happening in my life. If everything else is fine, then the weather makes no difference. If my life is difficult, or I'm troubled, then the weather is the last straw."

An exercise and ballet teacher says: "When it's humid, most of my dancers are low in spirits, they ache; but when it's cold, brisk, and brilliant, they are full of beans. You see, muscles are hydroscopic. Too much or too little moisture in the muscles is bad; if dehydrated, the fibers stick together and they may cramp. All my students feel it. Even if they deny it, they still feel the weather."

Here is a six-year-old friend, a blond, blue-eyed boy: "Summer is my favorite season. Clear, blue sky. It's sunny and warm. I don't like the rain, and I get depressed sometimes then, and my mother gives me hell. But I like to look at the sky, because . . . I don't know. Outside I can play."

An unusually talented painter, whose depictions of skies are extravagantly lush—abloom with clouds and subtle hues of blue and grey—looks at the weather in an intensely personal, emotional, almost sensual way: "I feel like the painter Turner strapped to the mast of a ship while he painted the wind, the sea, the water, and the light. Those elements *dominate* me and my painting. I paint the mood that they create in me, I paint my mood that corresponds to nature. If I see a tree flattened by wind, I feel like that tree. If I'm cold, I paint what it feels like to be cold. I'm struck by the elements. They happen for only an instant and you have to remember the feelings they made. You seek out beauty as a painter, no matter what the weather is. The weather almost always excites me, it almost always means vitality. It's the antithesis of living in New York, and that's the only time I'm depressed—in the absence of the elements. When I'm painting, I'm always weather-susceptible. It's like a sixth sense to me. I'm touched and moved by the weather. It's my inner emotions that dominate my response to the weather. It's a very *physical* quality, a turn-on, a sort of harmony, in the weather. The weather speaks to me directly."

A DIFFERENCE OF OPINION.

FINE BRACING WEATHER.   BITTER, BITTER COLD.

Newspaper commentary, circa 1859
Both the anatomical and socioeconomic depiction is faithful to current
research results in human biometeorology.

There's no simple pattern emerging, but here are more people weathering.

A plump, thirty-year-old man working as a civil servant is emphatic: "The weather? I never notice it! And I don't know anyone else it bothers either."

Here's a middle-aged physician, trying to describe how he sees the weather's effect on his patients: "Some people are 'conditioned' by pleasant or unpleasant experiences, in the Pavlovian sense that a dog salivates when a bell rings if he has been trained that way. So the season or the weather at the moment serves thereafter as a stimulus to bring about a recurrence of the feelings associated with the original experience—good or bad. Weather is the one great environmental influence that's common to very large groups of people."

An extremely alert, inquisitive, quite elderly lady (maybe close to eighty), a widow, observes: "When it is going to snow or rain I can feel it. My body refuses to move. I feel great heaviness, vertigo, depression. I have to lie down. I'm so weary all of a sudden. The *symptoms* are very definite, but I don't always *connect* up my tired feeling with the snow or rain until later, when it snows or rains. And it always does when I feel this way. I'm *so* relieved when it finally rains or snows I feel like a *new* woman—alert, wide awake, full of vigor. My sister has the exactly same symptoms.

"I also get nosebleeds when it's very dry. I have a humidifier in my room, and if it becomes empty in the middle of the night, without my knowing it, I wake up with a nosebleed.

"The weather affects me more at holidays and when I'm lonely than at other times. I know, old people are lonely and have to talk about the weather. But those who have no internal resources talk *endlessly* about it. When you're middle-aged you're too busy to think much about the weather. I think life begins at forty, but it ends at fifty.

"I like early fall. I enjoy the seasonal changes. I would be very unhappy in Florida. I don't like rain to start and stop. But I do feel excited when the weather changes. I would feel dreadful to be south and to wear summer clothes all the time. Changing clothes adds color—I guess I mean coloration—to my life. It has something to do with my sense for visual beauty, a highly developed visual sense for form and decoration.

"I adore paintings. My favorites are the Impressionists. By not being specific, they do something to me. Like the weather changes. I know I bring something to these paintings I see. I also bring something to the weather I see. I'm not sure what it is, but it's there."

A twenty-nine-year-old social worker tells me: "I feel that the outside is hostile and I resent it when it's cold. I don't want to be subjected to it in any way, shape, or form. I get depressed as soon as it starts to get cold, and I feel lonely. The cold is unfriendly. I'm almost a little embarrassed about it all. I crave constant warmth. The sun comforts me. It's like a parenting force. 'When the sun turns traitor cold,' is from a pop song and I *know* what the lyric means. The weather is an impersonal representation of the world . . . I feel persecuted by it. It makes me hate life sometimes. I feel fury and I cry about it."

A psychiatrist gives his opinion: "We are certain that the weather is sufficient to tip a fluctuating, unstable, predisposed individual into any form of mental illness. The onset of psychiatric episodes coincides with definite changes in the meteorological environment."

A patient, talking about his own psychoanalysis, says: "I had ten years on the couch. You see when I was a kid, I suffered sinus trouble—my nose was always stuffed, I had shooting pains in the back of my head. I snored. It got really bad, especially when I was traveling, and got worse in winter. My psychiatrist said it was migraines. My wife, who was a registered nurse, was a light sleeper. I became aware that my condition was tuned in to the weather because she got very annoyed at my snoring. It always got worse in winter; from fall to winter my snoring was unbearable to her. She made me take a pill, but I didn't like taking it. I was curing the effect, not the cause of the snoring.

"I left my wife four years ago. I changed my eating habits. I lost thirty pounds. I became aware I was a creature of the rhythms of the earth—the seasons. I'm a geologist, so I know those rhythms.

"After my self-analysis, I'm more tuned in to the weather because I'm more tuned in to myself. Being more self-aware, I attribute my symptoms—feeling groggy, dizzy, tired—to legitimate external causes, to major weather changes. Not solely to inner causes. I'm even off medication now.

"I've always been drawn to water like a moth to flame. My emotions are affected by the rhythms of the ocean waves. I listen to the waves and I'm in 'synch' with that rhythm. It gives me a sense of isolation and survival, like I'm on my own and I have to make it."

A character in a Hugh Walpole novel, *The Inquisition*, says:

When you get to be my age . . . and are out of condition as I am, some part or other of your body responds evilly to every kind of weather; if it is a lovely day and the sun is shining your eyes ache; if it is cold your prostate gives you trouble; if it is close your head shuts down on you; if it rains you have rheumatism.

How are all of these reactions possible? What unites them? Is there a single thread passing through the universal weather experience, these anecdotal stories and reactions to the weather? Is there one unifying idea to explain all of the different notions about weathering? Or are there several? What can we do about the weather and our responses to it?

The Law of Initial Value

The complex action of each passing air mass on the human body is simplified by a curious and deceptively subtle principle called Wilder's Law of Initial Value. Easy to state, its importance and ramifications are difficult to appreciate fully at first.

Simply, Wilder's Law says that your reaction to any stimulus now (medical drug, weather impact, emotional stress, natural disaster, social revolution) depends on your prior level of arousal or excitation (called "the initial value").

As examples, consider common household "drugs," the "pleasure-poisons" coffee, tea, alcohol, and cigarettes. The *arousing* effect of coffee is well known. But certain people will take an oath that they frequently use coffee as a *sedative*, in order to fall asleep—a paradoxic inhibiting response to a stimulant. One student of world-wide tea-drinking habits observed tea's sedative effect on the jittery and its stimulation on the fatigued. The English drink tea to remove dampness from their bones, the desert Arabs to avoid thirst and heat, the Laplanders to fight coldness.

It seems that the more a man is depressed or frustrated, the more pleasure, euphoria, and release he gets from alcohol. When the coward becomes heroic; the shy man, a braggart; the inhibited, sexy; the mature, childish; the quiet person, overbearing; the aggressive, sleepy—these are living examples of "in wine is the truth" (*in vino veritas*), or "in Wilder is the truth." These are paradoxic reactions, more or less familiar but often overlooked. Other drugs (morphine, bromides, barbiturates, tranquilizers, antidepressants, adrenaline, acetylcholine) bear out the observation, "Show me your response, and I can tell you your initial value." Even smiling, blushing, speaking, moving, breathing, and many other behaviors are subject to the Law of Initial Value, as are dysfunctions, defenses, anxieties, neuroses, suggestibility, blood pressure, pulse rate, digestion, sweating, diuresis, growth, aging, fatigue, and the "second wind" in sports.

Temperature regulation in the human body shows us that the colder we are, the hotter we usually get after staying awhile in a warm room. Rubbing the exposed part of the body with snow is probably the oldest folk-medicine against frostbite. And the fact that fever-producing agents cause a great *rise* in body temperatures at *low* body temperature but a *drop* in temperature at *high* body temperature is another example of paradoxic reactions in the Law of Initial Value.

Not quite a theory, it is a valid description of how human physiology seems to work. But it is still not widely appreciated, especially in all its implications. When noticed, it may be considered a nuisance to be disregarded in medical experiments, a dangerous unpredictable complication of therapy, a subjective "error," or an embarrassing problem.

Specifically, Wilder's Law says the *higher* your initial value of arousal, the *smaller* is your response to function-*raising* stimuli. And the *higher* that initial value, the *larger* is your response to function-*depressing* stimuli. Beyond a certain medium range of initial values, there is a tendency to "paradoxic," or reversed response.

Suppose both stimuli are equal doses of some medical drug. The second dose will then not simply yield an arithmetic summation of the two-dose effects. The second dose almost invariably (at 75 to 85 percent probability) will provoke an effect that is either (a) smaller than the effect of the first dose; (b) a nonexistent or absent response; or (c) a *reversal* of the initial effect.

Now imagine the drug dosage to be a weather front or atmospheric impact, a temperature rise or fall, a tropical or polar air mass. (There *are* drugs that mimic our weathering responses; see Chapter 3.)

Wilder's Law then says that *every* weather "dose," or weather stimulus, is a *second* or a *third* "dose," or stimulus.

In other words, two different people—or the same person at two successive instants of time—will react differently to the same weather change; or the same to different weather changes. Their recent stimulus *history* (from any source—medicine, weather, emotional excitement, even social disaster) will dictate their immediate *future* response. (See next page.) This is mentioned here to show that the

Wilder's Law of Initial Value

Initial Stimulation	Response to Stimulator	Response to Inhibitor	Initial Inhibition	Response to Stimulator	Response to Inhibitor
High	Small, none, or paradoxic	Large	High	Large	Small, none, or paradoxic
Medium	Medium	Medium	Medium	Medium	Medium
Low	Large	Small, none, or paradoxic	Low	Small	Large

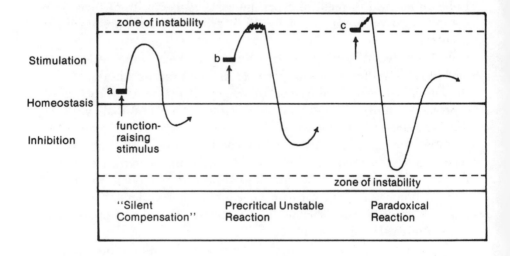

The arrow pointing upward is a function-raising stimulus. At *a*, a low level of arousal, the organism returns to homeostatic equilibrium by "silent compensation." At *b*, a moderate level of arousal, the same stimulus triggers a "precritical instability reaction" before homeostasis restores normalcy. At *c*, an extreme level of arousal, the same stimulus will induce a catastrophic instability, a crisis, and overshoot—a "paradoxic" reaction.

astonishing variability of our response to weather is explainable. And even though experiments with people and weather seek to maintain identical controlled conditions (diet, genetic endowment, weather, and so on) they are hampered in practice by Wilder's Law of Initial Value. Perfect correlations between weather phases and medical tests are therefore rare, but imperfect correlations are not fatal to my premise: Weather *conditions—preconditions* and *reconditions*—the human body.

This book is an attempt to unravel those mysteries of how we weather the weather, and why. Accumulating scientific research illuminates how we are tossed by atmospheric tides in our ocean of air. One recent study by two cardiologists on the staff of a prominent medical school noted that the conditions of our environment deserve more attention than all the pollution of the atmosphere and water, because, as they said, "Weather and climate injure normal and diseased man more than does pollution of his environment." Medication, food, clothing, and travel are always changed by weather, and they, in turn, modify our reactions to weather—so it is necessary to know how to change them and when. A synopsis of these results, for the reader who wishes to know the weather prescriptions quickly, is found in Chapter 11, Beat This Weather!

An illustration of the ancient Wind Tower of Athens, which bears a sculptured figure on each octagonal side facing a wind direction, opened this chapter. Personifications of each wind (Eurus, Lips, Kaikia, Apeliotes, Zephyrus, Notus, Boreas, Skiron) will open succeeding chapters.

The Weather Experience: A Summary

Weathering is how we survive life's weather—defending our body's inner territories against repetitive environmental insults. Adaptability and good health are part of *weathering*.

Sensitivity to the weather is largely a matter of temperament, age, physique, sex, status. Later chapters explain how and why these operate, but a simple questionnaire in this chapter presents an opportunity to measure the reader's predisposition to weather-sensitivity, or risk-factor profile. How and why this simple paper-and-pencil exercise works is a large part of the rest of the book.

Various people interviewed from all walks of life display what can only be called an astonishing variability in their personal response to the weather. Readers may compare their own emotional and physical reactions, their own weather experiences, to *Weathering*'s cast of characters. The lady whose psychiatrist scoffed at her complaint that she was "under the weather"; she left him. The fellow who describes how years of psychoanalysis freed him from weather indifference, placing him in intimate contact with nature's weathering elements. The flight attendant who loves rain, but whose passengers loathe it. The injured football player's knee, and how it responds to dampness. A painter calls her weather susceptibility a "sixth sense," a turn-on, an extraordinary sensitivity; the weather, she says, speaks to her directly. Doormen, cabdrivers, policemen, bartenders, and others who see the public react to weather, tell how the elderly, or the criminals, or the depressed respond, each in his own way, to weather. The weather injures normal and diseased people more than all air and water pollution combined, according to cardiologists in a recent study.

Not only will the same person respond to the same weather conditions at different times (or places) in completely different ways—but different people will respond to different weather conditions in similar ways, all depending on their level of arousal, or stimulation, in advance of their weather response. Every stimulus, every *weather* stimulus, is a *second* stimulus—and often a *third* stimulus. This deceptively simple physiological (and social) principle, called Wilder's Law of Initial Value, helps explain our arousal to weather, our state of excitation . . . our *weathering*.

Two:
Sensitivity to Weather...
Sensitivity to Life

Nought cared this body for wind and weather,
When youth and I lived in it together.
    —Samuel Coleridge

Love is in the air
    Quite clearly
People everywhere
    Act queerly
Some are hasty, some are halting
Some are simply somersaulting
        —Stephen Sondheim

You will find that fatigue has a larger share
in the promotion and transmission of disease,
than any other single condition you can name.
        —Sir James Paget

Preceding Page: Eurus
The wind of the southeast, which in Athens is hot and cloudy and brings a
lot of rain, is represented by an older man who seems angry. He is wrapped
up in his cloak; his right hand and arm are entirely hidden in part of this
cloak; the other part, which hides the left arm, stretches out in front of his
face.

Are you sensitive to the weather?

If your answer to that question is "yes," then you are by definition "weather-sensitive."

But if your answer to the question is "no," very likely you are, nevertheless, "weather-sensitive." How can this be? Who are the weather-sensitives of the world? And what is weather-sensitivity?

There are many paradoxes to weather-sensitivity. Weather-sensitivity is not, in and of itself, a disease. But it is an indicator of general health—physical as well as mental or emotional. Sick people complain significantly more often of weather-induced symptoms than do healthy people. Sensitivity to weather is curiously revealing, because weather not only represents the changing sky, the physical environment, and the air mass we inhabit, but weather is an externalization of the distinct changes we feel throughout our life, inside our skin. "Weather" is a metaphor for "life," a screen upon which we may project our inner feelings about the world in general. "Tell me what you think of the weather, and I will know what to think of you," is not an idle boast.

Weathering many a storm reveals itself on your *weather-beaten* face. If it gets you down, you are *under the weather* . . . otherwise you are *weather-proof.* A *fair-weather* friend is undependable and fickle, a *mercurial* person is as *changeable as the weather,* or *wetterwendisch* in German. To a Frenchman, someone who *fait la pluie et le beau temps,* or "makes rain and good weather," is an influential person to whom one pays tribute.

Most people are weather-sensitive even if they claim not to be, since they present (at lower intensity) the same symptoms presented by self-declared weather-sensitives.

Weather-Sensitivity

Suppose you are a man in your thirties or forties. You are a member of the middle class. You are stocky and broadly built. Your hallmarks are emotional stability, complacency, calmness, and composure. You tend to be self-sufficient, perhaps dominant, but amiable toward everyone. You fall asleep easily and stay asleep. You love comfort. You will be relatively indifferent to the vicissitudes of weather, on an objective or subjective basis. You are not weather-sensitive.

But suppose you are a woman getting on in years, say in your fifth or sixth decade of life. You may be a member of the upper or the lower class. Perhaps you are slender or rather tall, somewhat self-conscious. You are easily excitable. Occasionally you are somewhat nervous or depressed. You prefer having only a few intimate friends. You need solitude. You tend to be secretive. It is very likely that you are weather-sensitive.

And you are in good company. Byron, Casanova, Columbus, and Dante were. Darwin, Davey, Diderot, and Donizetti were. Benjamin Franklin was. Johann Wolfgang von Goethe was. Heine, Herschel, Hugo, and Huygens were. Johannes Kepler was. Martin Luther and Michelangelo were. Milton was. Mozart was. Montesquieu and Napoleon were. Also Nietzsche, Pascal, Petrarch, Rilke, Rousseau, Torricelli. Leonardo da Vinci was. So were Voltaire and Wagner. (This list excludes famous weather-sensitive females because they did not publicize their sensitivity to the extent these men did.)

You can estimate how your body and mind responds to your environment (including the weather) by a detailed paper-and-pencil exercise (see the self-discovery questionnaire, Appendix C).

Subliminal Arousal

Weather-sensitivity is a human response, an adaptation to the stress, arousal, or stimulation of an atmosphere constantly changing. We are aroused by changes in temperature, changes in humidity, changes in winds, changes in sunlight. Precisely because we live constantly and freely with these arousal agents, or stressors, we take them for granted.

Environments as such have a way of being inaccessible to inspection. Environments by reason of their total character are most subliminal to ordinary experience. Indeed, the amount of any situation, private or social, verbal or graphic, that can be raised to the conscious level of attention is almost insignificant.

The author of these words, Marshall McLuhan, is one observer of the subliminal influences on our lives. Edgar Allan Poe, in his story "The Purloined Letter," knew that to hide a letter most effectively it had to be in plain view. Democritus said in 400 B.C., "Much is perceptible which is not perceived by us." And in 1698, as if he were referring to the influences of the weather, Leibnitz said, "There are numberless perceptions, little noticed, which are not sufficiently distinguished to be perceived or remembered, but which become known through certain consequences."

Merely because most of our environment is below our level of conscious attention does not mean that its "consequences" are minimal or minute. Because a stimulus may be "inaccessible to inspection" does not mean it is less of a stimulus. To the contrary: since a subliminal stimulus is imperceptible by definition, or invisible, we do not notice its effects until they cumulate—in an avalanche.

Sex, age, and social class of weather-sensitive individuals has been examined by Volker Faust and his colleagues in a decade-long series of recent experiments. He asked some 800 clinically healthy persons, 1,600 students, and 1,000 hospitalized patients to indicate their symptoms. A questionnaire listed thirty-seven symptoms associated with weather-sensitivity. The subjects' ages ranged from 13 to 93 years old. They were asked to check off those (purely subjective) physical or mental symptoms they experienced and whether or not they described themselves as weather-sensitive.

About half of the healthy people did see themselves as weather-sensitive. Since Switzerland is typical of the general population in an advanced industrial country in the north temperate zone, at our latitude, we can assume that, with some exceptions—cultural and language differences aside—the results will apply to the United States. Neuropsychiatrist Hans Reese, studying correlations between weather and health, was able to prove that "conditions which have been demonstrated for our country will be found valid for any region."

The most important symptoms claimed by healthy persons to be induced by weather conditions are (see next page) "tiredness," "bad moods," "disinclination to work," "head pressure," "restless or disturbed sleep," "impaired concentration," "difficulty in falling asleep," "headaches," "nervousness," "pains in bone fractures," "difficulties in sleeping through the night," "increased tendency to make mistakes," "forgetfulness," "visual flickering," "dizziness," "heart palpitations," "scar pains," and "depression." All other symptoms were below a 10 percent response level.

Symptoms of Weather-Sensitivity

Symptoms	Sex	Non-weather-sensitive	Weather-sensitive
Tiredness	♂	19	47
	♀	23	64
Bad moods	♂	16	54
	♀	13	45
Disinclination to work	♂	19	42
	♀	14	48
Head pressure	♂	13	44
	♀	13	42
Restless sleep	♂	16	43
	♀	11	41
Headaches	♂	6	37
	♀	8	38
Impaired concentration	♂	9	39
	♀	8	37
Difficulty in falling asleep	♂	10	34
	♀	13	36
Nervousness	♂	9	27
	♀	8	33
Bone-fracture pains	♂	9	22
	♀	8	30
Visual flickering	♂	6	17
	♀	6	27
Forgetfulness	♂	5	24
	♀	6	24
Exhaustion	♂	4	16
	♀	4	27
General discomfort	♂	8	20
	♀	1	21
Disturbed sleep	♂	10	22
	♀	8	24
Increased tendency to make mistakes	♂	7	27
	♀	8	22
Dizziness	♂	4	18
	♀	4	26
Heart palpitations	♂	5	18
	♀	3	22
Scar pains	♂	4	21
	♀	6	18
Depressive moods	♂	3	14
	♀	3	21
Respiratory problems	♂	3	12
	♀	3	19
Rheumatic complaints	♂	4	14
	♀	3	15
Anxiety	♂	1	10
	♀	1	18
Perspiration	♂	6	13
	♀	6	13
Loss of appetite	♂	3	14
	♀	3	15

The most frequent meteorologically determined complaints

□ among weather-sensitive men and women

■ among non-weather-sensitive men and women

Symptoms of Weather-Sensitivity

Notice that all symptoms are in fact complaints because these were what was asked. (Asking healthy people "Why do you feel sick?" is like the lawyers' query, "Why do you beat your wife?") So there was no possibility for a subject to register a benevolent response to the weather. Nor was there any chance to present objective confirmation that a symptom was associated with a specific weather condition. Faust made no attempt to synchronize a complaint with a weather event, although the subjects did; hence this is subjective weather-sensitivity.

A striking result is that those who describe themselves as not weather-sensitive suffer the same symptoms and complaints albeit at reduced intensity or frequency, as those who say they are weather-sensitive. This means that even if you claim you are not weather-sensitive, you probably are—at least weather-receptive! You may not attribute your symptoms to weather. The surprising corollary is that subjective weather-sensitivity is virtually omnipresent in the population at large. "Tiredness"—the most pronounced single symptom—was reported by over half (57 percent) of the self-described weather-sensitives and by a fifth (21 percent) of the self-described non-weather-sensitives, or 40 percent of the total group of healthy subjects. Clearly every pronounced symptom felt by weather-sensitives was echoed by the *non*-weather-sensitives, one-third to one-ninth as often.

Another result is that females are more weather-sensitive than males for many of the symptoms. (The exceptions are "bad moods," "head pressure," "disturbed sleep," "impaired concentration," "increased tendency to make mistakes," "scar pains.") Men suffer the disparity most with "bad moods." Women are significantly more plagued than men by "tiredness," "nervousness," "anxiety," and "depression." Except beyond sixty, where men and women converge, women are consistently more weather-sensitive than men at virtually every age of their lives.

It is known that men sweat more copiously than women under dry or moist heat stress. Yet women have a higher number of active sweat glands than men. Women's bodies may physically tolerate a wider temperature range than men and adjust better to it than men, but women object more to high temperature than men do. In other words, perhaps women both complain more and adapt more to *weather change* than men do to temperature changes and perhaps other weather changes as well.

Normal infants and small children are very weather-sensitive. Because they don't speak, we do not know exactly what percentage, but their symptoms are clearly reported by nurses and observers ("unrest," "whining," "quarrelsomeness," "fatigue," "dislike of play," and "disturbed sleep"). Sick children show more (and more intense) symptoms of weather-sensitivity.

Among thirteen- to twenty-year-olds, one-third of the girls and one-fifth of the boys (or one-quarter of both sexes) are weather-sensitive. Their major weather-induced complaints are "fatigue," "ill humor," "diffuse pressure in the head," "increased tendency to make mistakes," "dislike of work," "discomfort," "irritability," "restless sleep," "headaches," "nervousness," "moist palms," "impaired concentration," plus a host of other less frequent symptoms.

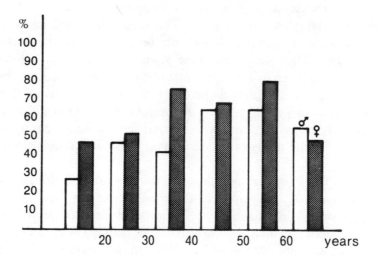

Percentage of Subjective Weather-Sensitives, by Age and Sex

Between the ages of twenty and thirty years, every second person is affected. Between the ages of thirty and fifty, two out of every three persons are weather-sensitive. In the critical years of menopause and climacteric, three out of every four persons are weather-sensitive. Beyond sixty, one out of every two persons is weather-sensitive.

Women consistently report more "tiredness" at every age than men; generally, one out of two women and one out of three men complain it is the leading symptom across all ages.

"Tiredness" is highest among weather-sensitives below age twenty (68 percent) and above age sixty (65 percent). Between twenty and sixty, it is considerably lower (42 percent, 41 percent, 43 percent, and 51 percent); versus age, its frequency resembles a U-shaped curve—high among the elderly and young, low among the middle-aged.

In his studies, Faust also obtained the following statistics for weather-sensitives:

- Some 13 percent of women and 8 percent of men believe they inherited their weather-sensitivity.
- Less than 10 percent of men or women think their weather-sensitivity just started up due to an operation, a psychological or physical ailment, a bone fracture, or fate.
- About half think that the geographical area they inhabit has some importance for their maladies.
- About one-quarter of men and women use aspirin to relieve their symptoms; one-tenth use tranquilizers, stimulants, or sleep-inducing drugs.
- If there were a medicine against weather-sensitivity, 30 percent of men and 23 percent of women would depend on it.
- Thirty-two percent of women and 15 percent of men use coffee to combat their symptoms.
- Forty-three percent feel their complaints are the same throughout the entire year.
- Twenty-one percent feel their complaints especially in the spring (12 percent in the summer, 6 percent in the fall, and 4 percent in the winter).
- About one-quarter feel pre-weather-sensitive by one day.
- About two-thirds feel more weather-sensitive on the day of the interview than before.
- At least intermittently, between 50 percent and 70 percent of the population is weather-sensitive.

Ravages of Age

Human adaptability shows distinct fluctuations from birth to old age. Total human mortality, for instance, is highest in infancy and old age, lowest during childhood years.

Human organs change their ability to function during the life cycle. Many vital functions and organs are at their peak performance generally between the first and third decades of life. Their performance drops off significantly on both sides of the peak period (say five to thirty-five years). This resembles the curve of weather-sensitivity with age (see Chapter Notes) and is a mirror image of "tiredness" versus age. Off-peak performance of vital organs occurs during those years when people are most weather-sensitive, easily tired, most susceptible to weather stress, and presumably to emotional stress and physical stress as well.

The age range for maximal athletic performance is in the early twenties for short distance events and twenty-five to thirty years for endurance events. Maximal oxygen uptake, which is the best reference level for aerobic work capacity, decreases with age. So do respiratory efficiency, cardiac stroke volume, muscle strength, and endurance under moderately heavy work. Research shows that the declining capacity for physical work with advancing age is delayed by continuous physical training.

As we age, our *range* of individual variation in organ functions becomes quite pronounced. According to Harold Bafitis and Frederick Sargent II, who assembled the information, age progressively accentuates our biological differences, and our loss of organ adaptability. Also, with advancing age, there are significant declines in the interaction among biological functions, those that depend upon metabolic processes (involving fats and carbohydrates), physiological processes, and the oxygen transport system (see Chapter Notes).

Peak organ function encourages our capacity to cope. Consequently the ability to withstand environmental assaults, or changes, must remain undeveloped in the very early years, improve in the early to middle years, and deteriorate at very advanced age.

Thus mortality would be minimal during the years of highest adaptive capacity. In fact, mortality *is* minimal between early childhood and the second decade of life, regardless of major changes in the causes of death. The seasonal variation in the death rate is considerable between zero to four years of age, it is small between five to thirty-nine years, but then above forty years the *seasonality* again increases. This is another way of showing *weather*'s ravages with age.

The very young and very old struggle to adapt to weather change or cope with weather stress. The probable reasons are poor or incompletely developed temperature control in the very young and impaired temperature control (for example, loss of ability to sweat) in the very old.

The age profiles of weather-sensitivity and of adaptive capacity of our body organs bear a suspicious resemblance to each other. Is weather-sensitivity a function of organ adaptability perhaps? Weather-sensitivity peaks at the age when most organs are working best. High weather-sensitivity probably means that your indicator lights are working well, that your protective reflexes are in order.

The remark that "life begins at forty but ends at fifty" is not really borne out by these graphs on age progressions. For some organ functions, life begins at twenty and lasts until ninety.

The Future Population

The age curves of weather-sensitivity also say something about future growth areas. The United States is a nation growing older. By 1990, the number of people over 65 will add up to 30 million, or 12 percent of the national population. Their number will grow as fast as the rest of the country. So the median age of the United States population drifts ever upward: from 27.9 years in 1972 to 29.4 years in 1977. By 1980, the average age of Americans will be over 30 years; by 1990, 32.3 years. In the year 2000, the average age will be 35.5 years.

If three out of four American men and women are weather-sensitive in their fifth decade of life, then, by 1990, we will see a large spurt in our weather-sensitive population of elderly (to 15 million). The 25 to 44 year age group will make up close to 80 million Americans in 1990. Two-thirds of that group's women may be subjectively weather-sensitive (30 million), over half of that group's men may be weather-sensitive (20 million). Of the 45 to 64 year age group (45 million in 1990), perhaps 30 million will be weather-sensitive. And of the 25 million 18 to 26 year age group, perhaps 10 million will be weather-sensitive. Under 5 years of age, add another 10 out of the 20 million.

The total is 115 million weather-sensitive Americans in 1990.

Furthermore, about one-quarter (or 29 million) will use aspirin; and about one-tenth (11 million) will use tranquilizers or sleep-inducing drugs to relieve their symptoms. And about 30 percent of men (17 million) and 23 percent of women (13 million) would use a medicine—if it existed—against their symptoms of weather-sensitivity. (There already are drugs, often antihypertensives, to relieve some symptoms; but notice the list of drugs in Appendix F whose actions are modified by weather.) Drug manufacturers should be betting heavily on these kinds of numbers, and on the trend to increased health consciousness. Also coffee manufacturers should take note that in 1990, 32 percent of women (18 million) and 15 percent (8.5 million) of men probably will use coffee to counteract many typical symptoms of weather-sensitivity.

The Touch of Class

Faust's queries also turned up the seemingly curious result that the middle class is subjectively less susceptible to meteorological influences than either the upper class or the lower class.

Members of the upper class are especially afflicted with weather-dependent "disturbances in concentration" and "mood," which provoke an appreciable lack of drive to work. Of course, highly placed executives or professionals usually engage in cerebral activity. But they also report high levels of heart and circulatory complaints and sensitivity to pain.

The middle class, though practically uninfluenced by the weather, complains most about "tiredness" and "increased tendency to make mistakes." You tend to make more mistakes when tired, and tiredness is the most frequently cited middle-class, weather-related complaint. Apparently these two symptoms are important, since in middle-class activities (say middle-management positions) both cerebral and manual activity is combined.

The lower class suffers most from "tiredness," leading frequently to "exhaustion." The largely manual character of lower-class work may explain this. "Heart palpitations," "pains from broken bones," and "rheumatism pains" may come from great physical exertion.

These results apply to the three socioeconomic groups or classes (defined by a combination of education level and type of work) without regard to sex or claimed weather-sensitivity.

If the group of self-described weather-sensitives are extracted from the total, the number of class-specific weather complaints increases. Thus upper-class weather-sensitives are irritated by central nervous system disorders (such as sleep, headaches, nervousness) in addition to their disturbed concentration and moods. Lower-class weather-sensitives, with their tiredness and circulatory problems, complain as well about pain sensitivity and depressed moods. Weather-sensitives of the middle class show a dim reflection of the pattern of upper-class complaints, like weakening power of concentration, sleep- and nervous-system disturbances, and headaches.

The most weather-resistant people are the male members of the middle class. Upper-class males show symptoms of stress. Lower-class males show intensified depressed moods.

Why should the upper and lower class claim to present more weather-induced complaints or more intensity of the same complaints than the middle class does? This is simpler to ask than to answer.

Suppose "weather" is understood as a stand-in for "arousal," for "life," or for "stress." Complaints, from any class or any source, are often credibly blamed upon weather. We are all exposed to it, and other people will often accept as natural your explanation, "I'm under the weather."

In the same way, some of us blame "luck" or "fate" for our fortunes; they are convenient scapegoats. But "weather" is more than that. It truly exists and it causes stress.

The upper and lower class may be under more pressure than the middle class. The lower class strives to achieve middle-classdom. The upper class strives to stay where it already is. Both are highly stressed by social and economic factors, perhaps enormously more stressed than the middle class is. Any added burden, such as weather stress, could provoke the reported symptoms of stress, such as fatigue, or nervous-system and circulatory disorders. Almost certainly, this explanation is as true as it is oversimplified.

Faust's method of questioning people has some acknowledged weaknesses. The list of items is symptom oriented and relentlessly loaded in favor of negative responses to weather (or to life or to stress). Perhaps this is merely normal for an investigator, a psychiatrist whose occupation is disease and dysfunction. There are other results from other studies (see Chapters 3 and 4) that reveal positive outcomes of weather stress.

It should also be possible to explain why women, the very old, and the very young report more weather-induced afflictions than others. Women resist stress better than do men. Women live longer and, paradoxically, are more weather-sensitive than men (see Chapter 10).

Physiometeorology and
Psychometeorology

Virtually all weather events seem to reflect themselves in your body. If the weather is normal, its effects will tend to be normal. But if it is contrary to what is expected seasonally, then—watch out!—its human reverberations will be amplified. Nevertheless, cold weather in the winter, and warm weather in the summer still exert strong effects. Cold and warm fronts are the most frequently mentioned triggers for physiological as well as psychological consequences of weather conditions.

A host of diseases and dysfunctions known to medical science are statistically linked to weather conditions. Diseases that are intensified or caused by meteorological events are called *meteorotropic* diseases:

- Seasonally conditioned diseases (hay fever, colds)
- Hypothalamic (thermoregulatory) disturbances:
  moderate thermal stress (asthma, bronchitis, rheumatic diseases, apoplexy, heart diseases, acute glaucoma, and other eye disorders such as Raynaud's disease)
  extreme thermal stress (edema, fainting, freezing to death, sweatgland disorders, chilblain)
- Radiation-induced diseases (sunburn, migraine from ultraviolet light)
- Infectious diseases (influenza, measles, colds)

The meteorological environment consists of combined influences: temperature, humidity, air movement or winds, air pressure, solar radiation, electrostatic and electromagnetic fields, air ionization, trace chemical elements, or physical-chemical pollutants. Vulnerable body parts are the skin, nose, eyes, nervous system, lungs, membranes, muscles—in direct intimate contact with one or more of these weather elements. The ease of passage of microorganism through tissue cells, and thus resistance to infections, will be weather-conditioned, according to Solco Tromp, Director of Leiden's Biometeorology Research Center.

Physiological and psychological symptoms have been found to accompany specific weather patterns, and these are summarized in the tabular material here, in Chapter 9, and the Appendix. Typically, physicians in the United States are quite unaware of the associations between weather and health that this material summarizes. Worse still, many of them scoff at these connections—despite the potential benefits to their patients. American medical schools emphasize pathology and ignore meteorological physiology, weather-induced modifications of drug action inside your body, Wilder's Law of Initial Value, and other deep and powerful effects of weather on your health.

Rheumatic pains are painfully aggravated by cold, damp, winter weather—particularly in an impending storm.

Psychometeorology: Mood and Behavior Consequences of Weather Conditions

Mood & Behavior	Weather Conditions
General state of health, as perceived by patient	*Deteriorates* in extremely good weather characterized by foehn (a hot, dry alpine wind; see Chapter 6) *Bad* when a change in weather is forthcoming *Improves* when a change in weather is terminating *Tired out* feeling results from warm, moist weather *More lively* feeling results from cool, dry weather
Desire to work	*Declines* with extremely good weather characterized by foehn *Slight* when a change in weather is in prospect or terminating
Work productivity	*Lessened* by extremely good weather characterized by foehn
Effect of alcohol	*Increases* with extremely good weather characterized by foehn
Need for medications	*Increases* with extremely good weather characterized by foehn
Need for treatment in general	*Increases* with extremely good weather characterized by foehn
Ability to concentrate	*Decreases* with extremely good weather characterized by foehn *Decreases* when change of weather is forthcoming *Decreases* shortly before sudden changes in weather, especially cold fronts *Decreases* in warm, moist air *Decreases* in a mild climate with continental polar air and cold continental air *Decreases* in active low-pressure regions (cyclonic weather) *Decreases* in extensive unstable weather conditions *Increases* with mild climate and polar ocean air
Headaches, migraines, vasomotor headaches	*Increases* with the beginning of cloudy conditions *Increases* with atmospheric high-energy radiation *Increases* with active low-pressure, cyclonic weather *Increases* with clouds moving in under subtropical influences *Increases* with warm fronts, occluded fronts (where cold and warm fronts meet to combine and raise warm air high up) *Rare* with active high-pressure, anticyclonic weather

Mood & Behavior	Weather Conditions
Reaction time	*Increases* with active low-pressure, cyclonic weather *Increases* with warm fronts, cold fronts, occluded fronts *Increases* with retreating cloud covers *Decreases* with active high-pressure, anticyclonic weather *Decreases* with the disappearance of clouds
Need for sleep	*Rises* with moderate weather *Fluctuates* when a change in weather is forthcoming *Increases greatly* when weather change is complete *Falls* with extremely good weather characterized by foehn *Disturbed* by low-pressure, cyclonic weather *Disturbed* by unstable and subtropic air movements bringing in high, piled-up cumulus clouds *Disturbed* by extensive, unstable conditions *Disturbed* by cold fronts, warm fronts, occluded fronts
Depth of sleep	*Shallow* with extremely good weather characterized by foehn *Disturbed* with forthcoming change of weather *Deep and strong* when a weather change is completed *Disturbed* when it is becoming overcast, and to a lesser extent when unstable conditions are caused by cold air *Disturbed* by subtropical, and above all, unstable conditions caused by cold air *Disturbed* by warm fronts, retreating cloud covers, clearing *Disturbed* by freezing foehn *Disturbed* by weather conditions behind a cold front
Depth of sleep for infants generally	*Unfavorable* when subtropical ocean air comes in, especially strong with unstable clouding over and warm fronts *Unfavorable* with air masses above all maritime tropical air and the appearance in the biosphere of increasing cloudiness *Unfavorable* especially with sultry weather, muggy conditions
Pain-sensitivity, in general	*Highest* at the passage of weather fronts *Frequent* just prior to the passage of a front (pre-sensitivity); sensitivity derived from sickness (e.g., concussion) does not seem to differ basically from constitutional sensitivity to pain; at most slight quantitative differences are found *Increased* by approaching and actual changes in the weather *Strengthened* by low-pressure, cyclonic weather

Mood & Behavior	Weather Conditions
Pain-sensitivity (*cont.*)	*Strengthened* by unstable and subtropical conditions of increasing cloudiness *Stronger* in unstable conditions in the air layers near the ground or at high altitudes *Stronger* during warm fronts and cold fronts
Chance of accidents	*Increased* by extremely good weather of foehn type *Increased* by approaching or actual change in weather *Increased* by heat (above 35° C, 95° F) *Increased* by cold (below 10° C, 50° F) *Increased* by air pressure under 740 mm Hg (29.1 inches of mercury)
a. Traffic accidents	*Increased* by unusually good foehn weather and by approaching change in weather (especially with alcohol use) *Increased* by unstable and subtropical conditions characterized by increasing cloudiness *Increased* by warm fronts *Increased* by dependence on cyclonic processes *Increased* with cold fronts, occluded fronts, clearing, or retreating cloud covers *Increased* with active, low-pressure, circulating air masses *Increased* with lower temperatures, higher humidity in air
b. Accidents at work	*Increased* by high-energy atmospheric radiation *Increased* by extremely good foehn-type weather *Increased* by approaching and actual weather changes *Increased* by polar air masses, cold fronts *Increased* by active, low-pressure circulations, cyclonic type *Increased* by subtropical increasing cloudiness *Increased* by high-rising, unstable conditions *Increased* by warm fronts, cold fronts, occluded fronts, retreating cloud cover due to high altitude strong winds
c. Hit-and-run accidents	*Increases* during weather changes, increasing cloudiness, and related phenomena
Crime	*Tendency* for acts of violence to parallel rise in temperature, heat, dryness

Favorable and Unfavorable Weather Influences on Diseases, Ailments, Symptoms
(Note: see Glossary for any unfamiliar terms.)

Ailment	Unfavorable Weather/ Increase Symptoms	Favorable Weather/ Decrease Symptoms
Angina pectoris	Clouding connected with passage of fronts. Active cold air weather. Low-pressure-influenced weather. Subtropical clouding. Unstable clouding. Clouding with warm or cold fronts. High-rising instability, unstable cold front. Low-pressure weather, especially at the high point of the Low, with passage of a westerly moving cold front. Passage of a front. Instability after passage of a front. Low-pressure weather with unstable cold air and unstable clouding. Winter: maritime and tropical air. Spring: tropical air. Warm front.	High-pressure weather conditions. Stable conditions associated with clouding. Unstable conditions in the bottom layer of air. Dissolution of clouds with a weak wind. Clouds dropping away, clearing.
Tonsilitis	On the days before the breakthrough of subtropical, warm, air masses and transitional air masses. In general, on the first days after the breakthrough of westerly and southwesterly plus transitional conditions, cold fronts, and breakthroughs of ocean air. In colder months with conditions associated with dissolution of clouds when low-lying atmospheric inversion is present.	
Apoplectic attacks	Active, cold-weather situations. Cold fronts. Drop in air pressure below 750 mm Hg (29.5 inches of mercury). Prefrontal phenomena associated with clouding and cold fronts.	High-pressure weather conditions.

Ailment	Unfavorable Weather/ Increase Symptoms	Favorable Weather/ Decrease Symptoms
Apoplectic attacks (*cont.*)	Low-pressure weather conditions. Subtropical conditions associated with clouding. Warm fronts.	
Appendicitis	Passage of fronts. Heat waves. Powerful vertical movements of air and strong occurrences of condensation. Phenomena associated with falling away of clouds in lower strata and with beginning of clouding at great altitudes. Transition from high to low-pressure regions. Subtropical clouding. Low pressure. Rising unstable conditions.	Low-pressure weather conditions. Dissolution and clearing of clouds.
Bronchial asthma	Cooling of air or great heat. Active cold air. Cold air from the northwest. Clouding, instability of cold air, atmospheric inversion layers. Low-pressure weather conditions. Passage of unstable layers, weather fronts, especially warm and occluded fronts. Clouding associated with tropical warm air as well as unstable cold air. Transition from calm, high-pressure center to low-pressure ridge. Passage of a cold front; to a lesser extent, occluded and warm front. Decrease of total radiation. Lower atmospheric pressure. Higher air humidity. Increased risk due to increased allergy-causing aerosols (after long-lasting high-pressure area and easterly winds) with layers of atmospheric inversions, with easterly winds containing continental aerosols and maritime air. High humidity. High-rising, unstable conditions.	Low-pressure weather conditions. Dissolution and clearing of clouds.

Ailment	Unfavorable Weather/ Increase Symptoms	Favorable Weather/ Decrease Symptoms
Premature bursting of amniotic sac	Active, cold air conditions.	
Bronchitis	Foggy days.	
Diabetes mellitus	Rapid succession of warm and cold fronts. Subtropical phenomena associated with clouding and low-pressure areas, or active, warm air movements in general. Overall weather conditions involving northerly high-altitude wind from brisk maritime or continental polar air.	
Diphtheria	Low-pressure weather conditions.	
Dyspepsia	Active, cold-air weather conditions.	
Eclampsia	Active, cold-air conditions. Low-pressure weather occurrences, especially passage of weather fronts. Polar-maritime air masses in winter. Subtropical air masses in summer.	
Embolisms	Active, cold-air weather conditions. Warm-front occurrences. Subtropical clouding, in part depending on temperature. Cold fronts and unstable conditions. Low pressure; clouding. High, unstable. Warm fronts, atmospheric inversions.	Low-pressure weather. Stable clouding. Dissolution of clouds.
Epilepsy (especially traumatic)	Blustery weather fronts. Drop in barometer, storm, precipitation. Passage of warm or cold fronts. Low-pressure weather conditions. Occluded fronts.	
General sickness	Passage of fronts. Inversions. Higher humidity. Lower atmospheric pressure. Decrease in total solar radiation.	

Ailment	Unfavorable Weather/ Increase Symptoms	Favorable Weather/ Decrease Symptoms
Gallstone colics	Change in front (especially frequent air influx of cold, moist air). Active, cold-air weather. Cold fronts and prefrontal clearing. Low-pressure weather conditions. Subtropical clouding.	High-pressure conditions. Dissolution of clouds, clearing.
Hemorrhage (bleeding at joints, hemophiliacs)	Break-ins of cold air. In low-pressure situations with powerful air movements, especially at the front side of a high-pressure trough with warm-air drawing in (advection), clouding.	Calm, high-pressure conditions.
Glaucoma	Passage of fronts (especially cold fronts). Clouding and turbulent conditions. Winter: sudden rise in temperature. Summer: sudden drop in temperature. Low-pressure weather. Warm fronts. Occluded fronts. Clearing.	High-pressure weather.
Influenza, rhinitis	Dry air, especially if the air temperature was lower the previous week. High-pressure conditions. Winter: especially with high-pressure weather conditions with weak wind, which leads to the building up of cold-air reservoirs. Under the same conditions when air masses warm up then sink, they build temperature inversions 300 to 1,000 meters altitude; these barrier layers hinder the vertical exchange of air and further spread the disease. Previous high-pressure periods, frequently with high fog or thick-layered clouds (cirrostratus).	

Ailment	Unfavorable Weather/ Increase Symptoms	Favorable Weather/ Decrease Symptoms
Hay fever	Atmospheric turbulence (depending on the flora).	
Deaths from heart disease	In general, low-pressure weather conditions. Unstable clouding conditions. Warm fronts. Cold fronts.	High-pressure conditions. Dissolution of clouds.
Cardiac infarctions	Air turbulence. Cold fronts. Warm fronts. Occluded fronts. Phenomena associated with clouding and rising air masses. High humidity. Unstable conditions. Cold front, clouding, or turbulence. Warm front with clouding. Breakthrough of warm, dry air to ground level. Low-pressure weather. Clearing. Subtropical clouding phenomena.	High-pressure weather. Dissolution of clouds.
Toxic goiter	Active, warm-air weather conditions.	
Hypotonic complaints	Warm-air activity. Subtropical air masses.	
Larynx croup	Cold fronts. Breakthroughs of cold air. Sometimes warm fronts.	
Postoperative complications	Cold fronts (60 percent); warm fronts (up to 30 percent of cases).	
Climacteric problems	Active, warm-air conditions.	
Stomach ulcer	Moist, warm weather.	
Stomach perforations	Cold front. Low-pressure weather. Stable, unstable, and subtropical clouding. Warm front. Occluded front. Combination of great water-vapor pressure with small variations in daily temperature or daily humidity.	Low-pressure weather conditions. Instability in the layers of ground air, higher layers. Dissolution of clouds, clearing.
Meningitis	Break-in of oceanic polar air, frequently after warm temperatures. Drawing in (advection) of warm air.	

Ailment	Unfavorable Weather/ Increase Symptoms	Favorable Weather/ Decrease Symptoms
Multiple sclerosis	Cold climate, warm-air advection.	
Scar pains	Increased, long-wave, high-frequency radiation.	
Neuritis	Increased, long-wave, high-frequency radiation.	
Kidney stone colics	Passage of fronts. Active, cold-air conditions. Change in air masses. Cold fronts and prefrontal clearing. Subtropical clouding phenomena. Low-pressure weather conditions.	High-pressure weather. Dissolution of clouds. Clearing.
Poliomyelitis	Too warm, moist air masses two to three days before beginning of disease. Warm-air advection. High humidity and high equivalent temperature. Cold fronts occasionally, especially those in warm half of year preceded by moist warm air masses (unstable, thunderstorms).	
Rheumatic complaints	During cold, moist, windy periods. Increased, long-wave, high-frequency radiation. Cold-front passages (complaints diminish as weather quickly calms). Warm fronts, occluded fronts. Drops in temperature. Frequent air turbulence.	
Infant infections	Active, warm-air, weather conditions.	
Scarlet fever	Prevailing low-pressure circulation (westerly weather conditions). Large-scale weather conditions with high-pressure, mixed circulation.	
Stenocardia	Active, warm-air conditions. Increased, long-wave, high-frequency radiation.	

Ailment	Unfavorable Weather/ Increase Symptoms	Favorable Weather/ Decrease Symptoms
Deaths (see Appendix E)	Low-pressure, weather conditions. Unstable and subtropical clouding. Warm front. Cold front. Occluded front. Clearing. Inversion.	High-pressure weather. Unstable conditions in ground layers. Dissolution of clouds.
Bleeding after tonsillectomy	Beginning cold weather. Foehn. Warm front. Cold front. Occluded front. Clearing. Inversion.	
Pneumonia	Dry air preceded by low temperature. After cold-air fronts. Influx of cold air and occlusion. Sometimes warm fronts. (After antibiotics, symptoms disappear.)	
Bleeding after eye operations	High-pressure weather. Clearing.	
Weak labor pains	Active, warm-air, weather conditions	
Root canal pain syndrome	Cold, moist weather.	

Subliminal Stress, Sublime Stress

Hans Selye, in discussing the prescientific, intuitive feelings he had as a medical student (in 1926), which foreshadowed his later work on stress, remarked recently:

> I began to wonder why patients suffering from the most diverse diseases have so many signs and symptoms in common. Whether a man suffers from a severe loss of blood, an infectious disease or advanced cancer, he loses his appetite, his muscular strength and his ambition to accomplish anything; usually the patient also loses weight, and even his facial expression betrays that he is ill. What is the scientific basis of what I thought of at the time as the "syndrome of just being sick"?

Later he defined stress as the "nonspecific response of the body to any demand made upon it." He said that all stressors cause the body to make generalized adjustments to reestablish normalcy. But the adjustments are independent of the specific agent, environmental force, or activity that triggered them. It is the nonspecific demand for adjustment, or adaptation, that is the essential nature of stress. Selye's formulation of our response to stress accounts for Wilder's Law of Initial Value (see Chapter 1) by considering the organism to be prestressed, prior to its exposure to stress.

A recent computer survey of the scientific literature of stress suggests that many, if not most, ailments known to modern medicine are stress-related. One list of these selected *physio*logical effects of stress (over one hundred items) shows that leading but diverse causes of death—such as suicides, accidents, carcinoma, myocardial infarctions, among others—are implicated. Another list of selected *psycho*logical effects of stress (over fifty items) covers many emotional, mental, and psychiatric disorders. *There is probably no human condition that stress cannot make worse.*

Most of mankind's ailments, judging from these lengthy lists, are stress-related. Perhaps intimidating, they demonstrate that the results of stress are likely to reach deep into the organism. They show that a large number of symptoms, complaints, and ailments that appear to be induced by weather conditions also appear to be induced by stress. (For a detailed assessment of your own stress-induced dysfunctions, see Appendix C.) The "syndrome of just being sick" is an adaptive body response common to both nonspecific agents—generalized stressors—and to specific agents—weather stressors.

Sensitivity to Weather . . .
Sensitivity to Life: A Summary

"Weather" is a metaphor for life, and your sensitivity to weather, like your sensitivity to a social or emotional environment, is vastly revealing. Weather-sensitives of the world cluster into seemingly obscure patterns. Thus, middle-class people are generally less weather-sensitive than upper- and lower-class people. Middle-aged people are generally less weather-sensitive than the elderly and the very young. Men are less weather-sensitive than are women. And many geniuses seem to have been extraordinarily sensitive to our weather, although most of our environment is inaccessible to inspection, invisible by virtue of its pervasive omnipresence.

Large-scale studies of the phenomenon define some thirty-seven symptoms of subjective weather-sensitivity, including tiredness, bad moods, disturbed sleep, disinclination to work. Perhaps half to three-quarters of the population is, at least intermittently, subjectively weather-sensitive—they attribute one or more of these symptoms to the weather. Perhaps 115 million weather-sensitive Americans will inhabit the United States by the year 1990.

Many of our body's organs seem to function at their maximum capacity between the ages of fifteen and thirty-five. According to the statistics, the adaptive ability to conform to the weather environment and to rally against environmental assaults is incompletely developed in the very early years, reaches a crest in the early to middle decades of life, and deteriorates at very advanced age.

A *broad range of physiological symptoms* (alterations in blood and urine composition), *psychological symptoms* (ability to concentrate, desire to work, reaction time, mental illness) *and health disorders* (hemorrhage, influenza, heart attacks, scar pains, stroke) *are associated with specific weather conditions*. Many of the same symptoms are also associated with stress agents, both general and specific. Weather as a stressor has both specific and general repercussions upon the human body and mind very much like those of emotional and physical stress.

Three:
Weather-Beaten ...
or Weather-Proof?

Men of a conquering army do not report sick.
   —Napoleon Bonaparte

Health is not conscious of itself, but frees the mind for the perception
of other things; and even the joy of health, when it comes to the surface, comes rather in the form of some generous enthusiasm for nature, for sport, or for loveable people.
   —George Santayana

The five aphrodisiacs are: exercise, fresh air, sunshine, good food,
and sufficient sleep.
   —Alfred Kinsey

Then you had better cover your skin well,
   as I instruct you:
Put on both a soft outer cloak, and a fringed tunic,
   and have an abundant woof woven across a light warp;
Put this on you, so that your hairs will stay
   quiet in their places, and not bristle and
   stand up shivering all over your body.
      —Hesiod's advice to his brother Perses, "Works and Days"

Preceding Page: Lips or Libs
The southwest wind is represented by a robust man. In his hands he holds
an "apluster," a wooden ornament usually placed on the highest extremity
of the stern of a ship.

The portly man had a few drinks at the party. He was warm and relaxed. The conversation and people were interesting. Before leaving, he swallowed his medicine, lighted a cigarette, and bundled up. It was bitter cold outside. Hatless he stood trying to hail a cab. No luck. As he started to walk, he felt palpitations in his chest . . . Nothing . . . Just nerves from overwork—or a heart attack? He wondered. First fear, then panic, swept through his body. A hospital was nearby. He began to walk farther and faster; then he ran. At the emergency ward, an aide saw him collapse. Thinking the man in shock, she covered him quickly with a warm blanket. Moments later, he died. The unfortunate man had unwittingly exposed himself to massive stress.

First, alcohol had opened his peripheral blood vessels, encouraging the loss of his body's heat. His body's natural, reflexive response to cold would have been the narrowing of the blood vessels (vasoconstriction), insulating and isolating the body's core from thermal change. Alcohol defeated that.

Second, cigarette nicotine had decreased the amount of blood reaching his extremities, interfering with retention of warmth.

Third, once his coat opened, the chilled air on his chest constricted his coronary arteries, causing spasm.

Fourth, without a hat he was like a topless Thermos jug—a large amount of internal heat rising through his poorly insulated body would also leave out the top.

Fifth, his anxiety over the palpitations "fed back" upon itself, fueling further intensification of his agitated emotions.

Sixth, walking, then running, added to the coronary overload by requiring physical exercise, vascular dilation, and increased skeletal muscle supply, in turn demanding additional coronary output.

Seventh, the well-intentioned blanket prevented his body from cooling properly by the evaporation of perspiration in a warm room, "hyperloading" his heart with an extra burden of sweating in a vain attempt to discharge heat.

Eighth, the medications he had taken interfered seriously with his ability to regulate his body temperature, unbeknownst to him—or his physician.

A similar disaster story, demonstrating the deadly consequences of not knowing how the body maintains its temperature (thermoregulation) can be told about hot spells. In blithe ignorance of its effects, our consumption of excessive quantities of tranquilizers, sleeping pills, or barbiturates would lead to the body's failure to maintain its temperature.

This horror story, a composite of real-life episodes, contains many elements of stress that heighten its impact. Our response to stress, research shows, is enhanced by its intensity or speed of change, our lack of preparedness or prior experience, by its duration or our prolonged exposure, by the amount of stress or the departure of the body from its usual condition, and by its unpredictability.

But because stress is such a broad and general concept, it is useful mainly as an organizing principle to identify patterns or causes of disease (for example, for research) or better still as an all-embracing view of human beings in their environment. Perhaps its use lies in that the concept of stress seeks to encompass what is the equivalent of an organic, physiological, socioemotional version of Newton's Laws: push or pulled, inanimate objects move in predictable "displacements." There are no powerful Newton's Laws for sociology, psychology, physiology—or biometeorology. And vague generalities do not provide guidance or practical prescriptions in dealing with weather stress; as Walter Gropius said, "God is in the details."

The details must direct us how to remove stress, adjust to stress, or suffer defeat by stress. Our weather-connected activities also entail other types of stress—physical or exercise stress, emotional stress, and even social stress.

Prescriptive measures demand both "specificity" (the details), and how to cope with weather—whether we address sports, physical exercise, foods and medicines, travel, clothing, and their effects under weather stress.

Exercise Weather

Athletes, like geniuses, resemble normal mortals—the rest of us— only more so. What specialists in sports medicine learn from athletes and physical competition under various extreme weather conditions will apply to the rest of us under normal conditions.

Maximal physical effort bears many resemblances to exposure to high altitudes. In each case, diminished oxygen (hypoxia) or lack of oxygen (anoxia) are the major cause of symptoms. Athletic performance demands muscular effort, increased metabolism, increased respiration (hyperventilation), and discharge of carbon dioxide (acapnia). At high altitudes, there is a diminished amount of atmospheric oxygen to breathe and, at the same time, a deficiency of carbon dioxide—but the presence of carbon dioxide is the body's way of regulating respiration. Consequently, after a delay of minutes or hours, acute sickness will develop. Called "effort sickness" in athletes, or "mountain sickness" in climbers, the symptoms are often pronounced weakness (without loss of consciousness), nausea, vomiting, and headaches.

Exercise can be dangerous at high altitudes unless proper acclimatization procedures are followed. In the 1968 Olympic Games in Mexico City, hundreds of finely trained athletes collapsed. Many cases were severe, but none fatal. Four diagnostic categories appeared. *Effort migraine* typically manifests itself after long races, with symptoms like seeing flickering images or luminous, jagged, wall-like outlines; nausea, vomiting, and severe throbbing headaches. *Sudden loss of consciousness* occurs during or after very long-lasting athletic performances; unconsciousness up to an hour may be followed by amnesia. *Shock* is characterized by bluish discoloration of lips and nose, reduced flow of blood to the brain and a severe drop in blood pressure. Finally, *attacks of powerlessness* come on the heels of great emotional excitement; when told he had just broken the world record for a long jump, one medalist collapsed. At Mexico City's altitude, the short track races, sprints, hurdles, and short events generally were run conspicuously fast, the long races conspicuously slowly.

The combination of emotional stress, exercise stress, and high altitude could be too much for an untrained, unacclimatized nonathlete. Tennis, football, wrestling, rowing, running, and basketball may induce "effort sickness." Its symptoms bear striking resemblances to symptoms of weather-sensitivity. But the similarities are not mere coincidences, since heat production and heat dissipation are necessary to shift the body temperature back to its comfort zone. Two extremes of stress in sports performance—at high temperature (hyperthermal) and at low temperature (hypothermal)—affect different locations in the body. The chart (see Chapter Notes) shows that the most common situation is high-temperature stress in the body's core.

At rest, your body will typically pour out the power equivalent of a

100-watt light bulb. Running a 26.2-mile marathon, a champion athlete will put out 1500 watts each hour for a little over two hours. That top runner will lose some four quarts of water, and his body weight will drop by 6 percent, perhaps ten pounds. If the mechanisms balancing his body temperature were not working, his body temperature would soar by some 79 degrees F (43 degrees C), to a lethal level.

Slower runners will put out less energy per unit time; four hours of marathon running at 750 watts each hour will yield the same 3000 watts delivered by the champion, enough to heat two fair-sized rooms.

Of course various other activities will coax appropriate levels of power out of the body; sleeping (75 watts); strolling at 1.5 miles per hour (105 watts), canoeing at 2.5 miles per hour (210 watts); cycling at 3.5 miles per hour (310 watts); driving a motorcycle (425 watts); golfing (625 watts); hand-sawing hardwood (940 watts); walking on hard snow at 3.5 miles per hour (1400 watts); walking on soft snow at 2 miles per hour (1730 watts); walking on soft snow with a 44-pound load at 2 miles per hour (2560 watts).

The more intense the exercise and/or heat or cold, the more critical proper retention of water in the body (hydration) becomes. Body temperature will soar, performance decrease, involuntary functions will become disturbed, well-being will deteriorate via the central nervous system, and blood plasma volume will decrease, diminishing the heart's stroke volume, its cardiac output, and oxygen-transport capability. Thus it becomes necessary to replace the water lost by any of these exercises or to anticipate water loss by defensive drinking.

What is the proper amount of water? Exercising under thermal stress, people tend to drink only half to two-thirds of the amount of water they lose in sweat, which leads to progressive dehydration. Apparently this does not become serious until 3 percent of a fit person's body weight is lost. So if you deliberately drink 2 percent of your body weight to maintain body fluids during exercise in heat or cold, you will have a margin of safety. At a normal body weight of 150 pounds, 2 percent of body weight will be the equivalent of drinking a quart and a half of fluid (at 200 pounds, two quarts). Defensive drinking in the summer is especially important for all athletes and casual joggers.

Physical fitness will reduce the body's response to heat stress because it makes the body more able to sweat and to breathe without labor. Heat acclimatization and fitness do the same: they keep the body's core temperature low. Without physical fitness or heat acclimatization, hyperventilation, or the abnormal loss of carbon dioxide from the blood, generally occurs, and may suppress the sweating response, thereby allowing body temperature to rise. The regulation of the body's temperature is determined by the amount of carbon dioxide in the blood and the ratio of metallic salts (the sodium and calcium ion balance) in the hypothalamus (with excess sodium or decreased calcium, thermoregulation occurs around a higher equilibrium temperature, or "set point"; excess calcium or decreased sodium lowers that equilibrium temperature.)

Champion athletes, those physically fit or best acclimatized, will perform better in heat because of their aerobic training. They have a high maximum oxygen uptake and can maintain it for prolonged periods. They produce less heat for the same metabolism, they sweat readily, their circulation resists dehydration, and they maintain proper hydration.

As Kenneth Cooper shows in his book *The Aerobics Way*, even highly conditioned athletes need a cooling-down period after exercise. "Taper off gradually," he says. "Take at least as long to cool down as you did to warm up—five minutes is the minimum." He prescribes stretching exercises before exercise or sports to warm up, and walking around after jogging, basketball, tennis, swimming, or bicycling to cool down. Particularly important are warm-up exercises indoors, before exercising in cold weather outdoors. The arteries to the heart must be dilated by warm-up exercises and kept that way with warm enough garments, like a scarf across the chest.

In cold-weather sports, the extremities are most likely to suffer. Hands, feet, facial skin may be deprived of warm blood from the body's core by the environmental demand. Exposed flesh can be frozen in one minute if it is cold enough outdoors to withdraw the power equivalent of some forty-two 100-watt bulbs from an average-sized man. In cross-country skiing, cold and exercise are important considerations. A man heavily dressed in arctic clothing at $-40°F$ ($-40°C$) will freeze his exposed finger in one minute if he is resting. However, if he runs enough to generate the equivalent of ten 100-watt bulbs, his exposed finger will not freeze in twenty minutes of running despite the wind-chill factor. Cross-country skiers may start inadequately dressed in anticipation of overheating. But before the body heat distributes warm blood to the extremities, the skier's fingers, face, or feet may freeze. If the skier is accidentally immobilized and cannot generate enough body heat or if the weather turns suddenly colder, he or she may suffer severe frostbite.

Cold fingers are common in winter sports, but permanent damage is not done unless skin is frozen for several minutes. Mountaineers, without freezing their fingers at all after several days at mountain altitudes, may suffer loss of feeling (anesthesia) in the fingers. This comes about from constant blood-vessel constriction and low blood oxygen, which causes cellular death by air hunger (hypoxia or anoxia).

Although unproven, exercise leading to physical fitness is likely to improve blood flow to the extremities at rest during cold weather. Physical fitness has these important advantages for cold adaptation: it sustains heat production, it lowers your resting evaporative losses, and it lowers your resting breathing rate.

Only long-distance walking, mountaineering, or lengthy cold-water immersion will provide the likely conditions—sustained severe cold, accidental immobilization—that can drop the body core temperature to a lethal level. Fitness in advance, of course, can help to prevent this drop. And so can endurance fitness training and gradual habituation to cold.

In extreme cold, it is wise to avoid being motionless for any extended period of time. The involuntary shivering that accompanies being cold is meant to generate heat energy from muscle tissues, so it is nature's warning: get moving. Get out of the cold or move your muscles, make wide circles with your arms, twist your trunk to the left and right, stamp your feet, jog in place, clap your hands, jump up and down.

Also wet skin, from any source—from perspiration due to overdressing (discussed later), from rain, or from total immersion in water—can be especially dangerous in cold weather. Water conducts heat over twenty times better than air does.

Altitude conditioning of athletes and sportsmen is not the only way to accommodate them or us to stress; heat acclimatization and cold acclimatization are others.

Boxers, wrestlers, judo performers, gymnasts, canoeists, and rowers who underwent special weather conditioning improved their athletic performance. Their pulse rate and arterial pressure increases were suppressed by training in high-temperature–high-pressure weather systems. Normal weather-induced inefficiency was quickly restored by their physical fitness and adaptability.

The air composition is a critical factor in athletic exercise and weather conditioning. Because athletes and sportsmen breathe especially deeply during competition, pollutants and oxygen levels are critical. Obviously, outdoor stadiums should not be placed downwind of a factory discharging contaminants into the air. Sports fans benefit as well. In Europe, it is fairly safe to build a stadium south of a pollution source (north winds are rare) to provide good air mixing by turbulence. In the United States, depending on the region, sports stadiums should generally be located west of pollution sources to take advantage of the prevailing westerly winds. Ice-skating rinks trap stagnant air near the surface, so outdoor ice-skating rinks, particularly, benefit from a placement windward of a discharge.

Tennis, ball games, and track and field events are confined indoors by the winter season, and the air must be kept pure, even if it means prohibiting smoking.

At an altitude of 6,000 feet (2,000 meters), the diminished oxygen is compensated for by deepened breathing, and after several days the blood shifts away from acidity toward relative alkalinity, according to one expert, thereby increasing the concentration of oxygen-carrying hemoglobins (erythrocytes) and facilitating the combination of oxygen with hemoglobin. Athletes will acclimatize and perform well at this altitude after perhaps ten days' stay. Upon the athlete's return to sea level, the new oxygen-carrying hemoglobins may last four months, and the athlete will continue to enjoy better performance at lower energy expenditure for some time. Bulgarian athletes at the Mexican Olympic Games gave their best performances two or three days after returning to the lowlands; four to seven days later, drowsiness and laziness set in; on the seventh and eighth days, good performance was restored.

Each new climate condition and its own acclimatization, whether for athletes or not, demands a prolonged reacclimatization period. Adaptation to cold differs from adaptation to heat; and both differ from adaptation to frequent or infrequent weather changes. The postacclimatization periods ("climatic regression") call for rest to avoid psychic depression or the inability of the heart to maintain adequate circulation (decompensation). Put another way, the best way to recuperate is to rest and relax.

Acclimatization to Weather

The air mass may come to you; or you may travel to the air mass. In either case, from the personal frame of reference, the weather changes.

From whatever cause, weather stress may not be noticeable at first but will gradually appear as several other stressors accumulate. Intense sports activity, inadequate nutrition, enhanced emotional excitement, or prolonged or excessive weather stress—any one of these may be the decisive trigger. You will be particularly vulnerable to weather after a stretch of prolonged exercise, or poor diet, or emotional upheaval, or severe changes in weather conditions due to travel or the rapid passage of weather fronts. But, the trained athlete adjusts better than the untrained person. According to a bioclimatologist, two or three weeks or even more are necessary for "full acclimatization to a significant change in locality." However, adaptation may be accelerated to ten days if training is intensified.

Particularly acute is a move from a Northern Hemisphere winter to a Southern Hemisphere summer, because of the number of changes taking place at the same time: additional thermal load, disrupted yearly rhythms, and possibly distorted daily rhythms.

"Thermal neutrality" is the subjective sensation of comfort, neither too hot nor too cold. As outside temperatures drop, blood vessel shrinkage (vasoconstriction) continues, peripheral body tissues become increasingly good insulators, and the personal sense of discomfort increases. Further vasoconstriction in response to lower temperatures is perceived as "uncomfortable" by men and as "unbearable" by women. Women are more sensitive to their own vasoconstriction response to outside cold, but at the same time surpass men's ability to shut down and insulate their periphery by vasoconstriction. Women will react to cold *sooner* than men and withstand it *better* than men. In the company of a woman who is cold, a cold-susceptible man would do well to bundle up, because she knows something—it is cold—sooner than he.

Personal discomfort from vasoconstriction also triggers conscious adaptation, behavioral thermal regulation, or habituation to the local climate. If the discomfort sensation is absent during exposure to cold weather, serious trouble will develop. Body temperature will fall without triggering appropriate conscious adaptation to maintain body warmth. This may happen in elderly people living alone, in hyperactive individuals, in those who avoid their inner feelings, and in those who are distracted by some greater pain.

One way to prevent this is to seek thermal corroborations: If you cannot trust your own sensations of discomfort when exposed to the cold, check your warmth by touching one hand to the other periodically or to your face.

Heat evokes sweating and blood vessel expansion (vasodilation) to increase heat flow outward from the body's trunk via its extremities to the environment. Above thermal neutrality, the sensation of discomfort begins as vasodilation rapidly sets in, increasing peripheral heat conductance (or decreasing peripheral insulation ability). Men begin to sense discomfort before women do as the temperature climbs, but women reach both greater thermal conductance and greater discomfort than men. Thus, a heat-sensitive woman might do well to listen to a man's complaints about the onset of heat, since he feels it sooner than she.

Acclimatization to heat means that your blood vessels will dilate more quickly and you will begin to sweat earlier and continue sweating.

But acute heat, such as a heat wave, if accompanied by exercise, work, or emotional stress, can strain the thermoregulatory functions, cardiovascular system, and sweating mechanism. The dangerous results, *heat exhaustion* or *heat stroke*, may be difficult to distinguish.

Failure of the cardiovascular system brings on *heat exhaustion;* symptoms are low blood pressure, fainting, dizziness, breathlessness, sudden loss of strength or of consciousness, pallor, weak pulse, *moist and cool skin*, and normal or low temperature. First-aid treatment calls for keeping the victim quiet, horizontal, and out of the sun, and supplying him with a few teaspoons of salt in water, coffee, or tea. Older people with heart trouble may have difficulty recovering.

Failure of the sweating mechanism brings on *heat stroke*, an extremely dangerous condition in which the *skin is hot and dry*, the body temperature is high and rising, and the victim is delirious or unconscious. First-aid treatment calls for placing the victim in cool shade, on his back, head raised; cooling the entire body with ice and a cool, wet cloth; and not giving stimulants. Sustaining the victim may still not prevent brain damage, which can cause death days later.

Deaths during severe heat waves are common in the United States. The number of deaths attributed to excessive heat are actually understated (see Appendix D). Heat-aggravated deaths are at least ten times more numerous than reported by the United States Public Health Service Mortality Tables. Infants and the elderly have the highest mortality. Heat-aggravated deaths occur during arteriosclerotic and degenerative heart disease, ischemic and hypertensive heart disease, vascular accidents, stroke, senility, infant diseases, diabetes, and declining sweat-gland efficiency. These examples of heat-susceptible ailments show reverse tolerance for heat, the antithesis of heat acclimatization and physical fitness. Probably the best long-term insurance to beat the heat is acclimatization and fitness.

Exercise, profuse sweating, and elevating the body temperature will do the job. Repeated exposure to heat for one to four hours for five to seven days, accompanied with exercise, will grant acclimatization to heat. Yale physiologist James Hardy exposed four young men to heat and a daily routine of programmed work. They began unacclimatized, and on the first day none could complete a physical test. Their pulse rates were high, internal body temperature rose rapidly to unacceptable levels, and their sweat rate declined before becoming appropriately high. But the results of the acclimatization program were dramatic. After two weeks, all four men "completed the work period with apparent ease, without undue elevations of body temperature or pulse rates, and with sweat rates at higher levels." Their metabolic rate decreased, a sign of increased physical fitness. Without proper heat acclimatization, young football athletes may suffer in the northern United States during the football season. Without repeated heat exposure and exercise, heat acclimatization disappears in three to four weeks.

Exposure to sustained heat or cold, on vacation or in change of season, will call forth normal acclimatization in healthy people. Voluntary acclimatization in advance not only represents good planning, it enhances the pleasure of weather.

"Dress as Though Your Life Depends on It!"

This weather service motto represents not only good public relations but good advice for healthy behavior. The question is, how?

The largest number of daily weather decisions made by the general public in selecting the quantity and type of clothing are made without a good guide.

Most people have a thermal comfort level at which they feel neither too cool nor too warm (thermal neutrality). The level varies from person to person only slightly. Some unfortunates have a diminished sensation of thermal comfort but not a diminished requirement for good thermoregulation, so they have to depend less on unconscious and more on conscious, thermal regulation. A keen subjective sensation of comfort is a reliably accurate indicator of what to wear. However it is often extremely difficult, if not impossible, to judge outdoor weather properly from a vantage point indoors.

The insulating properties of clothing depend on its thickness, weight, weave, fabric and style of the garment, air temperature, wind speed, and solar radiation. A typical vested business suit from the 1940s (somewhat heavier than today's) was defined as having an insulation value of 1.0 *clo* unit. Once the *clo* unit was defined, it became possible to compare clothing articles for their insulating ability and to recommend combinations for wear during different activities. For comparison, shorts have an insulating value of 0.1 *clo*, a polar weather suit 3.4 *clo*, a husky dog 4.1 *clo*, and a red fox fur 7.8 *clo* units.

| <0.5 | 0.6-1.2 | 1.3-1.7 | 1.8-2.4 | 2.5-3.4 | >3.5 |

The numbers show the *clo*-unit value corresponding to the clothing on the figure above.

One *clo* may also be visualized as a unit of thermal insulation that maintains a seated resting person (who is putting out about 100 watts in quiet air at a temperature of 68°F [21°C] and relative humidity under 50 percent) in a condition of continuous comfort.

Most people in the United States generally wear about 0.8 *clo* in a typical office, heated (until the energy crunch) to 75°F. Conserving energy, a temperature of 65°F to 68°F will make most people, including children, feel comfortable if they wear 1.2 to 1.5 *clo*.

If your activity level increases, clearly the insulation value of your clothing can diminish (see figure below). Or if the weather is very cold, you will need greater insulation. In a vivid, thermal-comfort image, ancient Chinese calendars call November a "two-suit month."

Clothing Insulation Required for Comfort		
	65-68 F	70-72 F
Seated, Reading with Light Mental Activity	1.6—2.0 clo	1.2—1.4 clo
Standing, Relaxed Seated, Typing Drafting Misc. Office Work	1.2—1.5 clo	0.9—1.1 clo
Cooking Washing Dishes Shaving Teacher in School	.8—1.0 clo	0.5—0.7 clo
House Cleaning Walking 3 mph Washing & Ironing	0.5—0.7 clo	0.3—0.5 clo

Clo units appropriate for different indoor activities, at two temperature ranges, for comfort.

The *clo* values for individual garments—from women's long-sleeved blouses to knee-high fashion boots, and from men's briefs to vests—can be found in Appendix E, with instructions on how to estimate the total *clo* value of your selected clothing ensemble. Clothing stores, from boutiques to department stores, or clothing manufacturers could include *clo* values on the labels or tags. A consumer advocate seeking a just cause for labeling could do worse than promote this. Promotional advantages in marketing, and energy savings advantages are also obvious.

Television and radio weather forecasts in the United States often present useless detail and endless technical elaboration of the weather conditions—but they fail to make suggestions about the likely effects of the forthcoming weather on *people*. They avoid admonishment, as they should. But they could begin to broadcast some hints (like the Bioprognosis system does in Germany (see Chapter 9). A good nonintrusive starting point is to suggest how to dress for the weather.

Television is a visual medium. For broad appeal, a visual presentation of both the weather—and the suitable clothing requirements for a given weather condition—is advisable. Simple, universal symbols for pictorial weather forecasts would be very useful and instantly comprehensible. Some suggestions are shown in the following figure.

Furthermore pictorial forecasts, combined with a prescription for comfortable clothing, have immediate appeal. Figures on page 62 show hypothetical weather forecasts with accompanying numerical and verbal descriptions.

Television weather forecasts would further benefit the public greatly if their forecasts were also conducted in *clo* units. The United States Army Quartermaster Corps speaks of the subtropics as a "one-layer zone," and the subarctic as a "four-layer zone." A forecast of 14°F with a wind of five miles per hour and cloudless skies is very difficult to interpret in terms of personal comfort, but *a 2-clo-unit day is very specific.* An apparently warmer day (37°F, wind of ten miles per hour, overcast skies) actually calls for the same clothing insulation to achieve thermal comfort outdoors.

If man and woman are the measure of all things (or at least all things commercial) then it might even behoove the United States Weather Service or the *Farmer's Almanac* to issue maps (as is done in Canada) revealing the climate itself in terms of clothing requirements or *clo* values. Nine out of ten Americans eagerly want *more* weather information, not less, as studies show.

As for clothing in hot weather, probably the most comfortable garments are made of light cotton, which absorbs sweat and then allows it to dissipate into the air. During exercise and work, low *clo*-unit garments, of course, are recommended. If you cannot trust your sensations or the television weather, you could consult the tabular material here and in Appendix E.

A historical "experiment with orange-red underwear" deserves a footnote. Frederick Sargent, II, described the following curious circumstances recently. Colonel Charles Edward Woodruf, "a brilliant but somewhat erratic member of the U.S. Army Medical Corps, believed that the tropics had a deleterious effect on white men, and attributed the injury to the effect of ultraviolet light." Consequently orange-red underwear was issued to several thousand troops to be worn for a year (1909) and the results compared with troops wearing

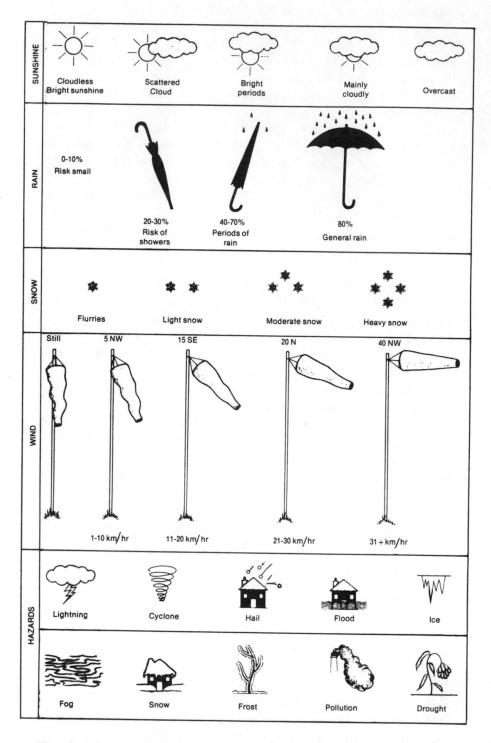

SUNSHINE	Cloudless Bright sunshine	Scattered Cloud	Bright periods	Mainly cloudly	Overcast

RAIN

0-10%
Risk small

20-30%
Risk of
showers

40-70%
Periods of
rain

80%
General rain

SNOW

Flurries   Light snow   Moderate snow   Heavy snow

WIND

Still   5 NW   15 SE   20 N   40 NW

1-10 km/hr   11-20 km/hr   21-30 km/hr   31 + km/hr

HAZARDS

Lightning   Cyclone   Hail   Flood   Ice

Fog   Snow   Frost   Pollution   Drought

Weather Symbols Proposed for Pictorial Forecasts

TIME				
REPRESENTATION FORECAST	-1°C 15N 2·4	+2°C 25NYW 2·3	+6°C 6W 1·6	+8°C 1·2
DESCRIPTION	Ta = -1°C V = 15 km. per hr. Overcast Light snow or periods of rain (40% Probability) Clo = 2·4	Ta = 2°C V = 25 km. per hr. Occasional sunshine General rain (80% Probability) Clo = 2·3	Ta = 6°C V = 6 km. per hr. Scattered cloud Risk of rain (20% Probability) Clo = 1·6	Ta = 8°C Still air Bright sunshine Clo = 1·2

Hypothetical weather forecasts pictorialized with suggested clothing, accompanied by numerical descriptions.

the usual white underwear. His analysis of the results in 1910 (in the *Philipine Journal of Science*) and by the Army Medical Research Board led to this expensive conclusion: "Wearing orange-red underwear had no beneficial effect whatever." Not light, but heat and humidity, make tropical life uncomfortable.

Weather-Sensitive Drugs

Belladonna means "lovely lady" in Italian. Once used by beautiful women as a cosmetic trick to enlarge the pupils of their eyes, thereby making them appear more wide-eyed and thus more interested and attentive to men, the drug comes from the dried leaves of the plant *Atropa belladonna*, or deadly nightshade, found in Europe and Asia. Belladonna, or atropine, is applied by ophthamologists locally to the eye to dilate the pupil and paralyze the ciliary muscles of visual accommodation.

The drug works in the body by blocking the action of acetylcholine, the substance that transmits signals to the nerve endings of the parasympathetic nervous system that controls vasodilation, shunts blood to the body's periphery, promotes heat loss, and lowers blood pressure. Atropine inhibits sweating and interferes with the normal regulation of body temperature. Because of this, research biometeorologist Wolf Weihe says, "Atropine has become the pet drug of climate-induced drug modification."

Use of atropine by ophthamologists in the hot, dry climate of Baghdad has led to fatal heat stroke. And as early as 1920, warnings against indiscriminate use of atropine were issued to military personnel stationed in the Middle East.

However, atropine is merely the most *famous* weathef-sensitive medical drug, though not perhaps the most *sensitive*. Fortunately, its weather effects are so spectacular that it not only drew attention to itself, but it implied that there were other drug families whose *in vivo* effects were weather-dependent, or temperature-dependent, or provoked sensitivity to the sun (photosensitivity).

Weather-driven reaction of animals to drugs has been known and studied for some time. But man has been so ingenious in maintaining a thermoneutral microclimate around his body and in his habitats, that he has masked many of the climate- or weather-induced drug actions on his body. Animals do not have our range of behavioral thermoregulation. But some of the findings applicable to animals may be partially extended to man. New studies and case histories are enlarging the knowledge of geographical, seasonal, or biometeorological pharmacology.

Calling a drug a stimulant or a depressant has little value unless one describes the environment in which the drug is given and the prior level of arousal of the patient taking the drug (in accordance with Wilder's Law of Initial Value, Chapter 1). The drug, the person, and the atmosphere must be evaluated together carefully. (See illustration in Chapter Notes.)

Weather-driven toxic changes in drug action were first looked upon as a nuisance. But testing drugs for toxicity in warm-blooded animals (who are subject to wide environmental conditions) is extremely important for drug companies to undertake in their screening of newly developed drugs. Weihe says that "whether a drug affects the controller system or effectors of thermoregulation . . . very few tests have been specifically designed to investigate."

Only since drugs have been used on a large scale has their photosensitivity or dependence on weather, climate, and temperature been brought to our attention through accidental overdoses in hot or cold weather. Weihe says, "In modern polypharmacy where antipsychotic, anti-depressant and anti-parkinsonism drugs are prescribed in conjunction, an even greater hazard has arisen than when the drugs are given alone. . . . *Even mild medication is a potential danger as it makes the organism more susceptible to heat and cold.*"

Unfortunately, major accidents have to occur before the attending physician is alerted. Anesthetics induce low body temperatures by depressing thermoregulation centers. A strong tranquilizer (chlorpromazine) is given routinely to psychiatric patients as an antipsychotic drug. During a heat wave in Topeka, Kansas, it brought on abnormally elevated body temperatures (hyperthermia), which was treated by anticholinergic drugs that suppressed the sweating mechanism and both drugs combined led to fatal heat stroke.

Physicians are not the only ones ignorant of the interaction or synergism between medical drugs and weather conditions. A boy under heavy antihistamine medication was allowed to play basketball in summer heat and expired. A fifty-six-year-old New York City man was admitted to a hospital emergency room with extremely high temperature. Because he had been depressed about his sexual inadequacy with a new girlfriend, anxious about his job, and frightened about a chronic disease, he took a large dose of an antihistamine. Afraid he might die, his girlfriend advised him to "work off" the dose. He set off for the hospital, wearing a jacket, on an abnormally hot day. "The combination of great distress, a high drug dose, ambient heat, overclothing and exercise made rapidly developing hyperpyrexia [high fever] inevitable," Weihe reports. Elderly people, who are particularly deficient in thermoregulation or sweating ability, are very susceptible to weather-sensitive drugs, a fact overlooked in nursing care.

Genetic makeup, in addition to climate, will condition the response to a drug. An antimalarial drug used in the tropics (primaquine) will be toxic to Thais or blacks, but harmless to Japanese and Caucasians under similar climate conditions. During travel, this genetic-climatic-drug effect may not be obvious.

Any medical drug that interferes with any of our mechanisms for equilibrating body temperature will have a weather-sensitive component to its drug activity in the body. Basic chemical reactions depend upon temperature, and, thus, so do the primary processes in living cells and tissues. Frederick Fuhrman classified the temperature-dependent factors that will determine the action of drugs: absorption of the drug at its entry point, transportation or distribution of the drug throughout the body, its interaction with the body tissue at its receptor site (called receptor binding), the body's metabolism (or detoxification) of the drug, and finally its elimination from the body by excretion.

Examples of one type of weather-driven reaction to drugs are produced by those centrally acting drugs that disturb the thermoregulatory portion of the brain: atropine, sleep inducers, drugs that mimic nervous disorders, morphine, tranquilizers, analgesics, digitalis, choline-blockers. (See Appendix F.)

A second response type are drugs that mimic the actions of the sympathetic nervous system (amphetamines, epinephrines, procaine, cortisone), stimulants (caffeine), and antihistamines (see Appendix F for a full list of weather-dependent drugs).

A third type of response may be open to question once sufficient testing is done, because it may merely be a variant of one of the other two types.

Common household substances can effect thermoregulation. Aspirin will reduce high fever and hasten the loss of body heat by virtue of its indirect action on the hypothalamus, dilating blood vessels in the skin. In larger doses it may induce sweating or hot skin and fever.

Caffeine constricts the blood-vessel walls, raises blood pressure, and retards the loss of body heat. It also enhances mental acuity and alertness (which may explain the popularity of coffee, tea, and cola beverages that contain caffeine). Caffeine and cold weather will separately increase urine output; in combination, a great deal of body fluid is lost and needs to be replaced. In hot summer weather, caffeine may keep a person warm because vasoconstriction insulates the body's periphery and caffeine "stokes" up the body's metabolism, burning fuel, giving off heat.

Alcohol intoxication is enhanced some 10 percent in the heat. That is why those mint juleps seem to pack such a warm wallop in the South. Alcohol prevents the peripheral blood vessels from reacting properly to cold. Heat is lost. And from increases in the body's metabolism due to alcohol, the body temperature rises. In cold weather, alcohol would insure protection for a short time, but not for long. The effect of alcohol is deceptive because you feel warm as the blood vessels first dilate (lowering blood pressure) whereas in reality it is *warmth departing the body*. It is a good idea to avoid cold weather after alcohol, and in combination with cigarettes, since nicotine further prevents blood from reaching the body's extremities.

Change Dosage or Environment When Taking These Medications*

Decrease dosage in HOT weather *Avoid HOT weather/environment* *when consuming:*	*Decrease dosage in COLD weather* *Avoid COLD weather/environment* *when consuming:*
Alcohol	Analgesics
Anticoagulants	Barbiturates
Antihypertensives (Hypotensives)	Hallucinogens
Anti-parkinsonism	Mono-amine oxidase inhibitors
Antispasmodics	Neuroleptics
Atropine-like drugs	Narcotics
Cortisone-like drugs	"Sulfa" drugs
Mono-amine oxidase inhibitors	Sympatholytics
Neuroleptics (producing disorders of	Tetracyclines
nervous system)	Tetrahydrocannabinols
Parasympathomimetics	Tranquilizers, mild
Phenothiazincs	Tranquilizers, strong
Sedatives/sleep inducers (hypnotics)	
Thiazide diuretics	
Tranquilizers, mild	
Tranquilizers, strong	

Decrease dosage in sunshine
Avoid sunshine when consuming:

Antibiotics
Antidepressant (tricyclines)
Antidiuretics   *** Consult your doctor**

    Tetrahydrocannabinols are the pharmacologically active components of marijuana. They are also extremely potent agents in reducing body temperature. Marijuana will reduce blood pressure, heart rate, and body temperature, thereby reducing heat production and increasing heat loss in animals and probably in man. The lower the environmental temperature, the more marijuana probably promotes heat loss (inhibiting vasoconstriction) by the sympathetic nervous system: it is probably inadvisable to consume marijuana before or during exposure to cold weather.

    As these examples show, the weather-driven effects of drugs on the body will depend on which element of thermoregulation the drug attacks: heat production via chemical metabolism or heat dissipation by physical means. Heat production comes about by food and water consumption, digestion, muscle work, and shivering; heat loss comes about through cardiac output, respiration or panting, peripheral vasomotor response, sweating, water distribution, diuresis, and behavioral controls such as posture, clothing, and activity.

Our bodies, according to William Petersen, normally swing between poles of increasing or decreasing oxygen adequacy, of relative hydration and dehydration, of relative acidosis and alkalosis, of increasing and decreasing nervous system efficiency, and other polarities—conditioned primarily (not always or entirely) by weather. *So the moment at which a drug is taken, preceded or followed by a weather change, can exaggerate or diminish the drug's toxicity.*

On a practical level, a "clinician must become more aware of the possibility that his patient will often experience toxic drug manifestations. . . . the amplification of the biologic effects with undue frequency of atmospheric change is of moment, so that with different seasons, different responses are to be expected." Petersen's advice is still valid, perhaps more so since *more* drugs are available to the modern physician, and he probably prescribes more drugs than earlier physicians did. *"Drugs given in dosages that verge on the toxic,"* Petersen said, *"should be employed with particular care during times when the meteorologic environment is unusually disturbed, when seasonal effects are more pronounced and during periods of undue cold."*

Petersen proved, in landmark research on a case by case basis, that the weather demands *prompt adaptation*—of the involuntary, chemical, endocrine, and nervous systems. "We, as physicians must ever keep before us that when we administer these drugs, we are dealing with sick individuals, with the old or the young, with fatigued organisms—not with the normal—and in this group the mechanisms of automatic adjustment are not normal. If they were, these individuals would not be patients!"

Petersen showed that the administration of a drug at a critical weather-induced biological condition will be fatal. In each case, a drug was given under the uncalled-for assumption of the experimental physiologist that all other things were equal. Toxic consequences resulting from conditions bear fatal witness that "all other things" are *never* equal!

Swelling and Taste Changes

If drug action can be modified *in* the body by weather *outside*, are other drug-weather actions similarly prevalent?

One characteristic of vitamin B_6 (pyridoxine) is that its absence may distort the body's fluid balance, mineral balance, and hormone balance. Temporary swelling due to excessive fluid concentration in the limbs, called *edema*, is associated with excessive heat and is common in pregnancy, rheumatism, arthritis, heart diseases, menstruation, and menopause. John Ellis has reported using pyridoxine to clear up numerous symptoms including edema and joint pains; weather-induced swelling or pain might also be treated by vitamin B_6.

Recently it has been found that the vitamin choline (part of the B complex vitamins and present in many foods) can reach the brain directly and supply acetylcholine to the nerve endings of the parasympathetic system. Since the acetylcholine-activated response to weather stress is at the opposite pole from the adrenaline-activated response to weather stress, this new finding by Richard J. Wurtman may be important for weather-sensitive people. Choline-rich food substances, like lecithin in egg yolk, seem to pass choline through to the brain in a matter of hours. Thermoregulation requires a supply of choline and acetylcholine, which is destroyed quickly at the nerve ends and needs replenishment. So lecithin in egg yolks may help promote sweating or maintain comfort, in winter and summer, as the body adapts to passing weather fronts.

Some people will notice that their sense of taste will change according to the time of day and the sort of weather outside. Many people do not direct their conscious attention to this effect. But if made aware, they will. Try the identical food or beverage (cheese, wine, tomato juice) in sequence on a given morning, noon, or night; or after coming indoors from a very cold versus a not-too cold day. You may have to strain to notice, but there is a difference. The reason is probably due to the parasympathetic nervous system and its acetylcholine nerve transmitters that are influenced by thermoregulation (and thus weather) and by the state of excitation of the nervous system.

Eating Weather

Eskimos eat foods high in protein and fats. In the tropical climates, diets are poor in fats but high in carbohydrates and vegetables. Instinctively, human beings select those foods that best adapt them to the climate they inhabit, that combat climate stress. People eat to weather their climate.

The voluntary caloric intake of soldiers stationed around the world during World War II varied from 3,100 calories daily in the desert (average temperature 92°F [36°C]) to 4,900 calories daily in the arctic where the average temperature is −30°F (−36°C). Since metabolism can change by at most 20 percent between arctic and tropical environments, this large difference may be due to the "hobbling" effects of heavy arctic clothing and equipment. Nutrition researchers Mitchell and Edman say "the evils of overweight and overeating that overburden the heart and shorten the life in a temperate climate may be mitigated in a cold climate by the extra insulation afforded by a thicker layer of subcutaneous fat."

Alaskans observe that newcomers almost invariably develop a strong fat, meat, or candy hunger, and that they satisfy these new hungers by eating fat, meat, and candy. Experiments show that in the cold, more frequent meals have a favorable effect on maintaining a constant body temperature if the meals are largely fat, but an unfavorable effect if they are carbohydrates. Apparently, industrial productivity and physical efficiency also increase with increasingly frequent meals. The body makes more efficient use of fat as energy with five meals per day rather than three meals per day. You invite havoc in a cold environment by nutritional depletion; nutrients that will increase energy generation (like fat) or just assist in thermoregulation (like lecithin) are critical.

In studies of the extra heat output after eating a high-*protein* meal, the maximum excess heat output was 33 calories per hour, attained two hours after the meal. After a high-*carbohydrate* meal (of same caloric value), the maximum extra heat output was 21 calories per hour, one and a half hours after eating. Apparently when extra heat is needed to function, for example in cold weather, the body is stimulated more from high-protein meals than from low-protein meals. Protein may contribute more to physiological comfort than does clothing or body insulation.

A seasonal variation in food intake, in the metabolism of fat and carbohydrates in humans, may be a leftover sign of hibernation. Frederick Sargent, II, reviewing this possibility, suggested that despite a few contrary observations, the "supporting evidence is remarkable." The nutritional demands and expectations of the tissues would demand seasonal changes in metabolism and food ingested. The stimulus for such a mechanism might be solar radiation, specifically its ultraviolet component.

If true, the seasonal rhythm has two phases. A period of activity and preparation for inactivity called the *anaphase* runs (in the Northern Hemisphere) from about April to October. It is marked by improved carbohydrate tolerance, lowered blood sugar, increased liver glycogen, relatively high respiratory quotient, less utilization of fat, increased liver fat, increased deposition of fat, and increased fat tolerance. The opposite phase, called the *cataphase*, runs from October to April and is characterized by complete inactivity and preparation to resume reproductive activity and general activity.

During the active anaphase, the tissues and organs use carbohydrates in the spring and summer as the chief source of energy, storing fat for anticipated hibernation. During the inactive cataphase, in fall and winter, the stored fat is completely metabolized. The appetite shows rhythmic seasonal preferences for fat and for carbohydrates. Soldiers, urban families, and mill workers consume more calories in the fall and winter than in the spring and summer. Physical and mental growth, metabolic diseases (like diabetes mellitus), strength, neural ability, conception, and the incidence of disease and death may have seasonal swings that correspond to this notion of vestigial hibernation. The rhythm of life swings from a phase of minor stress in fall and winter to a phase of major stress in spring and summer. The diet should swing accordingly.

Newcomers to the tropics show a marked decrease in appetite, at least until acclimatization takes hold. Decreased appetite and thus decreased heat production is an adaptive response to heat. High temperature will depress the level of vitamin A in blood plasma, leading to nutritional disorders.

The food-intake habits of animals seem to be a mechanism of temperature regulation. The same may be true of people. An experiment in which rats ate freely of a varied diet in a cool room and in a hot room suggests that need for thiamine, choline, and vitamin K are much higher in a hot environment than in a cool one. Need for riboflavin, pyridoxine, pantothenic acid, pi-aminobenzoic acid, and inosital are apparently unaffected by the environmental temperature.

The best work performance, or productivity, in the tropics is achieved by replacing hour by hour the "water lost in sweat," according to Mitchell and Edman. However, the need for water may surpass the thirst for water: during work, people drink only ⅔ of the water lost in sweat. "The amount of water can range from 4 quarts (or liters) per day for light tropical work, to 13 quarts per day for heavy work at 113°F. Usually it is best to drink when thinking of it, rather than wait for meals. But replacing salt can wait until meals."

Petersen held another view of diet. Early Americans, exposed to cold, ate a high-protein, acid-forming diet that must have stimulated their metabolism and exaggerated the acid phase of the acid-base balance. However, the modern American does less hard work and is exposed less to the cold, so the diet has shifted to a high-carbohydrate diet, one that augments alkalinity. Apparently, many more diseases are associated with a relative alkalosis than with a relative acidosis. "The propaganda-susceptible and propaganda-flooded American has been taught to believe that there is a saving grace in alkalinity," Petersen said in the late 1930s, and that "acidosis is the root of all evil—whether from the roots of the teeth, the roots of the hair, or the roots of the family tree." He argued the absurdity and possible harm that could come from such a diet, particularly for many suffering patients. Petersen suggested that a high-protein, acid-forming diet—coupled with moderate level of tissue-stimulating work to keep the capillary beds open—was perhaps the secret of longevity. Aging meant closing of the capillary and arteriolar beds and thereby diminished blood-vessel activity.

But tropical people age relatively early. Perhaps their "climatic tranquility" promotes relative alkalinity from their diet, and blood vessel inactivity from sweating, lassitude, and sunshine. In hot countries, ancient Egypt and modern Java, hardened arteries (arteriosclerosis) was and is commonplace. But in the benign atmospheric tranquility of the South, a relatively high alkalinity may not be so harmful as in the North "where frequent fronts may urge alkalotic crests to dangerously high levels."

De Forest Jarvis has conducted some interesting experiments that confirm Petersen's evils of alkalinity, the benefits of acidity, and incidentally, the wisdom of Vermont folk medicine. He found that people's urine turned alkaline when fatigue or sickness (the common cold, asthma, hay fever, sinusitis, neuralgia, and childhood diseases like chickenpox or measles) was on the way. Furthermore, by shifting the body toward acid urine, the subsequent ailment was either less severe than before, or never appeared at all. The shift was accomplished by acid-forming diet—avoiding sugars and wheat, consuming apple cider vinegar, corn oil, kelp, honey. Jarvis also discovered that cold weather shifted the urine to the alkaline side, but it was shifted back to the acid side by taking a hot bath, drinking warm fluids, and keeping windows closed in bedrooms on winter nights—all Vermont folk remedies.

Altitude Food

The effects of altitude may be felt in mountain climbing, in air travel, in a tall building (slightly), and in cities at high elevations.

Altitude effects are similar to some weather changes, both in the atmosphere and in the body. Diminished air pressure and oxygen content and increased solar radiation are the external manifestations. Through respiration, the body loses more heat at high altitudes than at sea level mainly because rapid breathing is needed to obtain sufficient oxygen. Decompression sickness (aeroembolism, or the bends) comes about when gases, mainly nitrogen, are liberated from body tissues. At great altitudes, abdominal gases may expand causing gastrointestinal pains that are sometimes severe.

The temporary and localized oxygen hunger results from our body's reflex to cold weather—vasoconstriction—which denies blood to peripheral tissues and confines it, relatively, to the torso. But oxygen hunger also results from diminished atmospheric oxygen itself (this is called anoxic anoxia) and may resemble drunkenness. In severe oxygen deprivation, sharpness of the senses, mental faculties, endurance, capacity and will to work, kidney and gastrointestinal functions, and carbohydrate metabolism will all suffer.

At altitude, the body's dietary requirements call for additional water, ascorbic acid, thiamine, and nicotinic acid. But its tolerance to altitude may be assisted by the nutritional value of preflight or inflight meals. "The ingestion of carbohydrates as compared with protein foods immediately before and during flight to altitude," Mitchell and Edman say, "increases mental efficiency, neuromuscular coordination, the capacity for muscular work, the field of peripheral vision and the acuity of vision in dim-light." The sudden loss of strength or consciousness due to cerebral anemia (syncope) is deferred, and so is the severity of decompression-sickness symptoms.

Aspirin may decrease the incidence of bends, and (like codeine) prolong the time during which altitude may be tolerated. Caffeine can stimulate respiration, but vitamin supplements have not been proven to increase our tolerance to oxygen hunger.

However, carbonated water or melons should not be consumed prior to flight, since they consistently cause gas discomfort.

Meals taken prior to flight or in flight should include a higher-than-normal amount of sugars or sugar-producing foods; postflight meals can make up deficits in high-protein or high-fat foods. Apparently, people prefer sweet foods and avoid high-protein foods at high altitudes, according to Mitchell and Edman, so free-choice meals (including candy snacks) do make sense.

The air pressure in most planes is equivalent to an altitude of 6,000 feet (about 2,000 meters), about the same altitude as Denver's. Most airlines keep plenty of fruit juice available, especially on long flights, to prevent the dehydration that accompanies low cabin humidities (a few percent or even *much* less). Alcohol, coffee, tea, or Coke only promote dehydration by diuresis.

Normal meals are generally prepared; "we serve *expectation*, not *nutrition*" says the food director of a major airline, who believes that people generally eat and drink the same at high altitude as what they consume on the ground. But free choice of foods at high altitude may not be the best guide for nutrition, even though for most people reduced pressure in aircrafts is not a problem or a stress. Foods may taste different to a gourmet or to a person made newly aware that altitude (or heat or cold, for that matter) may alter the "flavor statement" food makes. Taste sensitivity is a function of the nervous system, and in turn, of choline. The more complex the flavor stimulation, like champagne with its sparkling bubbles, the more enjoyable it apparently is at high altitude.

One factor in diet and nutrition may be connected to weather. Recently, certain foods have been found to trigger irrational behavior, mental unbalance, or aggression and acts of violence. Forensic psychiatrist Abram Hoffer suggests that a large fraction of prison inmates who committed sexual crimes may have vitamin deficiencies. Many other case histories are now documented. For example, one twelve-year-old patient tried to clout someone with a stick twenty minutes after eating a banana. The mechanisms are not fully understood, but food allergies may cause noninflammatory swelling directly in the brain. "The pressure of the swelling may make nerve areas that normally produce aggression more sensitive, or deactivate areas that normally inhibit aggressive behavior," according to K. E. Mayer. These so-called cerebral allergies may arise also from vitamin deficiencies of vitamins like B_6(pyridoxine), which may induce perceptual distortions. If modest swelling of cerebral tissues may change our behavior under normal atmospheric conditions, perhaps departures from normal atmospheres may induce immodest cerebral swelling and abnormal behaviors.

Travel: Zones of Contentment and Climate-Leaps

Travel to faraway countries will produce a climate-leap that, unfortunately, is rarely taken seriously. The faster the transition, the older and sicker the traveler, and the bigger the climatic difference between the old and the new climate are determinants of how severe the climate-leap is and what health problems it may cause. Furthermore, "getting there may be half the fun" in advertisements, but during travel by car, sea, and air our biological rhythms may be distorted.

The thermal-effect complex—which comprises air temperature and humidity—is characterized by a single quantity called the "effective temperature." It indicates the heat burden or content of air and is directly proportional to perceptible heat, or subjective comfort. High temperature-humidity environments will burden the thermoregulatory system of many people, especially older people, sick people, and children. At low humidity without wind, the effective temperature is essentially the normal temperature. The great heat found in some southern climates make those areas suitable for visits by healthy and adaptable people only.

Besides heat burden, the sun's visible radiation is not only emotionally important but it is our greatest source of direct environmental energy. Locations where the sun shines less than 50 percent of the day are called sunshine-poor and more than 60 percent of the day, sunshine-rich. The glaring sun can slow reflexes and inhibit the stimulation of the sympathetic nervous system. Especially when driving a car and concentrating on the road for a long time, a sort of meteorohypnotic condition can set in: The intense sun or heat *may* lull us into drowsiness; part of the central brain and hypothalamus is susceptible to conscious mood alteration or sensory overload by thermal messages.

The zone of contentment is then the preferred range of climates that have a comfortable heat burden and adequately rich sunshine for virtually every visitor. (Sun-sensitive visitors are likely to be comfortable with less sunshine.) The zone of contentment will change from month to month, place to place.

A few zones of contentment will enable some preliminary vacation planning, depending on month and place of origin of the traveler.

Northern Europeans frequently vacation in the Mediterranean areas and occasionally in the United States. They generally find that January temperatures in the northern United States occur in Europe only north of 60 degrees latitude (in Finland, for example) and high in the Alps. For them it is often merely a matter of finding the right time for a trip to the Mediterranean area. According to Freiburg meteorologist Otmar Harlfinger, who made detailed, quantitative studies, more than half of those locations fall into the biologically favorable zone of contentment.

For example, in January and February, the Egyptian and Israeli coasts and southern Tunisia are favorable; the northern Mediterranean is cool and sunshine-poor. In June, July, and August all other regions of the Mediterranean (except for the Atlantic coast north of Lisbon) have light to strong heat loads.

In the United States during June, July, and August, the favorable regions are the North and West, including the prairies; everywhere in the lowlands, the Southeast, and the Midwest below Iowa and toward the Gulf of Mexico are outside the zone of contentment.

Each form of travel—car, sea, or air—has its own climatic peculiarities. Air-conditioned ships may present thermoregulatory stress to the unacclimatized traveler but not to the acclimatized crew member. Excessive sunshine on ships or elsewhere can increase gastric excretion, increase protein metabolism, lower blood pressure, increase hemoglobin content and number of erythrocytes, increase the fraction of vitamin D and histamines, and increase calcium, magnesium, and phosphate levels in the blood, according to Solco W. Tromp.

In air travel, two effects are important: those due to altitude and those due to biological rhythms. Latent infectious diseases, the common cold, appendicitis, dental infections, heart disease, or meteorotropic diseases (asthma, rheumatic diseases) will be aggravated by air travel, Tromp says, unless the travelers are high-altitude acclimatized. Probably the worst environmental burdens of automobile travel are air pollutants and atmospheric contaminants.

Traveling east to west or (worse) west to east can seriously disturb normal biological functions related to thermoregulation and acclimatization. Normally the body temperature and pulse rate will swing in a daily rhythm. Maximum body temperature and pulse rate will generally peak at around 3 P.M., and will tend to bottom out around 3 A.M. Physiologists at Marburg (Germany) have found that the rewarming time of extremities after a cold shower or cold hand-bath had daily rhythmic response, peaking at around 9 A.M. Indeed, following a cold shower, some twenty minutes was needed to rewarm the extremities at 9 A.M.—almost double the time needed to rewarm them at 9 P.M. Perhaps even warm showers in the evening are better for those with thermoregulatory problems.

Other daily rhythms (pain, respiration) lead to the conclusion that *responsiveness* of our sympathetic nervous system (governing thermoregulation) itself varies in daily rhythm. The maximum sympathetic responsiveness occurs in the morning around 9 A.M.; in the evening its nonspecific responses are minimum. This is compatible with the fast rewarming of extremities in the evening, if it is recalled that the parasympathetic system induces vasodilation (releasing the sympathetic system's vasoconstriction) after a cold shower. Put another way, you will stay cold longer under sympathetic vasoconstriction, and that happens more strongly in the morning.

Rapid climate-leaps will make extra demands upon the nervous system. In addition to climate stress, there will be the stress of desynchronization of the body's temperature-adaptation rhythms likely in east–west travel. More-than-casual precautions should be taken to guard the body's temperature constancy with appropriate clothing.

North–south travel will alter the blood pressure significantly. In traveling south from a northern temperature zone to a tropical zone, blood pressure (both systolic and diastolic) will *fall*, usually after several days. This corresponds to the "time to unwind" at the beginning of a warm vacation for a cold-dweller. Going north from a tropical zone to a temperate zone will *raise* the blood pressure, generally after a few days. Returning home from a warm climate to a cold one may be more stress than one can handle; upper respiratory infections are common then. Forewarned is forearmed, but it is difficult to prevent this reacclimatization stress without preconditioning exercises.

The elderly, the ill, and children may have blood-pressure problems of the following sort: a cold-dweller with low blood pressure may suffer even lower pressure upon travel to a warm zone, and a warm-dweller with high blood pressure may suffer elevated blood pressure in traveling north. Both conditions require the guidance of a physician prior to travel, especially among these high-risk groups. And during travel, the effect of drugs, medicines, and foods will change with each climate-leap.

The Ecoclimate, or "Haunted" Houses

Houses, buildings, offices or shelters have a sort of weather indoors too. Called the *eco*climate, it is larger than our *micro*climate, or air skin that clings to us, and smaller than the *geo*climate, that air mass out-of-doors.

Temperature and humidity are the obvious factors of indoor climate. Room temperatures are generally under our control, although the amount of control is often limited. Especially in the winter, heated indoor spaces are unfortunately almost always deficient in moisture. (Airplane cabins are particularly arid.) Winter air brought indoors and heated up will suffer a rapid decrease in relative humidity, since warm air holds more *absolute* moisture than cold air. Cold window panes will acquire, by condensation, much of the moisture you are able to generate indoors.

Air conditioning may adversely affect the body's development of natural acclimatization to summer heat. A study by Michael Marmor of twelve heat waves in New York City (1949–70) found that the number of air-conditioned households increased from none in 1949 to 38 percent of households in 1970; and that the increased use of air conditioning, which decreased heat-wave mortality in *early* summer heat waves, did not do so in *subsequent* heat waves. Accordingly, air conditioning probably postpones our acclimatization to summer heat.

The atmospheric pressure indoors is virtually identical to its value out-of-doors simply because buildings are rarely airtight. Air is constantly leaking in or out of the indoor *eco*climate, largely unnoticed, and equalizing normal indoor and outdoor barometers. Even the variograph, which measures the infinitesimal barometric changes that may herald weather fronts, will read the same indoors and out. Enough air to support life, 15 cubic feet (half a cubic meter) an hour, will leak into the worst ventilated rooms.

Thermal stress indoors may be troublesome, aggravated by air conditioning or heating. But there are sources of air pollution in every home or office, every living space and work space that have been ignored consistently.

Air pollutants are part of the ecoclimate just as surely as temperature, and they can "haunt" both allergic and normal people with enormous volumes of odors, vapors, fumes, and gases.

Consider the copy machine, with its dyes, inks, and chemicals. The typewriter ribbon radiates odors, as does the carbon paper. Odors emanate from the fountain pen, ballpoint pen, marking pen, aerosol spray can, hair spray, shoe polish, newspaper, carpeting, plastic coverings and supplies, heating, ventilating and cooking equipment (escaping gas from gas appliances), cosmetics and toiletries, volatile organic plasticizers, and many others.

"The breathed route of entry into a body is very adverse," says Francis Silver, "since contaminants have direct access to the blood stream." By contrast, toxic materials that are ingested through the mouth are detoxified in the liver before reaching the blood supply. "This principle is so little recognized," says Silver, "that persons who would not ever consider tasting a drop of turpentine or petroleum solvent, much less drinking a teaspoonful, often do not hesitate to breathe large quantities of turpentine (or worse) in the air evaporated from paint fumes. They may even exclaim joyously how beautiful and clean a new coat of paint, floor wax, or furniture polish looks, while befouling the interior of their body with fumes."

The ecoclimate is but one scale of the total environment, which also includes the microclimate and geoclimate. The physician must, René Dubos said in 1967, "master a new science focused on the effects that the total environment exerts on the human condition." How all aspects of that environment impinge on our lives is the subject of clinical ecology. Our relations to environmental excitants— air, water, food, drugs, climate-leaps—are modified by our susceptibilities. And these in turn are conditioned or determined by genetic background, state of mental and physical well-being, and adaptability. The ecological model views the health status of an individual or a population in terms of its genetic base, its environment, and the sum total of all environmental impacts on that base. Human biometeorology then takes the less olympian view that the environment is limited to the geoclimate, or public weather.

Dreams and Mood

Our *moods* today correlate with what the *weather* was one or two days ago. And our chance of a cold today correlates with what the weather was two to four days ago. Thus our moods may provide advance cues to the onset of a cold, but only (as in dreams) if the mood ascends into consciousness and we are fully aware of it.

Moods on any given day bear an important relationship to the quality of our sleep and dreams (which are weather-conditioned) the night before. According to psychiatric studies by Milton Kramer and Thomas Roth, sleep determines how aggressive, friendly, unhappy, or sleepy we are upon awakening. We are happy then if a certain person or personality, or a large number of people, appear in our dreams. The quality of sleep will govern our mood, and our mood will govern our performance—the next day. Day-time performance is related to waking moods; the less sleepy, the more friendly, aggressive, clear-thinking, and unhappy you are, the better you perform. (It is not obvious why an "unhappy" waking mood improves performance.) Dream content shows the greatest difference with regard to the dreamer's sex; less so with regard to age, race, education, marital status, or socioeconomic status.

But if weather does influence the course of sleep or dreams; if sleep or dreams govern our waking moods; if moods, in turn, decide our day's performance, then weather may govern performance directly, even without the intermediary steps. Energetic mood states are associated with increased intensities of weather elements (see page 324).

Others have observed the direct effects of weather on mood. Psychiatrist Basil Johnson says that severe cold is perceived as a threat that demands psychological and physical withdrawal from the environment. And psychiatrist Raymond Headlee agrees that cold weather does induce introspection, as does any sustained change, but that may not be all bad. Subzero cold can interfere with the search for a mate or make one more alert to other's needs—helping the elderly cross snow-covered streets. "Anything that arouses human beings to think about themselves is good," says Headlee. "If we lived in an area where there is a constant temperature—like nirvana—we probably couldn't do much thinking of any kind . . . just sit around and eat bananas."

The first balmy, clear day of spring will tend to make most people cheerful and optimistic, as one person put it, "ten years younger." Charles Lamb said that when the sun shines on a clear blue sky, he felt strong again, valiant, wise, "and a great deal taller." But to those who are depressed or unhappy, such beautiful weather can do the opposite. The contrast or tension between *inner* weather and futility versus the *outer* weather of sunshine and gaiety, may be unbearably painful. And the monotony of bright sunshine, day after day, may bring those northeasterners who moved to Florida or California back home again to cool variable weather—to invigoration.

See the Sun

The response of some seven hundred university and secondary school students to the comment "Today's weather is pleasant" was analyzed in terms of the weather itself. Australian geographer Andris Auliciems found that among all students, the primary and most significant weather element associated with increased "pleasantness" was increased sunshine—accounting for some 20 percent of the variance. Unrelated to sunshine, increasing temperature had a secondary influence on the perception of "pleasantness." And the perceived degree of "pleasantness" was reduced by increasing cloudiness, humidity, and wind speed.

Mental Work: Cool Compatible Comfort

High performance at continuous work is statistically related by Auliciems to high barometric pressure, low temperature, low humidity, decreased wind velocity, and lack of sunshine. These weather conditions almost (but not quite) represent the high pressure zone of anticyclonal air mass immediately following a cold front. (The only discrepancy: *increased* sunshine characterizes these weather conditions, except in the winter.) Arithmetical tasks were performed better during cold air masses with rising barometers, in William Petersen's important triplet study (see Chapter 5). And high pressure—cool, mild, dry weather in Brezowosky's southern Germany—favored high working-efficiency, low accident rates, and fast reaction times (see Chapter 9).

"A room should be as cool as is compatible for work comfort," says Auliciems since " 'freshness' tends to increase as temperature is reduced." "Comfortably cool," was the temperature condition, about 60°F (16°C), that led to optimum performance in his Australian classroom experiments.

Above thermal neutrality, the body tends to relax. Below thermal neutrality, tensed posture is assumed. Slight muscular tension seems to accompany the act of paying attention, so it is likely that up to a point increased "tension" leads to improved performance.

Social Weather

Our perception of stress may indeed be idiosyncratic. Persons with versatile defenses and broad experience, persons with a variety of assets and resources who have demonstrated competence in the past—such persons will be most likely to adapt or cope with any stressor. "The more experience they have had previously with a particular stressor," health researchers Judith Rabkin and Elmer Streuning say, "the more probable that their present responses will be effective."

Personal factors that modulate our stress responses are a sense of mastery over one's fate, emotional defenses, personality type, morale, verbal skills, intelligence, and threshold sensitivity to the stress.

The stress experience will reflect the social position individuals or groups occupy in a community, their social supports, their network of friendships, their "embeddedness." These involvements will condition—buffer, support, or undercut—a person's response to stress from any source, including the weather, which can overload an already stressed person.

Urbanologists have been pointing out for years that disproportionately high rates of medical and psychiatric disorders are found in deteriorating central cities. "There is now considerable evidence," Rabkin and Streuning say, "to suggest those who live alone, and are not involved with people or organizations, have for this reason a heightened vulnerability to a variety of chronic diseases."

Membership in a low-status group or in one that constitutes a minority in an area is associated with increased health risks. The Chinese, the French and English minorities in Canada, the Italians in Boston, and the blacks in Baltimore, all demonstrate the effects of stress; their rates of mental illness are higher than (1) other ethnic groups in the same area and (2) the very same ethnic group in other neighborhoods in which they are a majority. The smaller the minority, the less social support any member may enjoy and the greater becomes the stress. This is true for tubercular patients as well. (Any advice on the avoidance of social stress for those patients is gratuitous.) Such observations are compatible with the findings that weather-sensitivity affects those of lower socioeconomic classes. On the other hand, the medical histories of 2,600 semiskilled workers for the New York Telephone Company, analyzed over twenty years, reveals that the healthiest workers were found to be people "whose social backgrounds, aspirations, and interests coincided with their present circumstances," consistently. The frequently ill had goals inappropriately high for the work they were doing. Weather stress would disproportionately irritate such individuals, and intensify their ailments.

Five Aphrodisiacs

Exercise, fresh air, sunshine, good food, and adequate sleep are the five true aphrodisiacs, according to Alfred Kinsey's landmark study of sexual behavior in the human male.

Kinsey's findings have been seconded by the personal experiences of various writers; by plausible suppositions and explanations of several physicians, psychiatrists, physiologists; and by a massive amount of anecdotal material from the world's literature, both great and insignificant.

Perhaps it is the refreshing tranquility that follows exercise and accompanies fresh air, sunshine, and fine weather; the soothing glow of goodwill; or other revitalizers—ingredients that serve to enhance sensuality and sexuality.

Scientific research into the effects of weather on sexual behavior is almost nonexistent. But the combined effects of exercise, fresh air, and sunshine—whether at the beach or on ski slopes—is undeniable. Many (aphrodisiacal) effects of exercise are duplicated by changing weather conditions. For instance, adrenaline secretions increase metabolism, increase oxygen delivery to vital tissues in the brain, the heart, the kidneys, and the genitals, elevate sex hormone (testosterone) levels in men, and even heighten alertness, attention, and sensitivity. "After about twenty or forty minutes of exercising, the senses are sharper," says psychiatrist Thaddeus Kostrubula. "Sight, hearing, touching, taste and smell all become more responsive, and you may have one of those especially vivid moments that becomes a private personal treasure for life."

What kind of weather does this? To what sort of people? If the enemy of healthy sexual fulfillment, as Masters and Johnson say, is overwork and its partner, hypertension, then on one level, reducing both may temporarily serve aphrodisiacal ends. (See detailed Self-discovery Questionnaire in Appendix C.) Although the weather alone may not be responsible, winter vacations to warmer climates may kindle or rekindle sexual desires, as may a ski vacation.

Sex researchers J. Richard Udry and Naomi Morris found a seasonal variation in the rate of sexual intercourse. They examined sexual histories, daily "coital calendars" at the Institute for Sex Research of Indiana University, representing over a hundred woman-years of sexual experiences. The women were all well-educated, white, married, premenopausal volunteers, who represented no population beyond themselves. The weekly coital frequency peaked in July (between the twenty-sixth and thirty-first weeks of the year) and bottomed out in August-September (between the thirty-fourth and thirty-eighth weeks of the year). The crest was some 10 percent above, and the trough was some 10 percent below, the yearly frequency of sexual intercourse. Of course, weather cycles are only one component of seasonal rhythms, and almost any data will look periodic if treated by cutting it up, superimposing, and averaging. (Some of the more extravagant claims that there are only three major so-called "biorhythms" are hard for a scientist to accept because we respond to an extraordinary multiplicity of human daily and annual rhythms including weather-front "rhythms." Very sophisticated statistical analysis is needed to substantiate biorhythm's predictions.)

I have avoided mention of weather-induced changes in the sexual behavior of animals, but here I must make exception. With standard strains of mice, von Mayersbach has not only shown that identical doses of drugs will produce mortality rates between zero and 100 percent depending on different times of day but he suggests that "seasonal influences overrule factors of sex, strain, and age."

Seasonal sexual activity of golden hamsters peak in spring and fall, according to Reiter.

The pineal body, a vestigial third eye found in many mammals including humans, may respond to the natural seasonal lengthening and shortening of daylight periods.

However, without extremely sophisticated techniques it is almost impossible to tie sexual activity to weather phases alone. Common instinct and direct personal experience speak more strongly to the link between weather and sex than virtually all of the minuscule scientific research done on this ever-fascinating activity.

Weather-Beaten . . . or
Weather-Proof?: A Summary

Combinations of emotions, medications, exertion, and your body's attempt to compensate for weather conditions may prove fatal.

Sports or exercise in hot weather is likely to disturb the body's core, but in cold weather your extremities usually suffer. Physical fitness appears to bestow ability to sweat and unforced breathing ability, which helps in acclimatization to heat or to cold during exercise. Weather conditioning can improve athletic performance and acclimatization ability. Often several days or weeks are necesary to adapt to a new climate or to perform physical exercise in new weather conditions.

Your decisions to clothe your body are often made without proper or scientific guiadance based upon what is now known about thermal and weather comfort. Frequently, television, radio, or newspaper forecasts are of little or no help since they have not yet incorporated these new findings; and trusting personal sensations may be counterintuitive.

A large number of drugs modify their reactions in the body depending upon the weather conditions, heat, cold, or sunshine outside. Unfortunately, many physicians and most laymen are entirely ignorant of these important, sometimes fatal effects. Anticoagulants, antihistamines, tranquilizers, sedatives, and atropine react differently in your body in hot weather: hallucinogens, narcotics, and marijuana, in cold weather; and antibiotics and antidepressants, in sunshine. Heat-induced swelling of the body may be treated by vitamin B_6 (pyridoxine).

Because metabolism changes by some 20 percent in hot or cold climates, our appetites change as well. Newcomers to the arctic will develop a hunger for fats, meat, and candy—and five meals a day. Newcomers to the tropics will often lose their appetite for food altogether. Those who remain in a changeable climate will also change their diets as the seasons roll around, perhaps a vestige of hibernation with its changes in nutritional demands. Even the altitude changes found in commercial airliners require additional water and also dietary modifications, such as increased carbohydrate ingestion prior to flight.

Climate-leaps as a result of travel will cause health problems the faster the transition, the older and sicker the traveler, and the bigger the climate difference between the old and new climate. The preferred climates, or zones of contentment, will provide comfortable heat burdens and adequate sunshine for all visitors. These may and should be discovered in advance of travel. Travel in a north–south direction will alter body physiology considerably (especially blood pressure), and east–west travel will often desynchronize biological rhythms.

The ecoclimate, or indoor weather, may cause health problems in the winter associated with dehydration, in the summer associated with air conditioning, and year-round associated with vaporous fumes and contaminants of common household or office items like gas stoves or copy machines or aerosol sprays.

Your mood today correlates with the weather one or two days ago, but the onset of a common cold correlates with what the weather was two to four days ago; your mood can provide advance warning of the onset of a cold. *Aggression, endurance, liking of school, and play will all depend upon outdoor temperature, humidity, and other atmospheric changes. Mood depends upon the quality of sleep, which in turn depends upon the weather the night before.* Pleasure from the weather depends mainly on the sunshine. And mental work is most efficient indoors when the room is cool and comfortable.

Social "embeddedness" will condition a person's response to stress, including weather stress, as will membership in a low-status group.

Fresh air and sunshine are included among the legendary aphrodisiacs.

Four:
The Elegant
Science of Racism

ΚΑΙΚΙΑΣ

If by next year all the five million Zambians choose to be lazy as they are now, I would willingly step down as President because I don't want to lead people with lazy bones. . . . If you are one of the lazy ones, do not vote for me. I don't want to be voted for by lazy people.
    —Kenneth Kaunda, 1977 President of Zambia

The leisurely habits of the natives have a sound basis in physiological necessity.
    —David Dill, 1938

. . . governments may stamp the manners, but it is the air they breathe which molds the form, temper and genius of the people.
    —Walter Berman, 1845

Preceding Page: Kaikia or Caecias
The wind of the northeast is sad, humid, cold, and cloudy. Hail and storms accompany this wind in some seasons. It is represented by an old man with a severe or strict countenance, holding in his hands a circular ring and preparing to release a crashing hailstorm.

I was jogging with a seventy-five-year-old, black surgeon. I mentioned my interest in race and place, the numerous theories that vigorous climates produce great civilizations, that it is the challenge of the environment that leads to achievement, that racial character and body size and climate appear to be closely interwoven. Almost apologetically I said, "But of course these scientific theorists are all probably racists."

"You can learn a great deal," he told me, "from racists."

His comment was startling in its direct acknowledgment: prejudging prejudice is not necessarily incorrect. Although extreme racists may overstate their case somewhat, the case may nevertheless be a "good" one.

Climate conditions different peoples to such an extent that when their exposure changes by travel, their behavior and physiology also change. Cold-adapted northern whites vacationing in warm southern climates will experience relaxation and blood-pressure declines—a direct result of climate unstressing. Southern blacks who migrated north faced severe climate stress and high blood pressure, aside from the stress of dislocation, culture shock, and financial insecurity.

Why can the Eskimo, but few others, maintain a high skin temperature with his hand immersed in ice water? It turns out that the blood flow in his arms is almost double the blood flow of unacclimatized people. Why does an Andean have a large pulmonary blood volume and a high total hemoglobin content in his circulating blood? Why can central Australian aborigines sleep comfortably, uncovered, on cold ground, at 32°F (0°C), despite major losses of peripheral body temperature and despite the fact that the nonaboriginal scientific investigators were unable to sleep because of shivering and discomfort due to the low temperature?

Acclimatization. Newcomers to arctic regions will wear all available clothing at first; as winter, extremely frigid weather, and low temperatures come, no further protection is sought or needed. Basal-metabolism rates are higher in cold climates for newcomers than for those who have already adapted to the climate. Caloric intake is higher in the arctic than in the tropics. (Arctic residents and arctic explorers find that eating fat becomes absolutely essential, even if eating fat was totally abhorrent previously, as some United States members of an antarctic exploration team, who consumed fat in great quantity, discovered.)

Polar land and tundra is 16 percent of the earth's total land area, yet it is inhabited by less than 1 percent of the world's population. It seems likely that mankind originated in tropical grasslands (like Sudan) or scrublands (like Rhodesia) that make up 36 percent of the total land area and now contain 40 percent of the world's people. But humans have adapted to extreme habitats and climates.

Some 40 percent of the earth's population live on 7 percent of its total land area in a habitat we call temperate. These temperate forests have some six times the current population density of tropical regions where our ancestors originated. Yet see what happens when they try to return.

Tropical Neurasthenia

Here is a decades-old list of precursor symptoms warning of nervous debility among European immigrants to the tropics (called tropical neurasthenia):

- Inability to study or concentrate; difficulty with reasoning; reduced keenness, alertness, capacity, and speed of thought
- Loss of memory, amnesia, forgetfulness
- Lassitude, loss of energy, lack of pep, inability to work at full pressure, inertia, slowed. tempo of performance, deterioration in drive, tiredness, sleepiness, feeling dopey
- Irritability, temper outbursts, quarrelsomeness, fighting over the slightest or imagined insults

Other precursors (some of which are amusing) observed by physicians include:

- Mañana attitude, indecision in business
- Disinterestedness, boredom
- Depression
- Lack of self-confidence, reduced decision-making power
- Excessive smoking

- Insomnia
- Aversion to responsibility
- Criticism and disparagement of others
- Maintenance of a perfect score in bridge-party attendance
- Incessant novel reading
- Inability to sit quietly reading and thinking
- Nightly cinema attendance
- Chronic cabaret attendance
- Desire for nightly dancing
- Headache
- Loss of appetite (anorexia)
- Awareness of temperature
- Acceptance of lowered standards in oneself and others

By the time modern environmental medical experts like Frederick Sargent II enumerated these woes of tropical neurasthenia, he had a systemic classification of over seventy symptoms and signs (see Appendix G).

Climate is the long-term trend of atmospheric conditions, measured in decades, centuries, millennia. Weather is the seasonal, monthly, or daily condition of the atmosphere. Judging from European immigrants to the tropics, the Eskimo, the Australian aborigine, and the inhabitants of the Andes, climate does condition the person; we are challenged by the changing environment because of the climatic epoch or climatic geography we inhabit.

Countless observers have chronicled what American scientist John Draper said in 1868, "For every climate and indeed for every geographical locality, there is an answering type of humanity." Sir Francis Bacon, in the sixteenth century said: "It hath seldom or never been seen that the far southern people have invaded the northern, but is contrariwise."

Raymond Wheeler examined the effects of climate on human behavior throughout history. He said:

. . . observers of the past have been in almost complete agreement regarding important correlations between man and climate. In cooler climates man is more vigorous, more aggressive, more persistent, stronger physically, larger, braver in battle, healthier, and less prone to sexual indulgence. In warm climates man is more timid, smaller, physically weaker and less courageous but more inclined to physical pleasures, more effeminate, lazier, and less aggressive. Peoples of cooler climates treasured liberty, were averse to slavery, built democratic societies. Warmer climates, it was noticed, were more conducive to the more reflective pursuits; the birth rate was much higher in the colder regions even though there were more women, proportionately, in the warm countries, and the warmer races were considered to be emotionally less stable and dependable.

Wheeler noticed that of fifty-three rulers coming down through history with the title "The Great," forty-nine of them ruled in transitional cold phases of climate; that the great cities of the world all lie within 30 to 60 degrees north latitude; that cold-climate literature and music emphasized gaiety, fun, comedy, freedom, and baroque, rococo, or Occidental styles; that warm-climate literature and music tended toward tragedy, fate, idealism, intellectualization, Orientalism, drama, and form.

Unfortunately, these observations, as astute and trenchant as they may be, *prove* very little; there is near, but mixed, agreement on a host of human traits that appear to be associated with a type of climate, or weather, or geography, or a combination.

For the sake of simplicity, cool, variable, north temperate zone climates typical of northern United States or northern Europe will be called "moderate" or "challenging" climates. Polar or tropical climates, very cold and rigorous or very warm and mild will be called "extreme" climates. We will see that in the challenging or moderate climates human behavior is "efficient"—in the mild or rigorous climates it is comparatively "inefficient."

Energetic Skies

Is humanity's answer to a moderate climate a civilization punctuated by economic, social, or cultural growth and achievement? Here is how David McClelland tested the *cases of* and *exceptions* to this proposition, systematically:

	Growth Present	Growth Absent
Temperate climates	10 civilizations (cases)	2 civilizations (exceptions)
Tropical or polar climates	5 civilizations (exceptions)	10 civilizations (cases)

Testing the Climate-Growth Connection

To do justice to the above diagram the cultural periods or geographical locations must be classified by objective criteria on *climate* (moderate or challenging versus extremely mild or rigorous climate) and on *growth* (slow or no-growth or decline versus growth). In this figure twenty out of twenty-seven civilizations support the notion. Ten of these demonstrate that moderate or challenging climates are associated with economic or cultural growth (upper left). In another ten cases such growth is absent *without* a challenging climate (lower right). In seven cases the notion is not supported (lower left plus upper right). If the seven civilizations (two plus five) did *not* exist—after an exhaustive search for them—then any hard-headed scientist would agree that the proposition was "proven": every case was an *instance,* no case was an *exception.* But even if there had been a one-to-one correspondence between a challenging climate and a growth society, it would not necessarily mean that a challenging climate *causes* societies to achieve growth. It would merely say that where or when you find one, you find the other; where or when you lack one, you lack the other. Or, put simply, achieving societies and challenging climates would always accompany each other. Perhaps they were both caused by something else external, common to both; perhaps good climate provides good diet, which provides energy for achievement.

Social sciences, though inexact or soft, must often settle for less than rigorous proof of cause and effect or strict one-to-one correspondence. Modern social scientists permit exceptions because they know that their universe is multiply determined; achievement depends on many factors, and climate is only one of them. Therefore, a social scientist would find negative instances not necessarily fatal to a proposition whereas a physical scientist might. A wind-blown leaf, in apparent defiance of gravity, may move upward; but this exception does not disprove the law of gravity. The degree of proof depends upon how many exceptions may be tolerated.

As the number of *exceptions* to the proposition approaches the number of *instances* of it, we approach a random distribution. This situation would mean that there was probably no relationship between climate and achievement. (Any random error in the assignment of climates or societies will tend to "wash out," some favoring and others damaging the proposition.)

Are the exceptions fatal? Not really, unless systematic errors have created too many instances and too few exceptions. There are twenty instances out of twenty-seven events, so it is not likely that a systematic error has created the proposition synthetically.

Perhaps Yale geographer Ellsworth Huntington has made the most persuasive case that climate stimulates achievement. No great civilization, he argued, ever flourished in polar or tropical regions. He mapped the world's climates according to how much energy they induce in man, what he called *climatic efficiency*. He mapped the regions of the earth where high civilizations and high achievement exist now or existed in the past. He mapped the world distribution of education; he mapped the world distribution of automobiles; he mapped the world distribution of general progress. The maps show considerable congruences, instances where these factors coincide. Areas high or very high in one factor overlap areas high or very high in the other factors. Areas very low in only one factor are low in all factors. Indeed, the most productive, lasting, important civilizations—and cities like New York, Chicago, Los Angeles, Amsterdam, London, Paris, Berlin, Rome, Moscow, Peking, and Tokyo—all lie within 30 and 60 degrees north latitude. (See figures on pages 96-97.)

Huntington said that the most energetic climates for mankind were generally found in these regions: frequent mild storms, moderate rainfall, and average temperature range between winter and summer of from 40°F to 60°F (5°C to 15°C).

He ranked nations by their health and vigor (based on their current death rates, life expectancies, and infant mortality), their agricultural productivity per farm worker, industrial productivity per worker, and income per capita. During the 1930s he found that the ranks were all dominated by New Zealand, the United States, and Great Britain; at the bottom was India. He noted that Gandhi and noncooperation illustrate the kind of national philosophy prevailing among peoples deficient in physical energy; that general inertia and low vitality led the Indian people into passive resistance; that quiescence, fatalism, and submissive philosophies also prevail in Egypt and Persia, and nonresistance typified Moslems and Hindus. Huntington also thought it inconceivable that a well-fed vigorous nation in an energetic climate should accept domination by others. Norway and Holland resisted, often heroically, all Nazi attempts at domination. Great World War II epics were told of how young Norwegians climbed snowy mountains, hid for days in trees, or swam miles in cold water to escape or to fight their conquerors. Even old men or women and children refused to obey Nazi orders and sabotaged Nazi plans despite fear of bitter reprisals.

From the United States census figures for 1900, Huntington observed that both northern white farmers and northern black farmers improved larger portions of their land holdings than did southern white or southern black farmers. Northerners, white or black, had more "vigor" to clean their land than did southerners.

Huntington examined mental activity of regions by their reading habits and temperature swings. Both fiction and nonfiction books were read most avidly during the cold winter months, peaking in January, February, or March. The highest, sharpest, narrowest peaks occurred in the northernmost cities. Nonfiction was read least in June, July, August, at the same time that most fiction was read. The extreme swings between maximum and minimum reading were most vivid in northern cities and the contrast diminished southward from Minneapolis to Nashville to Tampa to Panama. He found performance on examinations (in college or Civil Service) deteriorated during warm months and peaked during the cold months.

The Temperature of Folk Tales

"The men of genius in the North Sea countries," Huntington says, "would be more energetic than those of other regions because they would enjoy better health, even though medical services were everywhere equally good. They would be emotionally stimulated by their cool bracing climate, and would feel like working hard all the year [and] cause civilization to advance." The specific stimulants to mind and body were mean temperatures of about 40°F (4°C) in winter and 64°F (18°C) in summer; relative humidity, about 60 percent at noon, high enough at night to precipitate dew; and variability of weather with frequent but not extreme changes.

To test these conditions of invigoration, McClelland analyzed

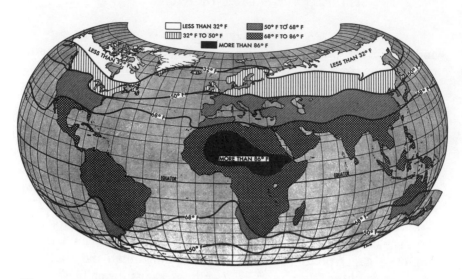

Temperature Zones in the World

Average annual isotherms, between 50°F (10°C) and 68°F (20°C), define most of the United States, the Mediterranean basin, Switzerland, the Balkans, southern USSR, the Near East, and most of China, Korea, and Japan.

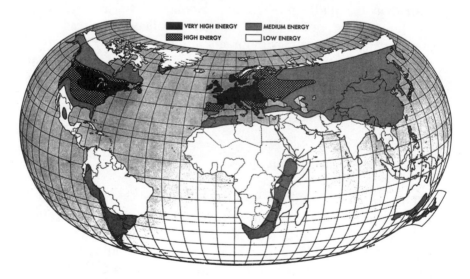

Climatic Energy

Huntington's classification of climate according to its effect on the energy and efficiency of human beings in current phase of civilization. The zone of "very high energy" (solid black) represents those varying conditions of temperature and humidity that are observed to stimulate workers to high productivity.

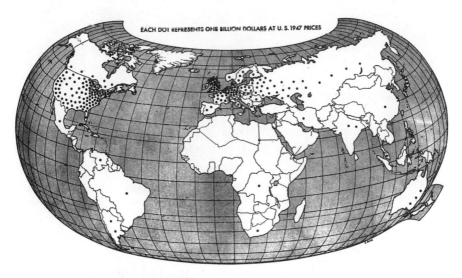

Industrial Production, 1950
Each dot is one billion dollars in United States 1947 prices. (USSR rate
deflated by 25 percent.)

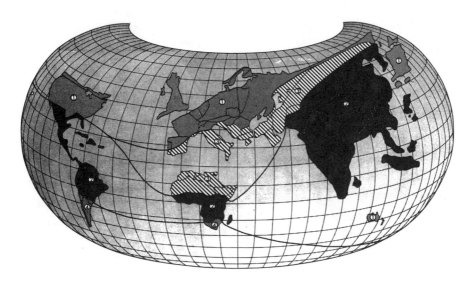

Diseases of the World
Region 1: heart diseases, cancer, tuberculosis, pneumonia, influenza,
syphilis, and diabetes. Region 2 (about half of mankind): malaria, amebiasis,
dysentery, hookworm, yaws, and leprosy; also tuberculosis and syphilis. Region 3: same ailments as adjacent regions plus skin and eye diseases. Region
4: typhoid fever, influenza, tuberculosis, syphilis, and flukes.

some fifty-two preliterate tribes for achievement and their physical habitat. He displayed the average level of each tribe's achievement (by scoring the "achievement" content of folk tales) plotted against mean annual temperature. The result is an inverted V shape, with the apex or peak achievement at 48°F to 60°F (9°C to 15°C). Thus, high achievement *is* more common in moderate temperatures. Furthermore, 92 percent of the high-achieving tribes (and only 50 percent of the low-achieving ones) existed in a climate where the mean daily or monthly temperature *variation* was greater than 15°F (a change of 11°C). Too much or too little temperature variability does not energize human achievement.

Rain falls mostly in hot tropical climates, in the absence of temperature variation. Thus low-achievement cultures are found in rainy areas and high-achievement cultures in relatively dry climates that also tend to have poorer soil.

How does one explain the clear findings that achievement occurs in challenging climates? Huntington's own view has simplicity in its favor: invigorating climates make people feel better and more energetic and encourages them to conceive more imaginative exploits —whether these exploits are building skyscrapers and bridges, waging wars, having many offspring, creating great art, music, or poetry.

McClelland's tentative interpretation hinges on family life: polygamy and concomitant mother-child households tend to occur more frequently close to the equator in the tropics; and monogamy, more frequently away from the equator. What this may do is not obvious, but household living arrangements and parent-child relationships in the north as well as the tropics mold character, aspirations, vulnerabilities, and perhaps achievement.

Another interpretation is that a challenging climate may trigger or maintain a certain preferred level of human *arousal*, or human *sensitivity* (weather-sensitivity as well). Once the human being is urged over that threshold, it is kept at high excitation by almost *any* change, but climate variability touches *all* in its path. Change of any sort, weather included, maintains a proper arousal; if there is too much change, there is too much arousal or distraction; with too little change, there is not enough push to cross the threshold. A certain amount of "jitter" is built into sophisticated electronic and mechanical systems, like servomechanisms. The jitter keeps the system "hunting" for its preferred level of performance. In humans the jitter, or variability, largely occurs on an unconscious level, and perhaps that subliminal jitter is weather-driven.

These interpretations are not the last word, since they are not provable in the hard science sense. The difficulties, again, are formidable. Arnold Toynbee, who noticed that race and climate were favorite explanations for the rise and fall of civilizations, also embraced a theory that geography and social conditions, place and race, *together* create the "challenge of the environment." Its stimulus had to be just right—whether it came about because of new soil to exploit, from living on a frontier, or from being discriminated against as a minority—neither too strong nor too weak. For example, the Jews acquiesced to Nazi genocide (a rigorous "environment"), but flourish in the United States under a moderate or challenging environment.

McClelland argues that the trouble with Toynbee's theory is that it is so general it cannot possibly be wrong. Any creative civilization must have had just the right amount of stimulus (from among many sources—climate, social conditions, and so on) and the historian could later prove the stimulus was just right—*after the event*. This kind of theory explains little and has no predictive power.

Huntington's prescription is specific enough, but the reasons that it works are probably buried in natural selection, human anatomy, physical anthropology, and physiological malleability.

If the environmental temperature variability accompanies or promotes productivity and achievement, then the body's physical long-term response must reflect itself in adaptations. Ability to regulate body temperature must show a north-south gradient with climate. Climate gradients must be evident in body weight, body size, thermal efficiency, and other, less obvious ingredients of our anatomy. They are.

Anatomy of Climate: Heavy
Cold, Light Warm

Suppose climate conditions physique, physique conditions temperament, and temperament conditions behavior. Does this daisy chain of suppositions explain why climate stamps behavior? Let us see.

Body heat is *generated* by body weight (fat and muscle tissues); and body heat is *eliminated* by body surface area. A connection between climate and physique, called *Bergmann's rule*, applies to warm-blooded animal populations in general, as well as to humans: low body weight is found in high-temperature habitats; and high body weights, in low-temperature habitats. This rule works. It has been justified by rigorous statistical analysis and holds up at a high level of significance for men, women, Europeans, Americans, Australians, Africans, and other geographical groups. Highest weights were found among Europeans—160 pounds (72 kgs) in a mean annual temperature of some 40°F (4°C); lowest body weights were the Africans—88 pounds (40 kgs) at 80°F (25°C).

Greater body heat (and therefore weight) is needed in colder climates. At a given body height, greater body weight could accommodate more fat, retarding heat loss. Body heat *balance*, that is heat *production* minus heat *loss*, would be facilitated. At lower body weights for a given height and at higher outside temperatures, the large ratio of body surface area to body weight favors heat loss. At higher body weights, the smaller surface area to weight favors heat production, needed for survival at low environmental temperatures.

The surface-to-weight ratio increases in going from cold climates to warm climates. Frenchmen have a lower surface-to-weight ratio than Arabs; Arabs have a lower ratio than Mexicans.

Anthropologist D. F. Roberts confirmed, with very impressive scientific evidence, that there is "a very marked tendency for most 'very high' weights to occur in cold areas and for 'very low' weights to occur in hotter regions." This is not only true from one country or race to another but it is also true for inhabitants of a single country and members of the same race. Northern Mongoloids or northern Americans are heavier than southern Mongoloids or southern Americans, for instance.

Anatomists have taken Bergmann's rule a step further. Protruding body parts are "implicated" in climate because they help regulate the overall heat balance. Longer arms and legs are hard to heat and easy to cool; emphasizing heat *loss*, long limbs should be found in hot climates. They are. Male Masai and other Africans of the upper Nile Valley, one of the world's hot spots, average six feet tall; they are among the world's tallest people. Shorter arms and legs, easy to heat, hard to cool, emphasize heat *retention*. Short limbs should be found in cold climates. They are. Lapp men live within the arctic circle; these men average five feet, their women four feet six. (This corollary to Bergmann's rule is called *Allen's rule*.) The Lapps and Masai represent two extreme end points of a climatic continuum running from cold to hot. "*Homo sapiens* come in so many different shapes and sizes," says Anne Scott Beller, "and the range of variation is so large and so predictable in terms of climate, that it constitutes what amounts to a living object lesson in Bergmann's and Allen's rules." Body weight, limb length, and surface area per unit of body weight are determined by age, sex, height, diet, genes, and other variables; short term, they are mainly extraneous. In matters of physique, temperature has the long term final say.

Body *movement* may also be conditioned by climate. Alan Lomax in his film, "Dance in Human History," noted cultural differences in how people move and walk. Hot-climate dwellers seem to move their torsos in *two* units (their torsos rotating in opposite directions, above and below the waist; think of the tropical woman ambulating with a heavy load on her head); and cool-climate dwellers move their torsos as a *single* unit (relatively stiff-backed).

But it is not necessarily the *average* temperature in a region that shapes and determines the size of the human body. The *mean* annual temperature in a region guides the *extremes* of summer heat and winter cold. Whatever controls the relationship between body build and temperature may be the annual temperature extreme, not the average.

Russell Newman and Ella Munro compared the body size of over 15,000 United States Army recruits with their home-town, mean January temperatures and mean July temperatures. They found that body weight (per unit of body surface area) was more strongly correlated with mean January temperatures than with mean July temperatures or with mean annual temperatures. In other words, even where summers are hot, *it is the coldness of the cold winters that produces the biggest Americans*.

Cold winter temperatures account for the variance in body weight (per unit of surface area) among the recruits by a very considerable margin compared to the effect of warm summer temperatures. Similarly, *cold* determines body weight much more powerfully than *warmth* does. Cold is a potent selector of heavy human bodies for survival.

Newman and Munro attempt to explain the greater weight in colder climates by several arguments. The most probable one is that cold weather stimulates appetite and activity, and heat stress depresses both. So the combination of expanded food intake and muscular effort must increase the body's muscular tissue, fat tissue, and even bone growth. The severity or duration of cold stress, or both, promotes stocky torsos and stubby limbs. A corollary may be that this body type is the most energetic, efficient, and productive archetype of humanity. Huntington would be pleased to accept these short-legged, barrel-chested, snub-nosed, enlarged-adrenal Alpine types (represented in the mountains of Europe and South America) as living embodiments of the morphological rules of weather: In the elegant science of racism, cold-dwellers have globular torsos, warm-dwellers have linear limbs.

The Climatic Architect

But climate is not only the architect of our torso and limbs but also of the details of our physique. Consider the facial anatomy. Heat rises slowly in long, narrow skulls, more so than it does in round cranial boxes. The Mongoloid facial features show reduced brow ridges and frontal sinuses, flattened and wide molar regions to permit fat padding and reduced nasal prominence. Eskimos and American Indians, both resistant to cold injury, show similar facial features.

The shape of the nasal aperture correlates strongly with temperature but very strongly with the air's vapor pressure. Vapor pressure governs the exchange of moisture between the respiratory surfaces and the air. So narrow noses are found in hot and dry deserts. Narrow nasal apertures in Eskimos may cause their observed high rate of nasal sinus and respiratory ailments. Low humidity of northern winter-heated homes may help explain similar incidence of such ailments, and may conceivably evolve us, slowly, into needle-noses. Upper-respiratory diseases are quite rare among those—like Malayan aborigines, African blacks—who possess wide, large nasal passages, which reduce blockage and subsequent infection.

The sweatiest animal of all is man. The sweatiest man of all is the Eskimo. Eskimos may have the greatest number of sweat glands per square inch of any species measured. Our tendency to think of the Eskimo crouched motionless over an icy seal hole in the bitter, penetrating arctic cold is quite inaccurate. Antarctic explorers point to the terrific heat and humidity that Eskimos meet inland in summers, with temperatures approaching 100°F(38°C), and twenty-four hours of sun beating down upon them. One explorer says, "The typical Eskimo house in the afternoon and evening resembled a sweat bath rather than a warm room . . . we used to sit stripped . . . streams of perspiration running down our bodies constantly . . . children occupied in carrying round dippers of ice water from which we drank great quantities." Indeed, on the basis of body weight, the Eskimo is temperature-adapted to mean annual temperatures (40°F) found in Maine or Minnesota.

Is it possible that our artificial control of climate by heating in winter and cooling in summer may give us a *larger* variability of body temperature than early man? After all, a cold cave in a cold winter did not change their body temperature by much compared to a warm home in a cold winter. Even a cool home in a warm summer gives us a thermal opportunity to adapt and be stressed by that environment—by the hour. The greater stress would encourage greater growth.

Tropical or Polar Sex?

The rate of human development, fertility, and sexual motivation depends upon climatic stimulation, according to studies by Clarence Mills. He has shown that the popular belief in early female maturity in the tropics is exactly wrong.

The onset of menses (or menarche) is a rough guide to sexual maturity and human development. On the average, Mills found that "nowhere on earth do girls mature so early as they do now [1939] in the central part of North America." He cited data to show that in the entering freshman class of 1935, there were sixty-two girls of seventeen years old whose mean age at the onset of menses was 12.9 years and four sixteen-year-olds whose mean age at the onset of menses was 12.5 years. In Paris he found it to be 13.5 years, but farther north and farther south, in the Americas and in Europe, the age of the onset of menses increased. In Montreal and Norway it was 14.5 years; among the Eskimos and in Finland even higher—fifteen to eighteen years. Panama was 14.2 years and Spain 15.9 years. Thus there is a latitude gradient in the age of onset of menses. Earlier sexual development comes in the temperate regions, due to the energizing climate. Tropical warmth and perhaps polar cold apparently retard sexual development.

Mills also demonstrated that female fertility peaked at an earlier age in the northern United States, and at a later age in southern United States. He noted that mean monthly temperatures between 40°F(4°C) and 65°F(18°C) were most favorable to fertility, which declined below 40°F and above 70°F(21°C). It was not clear to Mills whether the male or females were responsible for these thermal fertility gradients. He saw northern women going to Florida during its depressive summer season whose menses were suppressed; but northern women going to Florida in the winter months experienced a marked rise in sexual activity.

Like Petersen, Mills also suggested that fluctuations in temperature, pressure, and humidity were powerful stimulators of human growth and mental development. In particular, he decided that atmospheric turbulence, or "storminess", which appear as typhoons in the tropics, fronts and "highs" or "lows" in the north temperate zone, "deserve a place of commanding importance in . . . man's existence . . . [and] directly influence his energy level." These alternating highs and lows bring on sharp temperature, pressure, and humidity changes and major physiological disturbances. "Storminess" did not mean rain, lightning, thunder, and wind—but the low-pressure air masses followed by high-pressure air masses accompanied by clear weather and temperature drops. The great frequency of these storm tracks across the continental United States are responsible for the variations in temperature that are so stimulating.

A swath across the northern part of the United States encompasses the great cities and coincides with great industrial, artistic, and other types of productive human activity. But Mills went even further. He designed an index of climatic stimulation based upon temperature variability that characterized various places over the earth and the United States. He found agreement with Huntington's estimates of climatic energy and human achievement: the northeast, north-central, and northwest were highest; the gulf regions and semiarid southwest were the lowest. He forecast that as the population ages, the very stimulating northwestern plains would take the lead in bodily and mental exhaustion as the price we would have to pay for the greater vigor and material rewards that come with intense climatic drive.

In "The Coldward Course of Progress," a political scientist made a forecast in 1920: "The more vigorous peoples will move farther north so that by the year 2100, Montreal and Oslo will be focal points of civilization."

Ethical, Religious, and Army Gradients

The average temperature in a country conditions its religion, its ethics, and the size of its standing armies.

"Religions" do not spread to those countries and dominate them if the country is cooler than the place where that religion began. The only exceptions are communism and the protestant ethic. Their influences certainly reach deep into warmer-climate countries, but they have also migrated to colder-climate countries. The generalization stands: Religion dominates the areas that are at the same average temperature as, or warmer than, the country of its origin.

Religions dominant in countries	Mean annual temperature of country population centroids					
	Degrees Fahrenheit					
	30–39	40–49	50–59	60–69	70–79	80+
Protestant	I	卌 •III	I	IIII	IIII	II
Communist	I	卌 •II	II	II	I	I
No dominant religion			I			
Confessional Christian		I	卌•II	卌 卌	卌 卌	卌 卌
Shinto			I •			
Moslem (Shi'i)			I •	I		I
Moslem (Sunni)				卌•	卌 IIII	卌 I
Moslem (other)				II	II	卌
Jewish				I •		
Animist (tribal)				III	卌 II	卌 IIII
Hindu-Buddhist				I •		
Animist (Bud. Tao. Confucian)				I	I	
Animist (Roman Catholic)					II •	
Coptic					I •	
Animist (Buddhist)					II	
Buddhist					I	I •
Animist (Moslem)						II •
Buddhist Taoist Confucian						I •
Hindu						II •

卌 II Each cipher represents one country.

Confucianism did dominate China; now Communism does.

Lamaist Buddhism did dominate Outer Mongolia; now Communism does.

A Dot is in the column to identify the temperature at which the religion was founded.

If no dot (•) is in a row, all of the ciphers in the row represent countries dominated by a religion of local origin.

Religious Dominance of Countries by Temperature

The maintenance of standing armies depends upon mean temperature or latitude north and south of the equator. The warmer-climate countries (75°F or higher mean annual temperatures) invariably keep small percentages of their populations (0.4 percent) in standing armies. Cool-climate countries (30°F to 45°F [− 1°C to 7°C] mean annual temperatures) maintain larger percentages of their populations in standing armed forces (over 1.2 percent). But, as Iben Browning who assembled these statistics points out, *warmth* does not mean *peace*, because the *larger* the standing armies in a cool country,

- the *fewer* wars it starts
- the *fewer* wars it gets dragged into
- the *greater* percentages of wars it wins
- the *smaller* percentages of its population is lost in combat deaths

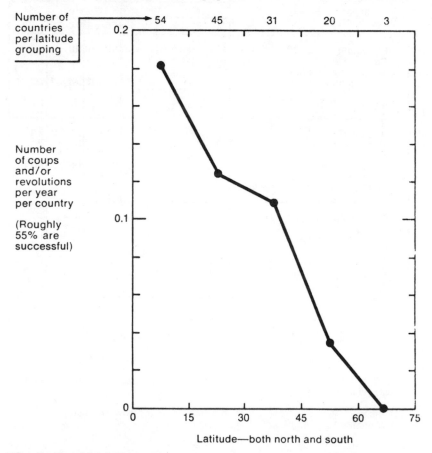

The Latitude of Coups

Social stability increases sharply, and revolutions and coups decrease sharply, both north and south of the equator. Perhaps, as Browning says, "*coups* are usually cheaper than elections, and may be the only change of administration that a poor country can afford . . .

> In cold climates anybody who doesn't spend a lot of time in planning for future contingencies—selecting leaders who will organize things so that snow will always be plowed from the streets and fuel will always be readily available—is in danger of being missing from the population come spring.

He is right.

A Question of Color

Every state of the Union has a flag. Twenty-one snowbelt states have chosen flags that are predominantly blue-green, but only two northern flags are predominantly red-yellow. In the South, only six flags are predominantly blue-green, but nine sunbelt states have chosen flags that are predominantly red-yellow.

According to McClelland, blue is a soft, malleable, and preferred "background" color, associated with great distances that do not "press in on us." Blue holds form poorly. Blues and greens are the so-called "Faustian will" colors. High-achievers prefer blues, "for such persons require that their environment be soft while they are 'hard'; they wish to exert their will effectively—to manipulate, not be manipulated." Blue-loving peoples (cyanophiles) are likely to be assertive, fierce, perhaps power-hungry, northern cold-dwellers.

But red-yellows or red-oranges, inherently brighter than blue-green colors, are "full-blooded," material and "near" or intrusive. The halo colors of Jesus Christ and sunsets are red-yellow. They complement a mild, gentle disposition of the sort found in southern, warm, or tropical climates.

In his analysis of 4,500 paintings with blue skies, meteorologist Hans Neuberger found that northern-country painters depicted the largest number of pale-blue skies and the fewest number of deep-blue skies. Pale-blueness in paintings is dramatically higher, by a factor of thirty, in the North compared to the South. The color associated with the omniscient, omnipresent, omnipotent Zeus is always blue (See Chapter 8).

Finally, British researchers who compared the effects of inactive substances given under the guise of effective treatment, placebos, reported that red placebos were more effective in treating pain than were blue or green ones. Foreground colors must appear more "active."

These results are highly significant statistically. We cannot argue with the blue sky, the red sunset—or the clouds, the ice, or the snow. We must adapt to them, whether by physique, temperament, or preference for colors—warm and cool. Such natural questions cannot be compromised. Political ones can.

Politics, Economics, Heat and Cold

Contemporary news stories—blizzards and summer blackouts—read differently in light of the sociology of atmosphere, the anthropology of climate, the anatomy of weather.

One day in 1977, an Air Nigeria flight departed from Lagos, circled above for half an hour, then returned to the airport for technical reasons. The technicality was that someone had forgotten to load the baggage. In another unrelated incident, an Air Mali pilot, shortly after takeoff, announced to his passengers that he had a problem: the jet was overweight; his solution: he left their luggage behind.

An American housewife living in Liberia put it this way: "When I first got here, it drove me crazy. People don't show up when they say they will; you can't get the simplest thing done; the inefficiency is deadly."

In West Africa the phenomenon is called "wawa," an acronym for "West Africa Wins Again." When scheduled airplanes do not show up on the appointed day; when toilets, air conditioners, and refrigerators stay broken forever because the new shipment of parts will not arrive; when craftsmanship is shoddy; when baggage is lost; when one waits a full day in line to pay a water bill; when natives present the unflappable attitude that these inconveniences are nothing to get excited about in the first place—that is "wawa." The explanation a newspaper reporter gives is that the sun is too comfortably warm and the land productive enough so that the native never has to work very hard to assure a subsistence level for himself and his family. Even old expatriates come to accept the explanation, too, though begrudgingly.

In southern Italy, a 1977 census proves that Naples and its environs hold the Italian—perhaps European—record for youth unemployment. Total joblessness is also alarmingly high. Northern Italians lament the deep south's underdevelopment. But the Neapolitans and other southerners are offended. They want no patronizing platitudes with a racist slant from arrogant northern industrialists and politicians. "What we don't need are sermons," says a Neapolitan radical student, "as if we belonged to the Third World and deserved all this misery because southerners are lazy and dirty."

A northern Italian newspaper reports in the southernmost tip of Italy's boot, "The Calabrian kidnapping industry is working overtime." Police reinforcements using "military methods," like helicopters, were dispatched from Rome to fight the mainland offshoot of the Sicilian Mafia, said to be the cause of the crime wave. The deputy police chief observes, "It's a problem of civilization." Others speculate and expound upon why the north-south cleavage is sharper in Italy than in any other European country. A reporter traveling from Milan or Rome to Naples and farther south is struck by "dilapidated houses, badly functioning services, and other signs of poverty in the south."

Rich and Poor

Eight industrial, advanced countries—who also happen to be northern and rich countries—conferred in Paris for eighteen frustrating months, with nineteen developing countries—who happen to be southern and poor. They met to "negotiate" their north-south differences. The Conference on International Economic Cooperation, or north-south dialogue, began in 1975. The northern countries hoped to organize world trade with some assurance of oil and raw material supplies at stable prices; to become essential partners with developing countries and to respect their aspirations. The southern countries wanted a drastic reform of the world's trading system and a rapid redistribution of the world's wealth, summed up in their slogan, "a new world economic order."

Both grew impatient. The northerners, because of "arrogant demands for instant and colossal handouts." The southerners, because of "high-handed contempt of the strong for the weak," or "greedy refusal to recognize their plight." According to a *New York Times* account of a meeting that ended in June 1977, common ground was never reached in the vast needs and hopes of the southerners and their high-living neighbors to the north. Both north and south realized they must trade together, but "the gap in their backgrounds, assumptions, and attitudes was too great for conventional diplomacy and the problems too huge for simple formulas."

On the delegation to the conference, Senator Jacob Javits, dismayed with the "rigidity" of southern demands, argued that not aid but investment, business, and trade could help create enormous capital. But southerners saw "business" as a code word for "exploitation."

The north-south dialogue is over; though officially ended, it will continue to occupy the minds of decision makers for a long time, like a malady that lingers on. Apparently, the Carter Administration took a position that "it no longer makes sense to tax the poor people in the rich countries for the benefit of the rich people in the poor countries." Now reread this position with "northern" substituted for "rich," and "southern" inserted for "poor." And now, with this in mind, consider the United States.

Sunbelt, Snowbelt, and Mindbelt

The sunbelt-snowbelt theory, popularized in 1976 by a series of articles and political utterances, argued that massive wealth would flow from the Northeast and Great Lakes states to the faster-growing western and southern states. A "second war between the states" was expected. The *National Journal* calculated that in 1975 the Great Lakes states sent $62 billion to Washington and got only $44 billion back, with a net loss of $18 billion. The northeast states had a net "balance of payments" deficit of some $21 billion, the southern states received $12 billion more than they paid in (and the western states $11 billion). It seemed as if this huge flow of funds was being directed by the federal government, siphoning tax dollars from the North and subsidizing the South and West. A great deal of press attention whipped up public interest in the issues; a coalition of northeast governors was formed to stem the "hemorrhage," to stop "the subsidy," reacting angrily to "regional favoritism."

Compared to the nation's gross national product (then running about $1.8 trillion), $10 or $20 billion is a percent or so—inconsequential. This sunbelt-snowbelt theory, whose advocates (mostly northerners), while attempting to draw attention to an inequality of redistributed federal tax monies, also incidentally underscored the financial/industrial *strength* of the northern states compared to the southern states. They have not been heard from during 1977 or 1978. The issue flared up briefly, then dimmed. Fortunately, few policy decisions were based upon the headlines—this time.

These recent instances of cleavage in northern and southern behavior show how deeply embedded the differences are. How resistant to change they are. And how these differences find expression in politics, economics, and daily living in the current "climate" of our day.

The issue is not "How does one resolve the differences?" In the context of the north-south exchange, it is a question of intrinsic behavior in the short term and is probably irresolvable in the long term. The issue is one of spreading the idea that the differences are as omnipresent and pervasive as the weather itself and that they are as resistant to change as is the climate. As much a part of our lives as breathing is—indeed because we breathe—we differ, we the northerners from the southerners. If politicians and the popular press recognized the fact that deep differences truly exist, buried under layers of civilized behavior, it would help many see how much they are unchangeably tied to their environment.

Hot and Cold Looting

In mid-July of 1977, New York City was steamy, hot, unbearable, unless one had air conditioning. The electricity failed. The entire city and surroundings was blacked out. What followed was described variously as a "billion-dollar orgy of looting and pillaging by tens of thousands" of slum dwellers, blacks and Hispanics; as an "act of God"; as a "cry for economic help, or expression of despair by society's forgotten people"; and as "Christmas in July."

However, the Manhattan Borough President, Percy Sutton, himself black, charged that the looting was "a function of criminality, not race." The largest black weekly newspaper, New York's *Amsterdam News*, charged that the blackout had exposed "a massive vacuum of black leadership," a tolerance of lawlessness, and a failure of "white dominated" government to understand the "depth of despair" among our young people.

Ordinary civility and morality were suspended during the blackout. "They took toasters, not bread; liquor, not milk; sports shirts, not shoes," said a journalist.

A Spanish language newspaper (*El Diario*) asked in a front-page headline, "PORQUE?" (Why?) The answers? That stealing is OK if you can get away with it. That society owes you not only a living but the good life. That since minorities have suffered, reparations are now overdue. That crime is the result of poverty. That society is to blame for what a poor person does when the lights are out. That the cops were not instructed to "shoot to kill." These were not reasons but excuses.

No one offered an explanation based upon climate, anatomy, and weather. An earlier New York City blackout in November of 1963 had produced virtually no lootings, no disorders.

The temperature during the first blackout was some forty or fifty Fahrenheit degrees cooler (instead of 90°F, it was 30°F or 40°F) than during the second blackout. Few noticed that poverty was greater and the standard of living was lower in the first blackout.

It may be hard to accept that a contributing cause was not only the temperature *difference* but *effect* upon northern compared to southern temperaments. Hispanic and black peoples for generations were preconditioned to warm habitats. Then in one or two generations, they were expected to accommodate their bodies and minds to one of the most stimulating and energetic climates of the North. The effects are so pervasive, they lose visibility and newsworthiness.

New York's blizzard of 1978 (seven months later) had the same population, yet did not produce a crime wave. Why?

"The way in which weather can instigate a riot is by creating a stress situation," says W. J. Maunder, "a state in which vital functioning of man is threatened." The reactions are defensive, adaptive, and disorganized; and if the first two fail, disturbed behavior occurs, "most likely when stress is intense and long lived, and when defensive and adaptive measures are weak or their capacity is exceeded."

Often the trigger is a trivial additional stressor (in accordance with Wilder's Law of Initial Value, Chapter 1) and the "weather could be said to act as a spark to light the ever-present fuel, but not the fuel itself."

The Elegant Science of Racism:
A Summary

Exposed to climate-leaps, southbound northerners will tend to relax and northbound southerners will tend to tense. Eskimos' hands remain warm in frigid water, mountain dwellers have large lungs, and aborigines sleep uncovered in freezing weather. Caloric consumption in the arctic surpasses caloric intake in the tropics. Loss of memory, alertness, ability to concentrate, and energy, among other symptoms of nervous debility, typify newcomers to the tropics.

Acclimatization explains these examples, yet hides the reasons for them. Warm-climate peoples appear timid, weak, small, lazy, compared to achieving, vigorous, brave, aggressive cold-climate dwellers. A challenging climate accompanies economic, social, or cultural growth, largely absent in a very mild or very rigorous climate.

Regions of the world frequented by mild storms, moderate rainfall, and average temperature ranges of 40°F to 60°F seem to be the most energetic and invigorating climates, likely to be most efficient and productive.

Climate not only determines achievement but also anatomy. Globular, heavy-weight torsos and short limbs favoring heat retention are generally found in cold climates. Linear, light-weight torsos and long limbs favoring heat loss are generally found in warm climates. The coldness of cold winters, not the average annual temperatures, breeds the heaviest Americans, perhaps because it stimulates appetite and activity.

Sexual maturity is later and sexual activity and fertility are lower in hot, tropical countries than in the northern temperate, variable, or energizing climates.

Even color preferences show a north-south gradient, as seen in the colors of state flags. High-achievers and energetic-climate dwellers prefer the "background" colors of light blues and greens. Mild, gentle tropical-climate dwellers prefer the active, intrusive, full-blooded colors of reds, yellows, and oranges.

Ethical and religious principles and the maintenance of standing armies also show a temperature gradient. Confessional Christians dominate countries having an annual temperature of 50°F to 59°F, the same temperature range found in the area where that religion first appeared. Protestant religions and communism dominate countries where the annual temperature is 40°F to 49°F. In general, religions do not dominate an area where the temperature is lower than the average temperature was in the area where the religion was founded. The largest standing armies (as a percentage of its population) are found in the cooler climates (30°F to 45°F), and the smallest in the warmer (above 75°F) regions. The cooler large-army countries generally start or get dragged into fewer wars, win a greater percentage of wars they do become involved in, and lose a smaller percentage of their population to combat deaths.

Rich and poor countries, vigorous and lazy nations, sunbelt and snowbelt politics, and looting exhibit a climatic cleavage.

Five:
Air—Our Ancestral
Home and Master

. . . Human beings have succeeded so well as thinkers and doers, as symbol users and culture makers, as fabricators and shapers, as inventors and constructors as to unwittingly place themselves conceptually outside of nature.
—E. Stainbrook

The conditions necessary to life are found neither in the organism nor in the outer (cosmic) environment, but in both at once. Indeed, if we suppress or disturb the organism, life ceases, even though the environment remains intact; if . . . we take away or vitiate the environment, life just as completely disappears, even though the organism has not been destroyed.
—Claude Bernard

I'd like to see people recognize the importance of the atmosphere.
—Margaret Mead

Preceding Page: Apeliotes
The wind of the east brings a rain that increases gradually. It is the good friend of vegetation. He is represented by a young man whose hair floats in all directions. He has a sweet and open countenance and the sides of his cloak, which is full of all sorts of fruit, a honeycomb, and some clusters of wheat. In Athens, this wind contributes to fertility and abundance, or as Dervish Mustapha explains, "It is a divine wind, it brings us from Mecca the blessings of Allah."

Air is your most important extrinsic ingredient of survival. Take away food, and you can live for a week or more. Take away water, and you will survive a few days. But take away air, and you will not survive more than a few minutes.

The words "am" or "is" come from ancient words meaning "to breathe" (*asmi* in Sanskrit) and "to grow" (*bhu* in Sanskrit); thus, existence was breathing air and growing.

Nowadays public figures will *go on the air* in order *to air certain issues*, to *clear the air* (if a politician is accused of a wrongdoing), to improve the *atmosphere* in the White House or the *climate of opinion*, and will most assuredly employ a firm and resolute *air of confidence*.

When rejected, he *gets the air*. When superficial, she *puts on airs*. The French will recognize her fraudulence if she *prend des airs de grandeur*, or "takes on a grand air." To give oneself an *air* or *aria*, an Italian will *darsi delle aire*, and a Frenchman *avoir l'aire de . . .* when he "resembles" someone or something.

In uncertainty, we are *up in the air*; *in der Luft hängen*, as the Germans say, is "to hang in the air"; or in French, *être en l'air*, "to be in the air."

When in love, or enraptured, we *walk on air*. Indeed, we rhapsodize in the springtime or in fine weather, when:

Love is in the air
   This morning
Bachelors beware
   Fair warning
If you start
   To feel a tingle
And you like
   Remaining single
Stay home
   Don't take a breath
You could
   Catch your death
      —Stephen Sondheim

Air makes constant and innermost contact with your skin and lungs over truly immense areas. An average-sized adult breathes some 2,000 to 8,000 gallons of air per day, and efficient air absorption by your lungs requires "great intimacy with the bloodstream over an area about half as large as a tennis court," says environmental engineer Francis Silver.

The skin of an average-sized adult covers an area of about 19 to 25 square feet (about 1.8 to 2.4 square meters) and weighs about six pounds, depending on physique and stature. And each *square inch* of skin contains some 15 feet of blood vessels, 72 feet of nerves, 100 sweat glands, and 3,000 sensory cells for perception of touch, pressure, pain, cold, and heat. The entire skin surface has perhaps ten million sensory cells and two million sweat glands in contact with the air around us. Despite what some psychiatrists or psychologists say, the term "a grounded personality" is neither flattering nor accurate. With his vast atmospheric exposure, with a mere 2 percent of his body area touching the earth, man is substantially less "grounded" than he is "aired."

Air hunger is potentially the strongest human drive of all, stronger than the drive for food, stronger than the drive for sex. Brain tissues, muscle tissues, cells, membranes, organs, skin—all demand air or oxygen for survival. Whether carried by blood or delivered directly, oxygen from the air indirectly furnishes energy during combustion or oxidation with glucose, a fuel providing muscle power. Activities like exercise that take place in the presence of oxygen are called aerobic. Localized tissues may starve and die for absence or lack of oxygen (called anoxia or hypoxia), although for a short time muscles can do without it.

"Probably the most basic factor is oxidation," research pathologist William Petersen argued. After a cold-front passage, for example, when the blood has left the outer areas of the body, these areas are at a disadvantage. The normal amount of oxygen the blood carries to the tissues is no longer transported, and this means that certain vital tissues of the body will not get as much oxygen as they have been accustomed to. If the organs are sturdy and smooth-functioning, the temporary decrease in oxygen will not cause any special trouble. If the organs are not completely up to par, however, they will be particularly susceptible to air hunger, and will act up immediately.

The air temperature, then, will exert a very strong influence on the amount of blood and thus oxygen available to various body tissues (see illustration of blood shifts, Chapter 7).

Your inner mechanisms to equilibrate temperature fluctuations depend almost entirely on your blood circulation and its changes. Once our prehuman ancestor lost his heavy coat and became truly naked, a great load was heaved upon his circulatory system, thermal reflexes, vasomotor apparatus, and pituitary-thyroid-adrenal glands.

In a relatively stable climate (say the seashore), our prehuman ancestor might thrive, but once he ventured into weather-unstable areas, he was forced more and more to use thermal reflexes, involuntary responses, and reflexive vasomotor mechanisms—vasoconstriction and vasodilation, or the subconscious narrowing and widening of the blood vessels to regulate body temperature. In changeable climates, the prehuman animal had two alternatives: (1) exhaustion, fatigue, and death or (2) training, improvement in speed of reaction, perfection of the reflexive response, and ultimate survival. The latter meant shunting his blood to and from the skin surface; it meant evaporative cooling with the release of sweat; it meant transferring heat from the extremities, by withdrawal of blood, to the body core to maintain its warmth. In short, it was thrive and strive, or die.

"It was just this demand and just this training," Petersen says, "that did much to make us human, made us the variable and adjustable animals that we have turned out to be. Greater vasomotor variability provided greater variability in the functional capacity of the cortex—wider amplitude in the range of cerebration—the opportunity for the appearance for genius."

But these thermal demands on our ancestors meant rigorous elimination of human strains that could not cope with such strenuous demands. The air mass, our ancestral *home,* was a demanding *master.* Survival meant absolute, intimate, internal adjustments to every passing air mass, to every environmental temperature change. For millions of years.

Temperature, air pressure, humidity, wind velocity—if the organism were conscious of all intimate adaptations, all subliminal adjustments to these cross currents, air forces, he would have had little thinking time for anything else. His brain would become overloaded. Conscious perception of the adjustments was not only *not* necessary, it was a hindrance to further cerebral evolution.

Fire, caves, animal skins, clothing or electric blankets and air conditioning are artificial buffers, thermal regulators between our naked tight-fitting overgarment we call "skin" and the great ocean of air above. For only a few centuries have we had some of these buffers and improved upon the sheltering embrace of our houses. "Winter is still an *occupation*," said Sinclair Lewis, "not a *season*," throughout most of the world—and throughout most of our evolutionary history.

Temperature regulation is still an *occupation* for most of humanity, a response to thermal stress. How much time, effort, energy, and capital are invested in keeping our bodies at their normal temperature of 98.6°F (37°C)? Put another way, consider the fraction of a day or year during which your body is neither clothed nor artificially heated or cooled. That fraction is very small.

What portion of your thermal regulation is conscious, what portion unconscious? You can quickly estimate: merely reflect how many times a day you regulate your temperature, by opening or shutting a window or door, by adding or removing garments, by raising or lowering a thermostat, and so on. Embedded deeply in your subconscious thoughts, but surfacing frequently, is an energetic battle to keep your body in thermal comfort and equilibrium.

Modern civilized city dwellers cling to a notion that they are sheltered from wind and weather. But the notion is wrong. Merely ask the doorman of an urban, high-rise apartment dwelling, "What is the most common popular subject of conversation?" Conversational weather pleasantries are legion. City dwellers have succeeded in diminishing one of our most pervasive and profound needs—the stimulation of weather. Our ancestors (see Appendix A) recognized the primacy of weather, not only in their conscious attempts at thermal regulation but also in their mythology (see Chapter 8), their religion, their language.

None of us—city dweller, suburbanite, or farmer—is immune to weather changes, even when we live in constant-temperature surroundings. We are eternally susceptible to changes in humidity, pressure, and light. We still modulate their intensity. When sheltered, we strive to moderate the severity and intensity of our reactions. In health, our reflexes and thermoregulatory mechanisms operate, our intimate tides still ebb and flow; we conform to the air mass, our master. When we are unable to conform, we fatigue, we suffer, we sicken, and we decline. We must equilibrate or die.

Not only temperature extremes, heat or cold, must be compensated within the body. But *every energy impact*—major or minor, transient or protracted—on the body and on the mind has to be equilibrated. For the same mechanisms the body uses in meeting heat or cold are also marshaled in meeting every energy impact. The blood distribution changes, endocrine activity changes, physical and chemical constituents of body fluids change; mental reactivity, muscle ability, kidney performance, bone marrow and leukocytes, mucous membranes, sensory response, even the retina of the eye—will all change.

Suppose one of your body organs is below par or congenitally inadequate due perhaps to a local injury or a state of fatigue after strain. Then suppose a shifting air mass induces blood vessels to constrict thereby denying blood, and therefore oxygen, to the disabled organ, which suffers local oxygen hunger, acidosis, hydration, swelling, pressure, pain.

The medical complaint may pass. Tissues may return to normal within several days or longer if unstrained. But suppose other air masses, of similar intensity and similar nature, come along before the tissues re-equilibrate, before the organ that is the focus of these changes returns to normal. The passing weather fronts will register focal changes; migraine, colitis, arthritis, neuritis, and stomach ulcers are a few examples. The transient local dysfunction may become permanent, "frozen in," as it were. Your occasional appendix pain may develop into an acute attack. Your simple headache may end in a throbbing migraine. Your ulcer may perforate. Your temporary loss of essential blood proteins (albuminuria) may become permanent. Periodic acidosis in a diabetic may end in coma. A temporary drop in total white cell count or blood platelets may lead to black-and-blue spots under the skin or internal hemorrhaging.

Public health statistics on reproduction and death, on mental and physical disturbances, on psychotic admissions, on the sex ratio of infants conceived, on the sex ratio of individuals who died, on scarlet fever, twinning, epileptic attacks, labor pains, cardiac deaths, tuberculosis, suicides, and on other dysfunctions echo atmospheric changes. The individual also reverberates to the atmosphere. Consequently, as we shall see later in this chapter, the population at large will parallel or mirror the organic rhythms seen in individuals.

Thus, the first necessity of evolution was adequate oxygen supply to the body's tissues. Thermal regulation, a reflex reaction to passage of weather fronts, created biological tides of air hunger. Focused upon weak body organs, the result could be dysfunction. Focused upon the population groups, the air-mass changes would trigger diseases, deaths, behavioral changes, perhaps mass migrations, the stimulation of higher cerebral activities, and the creation of synthetic buffers interposed between our skin and an overhead oceanic blanket of air, that is at once our ancestral home and our environmental master.

We Live in a Double-Blind Experiment

A "blind" experiment is one in which the patient does not know which pill he is taking—the powerful medicine or a placebo ("I shall please"), a purposely ineffectual dummy drug. In a "double-blind" experiment, even the physician who administers the drug to the patient does not know whether it is potent or neutral.

Most of us, when normally healthy, experience the weather as if we were subjects in a blind experiment. Often we do not know whether the medicine—the weather phase—is good or bad for us or what it does to us. When we are ill and under the care of the physician, we live a double-blind experiment, since neither the physician nor the patient knows what the drug, that pervasive air mass, is expected to do. Meteorologists and physicians collect their data separately. Rarely do they attempt, particularly in the United States, to correlate their findings.

But landmark investigations by William Petersen demonstrated the following:

1. Both normal and sick individuals, either exposed directly to weather changes or sheltered in the home or hospital, were conditioned by the weather.
2. The most diverse clinical symptoms reflected weather changes or were precipitated by weather conditions.
3. During the earliest stages of development, genetic trends were probably weather-conditioned.
4. Weather changes condition the mental reactions of normal persons and the psychopathic behavior of abnormal patients.
5. Weather changes are reflected in births and deaths of the entire population at large.

No two individuals are alike, no environmental situation is ever repeated, and no single individual is always the same. Consequently, Petersen undertook an exhaustive day-by-day study of three medical students (Harold, Eli, Seymour) as they reacted to normal weather conditions. They were normal in every respect, except for the fact that they were triplets and thus genetically similar. For six weeks, during June and July of 1940, he examined their daily, often hourly biochemical and biophysical alterations of blood and urine and their changing mental, physical, and emotional responses. He also examined any clinical symptoms they presented simultaneous with weather changes. He correlated the medical and meteorological findings, thereby annihilating the double-blind experiment the rest of us are part of.

Petersen's conclusions (see Chapter Notes) have far-reaching consequences. And so his triplet study bears close inspection.

The triplets lived in Chicago under identical controlled conditions. From June 19 to August 1, 1940, their daily routines and food intake were essentially the same; the only major condition that changed from day to day was the weather. That year June was dry and colder than normal, while July was dry and warmer than usual. In general, this weather was relatively extreme for that time of year, and consequently placed "unusual demands on the involuntary adjustment mechanisms."

Approximately fourteen cold fronts and seven warm fronts passed through Chicago during the six-week period of the triplet study.

Some thirty-six measurement series of blood, urine, and physiology were taken of the triplets at least once daily, and then compared. The daily readings varied in a consistent fashion with respect to each other. That is, significant statistical correlations occurred from one day to the next for these factors: systolic (heart pushing outward) blood pressure, body temperature (A.M.), body temperature (P.M.), pulse rate (P.M.), blood pH (acidity or alkalinity), total dynamometer (physical strength), creatinine, arm volume, red blood cells, total nitrogen, sedimentation rate, cell volume, weight, specific gravity, total fatigue, total acid output, total ammonia, uric acid, urine pH, protein, urine volume, total solids, hemoglobin.

The day-to-day readings of these factors for each triplet changed consistently with respect to each other (see Chapter Notes). This tells us that *day-to-day changes in the triplets' biochemistry were due to common causes*. Except for the weather, everything else (diet, living conditions, daily routine, genetic endowment of the subjects) was held constant. Therefore, Petersen concluded that the weather was the common cause of change in these medical tests.

Red blood cell count *increases* greatly when daily air temperature *increases*. Most of us are familiar with the fact that urine volume *increases* very considerably when daily temperatures *decline* precipitously (and when barometric pressure *increases*). All of these changes are not entirely independent. The air-mass system obeys rules; a wedge of cold, dense polar air often sends the barometer up. And human physiology follows its own rules: urine volume and urine pH generally move in the same direction, as do red blood cell count and sedimentation time, or blood protein and diastolic blood pressure.

The elements of each biological system or each meteorological system are not only linked to other elements in their *own* system. But the entire organism itself is yoked to the air mass it inhabits. While looking at each element alone we must keep in mind that it is isolated merely for examination. In reality, it is a part of a comprehensive, ever-changing system. "No single biological component or symptom is ever altered without corresponding effects on all other components."

Three Celestial Resonators

Harold, Eli, and Seymour are the triplets Petersen tested, whose bodily functions changed with weather changes.

The weather was cold one day prior to each of Harold's pulse rate peaks. Although his brothers "slurred" many of their reactions to passing weather fronts, generally pulse rate *increases* follow the passage of cold air masses and heat waves.

All other factors being equal, your afternoon pulse rate should peak about a day after the weather becomes colder. Some physicians are unaware of this relationship between pulse rate and cold weather, and so you or they could be unduly alarmed by a relatively high pulse rate. However, many other factors determine your pulse rate (including your physical activity, digestion, emotional state, endocrine balance, autonomic tone, ion balance, and blood pressure). In the triplet study, these other factors were kept uniform from day to day. In an uncontrolled environment, these other factors change considerably and can mask the weather's effect on pulse rate.

Diastolic blood pressure approximates the resistance against which the heart must pump. The heart muscle has relaxed and the heart arteries become filled with blood from the back pressure exerted by capillaries and blood vessels. Diastolic blood pressure is important since it is quite sensitive to outside happenings and *falls* following *cold* fronts.

Systolic blood pressure indicates the pressure level at which the heart is pumping blood *out* of its cavities; it is always higher than the diastolic blood pressure, and subject to wider fluctuations such as the location of the test, the identity and attitude of physician and patient, the position and emotional state of the patient, the patient's body build, and—as we will see—the weather. (That is why those do-it-yourself, coin-operated blood-pressure machines in airports and drugstores may give "incorrect" readings.)

You may be unwittingly fatigued by the passage of two weather fronts. Suppose cold weather constricts your body's peripheral tissues today, raising your blood pressure. Tomorrow, when your blood pressure falls due to relaxation of the blood vessels, a warm front arrives. If that tropical air mass follows a polar air mass—this happens often—your body reacts further by still lower diastolic pressure. The cumulative effects of two stressors (polar air followed by tropical air) are often accompanied by medical complications, vascular accidents, bacterial passage dissemination (low resistance to infection), psychotic episodes, nervous-system dysfunctions, and other disorders that accompany critically low levels of diastolic pressure. Quite simply, you are likely to feel tired one or two days after a sharp temperature drop.

Spring Fever

In northern-climate populations in late winter and early spring, relative blood acidosis develops when body fatigue is most pronounced. Resistance to infection, to intoxication, to trauma, and to emotional impacts is at its lowest level then. Conceptions are diminished, while stillbirths and deaths in the population peak during this time. Petersen charted the acid-alkaline balance of blood for a ten-year period in Chicago and it showed a pronounced high relative blood *acidity* (low pH) during April, spring-fever time, when spirits sag for some of us.

Relatively sharp increases of blood *alkalinity* (high pH) appear in summer and autumn. Pronounced peaks also appear in early July, early October, and late November. If the blood and tissue fluids shift toward an excess of the ratio of alkali over acid, blood alkalosis results. Excessive loss of acid or excessive elimination of carbon dioxide by overbreathing are typical causes, aside from weather fronts. One symptom is an exaggerated reactivity of the muscles which may go into cramp-like spasms.

The acid-alkaline balance also affects the nasal mucous membranes. The total acid output in the urine increases when the relative acidity of the blood increases. Nasal mucous membranes tend to become more acidic when the blood becomes more alkaline, more alkaline when the blood becomes more acidic. These interrelated phase swings of the body correspond (statistically) to passage of weather fronts.

Whenever the environmental temperature fell, the triplets had periods of relative acidosis. The swings in blood-alkaline levels showed definite and progressive increases (described by the Law of Initial Value) called "overshooting." The alkaline crests occurred during temperature increases and especially during *sudden* temperature increases to high levels. Blood alkalinity crested two days after the environmental temperature stopped falling and started rising steeply. Normally, peripheral blood will become more alkaline during warm periods; with extreme heat following a cold wave, the body "overcorrects" by increasing the respiration rate (thereby eliminating carbon dioxide) and increasing the sweating. The prior level of arousal drives the body to overrespond.

Furthermore, the triplets' blood acidity was maximum two to three days following a cold front. You will sleep longer and you will tire easily one or more days after a sharp dip in temperature, mimicking spring fever.

When a cold air mass passes, you may expect an increase in your body weight. Your evaporation rate diminishes during a cold front; relative acidity develops, causing retention of your body fluids and increasing the relative permeability of your capillaries. The triplet experiment also showed that on the day following a steep temperature drop and increase of barometric pressure (this combination usually signals a cold front) body weight is at a maximum and blood vessels constrict, creating air hunger, lower diastolic blood pressure, increased capillary permeability, accentuated acidity, and water retention.

If a warm or tropical air mass passes through shortly afterward, the whole process may slowly rise to the level of conscious attention. Tissue swelling would cause your body tissues to "hurt." During this *second* stimulus, or weather "dose," expect arthritic "weather prophet" complaints, expect toothaches, expect worsening neuritis, expect hurting bunions, expect migraine, expect acute episodes from mental patients, expect clinical awareness.

The successive passage of these two weather fronts—cold followed by warm—precipitates complex, subliminal, physiological changes that gradually may express themselves at the conscious level in clear-cut symptoms. Normally, a body restores (or overcorrects) itself by its own natural healing powers, by homeostasis. The normal response to successive stimuli is accurately portrayed by the Law of Initial Value: ever-present past arousal levels dictate future response.

You may glimpse the variety of your own *hidden* response to weather changes in the following brief sample results of the triplet experiment.

- *Leukocytes* are white blood cells, manufactured in bone marrow, that rush to the site of a bodily injury, engulf and digest foreign substances (especially bacteria), deliver important antibodies, supply fibrin and other healthy materials, and scavenge, or cart away dead and dying cells. It is not widely appreciated that passage of weather fronts will change leukocyte counts. *Cold*, or *polar*, *fronts* tend to accompany *increases* in leukocyte counts. *Warm*, or *tropical*, *fronts* tend to accompany *decreases* in leukocyte counts.
- *Dark-adaptation time* is the time taken for your eyes to adapt sufficiently to a darkened room in order to see. In Petersen's experiments, the triplets took from 15 to 150 seconds to adapt. Their dark-adaptation times swung widely with swings in the environmental temperature. The result: *dark adaptation was shortened with warm weather and prolonged with cold weather*—so it takes longer to find your theater seat in the winter than summer.
- The nose "knows" the air, since inhaled air is first warmed and moistened by the nose. Even on a cold day, by the time cold air reaches the trachea, it is close to body temperature and saturated with water vapor. Changes in the air mass—such as temperature or moisture—which register first in the nasal mucous membrane, will trigger important adjustments in our bodies. Consider the speed with which an aromatic substance can elicit a response from your nasal mucous membrane—with only a few molecules as a signal. The nasal mucous membrane is, to understate it considerably, *very* sensitive. The acid-base balance of the nasal mucous membrane (nasal pH) was examined daily in the triplet study. As environmental temperature increased, the nasal acidity increased (declining pH). The correlation was very strong. When nasal membranes change their acidity-alkalinity, so does their hospitality to the flora and bacteria in residence there. So the nasal bacteria count is very sensitive to

outside temperature. Among the triplets it increased consistently and strongly when the temperature increased.

- In the triplets, periods of irritability and elation associated with corresponding shifts in blood pH, and presumably reflected adequate or inadequate tissue oxygenation, undue hydration or dehydration of tissues, and undue spasm or relaxation of blood vessels.

- A measure of tissue oxygenation is breath-holding time, and it declined when relative air hunger of body tissues appeared. Significant drops in breath-holding time of each triplet were invariably accompanied by irritability, sleepiness, dullness, headache, sore throat, depression.

Mental Processes

Mental activity also depends on blood vessels that control the supply of oxygen reaching cerebral tissues in the brain. A network of capillaries under the skin react so closely to outside changes in temperature that the skin has been called the special sense organ of the involuntary or autonomic nervous system. The changing oxygen supply due to heat and cold is seen clearly in the alterations of mental processes—annual, seasonal, monthly, daily—and in the results of the triplet study.

The triplets were given daily tests of their arithmetic skill; each had to add sets of numbers. Every day the triplets were scored for *correctness* and for *speed*. These separate scores were compared to their biochemical and physiological conditions and to atmospheric conditions.

Correctness in these tests generally improved with the passage of cold air masses. Speed of accomplishment was retarded during periods of undue heat, but accelerated following five consecutive days of increasing barometric pressure, a condition that usually accompanies a cold front and reflects improved oxidation.

Rorschach test scores, however, frequently increased during transient alkalosis, rising blood pressure, declining breath-holding time— all symptoms of oxygen deprivation. Rorschach tests tap the "imaginative response," which may be stimulated during stress—fatigue, sleeplessness, disease, hunger, and thirst. The imaginative response of each triplet changed daily, in rhythm with each other. After the passage of cold air masses, the triplets reacted to Rorschach tests with greater imaginative response, and this response was depressed in warm weather. The imaginative response swung in synchrony with both systolic and diastolic blood pressure, which controls cerebral blood supply and oxygen in parallel with air temperature swings.

Celestial Resonance at Large

The triplets were normal adults. However, the population at large is composed not only of 100 percent normal people, but also of those who depart considerably from the norm. These are borderline mental cases, the "walking wounded," the very old and weak, the very young and weak, the pregnant, the diseased, and many individuals who are overloaded, or under great stress, or weak, so that any additional stress would push them over the edge into dysfunction. Weather changes are just such additional stressors.

The triplets' response reactions to weather stress were a sort of litmus paper, an early warning signal, a faint reaction-response that appeared amplified and magnified among those nonnormals in the population at large. Where the triplets reacted, a marginal fringe of the public *overreacted* to weather stress. These overreactions showed up in statistics—if the fringe group was large enough. Hospital admissions of psychotics, birth records, deaths, suicides, the sex ratio of those who died, the sex ratio of twins, and the ratio of conceptions to deaths, were among the statistics Petersen tracked. He found that physiological functions among the triplets shadowed these statistics simultaneously, before, or after they changed; he explained or sought to explain why this should happen on sound medical principles—the details of which are highly technical—and he succeeded brilliantly.

* * *

His conclusion, not only for the triplets, but also for the general population: *There are significant parallel alterations*—between the triplets' rhythms and weather rhythms; between statistical "markers" (such as psychopathic admissions, births, deaths, sex ratio of infants conceived and of the dead, twinning, and vital index) and the triplets' rhythms; between statistical markers and environmental conditions; between the triplets' organic rhythms and those of the general population.

"During the time the triplets revealed air hunger," Petersen says, "more potentially psychotic individuals become acutely psychotic;

more pregnant women near-term began to have labor pains, more normal individuals became sick, more sick individuals died, more males and fewer children were conceived. . . . All of which simply means that the human group is reacting as a mass to the weather that is ubiquitous."

In those whose organs are fatigued, the fatigue will pass over to exhaustion, to inadequacy, and to *disease*. In the sick or ailing, when the heart, kidney, liver, lung, or adrenal gland is failing, the individual fails irreversibly.

"So the simple tides of the inorganic forces of the world—reflected and amplified—dampened and stemmed in flesh and blood, in brain and marrow, may in the final analysis be of supreme importance not only for the individual but for the mass of mankind."

Air—Our Ancestral Home and Master: A Summary

Air hunger is stronger than sex hunger or food hunger, since after merely minutes of oxygen deprivation, life will cease. The conditions necessary to life obstinately bind the environment to living creatures, but we seem to have succeeded so well as thinkers and doers that we have unwittingly placed ourselves conceptually outside of nature's reach. Nevertheless, for most of humanity, winter is not a season, but an occupation.

Once our prehuman ancestor lost his hairy coat, a great burden was heaved upon his circulatory system, his vasomotor apparatus, his thermal reflexes, his pituitary-thyroid-adrenal glands—the job of regulating and equilibrating body temperature in response to surrounding air. Thus human skin perceives heat and cold, pressure and pain, with its ten million sensing elements over an area of twenty square feet, 98 percent of it in intimate contact with the air, its master. The blood stream enjoys great intimacy with air through the lungs.

Our involuntary response to air temperature controls the distribution of oxygen-bearing blood to all of the body's cells. Subconsciously driven narrowing of the blood vessels at the body's periphery conserves body heat but also unavoidably denies air and oxygen to cell tissues. Involuntary peripheral blood vessel constriction will trigger expansion, widening peripheral blood vessels to encourage the loss of body heat. These vascular changes occur in rhythmic response to the passage of weather fronts in a kind of organic "pendulation," reflected in subliminal moods, episodes of air hunger, hidden physiological shifts, medical dysfunctions, and clinical symptoms.

Historic experiments on genetically similar triplets demonstrate how the body reflects or "paraphrases" the passing weather conditions. Blood pressure, pulse rate, body temperature, physical strength or fatigue, mental activity, the imaginative response, composition of urine and blood, and nasal bacteria showed significant and systematic parallel alterations with weather changes. But where normal people react to weather, a marginal fringe of the public at large overreact, amplifying these parallel alterations into grim statistics. Hospital admission rates of pyschotics, births and deaths, suicides, mental illness, and other statistics will foreshadow, co-vary, or lag behind specific weather impacts.

Six:
World Winds

From the great sky a wind has blown and has caused a sickness in the eye of man.
   —Inscribed on Babylonian cuneiform tablet, ca. 2000 B.C.

When the wind is in the south
It blows the bait in the fishes' mouth.
   —Old Yorkshire fisherman's saying

In the stupendous work of [energy] transport the permanent agent was the atmosphere, thin and insignificant though it was in comparison with the monstrous earth itself.
   Within the atmosphere, the chief equalizers of heat were the great winds—the trades and anti-trades, the monsoons, the tropical hurricanes, the polar easterlies, and (most notable of all) the gigantic whirling storms of the temperate zones, which in the stateliest of earthly processions moved ever along their sinuous paths, across ocean and continent, from the setting, toward the rising sun.
   —George R. Stewart, *Storm*

Preceding Page: Zephyrus
The east wind is very hot in summer, but in spring its warmth is favorable to vegetation. It is represented in the figure of an attractive young man of agreeable countenance. His "movements" seem easy and smooth; he is nude except for a large cape overflowing with flowers.

Montana stood in the grip of fierce cold. It was the first day of December 1896. The thermometer stood at 45° Fahrenheit *below zero*. Scarcely a breath of wind stirred over the range, where tens of thousands of Montana cattle stood starving in thirty inches of crusted snow. The weather had been icy and grim for cattle stockmen since November; unusually heavy early snows blanketed the grazing ranges from the Rockies eastward. Cattlemen predicted that by spring their herds would be depleted disastrously, like that fateful, heart-breaking springtime of 1887, a decade earlier.

A starving steer, standing knee-deep in snow, waited fearfully. Wolves circled about, waiting to make the kill. This scene was commemorated by Charles M. Russell, the cowboy artist, in a painting, "The Last of the Five Thousand." For the steer—death; for the cattlemen and the livestock economy of Montana—financial ruin; for all—hopeless fear, no reprieve.

"Suddenly, over the edge of the mountains to the Southwest appeared a great bank of black clouds, their outer edge blown to tatters by the winds. In a few minutes a short puff of hot, dry air had reached the plains and in the following seven minutes the temperature had risen 34 degrees! The wind increased in velocity to 25 miles an hour and the temperature rose to 38 degrees above zero. Within 12 hours every vestige of the 30 inches of snow had disappeared, leaving behind bare hills and the plains covered with water." This vivid account of windy reprieve was written by Alvin T. Barrows, the United States Weather Bureau observer at the time.

Chinook

This welcome warm wind, a joyous thermal rescue from the dead of winter resembling "a scented virgin come to seduce the gods of winter" (according to Montana poet, Walker E. Taylor), is called the "snow-eater," or chinook.

In western Oregon, Washington, and British Columbia, chinook described a warm, moist, southwesterly wind coming from the direction of the district once inhabited by the Chinook Indians on the lower Columbia River. The name chinook was applied by early settlers along the eastern base of the Rockies to the hot, dry wind that rustled down in winter, often freeing the pasture of snow to bestow upon starving animals life-giving food. After Russell painted the scene mentioned, it was retitled "Waiting for a Chinook."

Rapid City, in the Black Hills of South Dakota, holds a record for the most spectacular chinook in the annals of American meteorology. On January 22, 1943, the mercury in nearby Spearfish skyrocketed from −4°F to 45°F in two minutes. "At eleven A.M. on the east side of the Alex Johnson Hotel in Rapid City," according to the *Monthly Weather Review*, "winter was in all its glory, while around the corner on the south side, not fifty feet away, spring held sway, only to be swept away in a flash by the sting of winter, and then to return."

Known as "the wind that warms," or *Ta-Te Kata*, among the Sioux Indians of the Black Hills, many of its comings were recorded in their calendars. Sioux medicine men apparently never predicted the wind's arrival, welcome as it always was.

Local old-timers, like Don Patton, the seventy-year-old son of one of Rapid City's original pioneers said, "I think of all the pleasant surprises, to wake up in the middle of the night and hear the drip, drip, drip as snow melts off the roof is the best. Not everyone ever gets the treat where you get home and go to bed shedding overshoes and big coat and mittens and cap and scarf, wake in the middle of the night and know it's warmer, then arise in the morning and the snow isn't there anymore. For me it's a *thrill*."

The Rocky Mountain chinook blows southwest to northeast, generally, with topographical variations. According to accepted meteorological reckoning, the chinook approaches the western slope of the Rockies heavily laden with moisture. As it climbs it begins to cool; and as it cools, moisture drops out in the form of rain and/or snow. The cooling process is mathematically calculable—the temperature of the air, when it is raining or snowing, falls three degrees every one thousand feet of ascent. If its temperature was fifty degrees at the bottom of the western slope (five thousand feet) it will be down to around twenty-nine degrees at a peak of twelve thousand feet. The process is reversed as it slides down the eastern side—it begins to warm. Since it has already dropped its moisture, there is no rain and in the absence of rain its temperature climbs at a fixed rate of 5.5 degrees every one thousand feet of descent. If the elevation at the bottom of the eastern slope is the same as that of its western counterpart (it is not necessarily so, but just for example) then by the time the air descends to five thousand feet, it is up to sixty-seven degrees, or seventeen degrees warmer than it was at the same elevation on the western slope. In other words, the rate of heating exceeds the rate of cooling when rain is involved to account for the difference. In winter the eastern slope of the Rockies is usually in the grip of an icy stream of arctic air; say it is around twenty-five degrees compared to the fifty degrees in Utah. That mass of sixty-seven-degree air rushes into Denver, Colorado Springs, Pueblo and—sudden spring.

That is the accepted, or textbook, meteorological reckoning. Chester Glenn and his colleagues at the weather bureau had another theory. "We don't think the classic explanation holds true for the chinook. It does for the foehn [alpine wind]—you've got an ample supply of warm, moist air coming off the Mediterranean. But there are too many mountains, too much leaching out between the Pacific and the Rockies. Very often we get a tremendous chinook when we know there hasn't been any rain from it on the western slopes. Without that rain the air on the western slope would get over here at the same temperature. But the temperatures differ. Why? We think something else happens. We think that chinook air peels off from a stream of cold air at a high altitude. You might say it uses the eastern slope of the Rockies as a slide, a down escalator, to reach the lower elevations."

Whatever its explanation, it is more or less the same—a warm, dry wind, blowing down the slopes of a mountain range, turning temperatures topsy-turvy, turning winter into spring, turning human nature inside out. Warm or cold, dry or wet, the world teems with winds.

Almost every language has a word for a special sort of warm, dry wind. In Italy, it's the *sirocco*, the "father of depression." In Spain, the *leveccio*. Egypt has the *chamsin*. Argentina has the *zonda*. France has the *autan* and the *mistral*. The Sahara has the *simoom*. The *sharav* and the *chamsin* are found in the Middle East and Israel. Hawaii has the *kona*, Norway the *bora*, and Austria has the famous and infamous *foehn* (called *phoenicios* during the Renaissance in the belief that it blew from Phoenicia). Salzburg has the *tauernwind*, the upper Danube has the *pyrnwind*, Lyons has the *vent du midi*, Romania has the *roteturwind*. East of the Rockies and the northwest up to Canada the United States has the *chinook*, and California has the *Santa Ana*.

In many languages, "wind" is synonymous with "spirit." In the Bible, the "Spirit of God" that "moved upon the face of the water" has also been translated as the "Wind of God." The very idea of God may have derived from the human experience of wind. To primitive natives, the wind indicated the presence of God: something that cannot be seen, can move objects, bend trees, and make whispering sounds. Wind is an invisible power, capable of communicating with man.

Our language itself is buffeted by the winds. An easy task is a *breeze*, a nonchalant person *breezes into* town, casual talk is *shooting the breeze*, or *windiness*, in French *causer en l'air* or in Italian *parole al vento*.

A German opportunist is "one who hangs his coat (on his shoulders) according to the wind," or *einer der den Mantel nach den Wind hängt*, a turncoat. A German "windbag" is a *Windbeutel*, "a windy character" is *ein windiger Mensch* or a *Windhund*, that is "a wind (or grey) hound." A German *schlägt doch alle Vorsicht in den Wind*, "throws all caution to the wind," because "he knows from which hole the wind blows," or *er weiss aus welchem Loch der Wind bläst*. (This last idiom may come down to us from the first century; Pliny's theory held that winds are vaporous accumulations escaping from subterranean caves through holes in the ground.) A good politician will always know when something *is in the wind* or *which way the wind blows*.

"To speak or preach to the winds" is futile, whether in French *parler en l'air*, in Italian *predicore al vento*, or in German *in den Wind reden*.

A *whirlwind* courtship is to marry in haste. You may repent at leisure once the *wind is taken out of your sails*.

In Aesop's fable, "The North Wind and the Sun," those two primal forces debate, each claiming to be stronger than the other. Finally they agree to test their powers, by seeing who can remove a cloak from a traveler. "The North Wind, gathering up all his force for the attack came whirling furiously down upon the man . . . but the harder he blew, the more closely the man wrapped his cloak around himself." Then it was the sun's turn. "At first he beamed gently upon the traveler, who soon unclasped his cloak and walked on with it hanging loosely about his shoulders. Then he shone forth in his full strength, and the man, before he had gone many steps, was glad to throw his cloak right off and complete his journey more lightly clad." Aesop's moral is "persuasion is better than force."

But a modern counterexample (one of many) begs to be told again. On November 8, 1940, four months after it was completed, the

Tacoma Narrows Bridge collapsed into Puget Sound. Extraordinary movies of the event vividly impress any viewer: winds buffeted the slender horizontal ribbon of road suspended by cable between two vertical support towers. Soon, the roadway went into oscillations, up and down, with cars still on it, deserted by their frightened drivers. The oscillations built up as the wind played upon it like the aeolian harp (that favorite of romantic poets which winds set into vibration, emitting sweet sounds to soothe the agitated and the disabled). Standing waves, seen in the roadway, grew ever greater in amplitude. Until finally and dramatically, the roadway ruptured and hung flailing in the wind, flopping like a wet noodle. It was, I believe, Theodore von Karman who showed that the bridge engineers had apparently neglected to take into account aerodynamic lift, the principle that carries airplanes aloft. At a seminar decades later, in allusion to this disaster (obvious to those present) and clearly warning of another, the space expert Wernher Von Braun said "I represent the wind."

Hippocrates Updated

Hippocrates, speaking to us from twenty-five centuries ago, blames the wind for many of our misfortunes.

> South winds induce dullness of hearing, dimness of vision, heaviness of the head (headaches), torpor and languor; when these prevail such symptoms occur in diseases.
> But if the north winds prevail, coughs, infections of the throat [sore throat], hardness of the bowels [constipation], dysuria [difficult or frequent urination], attended with rigors [shivering], and pains in the side and breast occur.

Hippocrates goes on to say that since it is possible to infer diseases from the winds and seasons, it is also possible to forecast winds (and the droughts that accompany especially the north and south winds) from diseases: soft sores in the mouth and private parts accompany southern winds, and pains at the joints flare up prior to rain and the winds. He thought that weather changes, especially violent ones, are chiefly responsible for human disease.

The Health Consequences of Winds

Ailment/Symptom	Winds (Weather Type)	Clouds (Weather change)
Exhaustion	Warm westerly	Unstable occurrences, strong meteorological activity
Difficulties with amputations	Warm prevailing southerly, cool prevailing northerly	Gradual clouding, high clouding
Angina pectoris	Polar front, cold westerly	Clouding, unstable conditions
Apoplectic attacks	Polar front	Clouding
Appendicitis	Tropical front, warm prevailing southerly	High clouding, unstable conditions
Bronchial asthma	Warm prevailing southerly	Clouding, unstable conditions, lower air inversion
Respiratory diseases	—	Clouding
General sense of malaise	—	Clearing, clouding, unstable conditions
Work accidents	Warm prevailing southerly, warm westerly	Clearing, unstable conditions
Blood-coagulation time shorter	Tropical front, warm southerly	Clouding
Blood-coagulation time longer	—	Unstable conditions
Bleeding	Tropical front, warm westerly	Clearing, clouding, unstable clouding, little atmospheric activity
Depressive moods	Easterly, warm prevailing southerly, warm westerly	Clearing, high clouding, unstable conditions, strong atmospheric activity
Diabetes	Prevailing southerly, prevailing northerly	Clouding
Inflammatory diseases	Tropical front	Clouding, unstable conditions, clearing with unstable conditions
Embolisms	Tropical front, warm westerly	Clouding, unstable clouding, clearing
Feverish diseases	Warm prevailing tropicals, warm westerly	High clouding, unstable clouding, unstable conditions
Epilepsy	Easterly weather	High clouding, unstable clouding
Cold-related sicknesses	—	Beneath atmospheric inversions
Gall bladder colics	Prevailing northerly, cold westerly	Clouding, unstable conditions
Heart attacks	Warm prevailing southerly, easterly	Clouding, unstable conditions, unstable clouding, clearing

Heart/circulatory disturbances	Warm prevailing southerly, warm westerly weather	High clouding, clouding, unstable clouding, strong atmospheric activity
Ileus symptoms	Cool prevailing northerly	Unstable conditions
Intra-occular bleeding	—	Clouding, unstable conditions
Headaches	Warm westerly conditions	High clouding, clouding, strong atmospheric activity
Attacks of cramps	Cool northerly infall	Clouding, unstable conditions
Laryngotrachitis	—	Beneath atmospheric inversions
Diminished ability to work	—	Clearing, unstable conditions, clouding
Decreased leukocytes	—	Unstable conditions, clouding
Increased leukocytes	—	Clouding, unstable conditions
Stomach perforations	—	Clouding, clearing, unstable conditions
Meningitis	Cool prevailing northerly	Clouding
Pains from scars	—	Clouding, unstable conditions
Nephrosis	Warm southerly winds, cool northerly winds	Clouding, unstable conditions
Kidney colic	Warm southerlies, tropical warm westerlies	High clouding, clouding, unstable
Longer reaction time	Cool prevailing northerly	Clearing, clouding, unstable conditions
Excitability	Warm prevailing southerly, easterly weather conditions	Clearing
Sleep disturbances	Warm prevailing southerly	Clouding, unstable conditions, clearing
Spasms	Warm prevailing southerly, cold westerly and easterly	Unstable clouding, unstable conditions
Suicide	Warm tropical front, easterly weather, warm westerly weather conditions	Clearing, clouding, high clouding
Thromboses	Tropical southerly front, warm westerly weather	High clouding, clouding, unstable clouding, clearing
Deaths	Warm tropical southerly, warm westerly weather	Clouding, high clouding, unstable clouding, clearing, under atmospheric inversions
Ulcer	—	Clouding, unstable clouding, clearing, unstable conditions
Increased traffic accidents	—	Clearing, clouding
Beginning of labor pains	Warm southerly prevailing	Clouding, clearing

The ancient Tower of the Winds, built in Athens about 50 B.C., has eight sides representing the eight principal winds of Greece (see Illustration opening Chapter 1). Each side depicts a different sculptured human figure who embodies the personality of the wind from that direction and its direct influence upon man (see chapter dividers).

Hesiod describes their character: "From Typhoeus comes the force of winds blowing wetly; all but Notus, Boreas, and clearing Zephyrus, for their generation is of the Gods, they are a great blessing to men, but the rest of them blow wildly across the water and burst upon the misty force of the open sea, bring heavy distress to mortal men, and rage in malignant storm, and blow from veering directions."

Aristotle's great treatise on natural science, *Meteorologica*, discussed all things in the earth and sky—rain, dew, rivers, thunder, and the winds: "Even the wind has a sort of life span—a generation and a decline," he said. Aristotle personified them according to their character—Boreas is the rude North wind, Zephyrus the mild West and Lips the homeward-leading Southwester, Notus the rainy South wind, and Kaikia the greedy Northwester. Notus empties a jar of water to show rain. Skiron, an old man, holds an inverted fire to suggest cold winds, squalls. The allocation of directions was not originally what we call north and south, but the rising and setting of the sun in summer or winter, or from the assumed direction of its origin.

An illustrious and elaborate folklore relates that the winds foretell, if not the future, then the future weather. Lord Francis Bacon said, "Every wind has its weather." And again, "A serene autumn denotes a windy winter; a windy winter, a rainy spring; a rainy spring, a serene summer; a serene summer, a windy autumn, so that the air on balance is seldom debtor to itself."

"Do business with men when the wind is in the northwest," goes the old Yorkshire saying. Bringing the finest weather, this wind was said to improve men's tempers.

The *mistral* "eats mud" the French say, or *mange la boue* (*lou mango fango* in Old French). Being cold and dry, it breaks open rocks by freezing them. "When the *mistral* comes through the window" the French say, "the physician leaves through the door."

Cutaneous Massage; Vascular
Gymnastics; Your Air Skin

You perceive winds as a mild skin massage, a form of "vasomotor gymnastics" for the superficial blood vessels. Winds make themselves felt even through your private air skin and your clothing. Gusts or other fast changes in wind speed or direction will markedly enhance their stimulus to the ten million or so nerve receptors on the twenty or twenty-five square feet of skin of the normal adult.

Your vast vulnerability to wind is close to nil at the soles of your feet, but steadily increases the higher your anatomy is above ground. When you move, the force or intensity of the wind at your hand is twice as high as it is at your knee.

Air in motion is felt as a stimulating force, pressing upon your skin. That wind pressure increases in proportion to the square of the wind's velocity. For instance, a ten-mile-an-hour wind at your knees feels four times more intense, more stimulating, more "pressing" than a five-mile-an-hour wind. At your head the wind would be eight times more intense than at your knees.

Aside from skin massage, the direct biological action of air affects your thermoregulatory system. Winds complement and aid your normal heat loss through heat conduction, convection, and evaporation. Your body owns a thin skin of air, a barely viscous layer beyond your physical skin that serves to insulate your body. The greater the body curvature, the higher the atmospheric pressure, and—most importantly—the greater the wind velocity (your bent elbows will be least insulated in a cold wind), the thinner is the insulating air-garment layer. In calm weather, your air skin is $1/6$ to $1/3$ of an inch (4 to 8 millimeters) thick. As the wind velocity increases to 5 miles per hour (or 2 meters per second) the air skin thins to 0.04 of an inch (1 millimeter) and at 22.5 miles per hour (10 meters per second), it decreases to 0.013 of an inch ($1/3$ of a millimeter).

In 60°F weather, your average skin temperature will drop from say 95°F with no wind, to 72°F urged by a slight seven-mile-an-hour breeze. The breezier the air, the cooler your skin is as long as the air temperature is below skin temperature. Skin evaporation increases with wind velocity, especially if the wind is dry and warm, like the chinook; in extreme versions—the alpine foehn, the Israeli sharav— the wind may evaporate more water than the body can afford to lose.

Man being blown by wind is suffering extreme bone-joint (osteoarthritic) pain.

Other serious physiological effects of these hot, dry winds will be dealt with shortly in some detail. However, your subjective perception of well-being is the combined result of wind velocity, humidity, outside temperature, and your body's specific abilities to regulate its own temperature under environmental change.

Clearly, a cool, dry wind will invigorate skin more than a cool, wet wind, a warm, dry wind, or a warm, wet wind—in that order. The world winds (see next page) are arranged according to their temperature and humidity to reflect the relative states of comfort or discomfort they bring.

Up to a speed of two miles per hour, winds are hardly perceptible. Beyond nine miles per hour, they are weakly felt. Above eighteen miles an hour, we have a strong sensation from wind. Wind turbulence—the creation of whirls, eddies, and vortexes—promotes vertical mixing of air, increased ventilation and purification, and reduced sultriness and heat. And turbulence increases sharply in discontinuous steps at nine miles per hour and then again above twenty-two miles an hour.

Wind and Human Energy

Emotions are intensified at high wind speeds. In one study, the average number of school playground fights per day virtually doubled when wind speeds surpassed thirty-five to forty miles an hour. (The result was very significant statistically; only one time in a hundred would it be likely to happen by chance.) Less statistically significant is the finding that as wind speed increased from five to fifteen miles an hour, the pulse rate after exercise returned more quickly to normal. Performance on a physical fitness test (which included situps and pushups) peaked significantly at a wind speed of fifteen miles per hour, falling off at higher and lower wind speeds.

In another experiment, wind changed the amount of time pedestrians took to walk between the post office and a main business street in the downtown district of a small western town. (The pedestrians were unaware they were being observed.) Excluding the elderly, the crippled, package-carrying shoppers, and children, a hundred persons per day from November to June were timed under different wind conditions. The results were statistically very significant; in five- to twenty-five-mile-an-hour winds, pedestrians walked increasingly faster; in winds of twenty-five to thirty-five miles per hour, their walk-

World Winds

	Dry		Wet
Warm	chinook (East of Rockies, Montana, Dakotas) Santa Ana (California) foehn (Bavaria, Switzerland) simoom (Africa, Asia deserts) chamsin (North Africa) ghilbi (North Africa) dzhani (North Africa) bhoot (India) karaburan (Asia) halny wiatr (Poland) ljuka (Yugoslavia) haboob (Egypt)	sharav (Israel) brickfielder (Australia) zonda (Argentina) sky sweeper (Majorca) aspre (France) puelche (Andes) Austru (Romania) kona (Hawaii) desert trade winds	solano (Spain) vent du midi (Southern France) sirocco (Algeria, Italy) ocean trade winds monsoons (India, Asia) lips (Greece) etesians (Greece)
	Canterbury northwestern (New Zealand)		
Cool	bora (Dalmatian coast, Adriatic, Caucasian Mts.) mistral (Rhone Valley) tramontana (Italy) bise (Southern Europe) harmattan (Africa, Sahara) polak (Sudetenland) drinet (Romania) cierzo (Spain) tehuantepecer (Mexico)		pruga (Alaska) buran (Siberia)

← TEMPERATURE

ing speed increased precipitously. The increase in wind speed was accompanied by a parallel increase in output of physical energy. Obviously, people were eager to avoid high winds and walked briskly; I have seen urban pedestrians literally *running* to escape very high winds.

Wind Disease

You may feel winds of under two miles per hour outdoors, but indoor breezes of one mile an hour or less (called drafts) will cool portions of your skin without mobilizing your body's thermoregulatory system. Outdoors, especially strong winds may induce skin reddening from increased blood flow and localized dilation of skin and muscle capillaries. A ruddy face or wind-burned skin are familiar examples. The red turns white under finger pressure and, unless exposure is constant, disappears promptly.

The stimulating and energizing quality of wind may be an asset. Those who live under constant exposure to wind—inhabitants of coastal regions, sailors, and fishermen—are said to be less prone to colds. The wind may "train" their bodies to react well to weather stress. Those who spend considerable time indoors, like modern city dwellers, may temporarily lose their intrinsic ability to adapt rapidly to changing environments. The ability to equilibrate temperature changes in wind can probably be enhanced by graduated exposures and "wind training."

Sudden, strong, cold winds can precipitate heart problems unless you are properly conditioned. Strong polar winds are often followed by increased incidence of myocardial infarctions (blockage of blood supply to heart muscle), stroke (hypertensive apoplexy), extra heart contractions (systoles), and angina attacks. Strong humid winds often aggravate tuberculosis.

Aside from doing damage to property, wind squalls, blizzards, cyclones, and hurricanes will, in and of themselves, precipitate health disorders directly. But the frequency of indirect blood-vessel disorders or vascular accidents (cardiac infarcts and strokes) appear to be associated with wind velocity.

Wind Velocity	Percentage of Vascular Accidents Occurring	Percentage of Myocardial Infarctions	Percentage of Apoplexy (Strokes)
up to 2 miles per hour	30–40	7	7
12 to 22 miles per hour	27–32	50	40
22 or more miles per hour	3–4	15	—

The simplest explanation for the effects of wind velocity on vascular accidents is that the strong winds stimulate the nerves of the skin to contract peripheral blood vessels, thereby raising the blood pressure and inducing stroke or heart failure. The mind may slowly perceive this as a "weather feeling."

Sharav and Foehn

Sultry winds (those of great humidity and heat) will provoke oppressive discomfort, irritability, headache, anxiety, insomnia, restlessness, and other physiological or psychological alterations that are ultimately traceable to body chemistry changes. The Israeli sharav or the alpine foehn probably trigger somewhat similar symptoms of climatic stress.

The Israeli sharav blows hot and dry in the spring and fall, originating in the Sahara. In the Mediterranean it is called sirocco or sharkiye. Its Arabic name, chamsin, means "fifty," but the sufferer finds little comfort in the euphemism that his discomfort will last merely fifty days; it may last for two or three weeks at a time, and intermittently half of the year.

For some years, Israeli pharmacologist Felix Sulman and his colleagues have been examining the physiological consequences of the sharav—the hormonal changes, metabolism, and secretions. With funds from the United States Public Health Service, he assembled some 200 Israeli sharav sufferers. They came from all walks of life—students, soldiers, the elderly, smokers, drinkers, immigrants, and veteran residents—whose ethnic backgrounds and diets were varied. Two or three times a week for a year he analyzed urine samples they preserved and voluntarily forwarded to him after following certain precautions. Earlier he had noticed that veteran residents of Israel decreased and newcomers increased their excretions of adrenaline and noradrenaline. Sulman measured the volume and contents of their urine.

By analyzing the urine of his sharav-sensitive patients, Sulman compared those components of his sharav-sensitive patients' normal days against sharav days. He found significant differences which he grouped into three patterns or syndromes:

- The first group (comprising 43 percent of his cases) showed up to tenfold increases in the excretion of the blood-vessel constrictor serotonin, and no other chemical changes. Calling this serotonin hyperproduction the "irritation syndrome," he observed that these patients' clinical symptoms included migraines, allergic reactions, flushes, irritability, sleeplessness, nausea.
- In the second group (44 percent of the cases) there was a drop in the adrenaline and noradrenaline secretions—in some extreme cases, to as low as zero. He called this adrenal deficiency the "exhaustion syndrome," since it was characterized by fatigue, culminating in apathy, depression, or hypotension.
- The third group (13 percent of the cases) seemed to mimic a mixture of the "irritation syndrome" and "exhaustion syndrome." They showed increases in all the urine components measured, including histamine and creatinine excretion on sharav days. Sulman noticed "hyperthyroidism," an accelerated release of cellular energy from glucose combustion, or a milder version called *forme fruste* (an abortive form of any disease, attacking without the usual symptoms). The chemical picture showed sleeplessness, irritability, tension, nausea, skin reddening, confusion.

Dividing the symptoms of climatic heat stress into three clinical pictures—two distinct, and one mixed—was an important contribution. Sulman selected what he deemed were appropriate therapies for each cluster of symptoms.

To correct the losses of all his sharav-sensitive patients, he urged abundant intake of fluid, sugar against high potassium loss, and salt to compensate for sodium loss through perspiration. (Because salt alone causes thirst, the salt medication Sulman recommended was salted herring, probably the most scientific justification ever made for eating this ethnic gourmet delicacy.)

For treatment of the adrenaline deficiency, he prescribed MAO (monoamine oxydase) blockers; since MAO promotes the oxidation of adrenaline and thus renders it inactive, MAO inhibiters prolong the life of adrenaline and relieve its deficiency and the attending depression.

For the treatment of serotonin oversecretion, Sulman experimented with two sets of agents. A fine balance between serotonin and noradrenaline and the brain's hypothalamus seems to maintain constancy of body temperature. One agent is a class of drugs called serotonin antagonists; the effects of these seem to vary with each patient. The other experimental agents are air-ionization devices, an extremely controversial matter, which requires a careful explanation of both sides.

And for the treatment of hyperthyroidism, Sulman has been using thyroid-suppression agents like lithium carbonate, often used to treat manic-depressive psychoses. (For details on Sulman's controversial ion research, see Chapter Notes.)

Foehnology

On the purported similarities between the foehn and the sharav—revisited. The foehn has its own personality. In Munich, winters are dark and gloomy; a grey fall day will include drizzles. Suddenly, a clear painted sun will push through the gloom and haze. The sun gets its own laurel of clouds. They get thinner and stringier. Finally, only a few wisps are left high in a brilliant blue sky. It has suddenly become a fake "prop" summer, as the foehn rolls back the grey clouds. Munich then becomes an Italian metropolis. The Alps appear so close you could touch them. In the Swiss wine country, the foehn is called the grape-cooker (*traubenkocher*), since it makes upland vineyards possible.

The foehn works slowly and deviously. To the traveler there is a great sense of well-being; the foehn is attractive, so much so that foehn sufferers hardly dare mention their headaches, believing they can see a black air mass bearing down upon them *personally*. To those long-time residents, the foehn is an ill-wind that blows nobody good.

Starting wet, a batch of subtropical air on the south side of the Alps climbs the mountains, drops its moisture as it climbs higher, and plunges, heated, down into the valleys of Switzerland and Bavaria, lifting roofs from alpine huts, drying out the mouths of alpine cattle, and imparting palpitations, tense headaches, anxiety, insomnia, nightmares, indifference to work, restlessness, breathing difficulties, coronaries, and jumps in the crime and suicide rates.

The foehn has its chroniclers—foehnologists—who will tell you all about the types of foehn-sick characters. A sample: The "foehn-sick secretary" who can't sleep, arises with witches' hair, black rings around her eyes; her coffee is tasteless; she can't remember what she was supposed to do; her eyes are popping; her typewriter continually makes mistakes; she feels hungover. Her superior, the "foehn-sick boss" does not suffer but gives everyone else a hard time since he brooks no compromise or discussion. He must have the last word. Everyone in the firm who is not destroyed by the foehn is done in by the "foehn-sick boss."

The foehnologists say that good scientific studies are not hampered by a lack of foehns. But mostly due to a lack of foehnds.

World Winds: A Summary

The "snow-eater," a wind known as the chinook, once sent the thermometer soaring from 45 degrees below zero to 34 degrees above in minutes, melting thirty inches of snow in twelve hours.

The world teems with winds, those equalizers of solar energy. Whether warm or cold, dry or wet, they turn temperatures topsy-turvy. They turn winter into spring. They turn human nature inside out. Even language celebrates winds. The Spirit of God—invisible, powerful, communicating to man—was wind.

The history of wind is also a history of health disorders that accompany or foretell the onset and direction of winds. Evidence points to these associations: exhaustion with warm westerlies, shortened blood-coagulation times with warm southerlies, epilepsy with easterlies, heart attacks with prevailing southerlies, headaches with warm westerlies, suicides with tropical infalls.

Winds are a variable stimulus to the skin's nerve receptors, a mild skin massage, that complements normal heat loss. A skin of air, which normally clings to your body, becomes thinner the greater the wind's speed. At high wind speeds, emotions and human energy are intensified, as are vascular accidents (strokes and infarcts). Blood pressure is elevated.

Hot, dry winds, like the desert sharav, trigger irritability and exhaustion. Urinalysis of the sensitive victims reveals striking alterations (increased serotonin, diminished adrenaline, and other changes) on those days when the winds blow. The alpine foehn, after dropping its moisture, plunges heated into the valleys of Switzerland and Bavaria, imparting to those in its path eye-popping hangovers, parched mouths, palpitations, tense headaches, restlessness, coronaries, and jumps in the suicide and crime rates.

Seven:
The Vortex of
History: Weather,
Temperament,
and Physique

Beware the exalted genius. The Great Man is a Public Calamity.
—Chinese saying

The environment tends . . . to annihilate differences, to bring the body temperature to its own levels, the blood pressure to the level of the atmospheric pressure . . . the environment wants to (and in the end does) "melt down" the organism, like the famous button-maker in Ibsen's Peer Gynt.
—Joseph Wilder

Preceding Page: Boreas
The wind of the north, cruel and threatening in Athens. It makes a noise in the conche shell through which he blows. The sculptor was probably trying to imitate the sound by placing a conche shell in the hand of this figure. He watches the spectator face on. He is dressed more warmly than any of the other figures except Skiron. His overcoat is a tunic that goes down to his knees. He has a short jacket with sleeves that cover his arms up to the palms.

Abraham Lincoln

Kentucky, in May of 1808, had rain, rain, and more rain, when Nancy Hanks—a slender, manlike woman, secretive and melancholy, exhausted by winter, conceived a child. He was Abraham Lincoln. He grew to be long, gangling, introverted, and President of the United States.

Aloof, even as a child, apt to be moody, taciturn, with bursts of humor and a droll slant on life, with thorough human understanding, a feeling for the common fellow. Fundamentally sincere, he was utterly independent; he was shrewd; possibly there was some inherent feeling of inferiority, he revealed fixed adherence to a predetermined course but he possessed with that a wealth of common sense and patience which saved him from being a fanatic. The absolute male, he was wholly cerebral; he cared nothing for luxury, nothing for decoration; to food and drink he was indifferent; flattery left him cold; music and the arts bored him. Being primarily cerebral, with emotions kept in check, he could be magnificently tolerant and generally diffident in his relations with women due to inhibition of the intense, instinctive reaction to the female sex. Extremely sensitive to the physical environment, a child of the soil, he reflected its every whim.

Lincoln was six feet four inches high in his stocking feet. Tall, thin, and gaunt, he seemed to have no blood in his frame. "His flesh was dark, wrinkled, folded: it looked dry and leathery, tough and everlasting."

Stephen Douglas

Sarah Fiske was a roly-poly, motherly type, with a generous heart and ample reserves. She conceived a child in July, 1812, when the temperatures were in the eighties. Her son, Stephen Douglas, was at least twelve pounds at birth. Voracious, with an insistent manner, he gave a "good loud cry to announce his wants." He grew to be short, with a powerful frame and round head, round chest and belly. He bustled with energy. A "steam engine in britches," he was later called. Douglas became a schoolmaster, lawyer, state's attorney, legislator, Secretary of State of Illinois, Justice of the Illinois Supreme Court, and Senator.

> Douglas was an extrovert, inordinately ambitious, energetic, a great mixer, a great speaker, self-confident, audacious, popular, convivial. His was the personality for success, almost always he was with the majority—when not, he was usually ready to compromise. Most decidedly successful was he in relations with women, if his two marital records are a criterion. Well insulated from the environment and therefore indifferent to the vagaries of season and weather, and buoyant in health as a young man, he could climb, step by step, the ladder of public success.

Douglas was five feet four inches short. He had a large head, a broad face, a complexion rich and dark. He was sturdy, solid, with a broad chest and square shoulders. His skin was as soft as a woman's.

Vortex

A vortex is a whirling mass of air or water—a fluid eddy, a circulating swirl. The irresistible absorbing rush of a whirlpool is a vortex. Miniature vortexes in stirred coffee, a bathtub or sink will draw free-floating particles down its funnel.

A vortex may exert catastrophic power as a tornado—that spectacular mass of air rotating at very high speed. Or massive vortexes may be deceptively tame, mild, and insidious. The "cyclone," derived from *cycle* or circle, represents, technically, a low central-pressure region relative to its surroundings. In the tropics it may develop into a storm of ferocious intensity; in mid and high latitudes, cyclonic weather is merely a depression, or Low. When high central-pressure regions (called "anticyclones," or Highs) advance toward Lows, they sweep large areas with winds, breezes, whirls, and eddies. A rotating earth, a warming sun, a tide of air conspire—now gently, then forcefully—to create a vortex.

But there are also vortexes within. A belly full of liquid sloshes, gurgles—you can hear it—in whirls and eddies. Blood speeds through the internal plumbing of pipes, valves, and pump, whirling past bends or crevices to nourish cells. The very fluids of life are vortexes.

A situation into which persons or things are steadily drawn, a tidal magnetism from which they cannot escape—that too is a vortex: "The whirlwind of his eloquence drew me into its vortex" or, "At the vortex of her being is self-love."

Every few days another vortex swirls through our lives as a huge rotating air mass, one of many, gliding eastward across the northern United States and southern Canada en route to the North Atlantic.

These rotating air masses pull along with them warm tropical air from the south or cold polar air from the north. Cold polar air is dense and heavy, often pushing the barometer *up*; it is usually clear and dry; warm tropical air is light so the barometer often goes *down*. An advancing wedge of warm air is called a "tropical front"—and of cold air a "polar front." The fronts are boundaries or interfaces between the pockets or masses of air (see chart on air mass movements and table on high- and low-pressure weather, Appendix J) that come

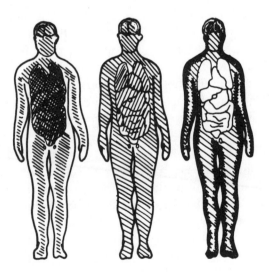

Blood Distribution for Opposite Environmental Situations.
Center figure—normal blood balance. Left figure—with increasing cold, peripheral tissues become relatively bloodless and internal organs contain increased blood. Right figure—with increasing warmth, peripheral vessels dilate, decreasing the relative amount of blood in the internal organs.

behind and those that lie ahead. Near the interfaces are winds, precipitation of rain or snow, turbulence, and other disturbances. And it is at these regular changes of air mass that prompt individual adjustment is necessary—when inadequate individuals generally suffer clinical symptoms.

Consider Lincoln: not much fat padding his skin; not many reserves in his liver, bone marrow, subcutaneous tissues, or his muscles. Every passing weather front had to be accompanied by an adjustment in his blood distribution; one moment the skin had to radiate heat; the next moment, insulate or conserve heat. The long, slender Lincoln would be a better radiator than a conservor of energy. And consequently, he would need more fuel than others to keep his body warm. His adjustment mechanisms—adrenal and thyroid glands, nervous system—would be under severe strain. Wider swings in amplitude of his adjustment to the passing fronts would be mirrored in wide swings in his body chemistry, his organ functions, in his feeling of well-being or fatigue—and in his moods.

To save energy whenever possible, Lincoln (and any slender type like him) would try to protect himself, both consciously and subconsciously. He would bundle up. He would shelter his body. He would stay near a fire or source of heat. He would withdraw within to lower his metabolic rate. His skin would toughen, dry out, wrinkle. He would eat much food, but drink little water. He would do whatever was necessary, above and below conscious perception, to help his thermal-adjustment mechanisms stay in peak condition. Because of constant use, his blood vessels or vascular system would likely stay young and vigorous.

Now consider Douglas. When young, he would be biologically comfortable, flourishing. He had plenty of fat padding his skin and subcutaneous tissues to blunt the swirling air mass changes from hot to cold and back again. His heart would not strive to push the blood mass back and forth between the skin surface and central core. But he did not need to conserve energy. He made efficient use of air's oxygen. He accumulated reserves of fat and water, sugar and protein, vitamins and minerals. Douglas rounded out even more in his late twenties whereas Lincoln became still more slender.

Douglas (and any broad type like him) would have modest needs for fire, shelter, clothing. He spent energy, feeling buoyant and exuberant. He enjoyed life, good health, and goodwill. He was venturesome. He invested time, money, and increasingly, conscious thought in the world about him. He avoided introspection and with-

drawal. The external world was endlessly fascinating to him—he became a millionaire in land-speculation deals—since he did not have
to devote energy or conscious attention to keeping the outside world
outside of himself. His fat padding did that for him. He was always
hale and hearty, seldom blue or depressed, though occasionally irritable. He would suffer in summer due to inefficient heat-radiating ability, but thrive in winter.

Human reactions to the passing vortex of air only seem alike. Yet
each individual responds distinctively to the rhythmic passage of
weather fronts—conditioned by age or sex, by prior experience (level
of arousal), by exercise, diet, or medication, by degree of exposure or
adequacy of shelter or clothing, by body build (or habitus), by chemical buffering, by emotional status, by season or time of day, and by
other simultaneously stressful events.

Lincoln types can swing too far in one direction—in the late
winter (when their blood may become too acidic) their resistance
declines. Likewise Douglas types can swing too far in the other direction—in summer or fall their blood may become too alkaline. In the
late winter or early spring, when his reserves were used up, Lincoln's
body chemistry could easily swing too deeply into a biochemical
trough after a cold front. With the undue heat of summer or autumn, Douglas could swing up too high and too far on the crest of
his biochemical reaction to heat, overshooting his compensatory
swing. When young, Lincoln would be too sensitive, too changeable.
When old, Douglas would be too stable, too inert to avoid disaster.
When Lincoln would become overly fatigued or moody—Douglas
would crack.

Indeed, either a Lincoln or Douglas body type could swing too far
in one or the other direction. The response to a sequence of successive weather fronts could cumulate, like a pendulum pushed again
and again, swinging ever wider.

A summation of environmental assaults would amplify, aggravate,
or trigger virtually any quiescent ailment. If Lincoln or Douglas had
any physical weakness, mental weakness, emotional weakness—the
weather would find it out.

The continuing ability to rally against repeated environmental assaults or insults (chemical, physical, infectious, psychological, or
social) is one modern definition of health. But the type of "rally," the
kind of assaults can make history (and determine its future) if the pro-
tagonist happens to be an Abraham Lincoln or a Stephen Douglas.

Weather and Constitution Are Destiny

The personality of Lincoln has been observed and recorded. In a profound way, his outlook was conditioned by his frame, his constitution, his reactivity—his weather-sensitivity.

Lincoln was under his own law and that ruled him with the iron of logic. One state predominates, and while it so rules, the other state is somewhat quiescent, shadowy, yet living, a real thing. . . . In one moment he is in a state of abstraction and then quickly in another state he was a social, talkative, and communicative fellow.

The unconscious regulation of body functions, the instability of his involuntary nervous system, the rapid changes of his blood pressure and blood circulation from body to brain, the shifting of blood from the internal organs to the periphery, the poorly buffered body, the slender store of reserves, the large surface area of fat-free skin—all were ingredients in his behavior and philosophy. His subconscious processes, well "aware" of these mechanisms and limits, had to impose a willful controlling action to coordinate and to govern his thoughts and actions. Flowing from these ruling forces were his powerful inhibitions, coldness, selfishness, and aloofness. His inner "accountant," who budgeted his energy expenditures, also ruled his episodes of escape, of sudden impulses, of ribald mirth, of stubbornness, of abandoned reason.

Mr. Lincoln was a curious being; he had an idea that he was equal to, if not superior to all things; fit . . . skilled . . . master . . . graceful in all things. Lincoln had not good judgments; he had no sense of the fitness, appropriateness, and harmony of things.

He was intensely thoughtful and persistent and tireless in his thinking. When he got after a thought, fact, principle, question, he ran it down to the fibers of the tap root, dug it out, and held it up before him for an analysis, and when he thus formed an opinion, no man could overthrow it; he was in this particular without an equal.

Perhaps because of the peculiar intensity of his thought, the peculiar usage of his brain, perhaps the deep stream of involuntary adjustments and impressions woven into the fabric of his tissues—perhaps all these lent him a dim appreciation of a uniqueness. His conscious self might "know" the intimate significance of environmental messages. His ability to fend off elemental stresses linked his body to the world. "And so, dimly aware, this kind of person senses the oneness of the individual with the universe, the close linking of feeling and mood to the needs and the unexpressed desires of his fellow men."

Observed in that light, here is Lincoln's philosophy:

Men were but simple tools of fate, of conditions, and of laws, and to praise men on the one hand or censure them on the other was in the abstract wrong in principle at all times. The thing, the event, was to be just as it had come, and no right and no wrong and no virtue and no vice should in truth be attached to it. . . . The man, the people, and the whole race are made by forces, conditions, environments around them, set in motion a million years or more ago, sweeping swiftly around the universe every instant of time, never flagging, ever onward.

Lincoln's philosophy was an intellectual version, or cerebral extension, of his weather-conditioned involuntary nervous system.

But now to Douglas. He "needs no philosophy of life so long as his digestion holds out—and it usually does." Not bothered by constipation, inhibitions, or complexes, he lived from day to day, organically pleased with himself, adjusted in his nervous system, apt to leave well enough alone.

Given the broad habitus with plenty of reserves, good skin buffering, large vessels adequately supplying all the organs, with no violent fluctuations of the blood supply, there is no fatigue from constant shifting of the blood mass. There is no necessity for the primitive brain center to be on edge or unduly alert, the subconscious governor may doze along, comfortable because the alarms coming from the outer world are conveniently put at the periphery of the human cell complex; the citadel may remain at ease, plastic and pliant. It is not necessary to build up inhibitions that will hide the turmoil of the internal commotion behind an exterior that seems aloof and mysterious.

Douglas probably had no compelling convictions, although he had wide-ranging interests—art, literature, society. "He relished good food and excellent vintages; he enjoyed a good Havana." He had an "amazing capacity for friendship." Once he arrived in pioneer Illinois, he "doffed his eastern dress and manners, and assumed a suit of Kentucky jeans, together with a frontier vocabulary. Before long he hobnobbed with the Border Democracy like one to the manner born."

Within a week he had written home that already he had become "a western man with western feelings, principles and interests." He was "the sort of man any of us would delight to have had the opportunity to know. Able, courageous, captivating in company, he was staunchly loyal as a friend."

Lincoln ate mechanically anything that was put before him. His slowness of thought and action were likely due to slow blood circulation, to lack of reserves and to the necessity of conserving sugars, fats, and minerals for his main goal—single-minded pursuit of politics. He planned, played, dreamed, and worked at politics his whole life. It was a fixation. Contemplate President Jimmy Carter (of average body build) while considering this description of Lincoln:

> Few knew him; he could be cheerful and chatty, somewhat social and communicative, tell his stories, his jokes, laugh and smile, and yet you could see, if you had a keen sense perception of human character, that Lincoln's soul was not present, that it was in another sphere; he was an abstracted and an absent-minded man; he was with you and he was not with you; he was familiar with you and yet he kept you at a distance.

In effect, Lincoln was saying, "This nature of mine is mine alone, and it is sacred ground on which no man shall tread." He concealed, suppressed, and withdrew parts of himself from the physical environment, the emotional environment, the social environment. He resisted alcohol (which in dilating the peripheral blood vessels would break down his first line of defense), he resisted trauma, he resisted energy depletion, he rejected all nonessential elaborations—food, art, beauty, sex, or friendship—he resisted the external suasions of air mass and temperature for his sole goal.

Lincoln and Douglas, at opposite polarities, played out their weather-conditioned destinies in their political lives.

Douglas, an adaptive individual, went along with "the spirit of the times." He did try to check the worst excess: public monies used for bank schemes, canal schemes, railroad schemes, and land speculation. But here is his simple technique for rounding up votes: "I live with my constituents, eat with my constituents, drink with them, lodge with them, pray with them, laugh, hunt, dance and work with them; I eat their corn dodgers and fried bacon and sleep two in a bed with them."

When the Mexican War came, Douglas supported then-President Polk and helped "wave the flag." But he was never a fanatic. He was too adaptable. He argued that "the President had made an honest effort to keep peace." Yet he pointed to "the catalogue of aggressions and insults; of outrages on our national flag and on the persons and properties of our citizens; of the violations of treaty stipulations and the murder, robbery and improvement of our countrymen which justified the war."

Lincoln was no energetic flag-waver. He was opposed, staunchly opposed, to the Mexican War and United States participation in it. "His sense of justice and his courage made him speak, utter his thoughts as to the War with Mexico. . . . No politician in America can vote and live if he opposes a war in which the spread eagle is concerned. . . . When Lincoln returned home from Congress in 1849, he was a politically dead and buried man; he wanted to run for Congress again but it was no use to try."

Lincoln had, as early as 1836, written in favor of women's rights; he wrote a book against Christianity in 1835–36. He advocated temperance in 1844 when it too was unpopular. "He opposed slavery everywhere and at all times when to oppose it was political death." Again and again he reinforced his powerful fixations to principles. He advocated "free immigration of foreigners and their right to vote, when Americanism here was popular and rampant." When one wing of the Republican party thought it would lose an election, and the other wing thought he was too cowardly, Lincoln issued the Emancipation Proclamation.

Avoiding sentimentality, Lincoln stuck to his ideas, even though they did not fit the times, and they were unpopular. He was tenacious, tough, with strong mental fiber. His mental pathways were fixed, set to accept even extinction rather than compromise. His inner "energy accountant" would urge, "Hold fast to what you have! Waste not! Life is hard for you! Do not yield."

He was misunderstood by most men. He was not a "hail fellow, well met." He had strong ideas and the courage of conviction. Consequently, he was not popular; indeed he was unpopular, because he did his own thinking and boldly expressed strong conclusions. He resisted mass psychoses. He hated financial speculation; he lacked the vision, that special boldness, the imagination, the gambling instincts, and the concern for things outside his body, his inner shrine, that characterize the entrepreneur.

The broad Douglas had surplus energy for ventures and adventures. Turned outward, his body, his mind, his constitutional interests could afford to speculate. He could take a chance. He could risk losing energy, the "currency of modern civilization." He could risk losing money. And by the late 1850s, he was a millionaire.

Stormy Ladies

In the spring of 1833, following a cold winter, when his low blood pressure was pushed lower, his blood relatively acid, his connective tissues lax, Lincoln went into a depression, looking hollow-eyed. His mind and body experienced the sensations of utter futility. Perhaps it was related to tuberculosis or consumption, but nevertheless he recovered—and by 1834–35 became interested in Ann Rutledge. He courted her. She became ill, nervous, neither ate nor slept, "was taken sick of brain fever," and finally died in late August of 1835. That year mid-August had been very warm in Illinois, reaching over 80°F at Fort Dearborn and over 90°F in Jefferson Barracks. Suddenly, temperatures plunged to the 40s at Fort Dearborn, and in New Salem where Ann Rutledge lay sick it recorded a low on the 23rd or 24th of August. The environmental strain on her sick body caused contraction of her peripheral blood vessels which increased her blood pressure, loaded her already burdened heart, and in the wake of this stress, she died on the 25th of August.

Lincoln was already fatigued by hard work, malaria, suspense about Ann's illness, and his blood acidosis. The trauma of her death, his grief, his loss, were aggravated three days later. It rained. The straw broke the camel's back, and "Lincoln went to pieces."

Douglas was "a rake and roué by nature, a demagogue and a shallow man," according to Mrs. Lincoln. In Springfield society, "it was no uncommon sight to find him surrounded by a bevy of girls, and he paid marked attention to Sarah Dunlop, Julia Jayne, and Mary Todd."

But Mary Todd had other plans. A broad, stocky, well-padded, pretty, and vivacious young woman, with "an exuberance of flesh," she set her mind on marriage to Lincoln—the opposite pole in body build and outlook. They became engaged. He tried to break it off at once. Then again, on January 1, 1841, when he was fatigued, defeated, worried, and blue. The previous few days were unseasonably warm. Suddenly, $-12°F$ signaled the passage of a polar front. Lincoln's weather conditioning first produced high blood pressure, alkalosis, increased brain commotion during the warm days; then withdrawal, acidosis, fatigue, and gloom. But Mary reacted with a relative alkalosis, prolonged increase in blood pressure, and a buildup of irritability. "Mary became hard, Lincoln soft; Mary became angry, Lincoln depressed. Mary became vituperative and aggressive, Lincoln silent and defeated." Lincoln broke the engagement; he got "cold feet"; he withdrew, psychologically and emotionally. Carl Sandburg has written about this period, "Lincoln's condition was not the result of some spontaneous occurrence, but was the outcome of causes of 'slow and continued influence.' Viewed in this light, the 'fatal first of January 1841' became merely an aggravated manifestation of his disease, rather than the reason for it."

But that was not the end, because on the 17th and 18th of January, 1841, another polar front passed through Illinois. "He became really distraught and incoherent for a week." He stayed away from the legislature, then in special session. He feared the danger of self-destruction and carried no knife for many months. His friends, thinking him suicidal, removed all razors and pistols from his presence. His medical state at that time was such that due to inadequate blood and air supply his tissues became inadequate. "Had he had an infected tooth, it would have been painful; had he had rheumatism, his joints would have hurt. Had he been subject to migraine, he would have had an attack." His brain tissues, like the rest of his body tissues, would have reflected and even amplified the passage of the second polar front leading him to contemplate suicide.

Clearly, Lincoln was sensitive to the air and its changes, to every environmental assault, to every energy impact. He was what is today called weather-sensitive (see Chapters 2 and 9). He was more acutely aware than other people, and at certain times—of weather changes. Below conscious perception, deep inside the brain, he had an "innate perception of what was going on in the minds and bodies of men in general, a clairvoyant sense of how the mass mind and body would respond. Such an individual can readily become the mystic, the reformer, or the spiritual leader because he is so close to the common man. He is close only because the tones and overtones of his autonomic rhythm penetrate through the subconscious and palpably influence the conscious attitude, the conscious reaction, the conscious expression."

It is tempting to speculate upon leadership and weather-sensitivity. Is there a correlation, a pattern? Does the Lincoln type "know" the common man because of his exquisite sensitivity to environmental assaults? Does this make him "in touch" with the masses? Does he thereby become a better leader? Does his unswerving adherence to moral and ideal principles aid and abet such leadership? Are there others like Douglas, who, by virtue of their buffering and relative insensitivity to weather, are also leaders? Is it their innate connection to matters external to their own bodies that makes them indifferent to self or another dimension, yet puts them in touch with a different reality that fosters leadership? Are there others, opposite polar types— one weather-sensitive the other weather-insensitive—whose responses to weather determine the management of world affairs? Whose leadership is crucial? Whose positions are fraught with power and influence, who plan the future, who make history?

Is it possible that these two extreme types—slender, weather-sensitive Lincoln and broad, weather-indifferent Douglas—define a special curious dimension of leadership? A continuum that ranges on the one hand in Lincoln, from a feeling for the common man secured through moody turning inwards, aggravated by weather changes; or on the other hand in Douglas, a feeling for the common man furnished by exuberant turning outwards, helped by indifference to vicissitudes of weather?

Could a persuasive case be made that leaders tend toward weather-sensitivity or weather-insensitivity—both manifesting concerns for the world—one through introspection, the other through extroversion? History provides more clues.

Six-foot-four Lincoln rejected five-foot Mary Todd in the bitter weather of January, 1841, when Lincoln was at his worst. But she won him over in the warm summer, when he was at his best. They married in the autumn of 1842.

There seems to be evidence—statistical and anecdotal—that sexual stimulation, erotic behavior, biological activation increase following increases in sunlight and warmth of late spring and late summer; tensions release, exhausted reserves of vitamins, foodstuffs, buffers are replenished; sex crimes and conceptions increase; and these may be associated with crests in blood alkalinity of autumn when summer temperatures fall.

Given her body build and constitution, Mary Todd, during the placid, autumn weather of 1842, with its rising temperature and clear skies, would have been buoyant and energetic; Lincoln would have had higher blood pressure and blood alkalinity, he would have felt more sexual and optimistic and less blue.

Their marriage turned out to be "hell on earth." She: ambitious, stingy, quick-tempered, a nag, impulsive, sarcastic, personally aggressive, acquisitive, vain, frequently irritable, later suicidal; given to headaches, migraine, tantrums, tongue-lashings, and later, hallucinations. All of these qualities were aggravated by specific weather episodes, which also triggered her bizarre assaults upon Lincoln. And he: in his early fifties, improving with age, vigorous, healthy, increasingly more cheerful and less sad, no grey hair, occasional bouts of melancholy, fatigue, or double vision linked to sudden temperature drops; but elected to the presidency in 1860, departing from Springfield and arriving in Washington—bundled in a shawl.

Douglas, the "Little Giant," who enjoyed good health when young, began to age early—typical of his broad, stocky body build. His metabolism would tend toward alkalinity, his blood vessels becoming closed and thick-walled, his major organs would reflect poor blood and oxygen supply, his tissues would become inactive, somnolent, and deteriorating. In fact, Douglas did have a series of ailments, each illustrating these trends and each accompanied by severe changes in temperature: gastrointestinal infection in 1848; a series of spring and autumn throat infections during the 1850s, one of which followed a sudden 25-degree temperature drop in 1855 and brought him close to death; inflammatory rheumatism in 1859, when temperature dropped 25 degrees sharply; his kidneys and heart may have been damaged; he died at age 48 in June, 1861, when his contracting blood vessels placed a great load on his heart. His winter reserves had been exhausted by unusual fluctuating temperatures prior to his death during the spring months, a time when the death rate of the entire population generally increases.

In 1861, Lincoln was "under the weather" due to greater than usual amounts of rain and snow and fluctuating temperatures due to the sickness and final death of his third son, Willie, and due to the state of the Union. A letter from Lincoln in 1861 was signed, "Your tired friend, A. Lincoln."

General McClellan was in command of the armies; and Lincoln felt he was inept. In February and March of 1862, Lincoln became impatient, but rather than discharge him, he put the matter to his military experts who voted to keep the general. On July 9, Lincoln visited McClellan to examine his conduct of the war. Apparently, this period marked a turning point in Lincoln's career as President.

"All the timidity, the hesitation that was conspicuous in him four months before, had vanished. . . . From this time forward there is very little in his attitude to life that is problematical. A great genius has found himself, has acquired confidence in himself, and henceforth will be master of his own house." Lincoln fired McClellan.

The genius had "found himself" in sweltering 90-degree temperatures.

Following a steady eight-day rise in temperatures, "Lincoln could expand, his feeling of insecurity and inferiority and his inhibitions would be dissipated. The warm energy of the sun dilated the vessels of the brain as well as those of the skin, loosened the brakes and reversed the incessant drain on the slender store of energy reserves. All this gave Lincoln assurance, firmness and finally leadership."

But if his conscious self was so affected, what of the subconscious Lincoln? His subconscious, itself under the sway of his involuntary nervous system and his lower brain centers, would in part govern his consciousness. We know that Lincoln "imbibed belief in dreams and wonders which influenced his mind to the last. . . . He saw apparitions from time to time during his life. . . . He brooded with freakish credulity over the meaning of what he had dreamed."

Cold waves trigger blood-vessel (vascular) contractions that mirror the passage of weather fronts. "Vascular swings can condition the cerebral mechanisms during the period of sleep, finding expression in restlessness, insomnia, twilight states, vivid dreams, nightmares; for change in vascularization during sleep will bring about functional changes just as they do in the actively functioning cerebral tissues when we are awake."

Although not possible to date precisely, shortly before his assassination Lincoln described a dream in which he saw a corpse lying on a funeral canopy in the East Room of the White House. The body was draped in funeral robes. It was the President of the United States, assassinated, prepared for viewing.

Through 1865, the convulsions of civil war lay heavily on Lincoln's soul. He was tired. A photograph of him shortly before the assassination shows him looking haggard, long-suffering, deep creases around his mouth, and beneath his eyes sagging pouches of wrinkled skin. His blood pressure was already low, according to his medical advisers, and in the spring it was likely to be lower still.

On February 6, 1865, his Attorney General "stormed in, announcing his decided disapproval of so many pardons of soldiers for desertion." Angry, excited, Lincoln jumped up and shouted at him,

"If you think that I, of my own free will, will shed another drop of blood. . . ." And then he fainted.

That day coincided with the third successive crest of barometric pressure and the second successive fall in temperature. Furthermore, tall people with low blood pressure are likely to faint as a life-saving measure, to provide adequate blood and oxygen to the brain.

On April 14, 1865, "in another brain the turmoil of the atmosphere and the travail of the South in dissolution, and the instability of spring laid the background for an act of desperate vengeance"—the assassination of Abraham Lincoln.

This is a tale of four bodies. Well-buffered, weather-insensitive Mary Todd and Stephen Douglas. Weather-sensitive Abraham Lincoln, whose buffeted body recorded and etched deeply within his mental processes and subconscious, memorable impressions of his immediate environment, of his fixed principles and habits.

And the fourth body is our atmosphere or air mass, the sky above. It presides over our being, the breath of life. While our consciousness almost ignores it, our primeval fiber, our subconscious self responds; deep inside we remember the sky.

Fat, Muscular, or Lean: Is Anatomy Temperament?

I have borrowed heavily from William F. Petersen's fascinating analysis of Lincoln, Douglas, and the weather. But does it hold up today? Is there a scientific basis for the Petersen scenario? Or is it merely brilliant foolishness? Would Lincoln's physique or Douglas's (or Nixon's or Carter's) have anything to do with his temperament or weather-sensitivity?

The answer is a conditional yes; a provisional, circuitous yes; a statistical yes—but it is a *yes*.

Questions like this were pursued by William Sheldon, a physician and psychologist, in a lifelong study of 45,000 men—their physique, temperament, and behavior. He collected, measured, and scrutinized thousands of physiques. He found they arranged experimentally in series, and classified themselves into three continuous categories, or "components."

Endomorphy ("within" or "inner" shape) refers to a person who is preponderant in soft roundness throughout the body; the digestive organs or *viscera* are massive and tend to dominate the body economy. These people float high in the water.

Mesomorphy ("middle" shape) refers to a person who shows a relative prominence of *muscle*, bone, and connective tissue; the physique is hard, heavy, dense, firm, and rectangular in outline. The hallmark is uprightness and sturdiness.

Ectomorphy ("outer" shape) refers to a person who is relatively linear and fragile, and who has the largest *skin* surface area in proportion to his mass, and hence the greatest sensory exposure to the outside world. Perhaps he is almost overexposed and naked to the world. Relative to his weight, an ectomorph has the largest brain and central nervous system.

Sheldon found that his entire sample of physiques could be arranged in ascending progression of the degree or strength of each component, that independent observers would agree on the arrangement and degree, and that no fourth component was necessary that was not obviously the result of a mixture of these three. The three components were sufficient to describe the physiques examined and were necessary for a system of classifications. Sheldon's trio of primary physiques resembled a triad of primary colors—red, yellow and blue—an admixture would reproduce any hue.

Concurrently and separately, he collected and measured personality and behavioral traits and found that they organized themselves into three categories.

By trial and error, Sheldon found sixty personality traits that appeared to cluster into three components (twenty each), comprising three primary temperaments. Each of these traits correlated positively and strongly with each other trait in the temperament cluster, and each trait *anti*correlated (correlated negatively) with traits outside its own temperament cluster. Here are the names and properties of the three components of temperament:

Viscerotonia, the first component, is characterized by love of comfort, food, people, and affection; by general relaxation, sociability, complacency, and evenness of emotions. The center of this personality seems to be the viscera; the welfare of the digestive tract, the primary purpose of life. Later in life, the past and childhood are important.

Somatotonia, the second component, is characterized by a love of action, adventure, exercise, and power—by vigorous assertiveness and push. Later in life, the orientation is toward the present and toward the goals and activities of youth.

Cerebrotonia, the third component, is characterized by a predominance of restraint, inhibition, concealment. The personalities in this group are mentally overintense, extremely attractive, apprehensive, and self-conscious. After thirty, they tend to remain youthful in manner and appearance and are oriented to the future, to later decades in life. All reactions, whether to food or sex, are overly fast and strong.

The simplest differentiation of the three temperaments is that the viscerotonic observes and exercises in order to eat, the somatotonic observes and eats in order to exercise, and the cerebrotonic eats and exercises in order to observe.

Sheldon analyzed and measured the physiques and temperament of 200 young men for five years. He found that the *viscerotonic temperament* was closely associated with the *endomorphic physique*, that the *somatotonic temperament* was closely related to the *mesomorphic physique*, and that the *cerebrotonic temperament* was closely tied to the *ectomorphic physique*. "Close" means that the correlations were about + 0.80 between the temperaments and the corresponding physiques. On a scale of 0 to 1.0, these are very high correlations. The "primary" nature of the three components of physique and the three components of temperament was reinforced by the observation that there were negative correlations between noncorresponding components of physique and temperament.

Correlations of this high an order suggests, as Sheldon put it, that "physique and temperament may constitute expressions, at their respective levels, of essentially common components. . . ." In other words, physique and temperament really measure the same thing "at different levels of expression."

Sheldon took great care to demonstrate that these connections between build and personality, his high correlations, were not due to errors of overenthusiasm for his point of view. He noted that Freudians usually "found" parent-child antagonisms in history of neuroses, and that Marxists generally "found" economic "causes" for war. And although he was inclined to see anatomical and emotional manifestations linked together, he satisfied himself and his co-workers that these correlations were not spurious or the errors of bias. Tight statistical results, at a very high level of significance, had been "teased" out of a complex, bewildering array of conflicting intuitions about body and mind.

Many of his observations ring true today; as the detailed traits are scrutinized (see Appendix H) one can recognize oneself and others in both the emotional and personality manifestations.

But Sheldon had opened a Pandora's box. He was accused of being fatalistic ("naturalistic," he responded). He was accused of ignoring the effect of the environment in shaping personality ("their argument is like that of one who would blame the match for the damage done by the firecracker"). He was "slow to receive the imprimatur of either the medical or academic establishments," says Anne Beller, "and his most lasting contributions will probably prove to have been neither in medicine nor in psychology (he had an M.D. and a psychology Ph.D.), but in the field of human biology, where a modified version of his technique is still applied today—especially in Europe. . . . Sheldon's conviction that temperament is largely grounded in physique is the other side of the coin of the Freudian assumption that the leitmotiv of biography is the individual's neurosis, psychosis, or character disorders. The truth is probably somewhere in between."

Many of Sheldon's findings, stimulated by earlier research, were largely supported by later scientific tests of his results.

Weather and weather conditions may seem remote, but *these findings on body build and personality bear directly upon human dysfunction, disease, and mental illness—all closely conditioned by weather.*

In 1915, Eppinger and Hess divided people into two types: *vagotonia*, characterized by a sluggish, relaxed vegetative individual with a slow heartbeat, who is governed by his *vagus* nerve (the most important component of the parasympathetic nervous system, controlling breathing, heartbeat, and digestion); and *sympathicotonia*, characterized by a person with a rapid heartbeat, overly tense body, partial paralysis of the digestive system, general apprehensiveness, hyperattentiveness, anxiety, and restraint (all part of the thoracic-lumbar segment of the involuntary nervous system, and under forebrain or cerebrum control). Normally the tenseness and emotional disturbance of sympathicotonia occur only during some emergency, but pathologically the condition may become chronic.

In 1925, the German psychiatrist Ernst Kretschmer observed 260 psychopathic individuals: *manic-depressives*, who periodically become excited, flushed, and expansive, followed by an interval of profound anguish and depression; and *schizophrenics*, who inhabit an imagined or hallucinatory world, cut off from reality; these two extremes, the *manic-depressive* states and *schizophrenia*, are pathological intensifications of fundamentally normal but divergent mental outlooks. In mental illness, the normally extroverted persons (also the endomorphs) become manic-depressive; and the normally introverted drift toward schizophrenia. Kretschmer found clear biological affinities: his manic-depressive patients had broad, fleshy, bodies and large internal organs; his schizophrenic patients were mostly slender, with small internal digestive organs. Sheldon himself found that *paranoids* were more likely to be of athletic or muscular physique—mesomorphs.

Sheldon's most controversial assertions have tested out quite well. Psychologist Irvin Child of Yale gave 532 Yale students, previously somatotyped by Sheldon, a self-rating questionnaire containing Sheldon's traits of temperament in abbreviated form.

Child discovered that *self*-ratings of temperament suggest, though they do not prove, that body type has an important influence on personality. Sheldon's ratings of personality were done "objectively," by trained observers who did not just accept a subject's self-described temperament, but who were especially trained to notice specific indicators of personality. Child's correlations between the triad of self-rated temperaments and the triad of objectively related physiques were all positive, but they did not approach the magnitude of Sheldon's correlations. Thus, although Sheldon's relationships between body build and personality were confirmed, and there was sufficient correlation to justify concluding that body type is an important determinant of personality, *self*-ratings of temperament are not as good indicators of temperament as are trained observations of temperament.

Behavior might follow from physique via enough environmental factors to keep the followers of Freud in business looking at adults' formative years. Fat cuddly infants, nervous bony babies, or muscular children must receive different parental vibrations in growing up. A body excessively heavy and possessed by a strong hunger drive and high reward for eating, and by a strong need and reward for love, can behave the same as high endomorphs and viscerotonics. However, a physique that permits forceful response, a high drive for physical activity, a relative insensitivity to pain, an appearance of looking older than one is, may be the primary basic attributes of a mesomorph who behaves as a somatotonic. An ectomorph's basic qualities which lead him to cerebrotonic behavior could be the easily-damageable physique, a body that allows rapid (but not forceful) response, a tendency to appear younger than he is, and a greater sensitivity to stimulation. (See Appendix H.)

Under similar stress, those of predominantly linear physiques experience more anxiety than those of muscular build. The stress was measured by psychological tests and blood plasma tests. Endomorphs, when shown Rorschach diagrams, fail to see form or shape more frequently than ectomorphs or mesomorphs do.

Sheldon observed the weather and thermal responses of his subjects in addition to less obvious traits. In highly viscerotonic people, he noticed "excellent thermal adaptability. Such people typically enjoy both cold weather and hot weather, although hot weather may be uncomfortable in cases where the physique has been permitted to degenerate into obesity." An excessive fat layer both prevents heat loss in hot weather and insulates in cold weather.

Sheldon believed that viscerotonia was the "central theme for a group of religions older than Christianity. . . . And probably more influential. . . . Buddhist doctrines are essentially a consistent exposition of viscerotonia."

> Earthiness, vagotonia and lassitude fully characterize the viscerotonics. They are materialists, but epicurean lovers of freedom and liberty. Their sexual appetites were slow and weak, despite their indiscriminate love of people and hunger for affection. Manifest sexuality (not procreative ability or potency) was statistically in opposition to endomorphy and viscerotonia. And finally, viscerotonics rarely made peace with the idea of death; they hate to die; they are rooted to earth.

"Somatotonics typically like high or mountainous country and sunny weather," said Sheldon, and they "feel good in the morning, they love to jump out of bed, take a shower, make a lot of noise, and greet the sun."

The bustling, energetic somatotypes, who crave danger or physical hardships, were found to prefer houses on a hill. They were those most likely to experience sudden conversions, sudden breakdowns, or sudden rearrangements of their world view. Relatively disassociated from their own deeper levels of consciousness, they also enjoyed freedom from doubt, and consequently made uncommonly good executives. Indifferent or insensitive to pain, they were also relatively fearless of death. One physician described his mesomorphic patient, "He died sort of careless-like, about the way I putt." Mesomorphy and somatotonia correlate only weakly with manifest sexuality.

"Cerebrotonics show a predilection for low country and for rainy weather," according to Sheldon. But he thought this trait was obscure and of questionable diagnostic value. "Ectomorphs are usually more comfortable in wet weather, possibly due in part to their peculiar susceptibility to dehydration (relatively greater surface area). They tend to be uncomfortable in strong sunlight, probably because of visual and general cutaneous oversensitivity. . . . Cerebrotonics love the twilight." They are thermally unstable, and tolerate heat and cold poorly, especially cold weather.

Late maturation and growth place a burden upon cerebrotonics. They have to put up with chronic overdoses of their own hormones over long periods of time. Internal jumpiness and nervous instability are typical of chronic sympathicotonia. Cerebrotonics are stoics and idealists who cherish self-discipline and understanding, often believing that their greatest happiness lies in the later decades of their lives, when they think they will be free of the inhibitory tenseness of their early larval period. This chronic future orientation, a Promethean world view, brings curiosity about death and often leads them to enjoy the *anticipation* of death and perhaps even death itself. Attending physicians often observe that ectomorphs or cerebrotonics "die smiling." Although there do not appear to be statistics, Sheldon thought that many suicides were probably cerebrotonics.

Sexually the most sensitive, cerebrotonics or ectomorphs in general find sexuality most disturbing or most exciting. Statistical correlations show significant strong, positive associations between ectomorphy or cerebrotonia and manifest sexuality. Perhaps cerebrotonics are more stimulated by their own sexuality in the same way that they are more stimulated by their own thinking (cerebration). Or perhaps their large exposure of skin per body weight makes their sensuality resonate like a quivering tuning fork. Sheldon says: "The genitalia of endomorphs are relatively small, while those of ectomorphs often seem conspicuously large, . . . but are probably not absolutely larger than mesomorphs."

Sheldon argued that temperaments and physiques were relatively basic and reasonably stable throughout our life, "comparable (although not equivalent) to that of changing the race of the individual." Sheldon did not survive to see the wave of exercise fever that has swept over the postbicentennial United States. In the latter 1970s we have become a nation of fanatical joggers—endomorphs, mesomorphs, and ectomorphs alike are out there at 6 A.M. or 11 P.M. jogging their hearts out for dear life. (And dear life it is, too, as a recent Harvard study shows that jogging or a good regimen of physical exercise can prolong life and improve the physical health and pleasure in living.) Other studies have shown that middle-aged men who begin jogging will manifest, six months later, measurable increases in assertiveness, self-confidence, and healthy aggression— traits we associate with mesomorphy and somatotonia. Since these men were a mixture of all body types, it is reasonable to think (as speculation) that ectomorphs and endomorphs can be induced or tilted toward mesomorphy and somatotonia, contrary to Sheldon's view that we are stuck with our body type.

Not that mesomorphy and somatotonia are ideals for all of us to strive for. Indeed, it is physically possible for someone to be endowed simultaneously with a great deal of fat and muscle and a wide expanse of skin—to be simultaneously very fleshy, very stocky, very muscular, very long-necked, and very leggy. Sheldon showed that this condition—high endo-, meso-, and ecto-morphy—hardly ever arose. However, many Greek gods, like Zeus, embodied elements of all three physiques and ideals.

What individual would be simultaneously very highly viscerotonic, somatotonic, and cerebrotonic? He might well be characterized by these traits: all-loving (viscerotonic), all-powerful (somatotonic), and all-knowing (cerebrotonic).

That is usually how many of us imagine God.

Zeus as a mesomorph—muscular, athletic, vigorous, fearless.

The Vortex of History:
Physique, Temperament, and
Weather: A Summary

Abraham Lincoln was tall, thin, gaunt, and introverted. Stephen Douglas was squat, stocky, broad-chested, and outgoing. Lincoln's slender body was a radiator of heat, and so he would try to conserve his energy, consciously or subconsciously; he bundled up, he stayed near a fire, he sheltered himself, he withdrew from the outside world, turning inward and moody. Douglas had plenty of fat padding to insulate his body against loss of heat. He did not have to conserve his energy; he spent freely, not only energy, but money, time, good will, and feelings. He was venturesome and became wealthy.

Lincoln's weather susceptibility was greatest in the late winter or early summer, when his blood chemistry swung too far in the acidic direction. Then he was overly fatigued and moody. His body reserves were exhausted and he would react deeply a few days after a cold spell. His personal philosophy, that men were tools of fate and environmental forces beyond our control, was an extension of his weather-conditioned involuntary nervous system.

Douglas's weather susceptibility was greatest in the summer or fall, when his blood would drift too far in the alkaline direction. He would be uncomfortable in the heat. His philosophy was simple: good food, wine, and friends; no compelling convictions; go along with the spirit of the times; adapt. All reflected his body build and temperament.

Lincoln broke his engagement during a depressive mood; weeks later, he became suicidal. Both events followed cold snaps in late winter. Douglas became ill later in life each time the temperature changed severely, and died after such a sequence, complicated by infections. Lincoln fired an incompetent general during a heat wave, after he was unable to do so in cold weather.

Not merely chance or coincidence, these links between physique, temperament, and weather are backed up by extensive statistical evidence and analysis. Three body types and three temperaments are found to be primary components, like the primary colors that can replicate any hue.

The slender, long-limbed body with a large expanse of skin and thus great exposure to the elements often houses a personality who is mentally overintense, self-conscious, restrained—and one who prefers rainy or damp weather and twilight, who avoids strong sunlight, and who poorly tolerates hot and cold (especially cold) weather.

A muscular, dense, firm physique often houses a personality inclined to assertive action, power, adventure, exercise, and drive—and one who prefers mountainous country and sunny weather.

The soft, rounded, massive body often houses a person who loves comfort, food, affection, relaxation, complacency, earthiness, and lassitude—and one who has excellent thermal adaptability, adequate insulation against the cold which also prevents heat loss in warm weather, when discomfort would set in.

The extreme and pure characteristic each primary type represents would be the idealized god-like qualities: all-knowing, all-powerful, and all-loving.

Eight:
The Touch of Zeus

When those who first used the word ZEUS went out in the world and looked upward, they found themselves over-arched by the blue of brilliant sky, a luminous Something fraught with incalculable possibilities of weal and woe. It cheered them with its steady sunshine. It scared them with its flickering fires. It fanned their cheeks with cool breezes, or set all knees atremble with reverberating thunder. It mystified them with its birds winging their way in ominous silence or talking secrets in an unknown tongue. It paraded before men's eyes a splendid succession of celestial phenomena, and underwent for all to see the daily miracle of darkness and dawn. Inevitably, perhaps instinctively, they would regard it with awe—that primitive blend of religious feelings—and would go on to conciliate it by any means in their power.

    —Arthur Bernard Cook, *Zeus, A Study in Ancient Religions*

There is a fraternity of the cold to which I am glad to belong. The members get along well together. For a few hours all life's dubious problems are dropped in favor of the clear and congenial task of keeping alive.

    —E. B. White

What men call gallantry, and the
    gods adultery,
Is much more common where the
    climate's sultry.

    —Lord Byron

Preceding Page: Zeus
The most famous statue of Zeus in antiquity, executed by Phidias in gold and ivory for the temple at Olympia. To call forth the feeling in the spectator that no earthly dwelling would be adequate for such a divinity, the seated figure's head grazed the roof of the temple. The base was twelve feet high, the figure an additional forty feet. The divine expression of the highest dignity represents the benevolent mildness of a deity who listens to prayers graciously.

Thunderation! or *thundering fool* is a mild American curse. In England, the exclamation is *Thunder!* Appreciative astonishment or utter displeasure in German is *Donnerwetter!* "thunder weather." The French *crier d'une voix de tonnere* is "to shout with a voice of thunder," and in Italian *tonare.*

You cannot physically be *thunderstruck*, but you can *steal someone's thunder*, and in so doing gain *thunderous applause*, or *donnernden Beifall* in German. *Donner* and *Blitzen*, two of Santa's reindeer, are "thunder" and "lightning."

To be fatally *struck by lightning* is rare (about one person per year per ten million people are); the French say *foudroyé* or *frappé de la foudre*; the Italians, *fu per me como un colpo de fulmire.*

A *stroke of genius* is *Geistesblitz*, in German, or "lightning of the mind"; in Italian it is *lampo di genio*, "flash of genius."

A powerful French speaker *lance ses foudres*, he "hurls his thunder," or has *un foudre d'éloquence*, "a lightning of eloquence." A brilliant Italian orator *i fulmere dele eloquenza*, "fulminates eloquently."

We are confused, the French say, *tomber du ciel*, "to fall from the sky." If someone was "born yesterday" the Germans say *aus allen Wolken fallen*, or "to fall from the clouds." Italians say *cascare dalle nuvole.*

"Quick as lightning" in French is *rapide comme l'éclair*, in German *blitzschnell*; as "quick as greased lightning" is *wie ein geölter Blitz.*

"Violent," in Italian is *fulminante*, similar to *foudroyant* in French. In German "lightning angry" is *zornblitzend; blitzblank* is "gleaming like lightning"; and *Blitzkerl* is a "capital fellow"; *Abgeblitzt*, literally "flashed off," means thoroughly rebuffed.

These figures of speech, stolen from the sky, are sky idioms that verbal attributes of weather or sky—personalize and personify weather and sky.

Profanities, curses, and oaths express deep-seated feelings like anger and fear. Swear words, curses and oaths, or superlatives commonly invoke the heavens—the lightning and thunder. "I take an

181

Deities and Weather

Egyptian	Nut	Sky goddess
	Keb	Air god
Greek	Zeus	Weather or sky god; good and evil
	Aeolus	Wind god
Roman	Jupiter	Weather god; various attributes
Nordic	Odin	Sky god
	Thor	Thunder god
Vedic	Indra	Thunder god
	Varuna	Sky god
Japan	Tenjin	Thunder god
Mexicans	Tlaloc	Rain god
Aborigines	Wind = God	Wind is god; you can feel wind but not see it
Christians	Spirit = Wind	"And the wind moved across the face of the waters" (*spirit* and *wind* are interchangeable in some translations of the Bible)

Dyaus, "The Bright Sky," Is the Root of Many Words for God

Dyaus	=	"to shine," "the bright one," "bright sky" (Sanskrit)
Zeus	=	Sky god (Greek)
Dies	=	Day (Latin)
Dies-pater	=	Day-father (Latin)
Iupeter	=	Jupiter (Roman), Jove
Díos	=	God (Spanish)
Día	=	Day (Spanish)
Deus	=	God (Old French)
Dieu	=	God (French)
Deity	=	God (English)
Dewes!	=	God! (Middle English)
deuce	=	bad luck, the devil (Middle English)
Djouia	=	God (Arabic)
Jehovah	=	God (Hebrew)

oath under the open sky," says the Goose Girl in Grimm's fairy tale. Profanities that invoke parts of our bodies or certain intimate body functions (like elimination or intercourse) also reflect deep responses; heavenly happenings have been supposed to arise from godly intimacies, godly rage, godly foulness, and godly benevolence.

"In the beginning there was fear," Lewis Browne writes, "and fear was in the heart of man; and fear controlled man. At every turn it whelmed over him, leaving him no moment of ease. With the wild soughing of the wind it swept through him; with the crashing of the thunder. . . . All the days of man were grey with fear, because all his universe seemed charged with danger. Earth and sea and sky were set against him; with relentless enmity, with inexplicable hate, they were bent on his destruction. At least so primitive man concluded. . . ."

This fear of nature's forces—climate and weather—must have been present at the very beginning of mankind. While primitives huddled beneath the onslaught of thunder, lightning, rain, these extravagant weather elements would insinuate themselves into consciousness, condensed to pictures and words and sounds. Weather evoked dismay, awe, sublime respect. Weather was capable of creating a "presence," of *being* a presence just as other creatures, animals and humans, had "personalities" and temperaments. Primitives endowed these natural forces with emotions—anger, rage, swift thoughts, flashes of imagination. And gradually these inanimate events evolved into *animate* forces that could destroy fearful man or leave him alone—at will, without reason. Out of such animations arose our personifications of thunder, lightning, air, sky, rain, snow. Out of such fear arose our religions. Out of personifications of weather elements arose our deities. All the great faiths of the world today derive portions of their beliefs from the climatic environments in which these faiths arose.

Personified Weather

"The Eskimo's hell is a place of darkness, storm and intense cold; the Jew's is a place of eternal Fire. Buddha, born in the steaming Himalayan piedmont, fighting the lassitude induced by heat and humidity, pictured his heaven in Nirvana, the cessation of all activity and individual life," says Ellen Semple.

The human being is a child of the earth. Yet when standing erect, only two-hundredths part of our body touches the earth's surface; only the sole of the foot is "grounded" on the inanimate soil of the earth. The rest of our skin touches air, sky, winds. All the millions of our nerve endings are caressed, bruised, stroked, and struck by the ocean of air above, its currents and concurrents. Browned and made pink by sky radiations, the skin, sense organ of the involuntary nervous system, responds to touch, pressure, warmth, cold, and pain—

speeding vast information about the environment brainwards, warning us of certain dangers and evoking our protective reflexes.

With this mediator interposed between environmental dangers and our intimate self, it hardly surprises us that skin would take on the role of insulator, radiator, buffer, and perceiver. Because it signals the need for thermal regulation, the skin's extraordinary role and biophysical hallmark is sensitivity to our atmosphere.

Indeed, the thought has been expressed again and again, going back to the early Greeks, that though mankind might try to overcome his sensitivity and susceptibility to physical environment, he could never wholly succeed in freeing himself from his bondage to the atmosphere.

Sacred Texts Refer to Weather Motifs

Muslim:	Allah is he who sends the winds so that they raise clouds, and spreads them along the sky as pleases him, and causes them to break and you see the rain downpouring from within them. —Koran, Surah 30:48
Hebrew:	The voice of your thunder was in the heaven; the lightning lightened the world; the earth trembled and shook. —Psalm 77:18
Christian:	And Jesus arose and rebuked the wind and said to the sea: Peace, be still. And the wind ceased and there was a great calm. —Mark 4:39

The myth of Prometheus, one of many Greek parables, tells how Prometheus stormed the stronghold of the gods to bring back to mankind fire and other arts of civilization enjoyed by the gods. But as punishment, Prometheus was chained to a rock high atop a mountain, exposed to cold and wind, rain and snow, thunder and lightning. He had to suffer eternal exposure to the elements for his audacious attempts to "deify" mankind, to civilize him with the warmth of fire, the spark of reason, the light of the mind. Eternal exposure. In the Greek language, the word Prometheus means foresight. And we may take it that his foresight, keen enough to seek fire, was also keen enough to perceive that his own future, his punishment, was eternal vulnerable exposure to the elements.

"Prediction is the name," William Sheldon said, "for the sin of Prometheus—the Christ of the Greeks."

Christ was mercilessly exposed to the eternal elements on a cross, not a mountain. But the Prometheus legend is repeated again and again, independently among disparate peoples. Early Sumerians of ancient Mesopotamia had a fire god *Gibil*, and *E-A*, a divine figure

Prometheus

For stealing fire from the gods, Prometheus is punished by Zeus with painful exposure to the elements. The legend has been retold by Hesiod, Aeschylus, Shelley, Browning, and others, each reinterpreting its significance.

who "conveys vital knowledge to humanity and acts as an ombudsman in its behalf," according to George Michanowsky, "a likely predecessor of Prometheus." And Plains and western Indians had an equivalent figure who made things happen—a trickster, fool, hero, erotic adventurer called Coyote by them and Loti in other cultures.

No matter how Promethean man (in Petersen's interpretation) might hope to "negate the cosmic forces about him, attain civilization and progress in art or mechanical ingenuity, the human organism would still be in bondage to the environmental forces of the atmosphere."

Again myth, perhaps. But a universal metaphor, a profound message, and a recurring human experience as well.

In the myth, the deity who punished Prometheus for attempting to snatch heavenly fire from Olympus was Zeus, father of all the gods.

Freudian Zeus

In Greek antiquity, Zeus was the God of the Sky and All Its Phenomena. Homer called him "the father of all gods and men."

Zeus was widely worshiped. He was enthroned on the highest mountains. He lived on Mount Olympus, the fabled abode of the greater gods of ancient Greek mythology. Olympus is actually the name of several lofty mountains, each approximately the highest in its own district. There is a mountain north of Thessaly called Olympus, so the divine abode was both a single location—and everywhere. On occasion, Olympus was referred to as the *sky*.

From Zeus came all the changes in the sky or the winds; he is the gatherer of the clouds, which dispense the fertilizing rains, while he is also the thunderer and the hurler of the irresistible lightning. As by the shaking of his *aegis* he causes sudden storm and tempest to break forth, so he calms the elements again, brightens the sky, and sends forth favoring winds. The changes in the seasons also proceed from him as the father of the Hours. [Horai]

Today the word *aegis* means auspices, sponsorship, patronage, protection, or defense. But in Greek, it is the same word as "goatskin." According to myth, Zeus was suckled in his infancy by the goat Amalthea. In his adulthood, however, he carried a shield "blazing brightly and fringed with tassels of gold, displaying at its center the awe-inspiring Gorgon's head." As imagined in Homer, this shield is the thundershield, thundercloud, or stormcloud of Zeus. In his contest with the giants, at the bidding of the oracles, Zeus drew his *aegis* over his thundershield, fastening on it the Gorgon's head. By holding or shaking his shield-and-*aegis*, Zeus sent down thunder and lightning. Zeus created the weather, under his *aegis*.

Although the *aegis* belonged to Zeus the "*aegis*-bearer," it is seldom seen in works of art as his attribute. Perhaps this is because it was occasionally carried by his daughter Athene, or by Apollo, the sun god and patron of music and poetry.

Yet Zeus had other attributes. As ruler of the world, he knew and saw everything—the future as well as the past. Those universal laws that regulate the course of all things came from Zeus. All revelation came from Zeus. He was the "author and preserver of all order in the life of men . . . he watches over justice and truth, the foundation of human society . . . both national and personal freedom." He gave to all things a good beginning and a good end. He was the savior to those in distress. Whatever was good, noble, strong—valor, victory, bodily vigor—was ordained by Zeus.

> At times, he announces to mortals his hidden councils by manifold signs: thunder and lightning and other portents in the sky; by birds, by prophetic voices, and by oracles.

"The friend of wisdom is also a friend of myth," said Aristotle. Perhaps myths presume to give us models of behavior, and thereby to give meaning and value to life.

Bruno Bettelheim argues that myths speak to us in the language of symbols, and, therefore, "Their appeal is simultaneously to our conscious and unconscious mind." The dominant feeling that myths convey is that mythical events are absolutely unique; they could not occur to ordinary mortals like you or me; mythical events are grandiose, awe-inspiring, miraculous.

A mythical hero like Zeus is obviously imagined on a superhuman scale, on heroic dimensions; we can never fully live up to what the mythical superhero, or mythical superevent requires of us. "The more we try to please it," Bettelheim says, "the more implacable its demands. . . . When mortal incurs the displeasure of a God without having done anything wrong, he is nevertheless destroyed. . . . In other words, we are under the control of destiny; we are pawns of fate or God; we are helpless before the forces around us. A mere mortal is too frail to meet the challenges of the Gods." Zeus personifies specific forces of nature—like thunder, lightning, wind, rain, snow—that we are unable to resist. We must succumb. We are tossed in the winds of life.

Freud would have said that myths represent repressed material that was too powerful to accept as it was in its naked form. Hence myths were similar to dreams, daydreams, fantasies—the language of subconscious parables—that feed our ego, id, and superego. Both the myth and the dream need deciphering.

It takes no Freudian genius to unravel the messages Zeus myths are trying to reveal. "Man is frail, nature is strong. Be careful."

Zeus, with the help of his brothers and sisters, overthrew Kronos, his father, and the great generation of Titans. Kronos was begotten by Earth (Gaia) and Sky (Uranus). The earth and Olympus were the possessions of the three brothers, Hades, Zeus, and Poseidon. Poseidon, according to Homer's *Iliad*,

> . . . when the lots were shaken, drew the gray sea to live in forever; Hades drew the lot of the mists and darkness, and Zeus was allotted the wide sky, in the clouds and the bright air. But earth and high Olympus are common to all three. Therefore, I am no part of the mind of Zeus. Let him in tranquility and powerful as he is, stay satisfied with his third share.

From Sky to Sky God

Perhaps the earliest written language was Sanskrit, which may have existed some five to ten thousand years ago. An ancient and sacred language of India, it is the oldest known member of the Indo-European family and contains an extensive Hindu literature. It also contains the word "dyaus," meaning "to shine" or "the bright one." At first it probably referred to the bright sky itself. Later it came to *personify* the bright sky, as the bright sky god Zeus.

"The precise steps by which man advanced from a belief in Zeus, the Sky, to a belief in Zeus, the Sky God, are hidden from us in the penumbra of a prehistoric past," writes Arthur Bernard Cook. "Nevertheless the shift from Sky to Sky God was a momentous fact, a fact which modified the whole course of Greek religion, and its ultimate consequence was nothing less than the rise of faith in a personal God, the Ruler and Father of all."

Jupiter (Zeus) Destroying the Titans with His Thunder

The Titans were the sons and daughters of Uranus and Gaia who probably represented supreme, primitive, alien deities who inhabited Greece before Zeus-worship. The ten-year battle was an attempt to reconcile the newer Greek religions with the earlier non-Greek ones. Thus, the will of Zeus triumphs (law and order) against the more terrible forces of nature, the Titans.

Religious feeling would come to those who saw in "the blue and brilliant sky a luminous Something frought with incalculable possibilities of weal and woe . . . inevitably, perhaps instinctively, they would regard it with awe . . . and go on to conciliate it by any means in their power."

Early man saw that vegetable, animal, and human life depended quite plainly on the weather, the condition of the sky. He would strive "to control its sunshine, its winds, above all its fructifying showers by a sheer assertion of his own willpower expressed in the naive arts of magic."

The blue sky had content: primeval sanctity, a vast and curious life, an impersonal life. And the blue sky had form: a sky god named Zeus, a magician-turned-king, the owner and operator of spectacular equipment for weathering—clouds, thunder, lightning, rain. Zeus (the form) dwelled in his sky home (the content).

In other myths, Zeus was said to have placed some seventeen constellations in the sky, including the zodiacal signs of Aquarius, Gemini, and Sagittarius. Later, Aristotle classified the planets according to new and old names:

Early name (and meaning)	Later name	Planet
Phaímon (the shining)	Kronos	Saturn
Phaéton (the brilliant)	Zeus	Jupiter
Pyroeis (the fiery)	Heracles or Ares	Mars
Stilbon (the gleaming)	Hermes or Apollo	Mercury
Phosphoros (the light bringer)	Aphrodite or Hera	Venus

Astrologers used a symbol ♃ for Zeus, perhaps not as the first letter of his name, but as a form of his thunderbolt. Later on it may have represented the trident of Poseidon, or Neptune. In many Greek or Roman depictions, Zeus and Poseidon are indistinguishable (and require diligent scholarship to differentiate them).

Blue Zeus

Hellenistic artists showed Zeus with a blue nimbus around his head, a blue globe at his feet, a blue mantle around his waist. His color is blue, always blue. Blue is also, as recent research shows, a placid and "acted upon" color to the human eye. (See Chapter 4)

Zeus was not only a ladies' man, he was a prolific womanizer and begetter of children. In Hesiod's *Theogony*, I count ten consorts:

The Consorts of Zeus and Their Attributes

Consort	Attribute
Leto	Obscure, concealed, or quiescent divinity from whom visible power issued
Demeter	A sister; agriculture, fruitfulness, marriage
Hera	A sister; queen of gods, goddess of women and marriage; later Aphrodite or Venus
Maia	Eldest and loveliest of Pleiades, later May
Metis	"Counsel"; first wife of Zeus, who devoured her for fear she would bear a son mightier than himself
Themis	Personifies law, custom, equity, order and justice; a prophetic divinity; holds a cornucopia and a pair of scales
Eurynome	A mother of the charities; represented as a mermaid
Mnemosyne	Goddess of memory; mother of the Muses
Alkmene	Fidelity, love, honor; a mortal, seduced by Zeus disguised as her husband Amphitryon
Semele	Destroyed by Zeus's lightning when she asked to see him as he appeared to the gods.

And Hesiod mentions twenty-eight children.

The Children of Zeus and Their Attributes

Offspring (mother)	Attribute
Apollo (Leto)	God of music, poetry, prophecy; associated with medicine and healing
Artemis (Leto)	Goddess of nature, hills, valleys, woods, meadows, wild animals; later Diana, huntress
Persephone (Demeter)	Infernal goddess of death; abducted by Hades
Ares (Hera)	God of war; later Mars
Hebe (Hera)	Goddess of youth, cupbearer
Ilithyia (Hera)	Goddess of women in childbirth, aiding or prolonging labor
Hermes (Maia)	Herald and messenger; later Mercury
Athene (Metis)	Goddess of wisdom, skills, warfare; later Minerva
Graces (Eurynome)	Brilliance, Joy, and Bloom; pleasure, charm, allegiance, and beauty
Muses (Mnemosyne)	Literature, arts, and sciences (nine)
Heracles (Alkmene)	Later Hercules
Dionysus (Semele)	God of vegetation and wine; later Bacchus
Horai (Themis) or Hours	Eunomia, Dike, Eirene (Good Order, Justice and Peace), cause seasons to change and all things to come into being at the right time; watch the clouds and guard Olympus
Fates (Themis)	Clotho, Lachesis, Atropos; control human destiny, spin and cut the thread of life

Semele
Semele was destroyed by Zeus with his thunder and lightning for asking to
see him as he appeared to the other gods.

Not only a man for all seasons, Zeus is a man for all important human activities and emotions. He rules by power, he endures like granite, he rages conspicuously like a Shakespearean actor, and lusts endlessly like a horny satyr. Justice, beauty, war, wisdom, peace, prophecy, music, deaths, wine, medicine, love—all come from Zeus. Directly or indirectly through his consorts or offspring, these qualities are the attributes of creaturehood, the eternal human verities recorded on the pages of history. In "Zeusifying" these constants of creaturehood, early Greeks tied them to sky, to air, to atmosphere, and to the weather—so that weathering humanity might itself humanize weather.

The powerful metaphors, legends, and lessons of the mythology of Zeus hid man's failure to placate the *weather*. Instead, he placated weather *gods*, their *children*, and all *human qualities* that flowed or seemed to flow from them.

Zeus cults flourished all over ancient Greece. One cult worshiped Dionysus, one of Zeus's sons. The word itself may come from Dios-Nysos, or Zeus of Nysos. Revelry and pagan and profane pleasures were part of the Dionysian cult. And (except in Hellenic religions) Zeus was identified with a whole medley of solar, lunar, and stellar elements and celestial luminaries.

Another cult, attested to by a considerable body of evidence, worshiped Zeus Asklepios as both a sacred healing god and a pilgrimage place for the sick. Aesculapius, god of medical arts, son of Apollo, cured the sick and recalled the dead to life. Zeus feared that mortals might escape death altogether, so he killed Aesculapius with his thunderbolt; but at Apollo's request, Zeus placed him among the stars. (Asklepios, the word, meant "gentle radiance," presumably of the bright sky or air after a storm, although it also resembles a strange word for serpent; nevertheless, the deity was connected to the healing atmosphere.)

The road of Zeus was called the Milky Way, or the Elysian Way. The word "elysian" meant a path or way, and was the area struck by the lightning of Zeus. Since death by lightning was considered a sort of euthanasia, the Elysian Way was also the abode of the divine dead.

The Conscious Flashlight

These Zeus cults—his entanglements and loves and offspring and stories—are extremely powerful and richly elaborate explanations of "just about everything." An educated Athenian, a Spartan, or lowly slave could "explain" the events in his personal life and the world beyond. The myths and stories provided a structure, a conceptual framework, a set of organizing principles, precepts, a code of behavior and ethical conduct. An ideology and a philosophy of life all led back to the weather—to vigorous, athletic Zeus, "king of the immortals," "whose eye sees everything," "whose mind understands all."

The Greeks were ingenious in their detail and elaboration. When a fact fit the myth, there were still two interpretations.

Homer says that "Zeus lightens," "Zeus thunders," "Zeus rains," "Zeus snows"; but Aristophanes, in his satirical play *The Clouds*, has this exchange about Zeus between a person of the old school (Strepsiades) and the philosopher Socrates of the new school:

Strepsiades: No Zeus up aloft in the sky?
Then you first must explain
Who it is sends rain?

Socrates: No Zeus have we there,
But a vortex of air,

Strepsiades: What! Vortex? That's something, I own.
I knew not before
That Zeus was no more
But Vortex was placed on his throne.

Whenever any fact did not fit the myth, neither fact nor myth was sacrificed. The myth was merely *elaborated*. One can see a slave or aristocratic citizen in gratitude to Zeus "with whom rests authority for all outcomes, good or evil." It was perhaps, as if there was a government "up" there, much the way today's press or various commentators seek to interpret, second guess, or "psych out" what Washington, the President, or his Cabinet members are going to do to the economy or to the defense budget or to welfare or to medicine. Interpreters might be good or bad, astute or foolish, trivial or profound, platitude-lovers or fine storytellers (literal or symbolic), but when they told Zeus stories they were telling life stories—for life is a story.

For the early Greek citizen or contemporary news interpreter, this story system works; that it does *something* is illustrated with an analogy by Julian Jaynes. Suppose you were to place a flashlight in a dark room to search for an item. For a moment endow the flashlight with a conscious mind and "ask" it where the lighted items are in the dark room. Since there is light in whatever direction it turns, the flashlight (whether bright or dim) would have to "conclude" that there is light everywhere. But of course *we* "know" there is not.

Belief in the Greek gods was a pervasive "beam," like the flashlight, "illuminating" all perception. Such belief was contagious, like unconscious learning and subliminal reinforcement. The stories of the Greek gods are probably similar to what Paul Watzlawick calls "self-closing explanations," or essentially irrefutable conjectures. Once a tentative explanation takes hold of our minds, any information to the contrary produces not *corrections* but further *elaborations* of the hypothesis. Thus Socrates's interpretation ("No Zeus have we there,/But a vortex of air") was amusingly difficult for Strepsiades to absorb.

Weather gods was a "theory" that explained weather *after* the event; such a "theory" is (in modern terms) third rate. A second-rate theory forbids. But a first-rate theory predicts.

In a brilliant but idiosyncratic view, Jaynes proposes that the Greek gods were

> . . . voices whose speech and directions could be as distinctly heard by the Iliadic heroes as voices are heard by certain epileptic and schizophrenic patients, or just as Joan of Arc heard her voices. *The gods were organizations of the central nervous system* and can be regarded as personae in the sense of poignant consistencies through time, amalgams of parental or admonitory images. *The god is a part of the man,* and quite consistent with this conception is the fact that the gods never step outside of natural law. . . . The Greek god simply leads, advises and orders. . . . The strongest emotion which the hero feels toward a god is amazement or wonder, the kind of emotion that we feel when the solution of a particularly difficult problem suddenly pops into our heads, or the cry of eureka! from Archimedes in his bath. . . . The gods are what we call hallucinations. [emphasis added]

Whether hallucinations, contagious delusions, an example of unconscious training, the result of a pervasive ideology, a self-sealing
explanation, a repressed subconsciousness, or a projection of ourselves—Zeus as sky god captivated and seduced many minds. Zeus,
as bright sky, still touches us.

The Touch of Zeus:
A Summary

Among the most fearful weather elements, thunder and lightning
insinuate themselves into our language, our emotions, our subconscious, our mythologies, and our deities. Personalizations of sky,
rain, snow, thunder, lightning, and sun animate our religions. The
great faiths of the world derive their character from the climatic environments in which they arose.

Zeus (meaning "the bright sky") as the mythical source of all
changes in the sky or winds, personified powerful forces of weather.
He ruled the world. He knew and saw the future and the past. He
preserved order. He punished and rewarded all of mankind. In ancient Greek myths, Zeus punished Prometheus ("foresight"), who
tried to steal fire, by chaining him to a mountaintop and forcing him
to weather the cruel elements, thus signifying man's everlasting
bondage to his atmosphere. Other early legends relate amorous exploits of Zeus among goddesses and mortals. By them he begat a
pantheon of children, whose attributes (justice, war, wisdom, peace,
prophecy, music, death, healing, love) are metaphors for the eternal
human qualities that flow from sky god, sky, and the weather.

The world-wide celebration of sky gods, their exploits and attributes, may be interpreted in modern scientific terms as hallucinations, delusions, unconscious training, ideologies, self-closing fantasies, repressed desires, projections, or helplessness. But sky worship
is a pervasive, universal experience.

Nine:
"Objective"
Weather-Sensitivity

When sorrows come, they come not singly, but in battalions.
—William Shakespeare

The "normal" man in the "normal" atmosphere functions so well that he is scarcely aware of the existence of the atmosphere. But both man and the atmosphere vary so widely in their functioning that it is not surprising that their interaction becomes medically significant.
—William E. Reifsnyder

It is not so easy to just commit suicide if one knows that it is the weather which urges the pill bottle into our hands.
—quoted (ironically) by Werner Ranscht-Froemsdorf

Preceding Page: Notus
The wind of the south is hot and very rainy. The sculptor represented him as a young man holding a vase of water.

It is fine to read Freud, but eventually you have to go out with the opposite sex. Similarly, it is convenient enough to ask if people *think* they are weather-sensitive, but eventually we must check their symptoms against the weather itself.

The problem of "objectifying" weather-sensitivity is not simple. First, the human reactions, symptoms, or sensitivity have to be independent of their own statement, objectively verifiable. Some, like "perspiration" are immediately evident and measurable; others, like "disinclination to work" or "headache" are "painfully" subjective. Second, the weather itself has to be objectively classified. Hot or cold and warm fronts or cold fronts seem acceptable for starters, but if there are finer details of meteorological subtlety, then any organizing principle of weather phases should incorporate them. This is tantamount to the difference between a single instrument and the full orchestra: at times extraordinary effects can be wrung from a solo clarinet, a solo violin, or solo piano; but for richness of range, a one-hundred-piece symphony orchestra can deliver the full sweep of emotions and moods.

Your moods, intensely personal and subjective, will actually change a day or two *after* the weather changes.

M. A. Persinger in recent Canadian experiments has demonstrated that the weather will induce delayed moods. High scores on a mood scale he used indicated happiness or pleasure; and low scores, unhappiness or discontent. He matched the mood scores of ten subjects with weather conditions for ninety days: mean daily temperature and pressure, relative humidity, number of sunshine hours, and other weather factors. *Statistical analysis showed that there were the most significant correlations (20 percent of all) between reported moods on any one day and the weather conditions during the previous two days.* Apparently one or two days' weather conditions (good or bad) are necessary before people are likely to register a mood change. What kind of change? Higher mood scores correlated more frequently with *increased* mean *sunshine* hours, *lower humidity* range, and lower mean humidity values.

Yet on the day a person's mood was evaluated, the weather condition was not significant. It may be that the mood and weather interacting on the same day hide a more profound relationship. This two-day lag is not an unusual human response; there are good reasons for its latency. Thus, common colds are associated with cold environmental temperatures two to four days prior to the onset of common-cold symptoms. (Weather-sensitives report more colds than non-weather-sensitives.) And the human body may take several days, say three to ten, to accommodate itself to a change in climate, temperature, or altitude. The next time you feel rotten on a fine-weather day, ask yourself what the weather was one or two days before; you may be surprised.

The complexity may be hidden from our conscious view. For instance, a single sharp change in weather can provoke a fluctuating human response, a series of subliminal or physiological oscillations in the organism that gradually dwindle. But unlike a struck gong, the human organism struck by the same stimulus—a weather change—can (and often does) respond differently each time. Both the intensity and the kind of response will depend upon our previous level of arousal or excitation. Thus, Wilder's Law of Initial Value is very important in understanding how the same weather has different effects on the same person at different times, and on different people at the same times (see Chapter 1).

The mood lag of one to two days and the cold-symptoms lag of two to four days suggest that weather seems to provoke a quicker *mood* response than it does a *common-cold* response. Thus, some of us can use mood change as a medical alert, an advance warning for colds. The involuntary nervous system clearly and deeply participates in our total interaction—physiological and emotional—with the weather conditions. How deeply may be appreciated by the fact that some individuals actually *dream* they are getting sick a day or two before they actually *do*.

Psychological Traits

Anyone who believes that weather-sensitive people are merely self-indulgent hypochondriacs might be persuaded otherwise by the following result.

Two groups, one subjectively weather-sensitive, the other not, were given psychological personality tests. The following figure shows the personality characteristics for weather-sensitives and non-weather-sensitives. Compared to non-weather-sensitives the weather-sensitive men and women were significantly more *nervous,* more *depressive,* more *excitable,* more *inhibited,* more *emotionally unstable*—and significantly less *calm* and less *masculine.* The weather-sensitives were more nervous because they had problems in their involuntary (self-governing) nervous systems and their physical functioning; they also became tired easily and were more irritable, restless, and easily disturbed during sleep. (These symptoms are similar to those of the self-declared weather-sensitives in the Faust experiment, Chapter 2.) Moreover, weather-sensitives present a strong physical "affect" (the intense involuntary and muscular effects of emotions). The non-weather-sensitives showed few of these physical or psychosomatic symptoms.

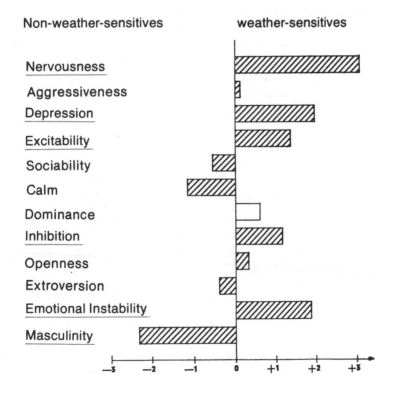

Weather and Personality
Personality differences between weather-sensitives and non-weather-sensitives. Underlined traits are statistically significant.

Numerous medical tests were performed—blood pressure, reaction time, reflexes, exercise tests, cold water immersion tests. Significant differences appeared in the outcome of the tests for the objectively weather-sensitive and non-weather-sensitive. Generally, the weather-sensitives had a much stronger reaction to all tests; they responded to the controlled external environments with frequent and strong changes in blood pressure. Their circulatory regulation system was more unstable and changeable.

Perhaps "low threshold of pain" rather than hypochondriasis might better describe weather-sensitives. But anyone who believes weather-sensitives are merely complainers will not easily be otherwise persuaded, since they are probably indifferent to weather or pain.

Karl Dirnagl, a professor of the science of therapeutic baths (balneology), examined a large population (several thousand citizens of Munich) using a questionnaire distributed and collected daily. The sample was a representative cross section as to sex, age, and profession, except no presumptive weather-sensitivity was attributed to any respondent. The period covered was fifteen weeks in 1970. Simultaneously, he recorded a host of weather indices like temperature, humidity, pressure. Detailed results of his interrogations are illustrated and discussed in the Chapter Notes.

Briefly, when *some* people felt good (or bad), almost *all* people felt good (or bad) at the same specified times. The question is, are these clustered days associated with any special weather conditions? And are there time lags? The answers are yes, and yes.

The weather days on which unfavorable health reports were noted were classifiably different from those weather days on which favorable health reports were noted. Later in this chapter, the weather differences or phases are described as the Bad Tölzer weather scheme. The time lags require a brief elaboration.

Dirnagl undertook the heroic task of correlating the "index of indisposition" with virtually all weather variables (some 140 of them) reported by the Munich Weather Service for that period. The correlation was expressed as a sky-influence (meteorotropic) equation. He found that as much as 47 percent of the change (variance) in the index of indisposition was accounted for by three quantities:

- The first, contributing 34 percent to the overall variance, was the temperature. (Actually, the temperature was the minimum or morning temperature on a given day minus the weighted average of minimum temperatures for the prior seven days.)

- The second quantity, which contributed 12 percent to the change in health complaints, was the relative humidity (or water vapor content of the air) in the morning of the day the health complaints were registered.
- And finally, the barometric pressure accounted for 1 percent of the health complaints.

The direction of each quantity was significant: *rising* temperature, *falling* humidity, and *falling* barometric pressure *increased* the number of health complaints, or index of indisposition, during September, October, and November. *Falling* temperatures, *rising* humidity, and *rising* pressure *reduced* the health complaints and improved general well-being during that time.

Because the minimum temperature of the day usually occurs in the morning and because prior days' temperatures are incorporated, Dirnagl concluded that there is also a delay, perhaps one day or more, between a weather change and its reflection in the human organism. This is a meteorotropic lag.

The Sky-Influence Equation

Dirnagl displayed people's reaction to weather in the form of an equation (see Chapter Notes): human response on one side and weather factors on the other.

It describes, rather uniquely, how human health depends on objective weather conditions; it says, in effect, "meteorotropisms are real," even though there is no one-to-one correspondence, or "mapping," of weather onto health.

Furthermore, this meteorotropic equation says that in our north temperate zone our state of health depends *mainly* on the environmental temperature. We are three times as sensitive to a change in temperature as we are to a change in relative humidity. And we are thirty-four times as sensitive to a temperature change as to a barometric pressure change. *Temperature clearly rules our lives.* Any weather classification scheme would have to incorporate the temperature and humidity milieu if it were to lay claim to any meteorotropic fidelity.

Industrial Accidents and
Emergency Calls

Industrial accidents, like traffic accidents, reflect an increase in reaction time, and a considerable change in alertness and mood.
Otmar Harlfinger has identified those types of weather phases or conditions associated with increasingly frequent or infrequent industrial
accidents. Increased accidents come during warm air currents and
heat thunderstorms, less frequently during cold air movements. Specifically, he found more industrial accidents during southwestern
winds, unstable weather processes, increasing cloudiness, and warm
fronts. Fewer industrial accidents occurred during northwestern
winds, cold high-pressure regions, cumulus clouds with broken cloud
covers, and within the central part and cold side of a weather front.

In a different attempt to connect state of health or rate of disease
with specific weather situations, Posse looked at over ten thousand
patients over a period of three months. He collected statistics on the
rate of diseases (called morbidity) by monitoring nightly calls to the
Munich emergency medical service. At first, the weather's effect on
morbidity was masked by the weekly rhythm and overall trend in the
frequency of calls. By a retrospective analysis over a long time span,
he demonstrated that the passage of weather fronts, weather inversions, and warm, damp air conditions near the ground all significantly increased the morbidity in the population. Furthermore, certain ailments clustered around specific weather phases, or patterns.

- With a forthcoming change of weather during the night or in the
  afternoon of the previous day, and the air's water vapor content
  increasing, there was a significant increase in feverish conditions, and a tendency for asthma, diffuse headache, heart and
  circulatory complaints to increase.
- The passage of a cold front, occurring in the afternoon of the
  previous day (note the time lag), *significantly increased* the
  number of notifications of disease called into the emergency
  medical service, and tended to increase the number of kidney
  and gall bladder pains and heart, circulatory, and migraine
  complaints.
- The building of an inversion, occurring during the night, *signifi-*

cantly increased the number of calls per night, tended to increase abdominal pains, asthma, and all problems with an obvious psychic-psychiatric accent.

- When mild, warm, extremely dry air (characteristic foehn weather) built up at night, the number of calls to the emergency service *dropped significantly*—reversing the trend of the other weather phases and tending to decrease ailment complaints.

- In measurements near the ground, if the air temperature and absolute humidity increased (compared to their values of *both previous days*) the number of calls to the emergency medical service *significantly increased* and there was an increasing tendency for feverish symptoms, heart and circulatory problems, asthma, and diffuse headaches.

- If the ground-level air temperature and absolute humidity increased (as opposed to their values on *previous day*) there were significant increases in calls to the emergency medical service and increased feverish symptoms, asthma, and heart and circulatory complaints.

These results also show "biometeorological lag"—one or two days usually pass before people feel a weather phase.

Temperature and humidity *together* have a much stronger effect on our comfort and body chemistry than temperature *alone*. But the Temperature-Humidity Environment (called T.H.E.) of our biosphere (that part of the atmosphere close to ground level) is itself dominated by winds, precipitation, evaporation, incoming or outgoing radiation, the presence of suspended particles in the air. Complicating this bewildering array even further are: the cloud cover, the type of air mass and whether it is a high-pressure circulation (called anticyclonic) or low-pressure circulation (called cyclonic), and whether the air moves horizontally or vertically—all of these factors will influence the Temperature-Humidity Environment which influences us.

Temperature and humidity together govern our comfort (remember the meteorotropic equation). But it sometimes *seems* as if barometric pressure, or some other weather condition does. The reason for this is that many weather variables change together simultaneously; we call these "co-factors" because their changes are coincidental.

For example, Becker has shown (see Appendix I) that *high pressure*

*or anticyclonal weather means a favorable circumstance for humans,
but low pressure or cyclonal weather frequently tends to be unfavorable.* Highs "elevate" and lows "lower" your state of health.

Your Personal Weather Phases

The Tölzer weather phase classification is an attempt to perceive
the weather in human terms directly, as it effects people—their comfort, moods, behavior, health, morbidity, and mortality. Developed
into a Bioprognosis system by H. Brezowsky of the German Weather
Service (and others), and used by them for several years, it now provides medical-meteorological forecasts for physicians and hospitals.
As a consequence of the weather yesterday and today, Bioprognosis
reveals which patients and symptoms are likely to become aggravated
tomorrow, or the day after.

You may use a simplified version of Bioprognosis to forecast your
body's biological response to weather—your likely moods and behavior, and your likely ailments, symptoms, and diseases. There is one
caveat: although statistical and medical evidence, and biological reasoning, confirm the presence of intimate associations between
weather stimuli and body responses, no single individual is a "statistical" human being. Nevertheless, here is how it works.

First, consulting the chart on page 208 determine the weather phase:

- has the temperature trend for the past 24 hours been increasingly
  COOL, MILD, or WARM? Select one.
- has the humidity trend for the past 24 hours been increasingly
  DRY, ARID, HUMID, or MOIST? Select one.
- find the appropriate weather phase in the chart that corresponds
  to the temperature-humidity trend.

Second, consulting the table on page 209, determine your probable
moods and behavior:

- choose the column with the proper weather phase number at the
  top
- read the likely moods and behavior indicated by the column entries
- the higher your Weather-Sensitivity Risk-Factor Profile Score (see

Chapter 1) the more likely will your moods and behavior be accentuated by the weather phase
- your changes may not appear for a day or two.

Third, consulting the table on pages 210–211, determine your probable ailments, symptoms, and diseases:

- choose the column with the proper weather phase number at the top
- read the likely ailments, symptoms, and diseases indicated in the column
- your personal medical history will determine which ailments, symptoms, and diseases you are likely to suffer, and their intensity
- the higher your Weather-Sensitivity Risk-Factor Profile Score (see Chapter 1), the more likely will your ailments, symptoms or diseases be accentuated by the weather phase
- a day or two may pass before your ailments, symptoms, or diseases appear.

Weather Phase Number 1 to 6 Occurs if the Temperature-Humidity Trend for the Past 24 Hours Has Been:

		Increasingly COOL	Increasingly MILD	Increasingly WARM
Increasingly DRY		*Clearing, Calm Weather* (6)	*Moderately Good Weather* (1)	*Improving Weather* (2)
	Summers:	brisk, pleasant, early fog	pleasantly cool nights	bright days, cool nights
	Winters:	high fog, good visibility	invariably cold	warming days, very cold nights
	Winds:	weak	little or none	weak
	Clouds:	disappearing vertical puffs	tall, broken; later none	thunderheads summers, or clear
	Sun:	brief, pleasant appearances	moderate radiation	moderate radiation
	Duration:	18–24%	5–7%	7–11%
Increasingly ARID		. . . . . .	*Extremely Good Weather* (3A)	*Exceptional Weather* (3F)
	Summers:		mild mornings, warming afternoons	very warm early, hot later
	Winters:		warm days, very cold nights	very warm days, no cooling off
	Winds:		rising	foehn, chinook, sharav types
	Clouds:		cloudless, clear	distant visibility extreme
	Sun:		very strong solar radiation	very strong and glaring
	Duration:		14–15%	0.5%
Increasingly HUMID		*Beginning Precipitation* (5)	*Forthcoming Precipitation* (4)	. . . . . .
	Summers:	cooling off	sultry, heavy, moist	
	Winters:	wet and cold	beginning of thawing	
	Winds:	violent thunderstorms summers	warm, from southwest	
	Clouds:	heavy, no visibility, squalls	come in at high altitudes	
	Sun:	no sun	slowly disappears	
	Duration:	7–9%	22–25%	
Increasingly MOIST		*Completed Precipitation* (6Z)	. . . . . .	Note: Weather conditions may develop in or out of the numerical weather phase sequence.
	Summers:	uncomfortably chilly, damp		
	Winters:	cool but very damp		
	Winds:	blistery, from northwest (w-nw)		
	Clouds:	heavy at high altitude, hail		
	Sun:	piercing, briefly in summer		
	Duration:	13–14%		

Weather Phase

Moods & Behavior	1	2	3 A	3 F	4	5	6 Z	6
Ability to concentrate	high	high	falls	falls	falls			rises
Reaction time	falls	shortest	rises	rises	rises			short
Traffic/work accidents	low	low	rises	max	max			
General state of health	rises	rises	steady	falls	min	fair	fair	improves
Consumption of medication				high	high			
Medical complaints (% deviation from average)	−8%	−5%	−4%	high	+17%	+3%	+1%	−7%
Headaches, migraines		rise			severe			
Sensitivity to pain		high		rises	high	max		
Fatigue, tiredness				common	high			
Need for sleep				falls	changes	disturb'd	rises, hi	
Depth of sleep				shallow	falls	disturb'd	deep	
Productivity of work				low	low			
Performance, correctness				poor.	poor			
Desire to work				low	low			
Crime rate		tends up	climbs	rises		high	high	
Suicide rate				max			high	
Aggression (versus temp)		falls	low	low	low	rises	rises	rises
Endurance (vs. temperature)		falls	low	low	low	rises	rises	rises
Energy level (vs. temp.)		falls	low	low	low	rises	rises	rises
Pleasurable moods (vs. sunsh)	rise	rise	rise	fall	min			rise
Play (vs. temperature)			falls	low				
Biological influence	favorable		unfav'bl	unfav'bl	unfav'bl	unfav'bl	unfav'bl	favorable
Stimulus intensity	minimal	small	moderate	strong	v. strong	strong	strong	small
Frequency distribution	5–7%	7–11%	14–15%	0.5%	22–25%	7–9%	13–14%	18–24%

Weather Phase

Ailments, Symptoms, Disease	1	2	3 A	3 F	4	5	6 Z	6
Blood proteins (albumins)	rise	rise						rise
Immune antibodies (globulins)	rise	rise						rise
Blood pressure					drops		low	low
Hemorrhages (post-operative)	low	low	rise	high	max	low	low	
Coronary failures			rise	high	v. high			
Cardiac infarcts	v. low	v. low	low	rise	max	high	low	v. low
Intercranial pressure (injury)	low	low			high	high	high	low
Migraines	low	low	low	low	max	low	low	low
Stroke, apoplexy	v. low	v. low	max	low	max	high	high	low
Blood clotting (thromboses)	v. low	v. low	rise	rise	max	falls	low	low
Vascular obstructions (emboli)				rise				
Circulatory problems				rise	high			
Labored breathing (dyspnea)	v. low	low	low	low	max	high	high	low
Asthma attacks	low	low	v. low	low	max	low	v. low	low
Asthmatic bronchitis	v. low	v. low	low	v. low	max	low	v. low	v. low
Acute bronchitis	v. low	v. low	low	low	rises	rises	high	max
Angina pectoris	low	low	low	low	high	max	high	low
Muscle tone	high	high	low	low	low	high	high	high
Cramps	v. low	low	low	low	high	falls	falls	high

Ailments, Symptoms, Disease	1	2	3 A	3 F	4	5	6 Z	6
Labor pain period			shorter	longer				
Convulsion in labor (eclampsia)			rise		rise		rise	
Miscarriages								high
Stomach/duodenum perforations			often	rise	max	high	high	
Gastritis					high			
Bladder pains							max	
Gall bladder pains							max	
Kidney pains							max	
Glaucoma attacks							high	
Body temperature (afternoon)	low	low	high	high	max	high		
Skin irritations (dermatitis)						high		
Dental difficulties					high	high		
Nerve pains				rise		rise	rise	
Rheumatic pains					high	high	high	
Osteoarthritis	low	low	low	low	max	high	high	
Fits & seizures (epilepsy)	low	low	low	low	min	max	low	high
Mortality	subav'g	subav'g	low	low	high	high	high	v. low

Biological effects may result from weather events that originate in the upper atmosphere or close to the ground. Some purely subjective symptoms of weather-sensitivity or of disease may originate at the very high strata of the atmosphere. Thus a very weather-sensitive person might feel tired, but an obvious weather change may not arrive until the next day; the person *thinks* (s)he is *pre*-sensitive. For instance, a warm front at ground level a day away from you may still cause fatigue, headache, and sleep problems, because the ascending warm air mass has already started weather changes high above your region. Even though measurable weather changes (in T.H.E.) have not yet been observed locally, circulatory problems and heart infarcts increase.

The landscape helps to determine the weather phases and T.H.E. in your area. Biological effects will differ if you are near mountains or large bodies of water.

During the summer, in weather phases 1 and 2, high pressure tends to make conditions stable. Few physiological maladies, scar pains, rheumatoid problems, nervous agitation, psychosomatic headaches, or central-nervous-system problems appear. Bronchial asthma, angina, circulatory or blood-vessel problems are rare.

In the winter, high-pressure weather phases 1 and 2 may cover a region with low clouds, heavy fog, or even smog. This can lead to increasing attacks of respiratory and circulatory problems (see chart on pages 210–211).

When the weather changes from high to low pressure, phases 3 and 4, there may be a warming of high layers of air which you cannot see, although the weather is deteriorating. These nice-weather clouds begin to dissolve, and later the sky is covered with high, tufted or plumed cirrus clouds, or cirrostratus clouds that make unblurred halos around the sun or moon. Disturbances of the involuntary nervous system (such as agitation, exhaustion, irritability, concentration difficulties, dizziness, headache, anxiety and so on) usually begin here. Efficiency and reaction time drops, causing industrial and traffic accidents (see chart on page 209). Scar and bone-fracture pains may begin. Unstable people, especially, may react with irritability to the impending precipitation. Gloom and doom are two prevailing moods. "Even benign Nature habitually lies, except when she promises execrable weather," as Mark Twain said, and he could have been referring to phase 4.

As the low-pressure area advances, phase 5, stratocumulus clouds appear. These are light grey roll clouds with flat bases, beginning at

3,000 feet (1,000 meters) and ranging up to 18,000 feet (6,000 meters). From the darker parts, rain or snow may threaten, and then actually fall. At this stage, the impending or beginning biological changes in individuals proceed. Thromboses, embolisms, and heart attacks strike.

Once the warm front passes and the low-pressure phase is complete, precipitation decreases, the clouds vanish, warm or mild air flows in, and biotropic effects diminish. During the summer, if a cold front arrives, there is turbulence with showers or thunderstorms locally. At the back flank of the Low (after the cold front has passed) people suffer from asthma, bronchitis, angina, and other spastic diseases.

The transition from low- to high-pressure weather will be accompanied by calming weather, phase 6, a decrease in precipitation, and dispersal of clouds until the high-pressure weather stabilizes. The spastic diseases diminish and subjective symptoms, like headaches, migraines or sleep disturbances, may affect well-being.

If there is a high-pressure system near the ground, moving from west to east, there can be a separate cold air mass above which drops suddenly, causing a severe cold snap. This is especially troublesome. Strong migraines, headaches and, heart and circulatory problems arise. These also result when the high-altitude winds, like the jet stream, may blow at higher speed in the opposite direction to the ground level winds.

Bioprognosis Samples

In Germany, the Bioprognosis system alerts physicians and hospitals daily to forthcoming weather changes and their likely influence on the health or illness of their patients. It is available only to physicians (by calling an unlisted telephone number); the general public cannot "imagine" or "self-induce" symptoms, since they do not have access to this information. The system is based upon the principles of weather phases described above. What follows are two sample forecasts that went out on tape or telex:

BIOPROG Bad Nauheim: medical-meteorological report for Franken, Hessen, Oberplatz, and Rheinland-Platz, valid from 9/1/77 to 9/2/77.

1. *Weather condition:* At further shallow pressure distribution we will have the formation of moist, unstable rearrangements.
2. *Intensity of weather biotropy:* around moderate.
3. *Tips for physicians:* a. Subjective condition: increased sensitivity to pain, decreased concentration, and quick fatigue; b. Influence on diseases: increased heart and circulatory problems; danger of infarcts; repeated inflammatory processes.

Hello ladies and gentlemen! Here is the automatic answer to your call about the medical-meteorological forecast for Baden-Würtenberg, to 8/17/77:

1. *Weather conditions:* There is an increased influx of warm air at the face of a low-pressure area over France. At the same time, there is a tendency for unstable rearrangements to increase.
2. *Intensity of the weather biotropy:* increasing to moderate and strong.
3. *Tips for physicians:* a. Subjective conditions: increased danger of accidents with decreased concentration ability, fatigue, and psychic abnormalities; b. Influence on diseases: increased deregulation of hypotone circulation; abnormal blood clotting; repeated inflammatory processes.

Bioprognoses are used daily by hundreds of physicians, not only in Germany but also independently in Poland and Hungary. Would adoption of a similar system be advisable in the United States? I believe the answer is yes, and the sooner the better.

Barometer, Variograph, Ailments, and Well-Being

Symptoms of weather-sensitivity not only touch those who are outside, directly in the air mass, but also those indoors. Weather factors can penetrate a building almost unchanged, but only a few fulfill the necessary stringent conditions: sunlight, infrared radiation, electric or magnetic fields, electrical charges or ions, discharges (called sferics), and slow or rapid air-pressure fluctuations. These fast pressure changes originate in the border regions or boundary layers of the atmosphere, for example in fronts, in inversions, and in foehn. These rapid changes are responsible for a great number of weather-induced human health problems. Indeed, they may help explain the phenomenon of pre-sensitivity to weather, because rapid pressure changes, traveling faster than the airmass, herald new weather systems. And we are more aware of large *rapid* pressure changes than large *slow* changes. Merely reflect upon the sensations you feel when the elevator ascends or descends rapidly and your eardrums "pop," or your eustachian tubes fail to equilibrate the inner and outer pressure differential.

Normal barometers, in registering the regular passage of high-pressure and low-pressure air masses, change on a time scale of one or perhaps several days. Such pressure changes are relatively slow and a normal *recording* barometer (called a *baro*graph), traces the air pressure slowly with time. But minute air-pressure changes, measured with a device called a variograph (see Chapter Notes), reveal the following results: men feel better than women, who suffer more ailments and headaches. People in non-air-conditioned rooms feel better and have fewer headaches than those in air-conditioned rooms. And finally, non-weather-sensitivies feel better, *much* better, than weather-sensitives, who suffer more ailments and more headaches.

Zurich physicist Hans Richner and his colleague scrutinized the existing scientific literature of biometeorology and concluded that biometeorology research was "a disaster area," that it had no scientific right to exist. His collaborator concluded, from scrutinizing the same literature, that weather changes did affect our well-being. Thus their experiments were designed so that the results would be independent of the personal beliefs of either investigator. They questioned two hundred persons working in an insurance company. On a daily basis, for seven months, questionnaires were passed out and collected an hour later. The subjects responded to two groups of questions. The first set, inquiring of specific ailments, was to be answered "yes" or "no." The frequency of all these ailments was then called the "sum of ailments." The second set were pairs of opposite adjectives at either end of a straight line. For example, "happy" was on one end and "depressed" was on the other end of one (numbered) line segment. The subject placed a mark at a point near or far from the word to depict how he felt (as if it were a mood scale), and an "index well-being" was the average score on these bipolar questions.

These two scores ("ailments" and "well-being") were grouped by age, sex, belief in whether personal comfort depends on weather, and whether or not the working area was air-conditioned. And the scores were compared to the fast or slow atmospheric pressure fluctuations or waves.

The results: no correlations exist between "well-being" or "ailments," and the pressure changes of *less* than 4 minutes (fast waves). But for pressure changes *longer* than 4 minutes (slow waves) *the correlation with subjective scores was significant.*

The self-described weather-sensitives showed *highly significant* correlations between "well-being" and "ailments." In the self-described non-weather-sensitives correlated pressure fluctuations significantly with "ailments" and very probably significantly with "well-being." Thus even non-weather-sensitives suffer the weather-induced "ailments" (but not the weather-induced "well-being") as do weather-sensitives. Subjective "well-being" does not depend on weather, but "ailments" do for non-weather-sensitives.

The amplitude of the slow pressure changes was observed by the variograph; the human responses were observed from the questionnaire. The human responses moved (up and down) for seven months consistently with respect to the intensity of the rapid pressure changes. If a human response and a pressure change move together (in the same or opposite directions) they are related or correlated. If there was one chance in a thousand that their joint co-movement was purely at random or by luck, then they moved together in a *highly significant* way statistically. If their co-movement occurred by chance one time in a hundred, then it was statistically *significant.*

The result *for women: "index of well-being," "total ailments," and "headache" changed in a highly significant way with the slow-wave intensity.* For men, only their "sum of ailments" did this. For those working in air-conditioned environments, there were highly significant correlations between well-being and pressure, between ailments and pressure, and between "headaches" and pressure. For those in *non*-air-conditioned work spaces, there is no correlation between headache and pressure changes; that is, *workers in non-air-conditioned work spaces felt better than workers in air-conditioned work spaces.*

Beyond these results, Richner also found that in over two years of monitoring pressure changes there are significant correlations with mortality rates from cancer and mortality rates from circulatory diseases. More *circulatory* deaths came during high-pressure fluctuations, but there were *more cancer* deaths at low-pressure fluctuations; he was unable to explain this. Outside the hospital, the correlations were still higher between pressure fluctuations and mortality for cancer or circulatory problems. Thus, hospital care may prolong some lives, or medical treatment may mask the meteorological influences—or both.

Richner is convinced that there are significant correlations between the human responses or physiological reactions and the measured pressure fluctuations in the atmosphere. However, as he admits, he has not proved that these fluctuations are the actual cause of
aggravated well-being, ailments, or death. But pressure fluctuations
have the necessary properties to directly influence the human condition—*rapid pressure fluctuations penetrate buildings*. They propagate
wave energy from their source like ripples in a pond. And humans
are more sensitive to rapid pressure changes than slow changes.

The admirable reluctance of Richner to attribute a causal connection between pressure fluctuations and suffering is consistent with the
best spirit of scientific caution. The sequence of sober scientific de-
tachment goes like this, as Nobelist Richard Feynman put it. First,
assume that the progression or synchrony of two different sequences
of events is pure chance, unlinked. Second, if chance is improbable
or unreasonable, then assume that each sequence of events occurs
due to interacting or intrinsic parts within a larger system. Third,
only when chance and intrinsic causes are ruled out, entertain the
third assumption—that simultaneous or co-varying sequences of
events have external causes. Applied here, we can say:

1. The atmosphere is a statistically significant stimulus, an external
   cause—not pure chance—of human response.
2. If both the pressure fluctuations and the human response are conditioned by the atmosphere, then there ought to be physiological
   models explaining the apparent synchrony of weather and
   moods, weather and well-being, weather and ailments, of weather
   and death.
3. The third assumption beckons.

"Objective" Weather-Sensitivity:
A Summary

To link human reactions to specific weather patterns requires that
the symptoms must be objectively verifiable, that the weather must
be classifiable into definite phases, and that a statistical correlation
must appear between the weather phase and the human symptom.

One objective measure of the human response to weather is blood
pressure, which changes readily in weather-sensitive individuals,

whose circulatory system is unstable, and who also tend to be nervous, depressive, excitable, feminine, and emotionally unstable.

Examination of large populations and weather conditions daily over months reveals a clustering of health problems on certain days and feelings of well-being on other days. The clusters indicate what kind of weather was statistically favorable or unfavorable to people. Fine weather days had few complaints, and poor weather days many complaints. Health complaints formed an "index of indisposition" which changed most readily with the outdoor temperature, less so with humidity, and least of all with barometric pressure—not only on a given day, but for several days prior to the complaint. In other words, the weather's impact is not felt immediately.

Calls for emergency medical service (rate of disease or morbidity) also vary significantly with weather fronts, weather inversions, and warm, damp air near the ground. Complaints on any day increased when a cold front passed the previous day, or when air temperature and humidity increased on two prior days. Cardiac infarcts, bronchial asthma, and death rates are most sensitive indicators of weather events, usually low-pressure, or "cyclonal," weather.

Most weather-classification schemes ignore the human response. But one grouping of weather events into a pattern that incorporates the temperature-humidity environment is designed specifically for its effect on people. In this Tölzer system, the weather phases (considerably oversimplified) include moderate and increasing fine weather, departing with a forthcoming weather change, the completion of the weather change, a final calming down before the pattern tends to repeat its cycle of weathering. The biological effects of each phase are technically different, but statistically predictable. So much so, in fact, that the Bioprognosis system in Europe forecasts medical ailments based upon this scheme of weather phases and the known lags in people's weather response.

Tiny, rapid barometric changes, which signal forthcoming weather changes and penetrate buildings, are responsible for many weather-induced health changes, both disorders and improvements. Experiments show that well-being, ailments, and headaches are significantly associated with these pressure fluctuations for women, for weather-sensitives, and for those working in air-conditioned environments.

Ten:
Fire, Ice, and
Inner Weather

ΣΚΙΡΩΝ

Some say the world will end in fire;
Some say in ice.
From what I've tasted of desire
I hold with those who favor fire.
But if it had to perish twice,
I think I know enough of hate
To say that for destruction ice
Is also great
And would suffice.
        —Robert Frost, "Fire and Ice"

The mercury sank in the mouth of the dying day.
O all the instruments agree
The day of his death was a dark cold day.
        —W. H. Auden, "In Memory of W. B. Yeats"

That day she put our heads together,
Fate had her imagination about her,
Your head so much concerned with outer,
Mine with inner, weather.
        —Robert Frost, "Tree at My Window"

Preceding Page: Skiron
The wind of the northwest is the most arid and dry of all. Extremely cold in winter, in summer it is scorching, violent, and accompanied by cruel and frequent thunderstorms. People's health and vegetation suffer considerably from this wind. The figure has an air of languor. The upper short tunic is similar to Boreas's. The curious vase probably represents a bronze pot of fire; its cinders are supposedly scorching the poor terrestrial creatures below.

A lion stalks. His victim, an antelope grazing on the African flora, eats peacefully. The lion readies itself to spring. A breeze stirs. A leaf flutters. The brush snaps . . . Suddenly, the antelope sees the lion, turns to flee. And then . . . But let us stop a moment and run through the scene again—with a *physiological* eye.

Peacefully grazing, the antelope is unstressed. Blood fills his viscera to help digest his food. At once perceiving danger, the antelope's nervous system triggers a massive discharge. His cardiac output shifts from the gastrointestinal tract to the skeletal muscle; his increased blood pressure and cardiac output, his heightened awareness—all provide an extra margin for survival, an edge of safety for escape. Within two seconds, the antelope turns to flee; the lion pounces. Will he survive uninjured? Precipitously stressed, his nervous system responded promptly. This time he lives.

In his relentless search for food, the lion, also stressed, activated his sympathetic nervous system.

A nervous system under stress rapidly controls blood circulation as a physical response to attack, danger, fear, anxiety.

Experimentally induced anxiety in animals provokes alterations of their circulatory systems: blood levels of adrenaline and noradrenaline rise, pulse rate speeds up, blood pressure is elevated, cardiac output rises, coronary blood flow increases, respiration speeds up, mental acuity rises, levels of fuel in the blood are elevated.

These symptoms represent activation of the sympathetic nervous system. In the laboratory, these symptoms were triggered by experimentally provoked emotional stress and anxiety. Despite the fact that the involuntary nervous system can respond in a limited number of ways with a seemingly tiny repertoire of reactions to stress—almost indifferent to the provocation—there are significant differences.

Biochemical alterations in the blood are induced by brain-controlled hormones that raise the level of muscle fuel. With *exercise* stress, these fuels are metabolized by skeletal muscles. After exercise, the levels of these fuels (free fatty acids and glucose) decline, consumed by muscle effort. But in *emotional* stress, the glucose and free fatty acids are *not* consumed by the skeletal muscles, because they are

221

not being exercised. After emotional stress, the glucose and free fatty acids return to normal levels, but only much later, and not without upsetting normal control mechanisms.

Another difference between the body's answer to *exercise* versus *emotional* stress lies in the blood pressure. In *emotional* stress, the blood flow to skeletal muscles remains at pre-stress or basal levels; instructed by adrenaline, the heart has to pump hard to distribute fuels and overcome the resistance of these peripheral skeletal blood vessels; so pressure rises; both heart thrust (systolic pressure) and vascular reply (diastolic pressure) create dual hypertensions. In *physical*, or *exercise* stress, the blood vessels, or vascular bed of the peripheral skeletal muscles, open up. Peripheral resistance to blood flow diminishes. The diastolic (return) blood pressure falls due to vasodilation. So only systolic hypertension is present.

The sympathetic nervous system is virtually indifferent to the cause of stress. It responds in an unconscious, monotonous, repetitive, thoughtless way to all environmental assaults, to prepare the organism for fight or flight, for aggression or defense. When the anticipated battle or escape does not materialize, the body is nevertheless prepared for a response that does not occur.

With some modifications, *weather* stress provokes many of the same conscious behavioral—and subliminal physiological—replies that the grazing antelope had to the predatory lion. The environmental stress may be heat or cold or other weather agents, like humidity, thunder, lightning, wind. To see the difference between exercise stress, emotional stress, and weather stress, it is necessary to know why and how the body maintains thermal constancy, how it equilibrates temperature by its reflexive and behavioral anatomical repertoire.

Conscious behavioral response to weather stress is often provoked by underlying physiological processes that can be simplified.

Similarities and Differences: Physical, Emotional, and Weather Stress

	Physical/Exercise Stress	Emotional Stress	Weather Stress
Manifestations	Elevated pulse rate Elevated blood pressure Increased cardiac output Increased coronary blood flow Rapid respiration (tachypnea) Increased mental acuity Elevated levels of glucose and free fatty acids in blood Typical sympathetic activity	Facial expressions change Gooseflesh Tail erection in animals Aggressive behavior Vocal response for warning Ready for fight or flight External symptoms of sympathetic behavior	Sensation of discomfort from heat or cold In cold stress, vascular constrictions Isolates body torso by insulation Increases blood pressure and sugar Relative oxygen hunger, alkalosis Approximate adrenal phase, sympathetic phase Heat stress or compensatory counter-reaction to cold Extremities receive core heat by convection Decreased blood pressure and sugar Increased carbon dioxide and acidosis Approximate parasympathetic, acetylcholine phase
Differences	Voluntary efforts, conscious awareness Increased skeletal-muscle blood sugar Diastolic blood pressure falls Metabolism of glucose and free fatty acids rises After exercise, glucose and free fatty acid levels fall Always conscious	Normal emotional stress in preparation for physical activity, if absent diastolic blood pressure does not fall Sustained elevated adrenaline upsets normal physiological control mechanisms with long-term consequences Recurrent symptoms may self-perpetuate (pounding heart, throbbing vessels, increased respiration, heightened awareness) provoke further anxieties Often subliminal	Conditioned reflex reacts to frontal passages in biological synchronization, negation, or amplification Constant repetitive swings may push inadequate organs to dysfunction, producing wide range of ailments, including mental disease, inflammation, bacterial and viral diseases Mostly subliminal (except for extreme thermal sensations) especially when preoccupied

A Simple Picture

Imagine a seesaw. The pivot point, or fulcrum, is located halfway from one end of the seesaw to the other end.

Now imagine a child sitting on the right-hand end of the seesaw. The child's weight provides a downward force, which we will call a stressor (for example, a weather stressor). This stressor causes the system—child and seesaw—to change; the seesaw's right end tilts downward. If it were to continue downward, the end of the seesaw would accelerate, strike the ground very rapidly, jar the child, and shock the system. The child may simply extend her legs to the ground, absorb any potential shock at first, then tense her muscles and push upward until the seesaw changes direction. The right end would move upward.

While all this happens, the left end of the seesaw moves in the opposite direction from the right end. Call this movement the reaction.

The tug of gravity on the child is the system's stressor; it was opposed by an equilibrium-restoring force, her legs. This system of child-plus-seesaw resembles a homeostatic mechanism in the human organism; the body returns to normal, it restores its own equilibrium. In the human, homeostasis is ruled by the nervous system, the hormonal systems, and the chemical systems—all components of our reflexive involuntary apparatus.

Oversimplified, the analogy can be extended to the frequent passage of cold and warm air masses. Warm air masses swirl counterclockwise around a central low-pressure zone; the whole whorl, or vortical package, travels rapidly across the earth's surface.

Steep wedges of cold air, at relatively high pressure, push this warm air forward along well-defined paths called storm tracks (even though they are not storms). This package sweeps eastward, stimulating the more densely populated industrial northern United States and then scatters in the Atlantic. The pressure and temperature profiles, cloud types, and cross sections of the two air-mass types—Low, or cyclonal, and High, or anticyclonal—are clearly demarcated (see Appendix J).

Any given region in the United States will be visited frequently by a low-pressure vortex of air. In the first half of this century, an average of some 1,400 Lows per year passed through; the number per month in a given area depends on the season or month. During January in the snowbelt states, three or four Lows per month sweep through a small grid (five degrees latitude by five degrees longitude), and one or two per month in the sunbelt states. In June, snowbelt states will get one to three per month, and sunbelt states perhaps less than one or two per month. Where you live and the time of year there will decide when a new mass of air—warm or cool, hot or cold—may arrive: as often as once a week, occasionally more; or once a month, occasionally less. As a consequence, the local temperature and humidity will seesaw around some average.

Each passing atmosphere alteration is associated—like the seesaw—with changes in the body's physiology, because each air-mass temperature change calls forth prompt automatic adaptations. Or prompt reprisals. Several times a month (more or less) your body functions, both visible and hidden, will mirror the passage of cold and warm fronts. It is clearly *not* the atmospheric pressure itself we are responding to—there is no known simple organ (other than the eardrum) that is commanded by the barometric pressure—but the warm and cool fronts themselves, which happen to be signaled by pressure changes of almost-regular recognizability (see Appendix J).

Virtually every passing front will stimulate an individual. A cold polar front will generally trigger blood-vessel contraction or vasoconstriction, a warm front relative expansion of the vascular bed or vasodilation. Our biological swings are, like the seesaw, part external stressor and part inner compensations to the stressor. If the frontal passages are infrequent, as in the sunbelt, then relative lassitude prevails. If the fronts are too frequent or severe, individuals become overstimulated, then fatigued; and if a person is weak, he will suffer or succumb. If the passage of fronts is "sufficiently" frequent, its stimulation may be "just right"—vague value judgment, surely. The proof is in the results, and northern regions (like the snowbelt states and northern Europe) are energized into high productivity and achievement (see Chapter 4).

Weather Tides, Body Tides

A constant ebb and flow prevails between these frontal passages, or weather rhythms, and our biological tides. As your body seeks to maintain a proper balance, your biological rhythms may synchronize with, amplify, or negate the external atmospheric tides. At the deepest levels in your body, this is weathering. Depending on its construction and how it is pushed, a pendulum coaxed periodically will continue to swing or stop swinging; will swing wide or barely at all; will swing slowly or vigorously.

Whether your "pendulations" (the swings in your body's biochemistry and physiology) are in synchrony with the atmospheric rhythms—whether they amplify them or negate them—depends on your constitution, physique and temperament, your prior state of stimulation (or weathering), and on the weather itself.

Your body will pendulate between poles of increasing and decreasing surface blood-vessel action, increasing and decreasing cell-membrane permeability, increasing and decreasing blood acidity or alkalinity, increasing and decreasing blood pressure, increasing and decreasing metabolism, increasing and decreasing smooth muscle tension. It is a complex symphony.

As long as your biological swings can keep pace with the repetitive changes in air masses, a state of relative health is maintained. "If the environmental demand is too much," says William Petersen, "if the changes are too great or follow each other too quickly, if the organism is too young or too old to adjust properly, if other rhythms, seasonal or menstrual, or other energy impacts such as trauma, emotion, or work act to augment the meteorological effect, autonomic dysfunction and, later, disease arise."

The biological tides are driven by the involuntary nervous system. Most parts of the body receive signals from *both* the sympathetic nervous system and the parasympathetic nervous system. Both are subsystems of the involuntary system, and each subsystem generally acts in opposition to the other.

The sympathetic nervous system acts by releasing adrenaline and noradrenaline. (The one exception is the sweat glands, which act by the release of acetylcholine.) The following are adrenal or sympathetic activities: the sweat glands are *stimulated*; the upper eyelids are raised; the pupils *dilate*; the arteries to muscles, including the coronary arteries of the heart muscle, are *dilated*; the rate and force of the heartbeat *increases*; more air enters the lungs; however, arteries to the skin and abdominal organs are *constricted*, and the activity of digestive organs is *depressed*. These responses, or "arousals" to adrenaline, like "arousal" to cold weather, will follow Wilder's Law. Certain drugs imitate the weather in their sympathetic stimulations. Amphetamines create all of the above actions, plus the great excitement that comes with a "rush," which is craved by drug addicts. Weather changes trigger these "adrenal" actions as well, and I often wonder if some of us may be "weather-change addicts," getting a sort of inexpensive "rush" from atmosphere-induced adrenaline, a celestial "high." Ephedrine is less likely to raise blood pressure than adrenaline but causes unwanted excitement. And finally, adrenaline itself is usually given for symptoms of asthma or allergy; it works only if injected, and its action is rapid but short-lived. Whether injected or stimulated by the sympathetic nervous system, adrenaline appears only briefly at the nerve ends of muscles under its dominion.

Other drugs *inhibit* our response to cold weather or our sympathetic nerves. They erase, oppose, or destroy all effects of adrenaline. They are used, for instance, to treat adrenaline-induced high blood pressure. Tolazoline selectively inhibits the characteristic effects of noradrenaline, such as constriction of blood vessels, without disturbing the rest of the sympathetic system.

Both the inhibitors and the parasympathetic system follow the Law of Initial Value (see Chapter 1). The parasympathetic nervous system may be called the "loyal opposition" to the sympathetic system. It works by the release of acetylcholine from the nerve ends under its control and thereby activates its target organs. Acetylcholine is locally confined to a small area because it is rapidly destroyed. Cranial, vagus, and sacral nerves are among the parasympathetic couriers that tell appropriate muscles what to do. Thus, heartbeat *slows*, blood pressure *falls*, air flow in the lungs *slows*, and digestive-organ activity *rises*, the pupil of the eye may *constrict*, its lenses may *focus*, the bladder and rectum may *empty*, the mouth may *salivate*, and the penis may become *erect*—all at the appropriate command of the parasympathetic system. The physical expression of emotions and the sympathetic and parasympathetic nervous systems are coordinated and regulated by a gland below the inner brain chamber, the hypothalamus (discussed later in this chapter).

Other than acetylcholine, drugs act upon our warm-weather response through the parasympathetic system by imitation (carbachol), by preventing the destruction of acetylcholine (eserine), or by interference with acetylcholine (atropine) to suppress the parasympathetic nervous system (see Chapter 3).

Cold-weather stress will induce adrenal symptoms or actions of the sympathetic nervous system. But, followed by a counterreaction in the parasympathetic nervous system, acetylcholine symptoms may arise from *either* a warm front *or* the homeostatic mechanisms of counterreaction. Swings between adrenal and acetylcholine symptoms will take place by a push in either direction, conforming to Wilder's Law of Initial Value (see Chapter 1).

A normal individual will experience a cold-weather front or disturbance by all or most of these changes, at first, below consciousness: contraction of blood vessels, or vascular spasm, localized relative oxygen hunger, systolic blood pressure rise, relative blood acidosis, tissue stimulation, and, in general, an adrenal phase. (See Appendix K.) However, after a lag of minutes, hours, days, or longer, the corrective parasympathetic, or acetylcholine, phase activates itself unconsciously, as a reaction against the body's adaptation to the weather stressor. This phase may also become activated by outdoor or indoor warmth. In so doing, the following changes happen in the normal person: the blood vessels *dilate*; the diastolic blood pressure *drops*; blood pH swings toward relative *alkalosis*; the pulse rate *drops*; air flow to lungs is *reduced*. The whole elaborate process amounts to a weather-conditioned reflex.

If you are normal, this seesaw rhythm or pendulation is harmless. You may observe a change in mood or dreams. One day you may be full of vigor and pep, the next day sluggish or in the pit of depression. Perhaps you barely notice a subliminal rhythm of tension, headache, constipation, restlessness, or buoyancy. Ordinarily, these pendulations will pass without permanent or conscious effect. They are the normal companions of weathering. But suppose certain body organs are inadequate or weak, without sufficient reserves. Atmospheric stimulation of such an organ—also weathering—may cause fatigue or injury to that organ or system. The unconscious or involuntary production of high blood pressure and the body's reaction to reduce it can produce cerebral hemorrhage, thrombosis, rupture of blood vessels, aneurism, stroke, heart attack, or any other symptoms of stress (see Chapter 9). Falling blood pressure may deny vital organs their full supply of oxygen, cause sticky blood vessels, enhance blood clotting, or further complicate the clinical picture of overall health.

This recurrent tide of alkalosis and acidosis, of high and low salt content, of more and less water in the tissues, of vascular rhythms will influence the course of the infectious diseases and even mental illness. During the phase of response to stress that corresponds to greater cell or tissue permeability, microorganisms may penetrate with considerable ease. This is why rheumatism, streptococcus infections, diphtheria and influenza prevail more at certain times in certain places. Thus, passage of weather fronts will condition the organism to welcome or to reject infections. Atmospheric tides are echoed in the body's internalized biochemical tides. The biological vortex answers to the atmospheric vortex. Rhythms may change, but the program—the symphonic orchestration, the melody—lingers on.

William Petersen and neuropsychiatrist Hans Reese discovered that mental superiority and mental deficiency were regionally and seasonally distributed in patterns and thus meteorologically conditioned. The cerebral tissues bore witness to the effects of weather: stimulated by blood and oxygen flow in vasodilation, they yielded superior performance; overstimulated, they led to fatigue, insanity, and suicide; and understimulated, they produced feeble-minded behavior.

The normal, lean, linear person often shares with the schizophrenic patient many similar reactions to the weather. Both tend to suffer most during the late winter or early spring when their blood (like that of the general population) is relatively acidic. Both slender and schizophrenic people are poorly buffered against weather changes; their skin surface area preponderates over body mass; their physique and temperament express the dominance of their central nervous system (see Chapter 7). Clinical symptoms in a normal, slender person or acute psychotic episodes in the schizophrenic may appear when the blood pressure is lower after an extended period of vasoconstriction (during the cold winter), when the blood is acidic, and when the body's tissues are stimulated, overstimulated, or fatigued.

The slender person would suffer mental or physical discomfort early in life (premenstrually if female), and would suffer more often with tropical fronts and yet also be disturbed by the cold. Biological swings would be short and abrupt with sharp peaks.

The manic-depressive patient and the normal, stocky, broad, rotund person, both tending to blood alkalinity, are both afflicted with weather-related ailments most often in the summer and late autumn. What precipitates a change in mood for the normal, stocky person or an acute episode in the manic-depressive is a period of relative oxygen hunger. This coincides with vascular spasm or constriction; relative alkalosis dominates, the vessels are relatively impermeable, blood sugar is higher than normal, and the tissues are in a state of relative dehydration.

The stocky person would suffer later in life when blood vessels tend to close, and there is diminished physical activity (postmenstrually if female), when alkalinity occurs, and, paradoxically, when polar or tropical fronts prevail. The metabolic swings are longer and gentler.

Hans Reese says, "Normal mental processes require the maintenance of proper vascularization," or blood supply to the brain. Undue constriction or undue dilation of the blood vessels accompany mental disturbances. Hydration or dehydration of the tissues also change our mental functions. (Remember that hangover? That is dehydration.) The sympathetic and parasympathetic nervous system dictate those vascular changes.

Petersen conceived of the body as having two opposite states, or phases, one of which may coincide with a polar front; the other, with a tropical front (see Appendix K). Each of us swings or pendulates between these two phases or poles of normality. In health, the swings are in step with the passage of successive cool and warm air masses. In illness, the swings are out of step with the air masses, the body overshoots and over- or undercorrects. Much of Petersen's work holds up today, according to Frederick Sargent, II, an early collaborator and colleague.

The two body phases are strikingly similar to Hans Selye's picture of stress response, called the General Adaptation Syndrome. Any agent of stress will trigger the characteristic "defense," or "alarm," reaction, followed by a "resistance" reaction, and terminating in an "exhaustion" stage. *Exhaustion* and *resistance* resemble the two Petersen body states, the acetylcholine and adrenaline phases.

Suppose a long stretch of warm weather is interrupted by a sudden cold snap. You may notice that almost everyone exposed to the weather change will feel tired for a day or so and will actually sleep longer (typically up to an hour). The same happens when a person returns north after a warm southern vacation. From the Petersen vantage, the warmth induces general relaxation and a lowering of blood pressure (a tilt to the acetylcholine phase). Then the cold stress suddenly tips the body toward the tense, adrenaline phase, which consumes inner reserves of energy. From the Selye vantage, the alarm phase mobilizes resistance mechanisms and leads to fatigue. And from the Wilder vantage, the level of arousal prior to the stimulus will determine the intensity and direction of the response.

Hot and Cold

An immense array of separate traits—anatomical, biochemical, functional, behavioral—characterize *Homo sapiens*. As Frederick Sargent, II, points out, the features of human biological variation can be placed into a "hierarchy of variation," and an orderliness emerges.

Eighty-nine human traits were assembled and grouped into high, medium, and low variabilities. The maximum spread in variability for each trait (arising from differences between individuals) was compared to its minimum spread in variability. Ratios of maximum to minimum spread, called the "range ratio," were collected, reflecting the variances in 99 percent of the population.

The highest variability is found in measured human *intellectual abilities*. Next in the hierarchy of variation were the *weight of the body and its organs*. *Motor capacities* followed.

Medium variabilities are found in the cluster of *physiological functions*, *body circumference*, and *linear traits*.

But the lowest variability in the hierarchy is the *body temperature*.

"This hierarchy of variation bespeaks a precision of regulation," Sargent says. "Those traits most essential to the normal function of cells should be most closely guarded, i.e., exhibit the least variability." And those traits least essential to survival of the organism are unguarded. Body organs and organ systems regulate *internal* mechanisms and show wide variation; behavior traits regulate *external* adaptations and show the widest variance. Clearly body temperature, wandering by merely 3 percent, is the most tightly maintained.

Body temperature swings slightly during the course of a day: from noon till evening it is above normal, then it falls during sleep, one or two hours after midnight, to considerably below normal. This daily rhythm may be hormonal, as it is monthly in women.

But constancy of body temperature is a prime fact of human life. Hippocrates said that of all external changes, we are least susceptible to the change in environmental temperature (see figure on next page). How this comes about is of critical importance in understanding human response to weather elements.

The body relies upon conscious behavioral thermoregulation—by creating a microclimate with clothing or externally controlled room temperature—for efficient adaptation to a wide range of *outer* temperature ($-100°F$ [$-73.3°C$] to $+250°F$ [$+121.1°C$]). But *body* temperatures above $110°F$ or ($43.3°C$) below $82°F$ ($27.8°C$) for extended periods of time can inactivate thermoregulation and prove fatal. Most efficient involuntary self-regulation lies a few degrees above or below the normal body temperature of $98.6°F$ ($37°C$).

In hot weather or at high body temperatures, thermoregulation sends body heat out to the body's surface. Warm blood is delivered to blood vessels lying under the skin near the body's surface or periph-

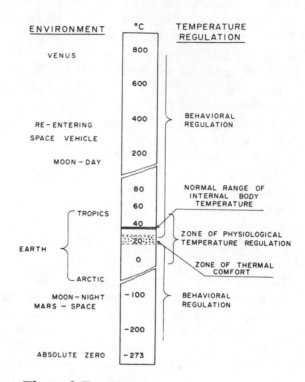

The Human Thermal Experience
The environment ranges over great extremes (left). Temperature regulation by physiological adjustments is limited (to 0–50°C), compared to behavioral thermoregulation.

ery. We say a "warm" personality is "expansive." In effect, the body's "thermal profile" expands.

In cool weather or at low temperatures, body heat in the form of warm blood is shunted to the internal organs in the central trunk, the torso and viscera: a "cold" person "shrinks" from the cold. In effect, our thermal profile *contracts*.

These *involuntary* mechanisms "fine-tune" the body temperature by means of the involuntary nervous system, special areas of the brain (the hypothalamus), the heart, and a wide array of ingenious defenses against temperature change. Failure to equilibrate temperature properly brings prompt and disabling reprisals. The hypothalamus commands peripheral blood vessels, via acetylcholine, to dilate; and via adrenaline, to constrict. *Prolonged vasodilation* may cause swelling of hands and feet, low blood pressure, difficulty in breathing, skin irritations, headache, increased sensations of warmth or heat; the greater heart and pulse actions may cause throbbing. These warm-weather conditions are also present in adaptations to warm climate. *Prolonged vasoconstriction* may cause dry, irritated, and chapped skin, frostbite, joint stiffness and pain, low oxygen content in tissues (which cause cramps and tissue damage), and intense sensations of cold in hands, feet, ears, and nose. These symptoms are found in both cold climates and cold weather.

Aristotle, and later, John Locke, said that we live our lives motivated by pleasure on one side and pain on the other. (Both urged us to educate ourselves to be "pleased" by moral and virtuous acts, and "pained" by immoral and wicked behavior.) Some speculate that the "warm-cold" dichotomy predisposes the suckling infant later in life to "comprehend" all sorts of opposite polarities: heaven and hell, right and wrong, good and evil, true and false, right and left, desire and hate. The sensations "hot" and "cold" may begin the long ascent of the fetus to adult concepts of "pleasure" versus "pain."

Thermoregulation mobilizes major elements of the anatomy of the skin; the skin, therefore, may be called the special sense organ of the involuntary nervous system since nineteen to twenty-five square feet of skin separates the body from the environment. Millions of nerve endings can sense skin temperature changes as small as one-hundredth of a degree Celsius. These changes may arise from heat flowing across the skin barrier to or from the environment, as a result of fluctuations in the skin's blood supply, or from environmental temperature shifts. Temperature-sensing nerves send their impulses to the brain, which can instruct the sweat glands to produce sweat, the skeletal musculature to produce extra heat by shivering, the heart to increase or decrease blood flow, the vascular bed to dilate or shrink, the respiratory system to pant.

Our central nervous system has neural pathways to pass skin-temperature information to the sensory cortex for conscious appraisal. Once there, our hypothalamus has special temperature sensors and a neuron network for consolidating all of these signals into demands for action, behavioral or physiological, that will adjust the energy balance between skin and environment. The elements of thermoregulation incorporate so many feedback loops and elaborate interconnections, that the entire system can be described as truly impressive. If an electronic circuit were to simulate these functions, it might resemble the hypothetical regulatory system shown on the following page.

REGULATORY SYSTEM FOR BODY TEMPERATURE IN MAN
(HYPOTHETICAL)

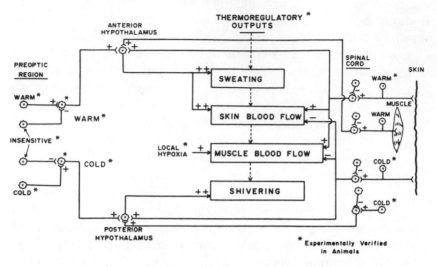

A portion of the neural interconnections needed to devise a computer analogy to human thermoregulation.

Actual transport of warm blood from the working muscles to the internal organs, or heat transfer by convection, is on demand. The vasomotor system diverts a small portion of cardiac blood output to the skin during exercise or heat exposure, and may change the thermal conductance of skin by almost tenfold, a remarkable variability.

But this may strain the capabilities of certain body organs or individuals to adapt. A person suffering cardiovascular disease may be stressed by involuntary or behavioral thermoregulation to a state of dysfunction, disease, exhaustion, fatigue, or death. Almost every intrinsic ailment is potentially vulnerable to *thermoregulatory* strain and, therefore, a target of *weather* stress.

Comfort and Temperature

Language, of course, celebrates our subjective sensations in familiar terms. A *sunny smile* or *disposition* is cheerful, joyous, warm, and pleasant. A *cold smile* or *disposition*, like *cold blood*, is forbidding, unsympathetic, ominous; it *chills*. Being *cool* used to mean unresponsive or self-controlled *under fire*, but now it may mean acceptable or good—especially among young people. A *hot-tempered* or *hot-blooded* person may be unstable, gets angry too easily. And a person who *runs hot and cold* may be ambivalent or unreliable or unpredictable. Television has been called the *cool fire*, a *cool medium* of communications. Robert Frost's poem "Fire and Ice" suggests that a *fiery desire* and *icy hate* are not only destructive extremes of existence but very personal choices as well.

When the background air temperature is about 86°F (30°C), most people subjectively estimate it as "pleasant" or "comfortable" or a "neutral" temperature. These are three different subjective dimensions. As air temperatures increase beyond warm to hot or decrease beyond cool to cold, subjective perceptions shift to "uncomfortable" and "unpleasant." We use such words as "comfort," "pleasantness," and "temperature" to respond to objective background air-temperature changes. "Comfort" changes *least* with air-temperature changes and "pleasantness" changes *most* sharply (see Figure below).

Subjective thermal "neutrality" (absence of either subjective sensation—warmth or cold) lies at the same air temperature as does subjective "pleasant" and "comfortable." This is important because these *subjective* conditions (at 30°C, 86°F) correspond to a specific *objective* condition: *absence* of thermoregulatory effort, such as vasoconstriction, vasodilation, sweating, or shivering.

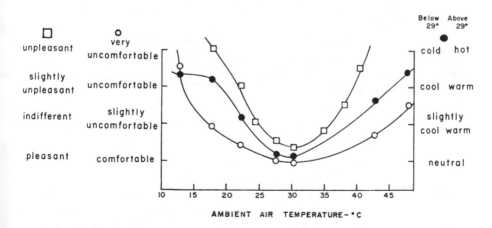

Our Response to Temperature
Subjective estimates of Pleasantness (□), Comfort (○), and Temperature (●) vary considerably with surrounding air temperature.

The sense of discomfort increases faster for changes below than for changes above thermal neutrality. The subjective sensations of comfort and temperature can be predicted on objective measurements of average skin temperature, body temperature, and evaporation.

But when rapid changes take place in surrounding air as a result of transient breezes, our subjective senses of comfort and temperature are *anticipatory*, leading the body itself. Although this "thermal foresight" is usually absent in warm surroundings, Yale physiologist James Hardy discovered it is most pronounced in cold surroundings.

Thermal discomfort is an early warning signal to take conscious action to modify the body's microclimate by "coarse," long-term thermal adjustments. But the early warnings of discomfort also subliminally cue the body in to making physiological adjustments ("fine-tuning"), or making short-term temperature alterations that continuously change and consume body energy itself.

Production, Storage, Loss

Chemical energy is converted into heat inside the body by combustion of carbohydrates, fats, and proteins. The body heat *stored* depends upon the body heat *produced* minus the body heat *lost*. Produced heat comes from metabolism of fuels. And heat is lost by physical work, by evaporation of fluids, and (in cool environments) by radiation, convection, or conduction.

Venture forth into cold weather, and conserving heat, your warm body fluids sink into your viscera, often precipitating a strong urge to urinate (temporary diuresis). In cold weather, in the absence of fluid removal by sweating, urine volume can triple. Not only is the fluid lost, but its heat content as well.

Relative paucity of peripheral blood (due to this cold-weather vasoconstriction) provides effective insulation for the body's core. But if a person returns to a warm room it may so rapidly trigger vasodilation that the subsequent rush of cold peripheral blood may chill so large a volume of blood returning to the heart that it may cause trouble there. Disturbances of natural heart rhythm, or collapse and nausea are possible. The internal organs and torso of severely chilled people must be warmed rapidly to prevent this; prompt immersion in a tub of hot water (104°F to 123°F; 40°C to 44°C) is the simplest method.

Loss of the body's core heat by exposure to cold ocean water for an extended period can be extremely painful to recover from. A capsized sailboat in relatively warm water one May for a mere half hour led me to uncontrollable shivering and shaking for several hours thereafter, despite heroic attempts at rewarming. Hot fluids and a shower helped, but a hot bath is the best measure.

Metabolism produces heat mainly in the body's trunk, despite the fact that the bulk of body mass (about 60 percent) residues in the muscle and skin. At rest (according to Stolwijk and Hardy) over half the body's heat is produced in the central organs of the trunk and viscera, which constitute only a third of the body mass. The muscles generate only 18 percent of the total heat production at rest, but during exercise or work the muscles take up the job of body heat production yielding 90 percent of the total. Thus exercise moves the body's heat production from its core to its peripheral muscles where it is controllable, under the skin, by the vasomotor system of constriction and dilation of the capillary bed. Depending on age, sex, physique, size, and the type of exercise, work, emotions, or weather experienced, a body's heat output can range from a resting low of one 75- or 100-watt light bulb to an energetic high of some sixteen 100-watt light bulbs.

Heat enters or leaves the human body by three mechanisms (familiar to students of physics): radiation, conduction, or convection. Radiation, or radiant energy, can pass from a hot object like the sun to a cool object like the earth with no intervening medium between them. Only the (absolute) temperature of each object and its surface matters. A perfectly absorbing object, like an open window which reflects nothing, is defined technically as a *black body*. Human skin and a nonglossy (matte), black surface are both 97 percent black bodies; for comparison, a polished copper surface absorbs 10 or 20 percent of radiant energy directed on it, reflecting the rest. Human skin reflects different colors of light differently in the visible portions of the spectrum, but both white and black skins reflect infrared radiation in the same way. (From an energy-transfer standpoint, James Hardy says "all skin is black in the dark," meaning that energy absorption and reflection is identical.)

Heat spontaneously flows from a higher-temperature object in contact with a lower-temperature object. An object "hot" to the touch conducts heat from itself to the skin; cold objects feel "cold" when heat is conducted from the skin to the object. So a marble tabletop at room temperature will feel colder than a wooden one by virtue of its greater thermal conductivity.

The ability of a substance to conduct heat—or its inverse, to insulate—depends upon its composition. Metals like silver are very good thermal conductors and poor thermal insulators. Silver is perhaps a thousand times better heat *conductor* than water or human muscle and bone. Put another way, water, muscle, and bone are a thousand times better heat *insulators* than silver. Fat is twice as good an insulator as muscle and bone. Hence, women's thicker fat layers give them an insulation advantage over men (Japanese pearl divers are often women). And air is some twenty times better insulation than muscle and bone.

Behavioral regulation of body temperature demands an insulating substance—clothing in humans, fur in animals, and feathers in birds. Natural fur and feathers and garments are excellent variable insulators. The total insulation ability of layered clothing is the sum of the insulation values of each layer (see Chapter 3).

Warm air rising from the skin is called natural convection, and cooling the skin in a fan or wind is called forced convection. That thin air layer clinging tightly to your skin as a sort of private microclimate thins out with increased wind speed or body curvature (see Chapter 6). Convection is the actual transport of warm blood to the skin, and it is the body's main method of equilibrating its temperature in changing environments. Entering or leaving a warm room on a cold day or an air-conditioned one on a hot day will shunt warm blood to and from the skin, in barely noticeable efforts to acclimatize.

Permeance of clothing fabrics to water vapor is a critical factor in thermal regulation, winter and summer, since water vapor is a fluid that carries heat energy with it physically when departing the skin's surface. Sweating eliminates heat rapidly, through some 2 to 2.5 million sweat glands distributed over our nineteen to twenty-five square feet of skin area. Moisture leaving the skin and respiratory tract also carries away heat, depending on relative humidity and temperature of the surrounding air.

In the winter, in airplanes, or at high altitudes, respiratory evaporation will dry out mucous membranes. This may be countered temporarily in a dry room (but not defeated) by boiling water or by drinking water copiously, or both. In the summer, moist skin cools faster when air moves across it. Sweating or wetting cools insofar as it covers skin areas, but once moisture drips off the body, it does not promote evaporative cooling.

The combined effect of temperature and humidity on personal

comfort is curious. It has been found that *damp* cold feels subjectively colder than *dry* cold, despite objective evidence to the contrary. Clearly comfort depends upon the rate at which the environment removes heat *and* moisture from the skin. Two indices of "how hot it feels" are the temperature-humidity index (T.H.I.) and the "effective temperature." "There is little guidance to be received from the T.H.I.," says James Hardy, "and its basis is not secured by physiological and psychological data, as is the scale of effective temperature." The "effective temperature" reflects subjective sensations of warmth at high and low objective humidities and temperatures; it can predict and prevent heat exhaustion and heat stroke, and guide physical activities, exercise, and exertion.

Our subjective sensations are often paradoxically connected to objective weather conditions. Thus, the need for increased or decreased warmth *indoors* seems to depend on the temperature *outdoors*, according to an experiment by Andris Auliciems. Over 600 teenage school children in Reading, England, recorded their daily, subjective impressions of indoor warmth an hour or so after entering their classroom, mornings and afternoons, for about a year. Their personal impressions of indoor thermal comfort were examined by a sophisticated computer analysis of objective, outdoor weather conditions.

Apart from indoor warmth itself, the single most significant outdoor atmospheric correlate of indoor comfort was outdoor temperature. The startling result is that the school children wanted *higher* indoor temperatures on a *warm* day and sought *cooler* indoor temperatures on a *cool* day. The effect was stronger for girls than boys.

The energy savings of this finding are considerable. Turning up indoor thermostats on warmer days and turning them down on colder days sounds like a gift from heaven. How much up or down depends on the outdoor temperature. But even a gift calls for an explanation.

Under warm *outdoor* conditions (like summer), subjects *under*estimated indoor warmth and wanted room temperatures higher; under cold *outdoor* conditions (like winter) they *over*estimated *indoor* warmth and wanted room temperatures lower. Estimating warmth after being cold outdoors may simply mean that additional clothing was worn on cool days. Certainly vasoconstriction, triggered by outdoor cold, can remain partially in effect indoors for some time. Indeed, Auliciems discovered subjective estimates of personal comfort were associated with outdoor temperature *three days earlier*. (On any day students wanted the classroom cooler if the outside had been warm three days earlier; and warmer inside if outside had been cool three days earlier.) On warm outdoor days, subjects tended to *overestimate* the indoor warmth *three days later*; perhaps relative vasodilation lasts for days. A cold outdoor day leads to an *under*estimate of indoor warmth three days later; relative vasoconstriction may also linger for days.

Your "Thermal Space"

The capacity of skin to emit and detect infrared or radiant heat is very high—so high that we can send and receive subliminal messages by changes in skin temperature over various parts of the body. Emotional states may be thermally signaled by blood-warmth changes in different parts of the body.

You will sense someone's body temperature by your skin's thermal detectors, if you are close enough; by greater olfactory signals (high temperature will increase perfume or skin-lotion evaporation); and by the sight of skin color. Edward Hall says that when young he would observe some of his female dancing partners were hotter or colder than average, and the temperature of the same girl would change from time to time. When he found himself establishing a thermal "rapport," and "getting interested without really knowing why," the young lady would invariably suggest that it was time to "get some air"—that is, to "cool off." Years later, he discovered that females were quite familiar with this effect. One said that she could tell, even at a distance of three to six feet in the dark, whether her boyfriend was feeling anger or lust. According to Hall, the temperature rise of the abdomen is a very early indication of sexual excitement.

The blush of embarrassment, the "slow burn," the "cold sweat," the damp palms, the "flush" of passion—all are thermoregulatory adjustments by which the body expresses emotions.

How a person experiences a crowd also depends on temperature. A hot crowd needs more room than a cool one. People stay farther apart on a warm day than on a cool day.

Some people hate to sit on an upholstered chair immediately after it has been vacated by someone else. "We do not know why one's own heat is not objectionable," says Hall, "and a stranger's is." People seem to respond negatively to an unfamiliar pattern of heat. And body heat is highly personal, intimate, and sexual.

"Hot under the collar," "a cold stare," a "heated argument," "he warmed up to her"—these thermal figures of speech betoken the universal experience of temperature, our common thermal sensibility.

Your lips and the back of your hand generate heat and are sensitive to it. With your eyes closed, move the back of your hand across your face at different distances, concentrating on the thermal sensations from your face and from your hand. At a certain distance, a few inches or less, you are aware of the sensation. You may even train yourself to seek thermal "cues" from others, to improve your temperature sense, and delineate your "thermal space."

Temperature Sensing

Temperature governs the speed at which chemical and biochemical reactions—which drive life processes—take place. Hence cellular activity will change with temperature, in special cells, manyfold for a few degrees. These specialized cells, then, are actually temperature detectors, located in the skin, the deep viscera, the spinal cord, parts of the brain (the hypothalamus) and brain stem, the tongue, respiratory tract, medulla, and possibly other yet unexplored areas.

Temperature sensing and regulation go on in a special region of the brain, the hypothalamus (literally "under the inner chamber"). Removal of the hypothalamus of "warm-blooded" animals makes them "cold-blooded." Parts of it are found by experiment to be more than normally temperature-sensitive. When probed and heated, a small region increased its neural discharge rate as the hypothalamic temperature changed. Other experiments show temperature changes in this region also bring about *behavioral* temperature regulation: animals will cool this part of their brain stem if their environment is heated. This preoptic region of the hypothalamus (as it is called) and the "reticular formation" are clearly important in thermoregulation— both physiological and behavioral. The reticular formation is a tangled net of nerve cells and fibers in the brain stem, which switches impulses from the body's periphery to the appropriate pathways in the brain.

The hypothalamus is a spontaneous unifying center. It controls our emotions, moods, thermal regulation, sexual activity, metabolism, growth, energy production and release, and our response to stress.

The hypothalamus is located in the front part of the brain between the two cerebral hemispheres, and it is connected by nerve fibers to almost all parts of the nervous system. Its functions are bewildering in their diversity:

- Regulation of the autonomic nervous system, especially the response of the heart and visceral organs to emotion
- Alteration of emotions and mood, such as excitement and depression
- Regulation of body temperature
- Control of appetite and thirst
- Increasing the blood flow to muscles during exercise
- Control of the pituitary glands; with their two berry-like lobes hung suspended from the brain floor, they are the complex governors of all other endocrine (ductless) glands.

There are complex circuits between the pituitary, the adrenal, the hypothalamus, and back to the pituitary. The hypothalamus is the link between the nervous system and the endocrine glands. The sum and substance of this extraordinary linked chain is the maintenance of our thermal *status quo* in a changing thermal environment.

Any ingested medicines, like psychopharmacological drugs, that act on the hypothalamus, midbrain, or brain stem—that in any way block the body's normal temperature regulation once inside your body—will be a temperature-sensitive or weather-dependent drug. These drugs and their usage (see Chapter 3 and Appendix F for a list) must be carefully monitored by physician and patient during specified weather conditions, for exposure to too much heat, cold, or sunshine will modify the drugs' action in the body and may prove disastrous.

Speculations

The history of man's weather sense is also a history of the hypothalamus. For inescapably and repeatedly, the conscious and subconscious manifestations of its function appear. A religious figure like Zeus, or Coyote, or Prometheus embodies many of the traits governed by the hypothalamus. Zeus is not only the controller of weather and a ladies' man but the maker of heat and cold, of good and bad fortune, and the begetter of those human attributes found in his offspring (see Chapter 8). He also personifies stress and stress resistance, both in individuals and in groups.

The stress syndrome in individuals has its counterpart in groups. Psychologists used to maintain that a group of individuals, acting together, function quite often as a single person acting alone. The various potentialities for action, at odds in the individual's conscience, are seen as opposing camps in a group decision. This notion probably holds up fairly well.

Consider a massive disaster like a snowstorm, tornado, a heat wave, or for that matter, a blackout. Those who have studied disaster situations—like sociologists or disaster novelists—find similar patterns of individual and group response to the disaster: *warning, threat, impact, inventory, rescue, remedy,* and *recovery.* Examine disaster novels (or large-scale personal disaster experiences) and this progression, with minor variations, will stamp the event.

Elmer Luchterhand relates a carefully documented study of the Arkansas tornado of 1952, which exposed 1,500 people, killed 46, and injured 615. Six hours before it struck, a tornado *warning* was broadcast. But the *threat* was perceived no more than a few minutes in advance of *impact* for some two-thirds of the population in danger. After the tornado had disrupted communications, community structure was fragmented, and normal controls disappeared. Within a half hour, an *inventory* was begun, showing that a third of the women and 5 percent of the men were "stunned." Nevertheless, half of the capable men nearby began to join *rescue* efforts. Outside helpers and sightseers converged on the scene (hindering transportation of wounded) to help *rescue* and provide a *remedy* for sufferers. An upsurge of neighborliness, goodwill, and helpfulness was observed; people actually brought gifts from many far-off states to assist in the *recovery.* Some 90 percent of the adults living in the impact area suffered psychological or physical disturbances: "loss of appetite, difficulties sleeping, headache, difficulties in concentration, extreme sensitivity to storm signs, and general nervousness." One-sixth in the disaster area reported some effect on their ability to work.

These symptoms are strikingly similar to weather-stress symptoms, or the syndrome of weather-sensitivity. They are common stress symptoms, whether from physical exertion, emotional trauma, weather changes, or disasters. This homeostatic reaction to stress does not have to be pushed very far as speculation to be convincing.

Effects of Stress—Physical, Emotional, Weather, and Disaster

	Physical Stress	Emotional Stress	Weather (Thermal) Stress	Disaster Stress
Trigger:	work, jogging, intercourse	crisis, anger, fear	cold front, warm front	tornado, blizzard, war, warning, threat
Stages:	adrenaline phase	alarm	thermal profile *shrinks* (vasoconstriction)	impact, inventory
	acetylcholine phase	resistance	thermal profile *expands* (vasodilation)	rescue
	fatigue	flight/fight	fatigue	remedy
	exhaustion	fatigue	exhaustion	recovery
	relaxation	exhaustion	dysfunction	homeostasis
	recuperation	recuperation	recuperation	
	homeostasis	homeostasis	homeostasis	
Systems Activated:	muscles (hypothalamus)	endocrine	endocrine	volunteers
		nervous (hypothalamus)	nervous (hypothalamus)	healers
			using ice to relieve frostbite	militia
Wilder's Law of Initial Value: (examples)	"second wind"	"blushing," trauma-resistance, susceptibility		"backlash" in public issue–attention cycle
Malignant Effects: (Dys-stress)	deteriorating tissues	mental illness schizophrenia psychosis paranoia	overstimulation understimulation meteoropathologies	sleeplessness fear inability to work
Benign Effects: (Eu-stress)	strength longevity adaptability stress resistance	growth resolution maturation	stimulation acclimatization habituation enhanced performance acuity energy productivity	altruistic community response "postdisaster utopia" "routinized zest"

244

Paradoxes of Weather-Sensitivity:
Natural Selection and Genius

Natural selection is the process by which the weak species dwindle, the stronger species flourish, the fittest survive. But fitness or strength is adaptability, a talent for homeostasis. So natural selection operates on homeostasis, choosing those races, species, and individuals who are most gifted at absorbing environmental challenges or assaults and equilibrating in spite of them.

Weather-sensitivity from this point of view provides cues for homeostasis. Does this mean that the more weather-sensitive (or unstable) an individual is, the more fully homeostatic he is. Paradoxically, weather-sensitivity (thus instability), and homeostatic talent for survival are tightly linked. Recall that women are significantly more weather-sensitive and live significantly longer than men. Does this mean that superior feminine weather-sensitivity has survival value? Other factors clearly operate. But women can stand the stress of heat and cold more than men, although they may complain more than men. Slender people, who are more weather-sensitive than others by virtue of their greater surface area, also live longer, according to life-insurance mortality tables.

The fact that the very young and the elderly are more weather-sensitive than the middle-aged is because their organs may not work at full capacity (see Chapter 2). For them, weather-sensitivity may not evoke the full homeostatic response and hence full survivability. Perhaps weather-sensitivity due to age should have its own special name, since it is organ deterioration that it reflects. As far as socioeconomic class is concerned, weather-sensitivity in the upper and lower classes is greater than in the middle class. Does that bespeak high homeostatic talent in response to great class-dependent stress? This form of weather-sensitivity, like race-dependent weather-sensitivity, needs a name to differentiate it from the others as well.

The species that are the most weather-sensitive, Bernard Primault says, are those that have evolved the furthest. For instance, roses with the best color and perfume evolve under artificial weather conditions; you increase their weather-sensitivity because of selection as a step in evolution.

The more complex the metabolism and physiology—the more selectivity in the body's needs, in the food supply, in the climatic influences. Human beings could no more eat what their predecessors ate five thousand years ago than today's Texan cow (who could not survive a few weeks in natural conditions away from man) could survive on a bison's diet. By habitation with man, cows are one or two steps more weather-sensitive than their predecessors (like bison). The same is true of dogs, cats, parakeets, nuts, and wine grapes.

The further from nature or natural conditions we are, ironically, the more weather-sensitive we become. Once adapted to air conditioning, we struggle harder to resist the aggressive assaults of hot weather. Yet in close contact with weather, the body both defends and stimulates itself. So man can not only *resist* weather's aggression, but he *needs* it, in symbiosis.

Is weather-sensitivity a blessing or a curse? Can the question be answered? Several answers are needed.

First, thermal sensitivity is equivalent to thermal indifference. What this means is that sensitivity and indifference to heat or cold are merely two aspects of a paradox. Recall that the most closely guarded human trait of all was body temperature by mobilizing a full array of body responses. Sensitivity is necessary for indifference—at least in human thermodynamics. It is that mysterious hypothalamus which seems to rule out thermal indifference, thermal sensitivity, our unconscious involuntary behavior, and subliminal emotions.

Emotional and physiological discomfort under heat or cold is the price we pay for thermal stability and neutrality. But we may pay a steeper price. Heat and cold are among the first sensations of the embryo, or the fetus. (Experiments show that they may react violently to injections of cold medicinal fluids.) Cold and heat are therefore the first "lessons," in a thermal sense, the hypothalamus "learns." As its thermal experience deepens, the hypothalamus develops a concurrent emotional response, and the hot-cold polarity asserts itself. Subconsciously, the activities of the hypothalamus are felt in the process of temperature regulation; consciously, in ordering us to curl up or dress to conserve heat. The growing infant makes a long journey into a world of ever-widening polarities that "heat" and "cold" were merely preparations and models for or symbols of. Pleasure and pain, good and evil, logic and emotion, future and past, left and right—all are perceived as dichotomies that may express an intrinsic thermal sensitivity or indifference, at different levels of consciousness. In this sense, weather-sensitivity—thermal sensitivity—like emotional sensitivity, is both a curse and a blessing.

The second answer ties weather-sensitivity to population and weather changes. Examining large masses of population data on large numbers of species, K. E. F. Watt has discovered a result that may be difficult to grasp. A species-evolved sensitivity to weather is crucial to its homeostasis. A homogeneous specialized species will be very sensitive to small changes in its environment, and its population will fluctuate in number far more than a species that has evolved an insensitivity to weather in a widely fluctuating environment. That is, widely fluctuating population changes may be the way a species survives external change, inadequately homeostatic members yielding to weather-stress—induced exhaustion; and adequately buffered members being stimulated by stress of weather, like cold-dwellers. Large population swings reflect "balanced polymorphism," a large amount of individual variance in a species; and this keeps the species balanced against stagnation and change. Evolved weather-insensitivity to large, stressful changes in weather leads to small population changes and probably overstimulation. It is the combination of sensitivity and stimulation that matters for the *long-term* survival of the species. True, weather-sensitivity may be a short-term inconvenience day to day, but it is the hypothalamus' way of replicating itself on a long-term basis.

The third paradox of weather-sensitivity is its link to genius. Many talented achievers in the arts, sciences, politics, the military and virtually every area of human endeavor are weather-sensitive; and many geniuses also "happen" to be unusually weather-sensitive. Byron, Dante, da Vinci, Goethe, Michelangelo, Napoleon, Mozart, Voltaire—to name a few—were distinctly "under the spell of weather." Their exquisite weather-sensitivity has been chronicled by their friends; it has shown itself in their work or in their own experiences or self-acknowledged sensitivity to weather.

Among 16,000 paintings done between 1400 and 1967, meteorologist Hans Neuberger found that 53 percent of these art works depicted meteorological information. He concluded that the artist, as a conscious or subconscious chronicler of his environment, the climate and weather—an all-pervasive agent in human activity—reveals the artist's deep experiences and expressions of that environment. (This is merely suggestive, not proof.) In a standard anthology of great poems, 56 percent allude to weather elements. Vivaldi, Haydn, Tchaikovsky and Glazunov have composed musical tributes to the seasons. Prokofiev, Debussy, Rimsky-Korsakov, Stravinsky, Cole Porter, and Stephen Sondheim—and other geniuses—have incorporated weather imagery into their art. Beethoven's *Pastorale*, or Sixth Symphony, written directly on the score itself, has wind, rain, thunder, and lightning. Shakespeare calls the sky "this most excellent canopy, the air, this brave o'er hanging firmament, this majestical roof fretted with golden fire."

As startling and bizarre as it may at first appear, the coincidence of genius with profound weather-sensitivity may not be merely chance. Probably the best (perhaps the only) argument for associating genius and weather-sensitivity has been made by William Petersen, citing data on 1,300 geniuses from 1600 to 1950. (He raises additional hypotheses even more difficult to accept: that genius and leadership occur in cycles, that these cycles coincide with climatic and seasonal cycles related to environmental strain—their month of death, for instance, often coincides with their month of birth.) That geniuses are more than usually susceptible to the environment is a proposition I wish to make plausible (not prove—that would be another book at least).

I have been privileged to know and work with several geniuses. At first hand I have observed what several psychological studies have suggested. Among other qualities, genius seems to be distinguished by a kind of "disinhibition"—a remarkable, sometimes excuciating, sublime, intimacy with the surrounding world. That milieu may be social, political, verbal, musical, visual, tactile, gustatory, olfactory— or meteorological. This environmental intimacy—a "cosmic" or "oceanic" feeling, that implies whatever it is (the superego?) that acts as a screen between the personal, inner "weather" and the objective, outer weather—is permeable, or absent, in the genius.

"I am what is around me," says the poet Wallace Stevens, and that describes this feeling simply and eloquently. When Byron says, "I am always more religious on a sunshiney day," is he referring to that cosmic intimacy?

Shakespeare was acutely aware when he spoke of those "tides in the affairs of men"—surely atmospheric tides, or what he called "skyey influences," that importuned our creaturehood.

Goethe had a cyclic "feeling" for the barometer, alternating periods of enormous productivity with humdrum routine and depression. In 1926, a German, F. Krause, referred to such extraordinary individuals—Nietzsche and Proust were others—as *Tiefenpersonen*, that is, deep or profound persons. These are people, according to Petersen, whose "autonomic and subconscious phases are closely interwoven with the inorganic world . . . and particularly in the genius . . . may be so pronounced that the individual becomes clearly conscious of it." His mind and body are conditioned not only by exceptional experiences, but by the routine experience of *weather*.

One of the more exasperating qualities of genius is their uncanny or mysterious ability to be "right" without knowing why, or without the normal proof and data that the rest of us need to buttress an argument. Perhaps geniuses are frustrating to non-geniuses because they are so mysterious. (Geniuses often show us they perceive truth not only because they may discover truth, but also because they are so convincing and persuasive.)

It is not clear whether this quality of genius (or weather-sensitivity, either, for that matter) predisposes a genius for survival. If they survive their first decade or so, geniuses appear to thrive, accomplish great things, and enjoy life. I would argue that it is likely though unproven that genius and weather-sensitivity are often found in the same person. If so, how would such an association come about? On several different levels I can make it plausible.

First, natural selection would select out from our ancestors, who wandered northward mile after mindless mile, only those who were "smart" enough to get in out of the cold or rain. They would cleverly warm themselves with animal furs or hide in caves or otherwise buffer their bodies' thermal homeostasis with behavioral equilibrations. They would live to "tell" how they did it, to spread the doctrine of "thermal habituation"; and in so doing might become leaders.

Second, natural selection would select those individuals whose hypothalamus worked well. Since it governs thermal regulation, emotions, dreams, moods, the unconscious, perhaps the imagination or "creativity"—to that extent would those hypothalamically well-endowed creatures survive and thrive.

Third, sleep and dreams may be conditioned (to an unknown extent) by weather situations. Dreams in which the weather is incorporated as background to the dream story, or content, are common, but dreaming of weather as a primary element of the dream is rare (unless you happen to be a meteorologist). Analysis of some 25,000 dreams turns up the following ranking of dreams' sensory content: most frequent are visual stimuli, followed by auditory, kinesthetic, tactile, gustatory, and olfactory. Sense organs consciously and directly respond to primary meteorological factors—temperature, humidity (not barometric pressure), rain, snow—so they trigger dreams and become transposed into sensory imagery. (Dream content shows greater differences on account of the dreamer's sex than because of age, race, education, marital status, or socioeconomic status.)

Visual and auditory subconscious aside, there is evidence for an "olfactory subconscious" (electrical skin resistance, blood pressure, respiratory and pulse rates all change during nonconscious exposure to smell), and for a "gustatory subconscious" (during adrenal insufficiency, your conscious taste sensitivity can rise by a factor of 60,000). Just as there are prodigies of visual and auditory senses (called painters or musical geniuses), there are "prodigies of smell" and "prodigies of taste." A famous physiologist was able to differentiate adults by smell, to identify change in odor due to exercise, states of emotional excitement, menstruation, and diseases. A professional perfumer can distinguish the odors of moods; he knows the "smell of fear" from the "smell of anger."

If there is olfactory and gustatory subconsciousness, and prodigies of smell and taste, then is there not a meteorological subconscious and prodigies of meteorological sensitivity? There are, and I think they are called geniuses.

Fourth, weather stress itself might directly stimulate the brain's performance by vascularization and its concomitant oxygenation and deoxygenation of brain tissues. Denied oxygen, brain tissue suffers; cells may cease to function briefly or for an extended period, causing a stroke. Frequent, slight interruptions of oxygen supply may occur constantly in most of us, perhaps reflected in instantaneous lapses of memory or the like.

Studies of the human brain reveal that each of us is not a single individual—but we are really two individuals joined together. Each hemisphere of the brain sees the same objective world, but each possesses an essentially different emotional version of the world. The left brain hemisphere (which controls motor functions of the body's right side) is responsible for speech and language, reading, writing, arithmetic, sequential processing of information, serial analysis over time, digital logic, perception of detail, and vigilance. The right brain hemisphere (controlling the body's left side) is responsible for three-dimensional vision, pattern recognition, holistic reasoning, nonverbal ideation, meditative states typical of Oriental religions, and simultaneous processing of information, or parallel analysis in time.

"Mind left" drives the "hand right"; and "mind right" drives the "hand left." The attributes of right or left down through the ages, are of considerable interest, as David MacRae shows:

Left is about emotion: the heart, the seat of emotion in our culture, is on the left: Right is about reason. Left is sinister (literally), while right is right and law. Left, then, is heteronomous and heterodox, while Right is autonomous but also orthodox. Right is the prompt side of the stage, and, therefore, about direction and instruction; Left is feminine and labile where Right is masculine and firm. Left is clumsy. . . . Left is weak; Right, "I'd rather be right," strong. The sacred, the dead and death itself are all associated with Left; and it is at the Christian Judgement, the direction of damnation; it is also the side of the *fall* of the damned in much iconography of the Last Judgement. Right is the side of salvation, the ascension, the manifestation—back to the familiar puns of ordinary language—of salvation and of life. But Left is also sacred, while Right is secular and commonplace . . . Left is weak, is less, is "off," and Right is strong, more, and "on." (Think about the directions in which the switches, controls, knobs, of familiar technical devices like gramophones, cameras, cars, etc. all operate.) Right is clockwise while Left is widdershins. The Right is stable and preserving—the Right hand of God is the hand that preserves. Does it follow that Left is about novelty and change? Certainly the Left is *pliable* and therefore perhaps innovatory; it is also expressive in social metaphors.

These attributes of left and right do not seem to be identical in all cultures, MacRae points out, but they are consistent enough to see universal social attitudes toward them in all human groups. Thus the left is associated with awkward, weak, gauche, sinister, fantasy, imagination, novelty, and change. And the right is associated with reason, correctness, firmness, certainty, orthodox, stability, energy, nerve, and "ahead."

But now consider the distinction between cooler-climate and warmer-climate peoples (see Chapter 4). Vigor, aggression, persistence, bravery, physical strength, large, good, healthy, avoiding of sexual indulgences—all characterize the northern temperate zone peoples, those with cool but variable environments. These traits are reminiscent here of others: mind Left (vigilance), hand Right (strength). The tropical, constantly warm-climate peoples are characterized as timid, frail, weak, effeminate, lazy, inclined to physical pleasure, reflective pursuits, emotionally less stable or less dependable, given to lassitude, mysticism, and domination of imagination over reason. Certainly there is a considerable overlap residing in these warm-climate traits (timid, reflective, effeminate), in mind Right (creativity, meditative states), and hand Left (fantasy, imagination).

What I am suggesting, tentatively, *very* speculatively, is that the considerable overlap of three sets of opposing traits—mind, handedness, climate—is no coincidence. Certainly, not the first two; there are neural connections; even the eye movements betray split-brain functioning. But with them and climate, how could that happen, if true? Natural selection again? I am not sure. This is speculation based on similarities of clustered traits and their polarities.

There is another polarity that seems to overlap the climate dichotomy and left or right mindedness and handedness. That is the duality of emotional traits associated with the past versus the future—hindsight personalities versus foresight personalities (see Chapter Notes).

There are three dualities: 1. (a) mindedness and (b) handedness; 2. climatological or thermal; 3. hindsight and foresight.

At the intersection of all three dualities are the traits "achievement *versus* imagination," "masculinity *versus* femininity," and "strength *versus* weakness." They are universal, age-old friendly antagonists . . . loving adversaries, like mankind and the weather.

Fire, Ice, and Inner Weather: A Summary

Exercise or physical stress elevates the levels of muscle fuels, which are then consumed by subsequent muscular effort. Our bodies respond similarly to emotional stress by elevating fuel levels, coronary blood flow, respiration, cardiac output, pulse rate—except that the expected muscular effort does not occur, and so the fuels are not consumed. Because the involuntary nervous system that governs these responses to stress has a limited repertoire, it is virtually indifferent to the source of stress. Thus environmental assaults, such as heat or cold, thunder or lightning, humidity or wind, will provoke many symptoms common to exercise or emotional stress.

Weather fronts are agents of stress. Depending on the time of year, they pass through the snowbelt region of the United States several times a month, more or less, and fewer in the sunbelt region. Each passing front calls forth prompt involuntary adaptations—or failing that, prompt reprisals in the form of health disorders. Cold fronts trigger blood-vessel shrinkage, localized oxygen deprivation, and involuntary counterreactions similar to our response to a warm front. Successive warm and cold fronts will push and pull the body's nervous system, causing it to "pendulate" as it seeks to maintain equilibrium.

Frontal passages are reflected in your biological tides that may synchronize with, negate, or amplify the atmospheric tides. Your physique, temperament, constitution, and prior level of arousal will modulate or determine your weathering response, deep inside your body.

Two opposing controllers govern your physical, emotional, or weather response. Your sympathetic or adrenal control stimulates your sweat glands, muscle and coronary arteries, respiration, eye-pupil dilation, heartbeat and pressure, and depresses your abdominal and digestive-organ activity. Medical drugs, weather, emotion, or exercise initiate or inhibit this control system and its counterresponse—the parasympathetic nervous system, or acetylcholine control. In normal persons, this seesaw rhythm may induce changes in moods or dreams, your energy levels, and even the normal wear-and-tear weathering of tension, headache, or restlessness. But inadequate organs or individuals may be pushed over into dysfunction; body tissues may invite microorganism penetration and infectious disease; the blood supply may deprive cerebral tissues of adequate oxygen, and mental processes suffer. As the body accommodates to weather changes, it lags behind them.

Slender or schizophrenic people may suffer most in cold weather, in late winter, and early in life. Manic-depressives or broad people may be most afflicted in summer or fall, in hot weather, and later in life.

Body temperature, the most tightly guarded human trait since it is essential to proper cell functioning, is regulated by an ingenious array of mechanisms, both involuntary and conscious. Skin sensors forward temperature information to the hypothalamus, which mobilizes major elements of our anatomy in order to equilibrate body temperature.

Comfort is a subjective sensation that corresponds objectively to the absence of thermoregulatory effort. If subconscious thermal fine-tuning fails, thermal discomfort is a conscious warning to rectify the body's microclimate. Most body heat is produced in the torso at rest, and in the musculature during work or exercise.

Clothing regulates body temperature by its insulation ability and permeance to water vapor, and by its modification of the private air layer that clings to your skin.

On warm days, higher indoor temperatures are preferred; and on cold days, lower indoor temperatures are preferred. Clothing or lag responses may account for these subjective under- and overestimates.

We sense temperature, or another person's "thermal space," by subliminal cues processed ultimately by the hypothalamus. It is also responsible for controlling appetite, thirst, emotion, mood, excitement or depression, sexual activity, metabolism, growth, energy release, and response to stress.

The similar physiological manifestations of stress found in exercise, emotions, and weather responses have a communal analogue in our large-scale response to disasters or other arousals to action. Social "backlash" may be the paradoxic response (of Wilder's Law of Initial Value) that is a counterpart of the "second wind" in physical stress, shock or sudden tears in emotional stress, and rewarming frostbite with ice in weather stress.

Weather-sensitivity insures survival, yet we require aggressive weather impacts for stimulation. Genius and weather-sensitivity seem to coincide, perhaps due to unusual intimacy with the environment and evolutionary forces of natural selection.

Left and right brain functions or handedness, temporal orientation to the past or the future, and warm or cool climate dispositions appear to overlap as three dualities: strength or weakness, masculine or feminine, and achievement or imagination.

Eleven:
Beat This Weather!

Civilization advances by extending the number of important operations which we can perform without thinking about them.
—Alfred North Whitehead

. . . the medical sciences have suffered and continue to suffer from the fallacy of thinking of a phenomenon as simple, of its cause as single, and to feel that, accordingly, there is but one clear straight path to be followed in action.

The discovery of specific pathogenic micro-organisms seems to have led back to an oversimplification of thought about the origin and nature of disease . . . to think of the specific micro-organism as the cause—the sole cause—of a specific disease, and later to think of the specific anti-toxin as a specific cure of that disease. . . . All this oversimplified thinking has flourished and survived because up to a point it is convenient. . . . it is more than this; it is probably necessary, for it affords the simplest possible conceptual scheme useful for certain purposes.
—Lawrence Henderson

Preceding Page: Hippocrates of Cos
The first biometeorologist, probably a weather-sensitive genius, the father of modern medicine, advocate of "treat the patient," and the man who "gave medicine a soul."

I remember sky
It was blue as ink,
Or at least I think
I remember sky.

I remember snow
Soft as feathers,
Sharp as thumbtacks
Coming down like lint
And it made you squint
When the wind would blow

And ice like vinyl, on the streets,
Cold as silver, white as sheets,
Rain like strings
And changing things
Like leaves . . .

I remember days
Or at least I try
But as years go by
They're a sort of haze.

And the bluest ink
Isn't really sky
And at times I think
I would gladly die
For a day of sky.
                    —Stephen Sondheim

The Good Physician

The good physician has at his disposal a wide choice of practical methods to treat the different weather-aggravated ailments, dysfunctions, and diseases differently.

Practical approaches to treatment of the same patient or the same disease are apparently endless. Consider this menu, for example. The *psychotherapist* acts through conscious routes to the involuntary nervous system and indirectly through the endocrines and blood chemistry; the *yogi* adds controlled respiration and thereby changes carbon dioxide and oxygen levels in the blood; the *dietician* brings about comparable results through nutrition. The *physiotherapist* will stimulate and exercise the skin, massage the musculature, and bathe, heat, or chill the body; their likely ultimate objective is to alter the balance between the body's peripheral and central organs. The *surgeon* will seek to cut, remove, or change an organ directly; one may work in the vascular bed to improve thermoregulation, another on the adrenal or thyroid glands, and still another may cut the sympathetic nerves. The *pharmacologist* will prescribe vasoconstrictors or vasodilators; the *psychiatrist*, psychoactive drugs. The *physiatrist* will inject medicines into spinal trigger points or bone joints. The *cardiologist* may stimulate the heart muscle directly or indirectly. The *neurologist* will attempt to locate brain tissues that may be dysfunctional due to vascular spasm, tissue hydration. The *orthomolecular psychiatrist* or the *clinical ecologist* will seek cerebral allergies to modify or eliminate. For mild thermoregulatory or respiratory disorders, the *balneotherapist* (mainly in Europe) will apply natural subterranean products—mineral waters, thermal springs, earth gases, and mud substances; the *climatotherapist* will treat the sick by changing their exposure to the atmosphere (carried out at seaside, it is *thalassotherapy*; in the mountains, it is *orotherapy*; as prescribed sunbathing or air exposure, it is *heliotherapy* or *aerotherapy*). It is almost an embarrassment of riches, a veritable Rashomon story, in which each player sees the situation filtered through his own special prism of expertise and motivations.

258

Routes to health may overlook the intense interlock between man and weather, the close integration of clinical events and meteorological phenomena. A whole gallery of symptoms and pathology presents itself in Petersen's work; the body's reflections of environmental stress; the periodic disruptions of the involuntary nervous system. The weather reflex also will trigger skin diseases from excessive vasoconstriction; neuroses from inadequate blood supply to the tissues; alterations of the gut, kidney, joint, stomach and cerebral tissues; localized tissue sensitivities to the body's physiochemical swings; activations of quiescent infections in the eye, ear, nose, throat, and other places. Petersen says these are "not diseases in the textbook fashion, but disease in its protein manifestations reflecting the interplay of innumerable environmental factors on the variable living substrate. . . . . I have expressed discontent with school pathology, because, in dramatically revealing *end* stages of disease it quite overshadows the far more important *beginning* of disease; crystallizes the impression of the static rather than the dynamic; the thought of finality and fixity, rather than variability and fluidity and the restorative phases in the biological mechanism."

But what is one to do? The statement, "Everyone talks about the weather, but no one does anything about it" was true—*except* for a few courageous innovators. (Some are mentioned in the short history of human biometeorology, Appendix A.) Hippocrates was one. Petersen was another. He urged physicians to think less of *pathology* and more of *physiology*. His views on therapeutic intervention in the man-weather-disease complex were basic and simple: The good physician must either seek to (A) *stabilize the environment*, (B) *make the organism as a whole more stable*, (C) *make the inadequate focal points or localized areas of dysfunction less responsive*, or (D) *proceed in all these directions at the same time.*

Petersen advised the good physician to understand and incorporate into patient-care the following knowledge: (1) environmental alterations that can cause undue biological swings; (2) general biological factors in the patient that cause undue reactivity to environmental alterations; (3) the normal biological rhythms (daily, sexual cycle, seasonal, annual) of the individual that may cause biological accentuation of meteorological actions; (4) individual components of the involuntary self-regulatory apparatus: the endocrine, nervous, chemical, and composite systems (the latter might include, for example, exercise, massage, or thermal, hydro-, electro-, shock or psychotherapies; (5) possible alterations in the unstable focal regions of sensitivity; (6) caution in those therapeutic interventions which are conditioned by the organism's prior state, its biological rhythms, and its phase of response to the atmosphere (adrenal to acetylcholine phase or vice versa).

Petersen's general measures to avoid overreaction to the possible air masses, particularly in the north temperate zones, are also simple. He emphasizes diet, avoidance of unnecessary trauma in the environment (physical, psychic, emotional), avoidance of undue fatigue, and institutionalizing a definite biological routine in daily life. He urged the elimination of all tissue-sensitive irritants, the encouragement of smaller and more frequent meals that produce acids in moderation, and regular changes of climate and rest.

Modern physicians who know and understand human biometeorology are few and far between, especially in the United States. But several scientists and physicians have addressed themselves, from different vantage points, to therapeutic advice for weather-sensitive people. The sun never sets on weather-sensitives.

Volker Faust, the German psychiatrist who has studied weather-sensitivity on a statistical basis, provides some tips for weather-sensitive people and their physicians. He suggests that dramatic improvements in health or long-lasting results may not occur unless these points are followed with persistence. (1) *Do not misuse stimulants* (alcohol, nicotine, caffeine). The persistent physician must see that the patient uses these only in moderation if he wishes to eliminate those weather-sensitive symptoms familiar to him (concentration difficulties, tiredness, forgetfulness, bad moods, nervousness, sleep problems, and circulatory problems). (2) *Seek to solve personal problems and conflicts* (family, professional, marriage). Although this is seemingly far-fetched, our response to the weather is a prime indicator of our emotional state. Symptoms that are meteorologically provoked are bad or depressive moods, nervousness, anxiety, headache, and especially head pressure, bad disposition, restless sleep, and difficulty falling asleep, dislike of work, increasing tendency to make mistakes, loss of appetite, and others. Faust believes that before medical drugs (like tranquilizers) are used, "conversation therapy" helps. "Problems for which one has words are already solved." (This common psychiatric view is overly optimistic, in my judgment.) (3) *Seek to avoid stress.* Many meteorologically induced symptoms are identical to the symptoms of stress, especially for men and those between thirty and forty years (to a lesser extent fifty or sixty years). These symptoms are difficulty in concentration, forgetfulness, distaste for work, increasing tendency to make mistakes, perspiration, loss of appetite, dizziness, and heart palpitations. These are warning signs that will be intensified by weather stress. Both patient and psychiatrist usually know that this sort of stress will be difficult to treat, but tranquilizers may be necessary. (4) *Seek adequate sleep.* Often attributed (correctly or incorrectly) to meteorological influences, lack of sleep is stress-related. (5) *Eat properly.* Non-weather-sensitive people are usually of normal weight, and weather-sensitives of both sexes are often overweight or underweight. Older generations of German physicians used to recommend fasting, drinking fruit juices, or eating foods high in protein and vitamins and without much animal fat. These prescriptions probably made sense in the hot, dry foehn climate of southern Germany but are difficult to advocate in changeable nothern winters. (6) *Be active; move and exercise.* Non-weather-sensitives beyond thirty years old generally find their physical capacity satisfactory, more so than weather-sensitives who at later age frequently suffer degeneration of the spine. Regular swimming, especially backstroke, is recommended. (7) *Take brush massages.* Skin brushing is an old European "remedy," cheap and harmless, but a good stimulant to the enormous skin area and reserves of blood near its surface. (8) *Take gymnastics, sauna, massage, and alternating hot and cold showers.* These can be very stimulating. (9) *Plan vacations.* The climatic conditions are especially important for weather-sensitives, and during the leisure time on vacation, it is often very useful to climb mountains and stay at the ocean to obtain the benefits of climate swings (see Appendix L). (10) *Take special baths.* Under the advice of knowledgeable physicians, thermal baths are prescribed for those weather-sensitives who complain of rheumatism or degenerative changes of bone structure (see Appendix L).

* * *

Werner Ranscht-Froemsdorf, a balneologist and climate physiologist practicing in Freiburg, echoes these prescriptive measures to help against climate and weather-sensitivity. But he adds several injunctions. To change the rhythms of stress he advocates changing eating and sleeping times. He urges heliotherapy (air and sun baths and infrared lamps) and hydrotherapy to strengthen one's constitution. He says that diet should be changed regularly, liquid and spice intakes reduced; and encourages fasting in steps (rice-days and juice-days).

His colleague, W. Schmidt-Kessen, has treated patients with bath cures (which Americans are inclined to scoff at) and finds that mineral waters can transport substances out of or into the skin because of certain special properties: vasoconstriction due to cold is suppressed in certain mineral-saturated cold waters. And the blood circulation is enhanced. (From personal experience, I can assure you that a mineral bath is invigorating and even sensual.) Skin diseases are treated with special baths. The therapeutic value of balneotherapy, Schmidt-Kessen admits, is open to question. "If applied without any other medical therapy, it does not seem to influence the long range course of the illnesses examined." The *subjective* success of the treatment is often much superior to the *objective* one. However, this does not negate its value to Americans. Calculations suggest that monies spent in Germany on health "cures" later save *triple* that amount in public-health funds. These spas, health resorts, and sanatoriums in European countries constitute a "large third system of medical care alongside the regular medical practice and the hospital." For 60 million Germans, there are three-quarters of a million *hospital* beds, but over a half million *health-resort* beds. If it didn't work, or if the "cure" was sheer charlatanry as many Americans suspect, those beds would not exist. Climate-exposure therapy has also been employed in respiratory disorders, in thermoregulatory disturbances, after acute chronic illness, in sympathetic nervous system disorders, and with supersensitivity to weather changes. This tradition flourishes in Europe partly from habit, and partly on the basis of its results and the relief it offers (see Appendix L).

Solco W. Tromp (author of more than a hundred research papers in biometeorology) urges asthmatic and rheumatic patients who have poor thermoregulatory systems to avoid low temperatures (and not sleep near an outside wall) but to vacation at high altitudes; after four to six weeks, he says many are almost "cured." In flying, the reduced cabin pressure will enhance your circulation after six hours or so. While skiing at mountain altitudes, he advises to allow at least three days to adapt; many ski accidents are caused by inadequate acclimatization to altitude, slowing the reaction time. He says that if you stay ten days above 4,500 feet (1,500 meters), your blood hemoglobin levels rise, and due to greater oxygenation you are physically fit for some time thereafter.

The Other Good Physician

The doctrine, now twenty-five centuries old, that physicians should explain things to their patients, has lain dormant until the present century, and it still has some way to go.

Hippocrates (460 B.C.), the father of medicine and by common consent, one of the greatest physicians, said in the book *On Ancient Medicine*, "Of the diseases under which common people have labored . . . illiterate persons cannot easily find out for themselves, but it is still easy for them to understand these things when discovered and expounded by others."

The *other* good physician, of course, is *you*. Perhaps there is much to be said for the belief that "you are your own best doctor." A recent survey of medical self-care show physicians and many of their patients strongly in favor of it. "The increasing involvement of patients in their own health care will be one of the most exciting things in medicine during the next ten years," says B. L. Huffman, Jr., past president of the American Academy of Family Physicians. "For a long time it was believed that ordinary people can't comprehend anything about medicine," says cardiologist Glenn O. Turner, who developed a widely published self-warning system for heart attacks. "We're finding out that simply isn't true."

One self-care or health-activation program is taught to laymen in thirty-two hours and shows how to measure the vital signs and to perform emergency resuscitation, the importance of nutrition, the importance of exercise and relaxation, and the danger of stress. Physicians who agree that "doctoring is not just for doctors" say that *one-third to three-fourths of all office visits are unnecessary if patients practiced self-health care.* Most office visits merely reassure the patient. Conventional medicine, they say, "is stumbling towards an era of diminishing returns [and] its scientific cure-oriented approach to health often ignores sufferers of chronic ills, the bulk of the disease burden today."

Since stress has been repeatedly involved in our response to meteorological change, it is particularly appropriate to notice that there are ways to cope with reducing stress. You can remove the agent of stress, you can adjust to it, or you can be defeated by the stressor. Insight and zest will go a long way toward removing or adapting to stress. Richard Suinn, among others, suggests how to break the habit of stress-induced, frantic anxiety and the vicious cycle that can lead to heart disease and other ailments. Because the added load from weather stress may be the straw just enough to break the camel's back, stress-reduction training may help. Some pointers: (1) *Learn to relax*—by music, deep muscle tensing and release, meditation; (2) *Retrain your reactions* by imagining new behaviors in old stressful situations; (3) *Control your environment* by forbidding telephone interruptions and demands, by scheduling appointments realistically, by setting priorities each day and sticking to them; (4) *Slow down*, by practice, and train yourself to wind down, to talk and eat and walk slowly.

The never-ending drive of successive air masses pushes the biological rhythm again and again to unusually high peaks and deep depressions; but these swings of large amplitude do not overload the normal population. Normal adjustment mechanisms, before tissue damage, are able to bring about prompt and adequate compensation. Those with organ deficiencies or congenital inadequacies may be pushed over the edge of health by the constant repetition of subliminal environmental assaults. Ultimately, the push and stress will lead to wear and tear, unless the good physician or that other good physician—you!—intercedes.

Weathering the weather means weathering life's stresses. The following advice on weathering (from earlier chapters) briefly explains why each admonition will help you weather life's weather.

Weathering the Weather

- Medicate yourself in cold or hot weather or sunshine as though your life depends on it. It does. The weather will modify drug action in your body, especially common stimulants (like coffee, tea, alcohol, nicotine), sleeping drugs, appetite suppressants, psychoactive drugs, antibiotics, barbiturates, tranquilizers, hallucinogens (like marijuana) and narcotics.
- In *extreme* cold climates or cold weather, eat high-protein, high-fat foods. Five meals a day provide more efficient utilization of fat as energy than three meals a day, according to diet studies of cold-dwellers.
- In hot climates and hot weather, eat vegetables, salads, and carbohydrates and drink plenty of fluids. Replace lost water hour by

hour, drinking whether thirsty or not. But unless severe salt loss occurs, salt replacement can wait until meals. Diminished appetite is normal, an adaptation to heat.

- Allergies to food may be aggravated in stressful weather situations. Certain "cerebral allergies" may trigger irrational behaviors. People are most "addicted" to foods that they are allergic to and that do the most harm.
- Generally eat relatively high-protein foods, coupled with a moderate level of tissue-stimulating activity.
- Notice how the identical food or beverage (say cheese and wine) may taste different in different weather and at different hours of the day or night. Observe how your senses are stimulated by the weather.
- The best sexual weather is fresh air and sunshine. According to Alfred Kinsey, the other three aphrodisiacs are good food, adequate sleep, and exercise.
- Exercise, play tennis, jog, ride a bike, do gymnastics—but gradually escalate aerobic activities until you condition yourself to weather changes. You will surpass your own pre-exercise ability to acclimatize to changing weather or new climates. You will welcome the arrival of new weather—hot or cold—the seasonal shifts, and travel to new climates.
- Anticipate water loss in exercise and replace it, preferably in advance. A quart of water per hundred pounds of body weight is about right for moderate exercise.
- Do warm-up exercises indoors before going outside to exercise in the cold. Five minutes is the minimum. Habituate gradually to exercise in cold weather.
- In extreme cold, avoid being motionless for an extended period of time. Get out of the cold or move muscles: jump, stamp, swing around, jog.
- Drink plenty of water in winter, even though urine volume can triple in cold weather. Water will help you keep dry mucous membranes hydrated and your body temperature constant.
- Physical fitness, mental alertness, emotional well-being, and absence of strain seem to go together with the enjoyment of weather.
- Social "weather" is important. Those who live alone, who are uninvolved with any people or organizations, who lack a network of friendships or social supports, who may belong to a numerical minority or low-status group will show heightened

vulnerability to chronic diseases and stress, including weather stress. Any additional stress, from weather for example, can overload an already-stressed person.

- Potent shields against stress overload (from a combination of sources) are past experiences with a particular stressor, a sense of mastery over one's fate, good morale, and demonstrated competence. All will promote weathering.

- Dress as though your life depends on it. It does. Plan your private microclimate in anticipation of weather changes. Comfort is the rule, in heat or cold. Use properly insulated garments (for insulation values, see Appendix E).

- Wear layered clothing in cold weather and in cold-weather exercise. The air-filled spaces between the layers is effective insulation. Avoid fabrics that do not breathe, like rubberized or plasticized fabrics. Free diffusion of moisture through clothing is essential to good temperature regulation.

- In cold weather, your head resembles a Thermos jug filled with warm liquid and without its cap on. Body heat, rising upward through relatively good thermal conductors (bone, muscle) will depart through your head in large amounts, like steam departing the Thermos. Keep head covered in very cold weather.

- In hot weather, wear light garments like cotton that readily absorb and then dissipate sweat into the air.

- In heat waves or acute heat, avoid emotional stress, excessive exercise, and strenuous work, which can strain your thermoregulatory system and lead to heat exhaustion or heat stroke. Keep cool.

- Air conditioning may retard your natural acclimatization to summer heat, so try doing without it as long as possible, or keep it on as little or low as possible, or both. Air conditioning will decrease heat-wave mortality in early summer heat waves but not in subsequent heat waves.

- Avoid deodorants and especially antiperspirants. Most of them interfere with efficient body thermoregulation—sweating. Have you ever wondered where the underarm perspiration goes when it is blocked by an antiperspirant? (It probably leaves the body elsewhere.) Acceptable substitutes are colognes and talc that mask body odors, morning and evening showers; undergarments, as shields, help.

- Swelling of hands and feet, low blood pressure, and headaches are symptoms of prolonged or chronic dilated blood vessels (vasodilation) near the skin's surface. Check with your physician.

- Dry or chapped skin, frostbite, joint pains, and hypertension are symptoms of prolonged or chronic constricted blood vessels (vasoconstriction) near the skin's surface. Consult your physician.
- To maintain or improve high performance and efficiency in continuous mental work, keep cool and dry. Studies show that high-pressure, low-temperature, and low-humidity weather (an anticyclonal air mass following a cold front) is statistically associated with good all-around performance. Keep rooms as cool as compatible with comfort, since slight muscle tension accompanies the act of paying close attention and mental acuity.
- High indoor temperatures are comfortable on a warm day and low indoor temperatures are comfortable on a cool day. Keep the temperature inside close to the temperature outside and that will save energy as well.
- Humidify in winter. Use a humidifier, water-filled pans over radiators, boiling water on the stove, humidifiers inside central-heating systems—*anything*, but moisten the air somehow. You will feel comfortable (especially if you are slender and tall) and your skin and mucous membranes will be grateful for humidity.
- Guard the ecoclimate of your home or office against volatile vapors, odors, fumes, and gases—from paint or shoepolish to aerosol sprays and carbon paper. Your lungs absorb gas so efficiently that they provide great intimacy with the bloodstream over an area half the size of a tennis court.
- Older people, especially living alone, should make strenuous efforts to become fully aware of their body temperature. If their discomfort sensation is absent, their body temperature will fall in cold weather. Called accidental (or "sneaky") hypothermia, subnormal body temperature can prove dangerous. Not only older people but those who are indifferent to their thermal sensations should be especially vigilant.
- In hot weather, especially when living alone, older, confused, or depressed people are likely to become dehydrated. They must be urged to drink sufficient fluids.
- Do not always trust oral temperatures. The mouth may be cooler or warmer than other parts of the body, especially for children and adults who are seriously ill.
- Place a severely chilled person in a hot tub of water to warm the internal organs rapidly. Quick exposure of a chilled person to a warm environment may release vasoconstriction so fast that cold blood may reach the heart.

- Allow at least three days to adapt to a ski vacation to prevent ski accidents due to initially slowed reaction times.
- Give acclimatization a chance. If healthy, you should be able to adapt to cold or to hot weather after days or weeks in total climatic immersion. The initial discomfort will soon give way to neutrality and eventually enjoyment. Acclimatization calls for forbearance.
- Avoid accumulating stress from any and all sources. Vulnerability to weather stress will be greater following prolonged emotional strain, prolonged exercise or hard work, poor diet, travel, and prolonged medication, especially those affecting thermoregulation (see Appendix F).
- Prepare for stressful events. Try to minimize their intensity, their speed of change. Recall prior experience with stressful events. "Rehearsal" will help. Minimize their duration or your prolonged exposure. Anticipate or predict, since the unpredictability of stressful events is harmful. Plan for stress.
- Change the rhythm of stress by modifying the times at which you eat and sleep. Change your diet and sleep habits regularly; experiment and observe the results.
- Diminish your total environmental stress load. Try relaxation training, meditation, deep muscle tensing and untensing, and massage. Retrain your stock reactions to old stressful situations by imagining and practicing new behavior.
- Control your total environment: prevent interruptions, schedule appointments, set priorities, slow down.
- Plan your vacations with climate in mind. Try new climates, your health permitting. Heat stress, cold stress, and altitude stress can challenge younger athletic vacationers and provide unexpected sources of pleasure once you are acclimatized.
- Prior to air travel or mountain ascent, consume carbohydrates and plenty of fruit juices. This will probably help maintain or increase efficiency, coordination, and capacity for work. Avoid caffeinated fluids (tea, coffee, Coke) that help dehydrate you in a low humidity cabin. Avoid melons or carbonated drinks prior to flight, since these may cause gas discomfort.
- In vacation travel, seek your own climatic "zone of contentment." Especially if you are elderly or weather-sensitive, cool or comfortable temperatures and adequate sunshine are most important.
- Traveling from west to east may seriously desynchronize your biological rhythms, thermoregulation, and acclimatization. Prepare for it by good diet, exercise, and stress reduction.

- Blood pressure will fall when you travel to a warm climate and will rise when you travel to a cold climate. Americans with low blood pressure who are going south in the winter, should seek a physician's advice. So should those with high blood pressure who are traveling north.
- Upon return north from a southern winter vacation of lengthy stay, take special caution until reacclimatized. You are especially susceptible to cold weather and related maladies like upper respiratory or viral infections and the common cold.
- Vary your vacations. Try seashores, mountains, even health spas, and places where you can take saunas, mineral baths, thermal baths, air baths, or sun baths—especially if you have never experienced them (see Appendix L).
- Scrutinize your reactions to weather conditions. A psychiatrist says, "Anything that arouses human beings to think about themselves is good."
- Sensitize yourself to weather conditions and weather changes. Consciously notice minor temperature and humidity changes, snow and rain, clouds and haze, sunrises and sunsets. Allow yourself to feel the moods that weather—and weathering—induce. Feel these moods. They may be precursor cues to forthcoming body changes, to possible ailments, to upper respiratory infections. Your mood *today* is associated with weather one or two days ago; the start of your common cold *today* is associated with weather two to four days ago. So your mood response is faster than your response to infection.
- Observe the sun and enjoy it. Studies show that the primary and most significant weather element that increases people's judgment of "pleasantness" is increased sunshine.
- Above all, enjoy the weather, Revel in it. Even those days that are not especially extreme have some weather appeal. Elevate your consciousness—to the sky. Twenty-eight centuries ago, Hesiod advised his brother, "Every man shall have his favorite day, but few will know about them. . . . Observe the Days [the good weather and luck] that come from Zeus."

These prescriptions are designed to help in weathering weather— the ever present micro-, eco-, and geoclimate we are in bondage to, like Prometheus chained and exposed to the elements. If we are to be forever vulnerable to the weather and forever enriched by the weather, perhaps we can live with these Promethean prescriptions.

Life is Short and the Art long; the occasion fleeting, experience fallacious, and judgement difficult. The physician must not only be prepared to do what is right himself, but must also make the patient, the attendants, and the externals cooperate.

Hippocrates in the *Aphorisms* was pointing here to the importance of "doctoring," of "doctoring" oneself, and of encouraging the external environment—the weather, the sky—to "doctor" us: the benevolent weathering from "Doctor" Zeus.

For From the Most High
Cometh Healing

Chiseled in granite on the twenty-second floor over the towering entrance to a prestigious medical center of a great university, this sober inscription comes to us from *Ecclesiasticus* (from the Apocrypha, Chapter 38, verse 2, of the Bible).

In that holy context it means that one should honor the physician because God created him. Or that God was the ultimate healer, the divine physician.

But in speculating upon its meaning, William Petersen mused, "One wonders whether the hopeful patient is to aspire wistfully for treatment on the [medical center's] topmost floors." For the Hippocratic physician, such healing "from the most high" meant employing the environment, the atmosphere, the winds, the sky—the very heavens themselves—in conjunction with other treatments, to serve the patient. The ancient Greek medical school at Cos was led by the father of modern medicine, Hippocrates, who taught his many followers to "study the patient." Hippocrates, probably himself a genius, was uncommonly aware that weather conditioned the person and the patient—inevitably, inextricably, irreversibly, ultimately, and forever.

The weather conditions us, not only by direct physical force or by thermal changes but by subliminal suasion, mood shifting, and religious power. The sky itself is a therapeutic doctor.

Primitive peoples understood sky; they invented weather gods. The word "Caelotherapy" means the use of the heavens, religion, or religious symbols for therapeutic purposes. One thinks readily of Zeus, Ea, Apollo, Aesculapius, and other healers "from the most high," like Jesus, Moses, Buddha. But one also remembers the poetic skies, the celestial arts—painting, music, and verse.

* * *

"It is hard to feel affection for something as totally impersonal as the atmosphere," Lewis Thomas writes, "and yet there it is, as much a part and product of life as wine or bread." He calls our atmosphere "the worlds biggest membrane" since it is so "marvelously skilled at editing the sun."

Taken all in all, the sky is a miraculous achievement. It works, and for what it is designed to accomplish it is as infallible as anything in nature. I doubt whether any of us could improve on it, beyond maybe shifting a local cloud from here to there on occasion. . . . We should credit it for what it is: for sheer size and perfection of function, it is far and away the grandest product of collaboration in all of nature.

Our atmosphere, the sky—our weather—is life. And weathering is living.

Beat This Weather!:
A Summary

Each medical specialist will treat a disorder based upon the principles of his own experience. But modern physicians often overlook the weather's intense stranglehold upon man. Those few in the United States who understand biometeorology suggest that physicians intervening in the man-weather-health complex should stabilize the environment or the patient, desensitize the inadequate regions of the body, and their patients should avoid stimulants, conflict, and stress. Proper food, sleep, and exercise are important, as are massage, sauna, gymnastics, special baths, and planned vacations.

Health spas, popular in Europe, often employ these and other principles of human biometeorology and weather therapies—sun, air, water, and altitude.

Climate "cures" save triple their cost in public health funds; Germany has almost as many health-resort beds as hospital beds.

Climate-exposure therapies have been employed successfully in the treatment of respiratory disorders, thermoregulatory disturbances, after acute or chronic illness, and nervous-system disorders.

Medical practice in the United States has largely ignored these therapies and the principles of human biometeorology—despite their legitimacy.

However, you are your own best doctor. You are entitled to employ these findings to maintain or improve your own health. Weathering life's weather is simplified if you have the "prescriptions." The sky can be a natural healer. Medication, food, travel, clothing, exercise, vacations, stress, and climate conditioning are all intimately entwined with the weather and how you enjoy good health.

Afterword

This book had its origin in the future. My agent, Peter Matson, had casually remarked, "I would like to read a book about the weather written by someone who thinks professionally about the future." We both knew of a number of books that had recently appeared, telling how we'd all be enveloped by glaciers or deserts in 20,000 years, or otherwise suffer the ravages of extreme weather changes—long after Peter or I would be here to know or care. Drought, invasions of the arctic tundra, expansion of the Sahara, great catastrophic floods, unexpected frosts, crop failures, famines were just a few of the predictions made by these authors, many of them scientists. (Several of these books read like disaster novels; I guess there have always been more catastroph*ists* than catastroph*ies*.)

Professional forecasters will tell you that in many ways it is easier to say what will happen twenty years from now than what will happen two days or two weeks from now. The shorter time horizon is more intriguing, more challenging. Certainly it is more interesting to the general reader.

The direct effects of weather on people seemed to have a duration of the proper length—from days to weeks. At least that was what the scientific papers on the human response to weather, called human biometeorology, reported. Very well, then. I would make a virtue of necessity.

The scarcity of responsible research in human biometeorology in the United States was more then compensated for by the variety and quantity of serious research in Europe; it was prolific. Some scientists there believed that weather had a powerful effect on the human organism; others felt it was mild, if at all. "A great truth," said Thomas Mann, "is one whose opposite is also a great truth." Was I faced with a "great truth": that "the weather hardly matters," *versus* "the weather does matter enormously"? Then I read the following, by Dennis Driscoll, about belief in human-weather response:

The spectrum of attitudes, world-wide, appears to cover the extremes from very unlikely, through skeptical, to convinced. It is interesting to note that belief has an east-west gradient. Weather-human response relationships are given little credence in the United States, and . . . very little research has been done. As one proceeds eastward through Europe, however, the conviction grows. The French and English research is not much greater than that of the Americans. German and Austrian research is by far the most extensive, with some skepticism evident. In Hungary, Romania, and Yugoslavia, weather influences are actually assumed, at least by those people who have worked in this area. So much so, in fact, that there as well as in Germany, medical-meteorological forecasting has been practised for some time, and hospitals schedule admissions and surgery only after consulting the latest weather forecast.

I began to wonder why this "east-west gradient" should be so strong. What evidence, hard-headed scientific data, was there to support the intense beliefs of respectable German, Swiss, and Dutch scientists? I read hundreds of scientific research papers they wrote, and then I went to speak to them face to face.

Perhaps the phenomenon was connected to a tradition going back centuries, even millennia (see the short history of biometeorology in Appendix A)—the prevalence of European health "spas," climate "cures," water-bath therapies, and other curiously European habits that never "traveled" well, that never took hold in the United States. I had lived in Paris in 1968 (doing research in astrophysics) and thought I understood something about Europeans and European science. But then, my mind was concentrating on the origins of cosmic radiations, those mysterious nuclear particles that arrive here from interstellar and intergalactic space. These extremely energetic nuclei, as they impinged upon the top of our atmosphere, create vast invisible avalanches of atmospheric nuclear reactions. A single, hugely energetic, cosmic-ray proton could trigger a cascading nuclear shower that would spread out over many square miles by the time it had propagated to the base of the atmosphere, our biosphere. My mind then was on the celestial sphere, the heavenly stars, and not the atmosphere through which we perceive them. It was invisible to me professionally. I knew that cosmic rays, like other forms of nuclear radiation, cannot be seen or felt by people directly, although their biological effects are—genetically and physiologically—significant, or deadly.

With this background, I wondered if the atmosphere could also exert invisible effects on us directly, aside from the obvious weather experience: exuberance at a clear, cool, crisp, dry day; the gloom at overcast skies, or sultry weather; and occasionally curious inexplicable feelings I and others seem to have during certain types of weather—not mystical, but unexplainable—like the awe at a sunset, the excitement of a snowfall, the paradoxically rhapsodic response to rain. How and why is a tall order.

When environmentalists talked about the environment it is a political, social, economic issue—air or water pollution and what to do about it. Environmentalists had converted "environment" into a dirty word. But here was a physical atmosphere, a literal "environment" if ever there was one, and there was no up-to-date scientific exposition on a popular level of human biometeorology. It had fallen between the cracks.

I soon found myself engaged in a Laocoön-like struggle with a spectacular phenomenon: on the one hand was the complex of weather conditions, weather types, weather changes; on the other hand were biochemical patterns, anatomical differences, blood chemistry, body types, and personality differences. And on the other hand (that's three hands—that's how confusing it was) there were patterns in social and economic geography. There was no simple lucid explanation in English to satisfy me, consistent with thousands of scientific reference papers a computer search printed out. Many were bewildering in their claims and counterclaims. The initial disadvantage of my specialty in physics was placed in a different perspective by one of Europe's leading biometeorologists, Wolf Weihe, "You are not loaded down with excess intellectual baggage."

I was stimulated and excited by these European specialists and their dedication to specificity, the elucidation of provable details that constitute good research. But my feeling sharpened, as I traveled and spoke to the experts, that there was no "big picture," no overview, no view from Olympus. Only separate research efforts, fragments, possibly-idiosyncratic images of the human-weather connection were begging to be tied together in a consistent pattern. Physicists (often) and futurists (always) seem to crave the "big picture"; because I seem to be both, that's what I have attempted to create in *Weathering*.

Appendix

APPENDIX A: **How Weather Affects People Directly:**
A Short Chronological History of Human Biometeorology Since Civilization Began

Chaldeans
4000 B.C.
and

Babylonians
2200 B.C.
and

Assyrians
1500 B.C.
and

Egyptians
3000–1000 B.C.

Physicians and priests in these early civilizations associated the zodiac (Greek for "circle of animals") with parts of the human body (Taurus the Bull = neck and shoulders, Sagittarius the Archer = hips), and astrological horoscopes to determine the treatment of sickness.

Huang Ti
2650 B.C.

Chinese
emperor

In ancient China, the seasons and elements corresponded to human body organs: wood = spring = liver, fire = summer = heart, metal = autumn = lungs, water = winter = kidney. Heat impairs the heart, cold impairs the lungs, moisture is bad for the spleen, and wind is bad for the liver. *Feng Shui* ("wind and water") was used to determine best location for houses, gardens, beds, and tombs; still practiced by Tibetan Buddhist and Chinese Taoist priests who believe man's nature is altered by his surroundings.

Book of Hiob
(Old Testament)

Gives medical-meteorological tips.

Nisaba Song

Oldest admonition to physicians: to consider the weather.

Hesiod
800 B.C.

Greek
writer

In *Works and Days* he explains relationships between health and weather. He advises his brother Perses to "Beat This Weather," to dress properly, avoid storms. In *Theogony* he tells the story of Zeus and the gods.

Susruta ca. 600–500 B.C.	Physician of India	Wrote medical compendium *Ayur Veda* on effects of seasons on men and animals. Recommended a sojourn for the king and the people at dry places, which led to popular health reports frequented by healers.
Meton 632 B.C.	Athenian astronomer	First weather calendar, *Meteoric Cycles*.
Anaximenes 6th century B.C.	Greek philosopher	Assumed changing psycho-physical effects between man and climate or weather: concentration and dilution of air affects all beings.
Pythagoras 580–500 B.C.	Greek mathematician	Thought all matter was composed of four underlying qualities: hot, cold, wet, and dry. Diseases were explained as incorrect proportions of four elements: fire, earth, water, and air. "Harmony of the Spheres" introduced.
Empedocles 495–435 B.C.	Philosopher, poet, statesman, scientist of Agrigentum (Sicily)	Established the dogma that the divine and eternal elements interacted with qualities and humors: Hot and moist = blood = air = south = spring = sweet = heart = child = sanguine. Hot and dry = yellow bile = fire = east = summer = bitter = liver = youth = choleric. Cold and dry = black bile = earth = north = autumn = acid = spleen = adult = melancholic. Cold and moist = phlegm = water = west = winter = saline = brain = old man = phlegmatic. He is credited with preventing an epidemic in Sicily by sealing the opening in nearby mountains, keeping out foul air, or miasma.
Asklepion 5th century B.C.	Greece	Sacred place of the healing god Asklepios (or Aesculapius, son of Apollo the air god, meaning "gentle radiance," or god of the clear bright radiant air after a storm); pilgrimages for the sick; climatic health records for patients treated by priest-physicians. Greek islands of Cos ("treat the patient") and Cnidos ("treat the disease").
Parmenides of Elea 5th century B.C.	Greek philosopher	Probably the first to establish climatic zones. Spoke of "burnt zones," or desert areas.

278

Name	Occupation	Description
Hippocrates of Cos 460–375 B.C.	Greek physician and surgeon	Leader of the School at Cos. Made regular weather observations and incorporated them into treatment of patients. He or his followers wrote seven books on disease, and each disease description began with the weather conditions. Admonished all who wished to study medicine to know the weather, the seasons, the winds, and the waters. He observed that the cold-dwellers were hardy, courageous and productive; warm-dwellers were placid and indifferent. Many of his medical-meteorological observations still hold today. "The whole body participates in intelligence in proportion to its participation in air." (Proper oxygenation of brain tissue is essential.) He was the father of modern medicine, a great genius and "gave medicine a soul."
Aristotle 384–322 B.C.	Greek philosopher	Wrote the *Meteorologica* (Greek for "study of the atmosphere or things in the air"). The stars were living noble beings, controlling the course of the seasons, nature, growth, and decay. Believed moon had a moistening effect. Noticed deaths increased in accordance with stars and weather. Explained composition of winds, thunder, lightning.
Theophrastus 372–287 B.C.	Pupil of Aristotle	Wrote reference work *About the Winds and Weather Signs* which explained over 200 omens of rain, wind, and nice weather (behavior of sheep, flickering of a lamp in a storm) and how to predict forthcoming weather a year in advance. "If the feet swell, the south wind shall rise." Influential for two millennia.
Diokles of Karystos 340–260 B.C.	Greek physician	Divided the year into six segments, and each time the life-style was supposed to be changed.
Asklepiades 124–56 B.C.	Roman physician to the aristocrats and rhetoricists	Asserted physician should actively intervene in disease: "Natural healing power is a delusion." Geography and climate were to be taken into account in diet and bloodletting. "Ethiopians become old rapidly in their

279

Aulus Cornelius Celsus 25 B.C.–A.D. 50	Roman encyclopedist	sixtieth year since their bodies are burned too much by the heat of the sun, and Britons die in their hundredth year for they inhabit a cold region." Though not a physician, wrote eight volumes on medicine, which are still the only special medical works in Latin of the classical age. Advised long sea voyages and changing climate for the improvement of health.
Claudius Ptolemius A.D. 85–165	Egyptian scientist (Ptolemy)	Gave climate zones on the map of the world. Wrote on astronomy (*Almagist*) and astrology (*Tetrabiblios*), good and bad planets, plagues, earthquakes, and floods. Argued that possibility of error should not discourage astrologers any more than it does the physician.
Galen A.D. 129–199	Greek physician Rome	Recommended mountain climates at high altitude, sending his patients to Castellamare near Vesuvius, and his pneumonia patients to desert climates.
Beda Venerabilis A.D. 673–735	Scottish scientist	Concerned with meteorological knowledge.
Monk's Medicine 5th to 10th century	Central Europe	Monks of the Middle Ages brought knowledge of bioclimatology from the Greeks, Romans, and Arabs to Central Europe. Galen was influential. In the seventh century, the church regarded medical astrology as legitimate, and Bishop Isidore of Seville advised physicians to study it. In the eleventh century, the School of Saleria incorporated these teachings.
Lex Frisionum 9th century	Friesenland (Ancient part of German coast bounded by Rhine, Ems, and Bructeri)	For the first time medical meteorology was included into jurisprudence. Those who inflicted wounds that left weather-sensitive scars were punished with greater severity. Probably the forerunner of thirteenth- and fourteenth-century law that penalty taxes were levied in accordance with the weather-sensitivity of the scar wounds.

Name / Dates	Role	Description
Avicenna 920–1037 and Gerald 1147–1223 and Al-Quazwini 1262 and	Islamic physician / Welsh topographer / Arabic philosopher	Each of these scholars wrote works on the influences of weather on mankind. Kings, popes, princes believed in weather prognostications and health prognostications, climate and temperament; and were their patrons.
Nicephores Blemydes 1197–1272 and Albertus Magmus 1193–1280	Byzantine philosopher / Western philosopher	
Roger Bacon 1214–1294	English scientist	The first Westerner to discuss the importance of topography for the local climate.
Bartholomaeus Angelicus Early 13th century	German scholar	Made medical-meteorological observations.
Paracelsus 1493–1541	Swiss physician	Wrote "To each elemental being, the element in which it lives is transparent, invisible and respirable, as the atmosphere [is] to ourselves."
Tycho Brahe 1546–1601	Danish scientist	Made meteorological-climatical observations.
Antoine Mizaul 1547	French physician	Wrote first textbook on meteorology; later vernacular version appeared as *Mirouer de l'Air*.
Galileo Galilei 1564–1642	Italian scientist	Developed the thermometer.

Johannes Kepler 1571–1630	German scientist	Made meteorological-climatical observations.
E. Torricelli 1608–1647	Italian scientist	Developed the barometer.
Thomas Bartholin 1614		Wrote "On Medical Travel," a letter to his two sons about the influence of the air of Naples; advised them how to eat, drink, and travel in cold and hot weather.
E. Gariotte 1620–1684 and Robert Boyle 1627–1691	French physicist and English chemist	Boyle–Gariotte law of gases.
Thomas Sydenham 1624–1689	English physician	Called the "English Hippocrates." Pointed again to the Hippocratic observations about the change of diseases and weather, seasonal dependence of health problems. Suggested that febrile illness was caused by alterations in the constitution of the atmosphere, a mysterious tainted something called miasmata. These "noxious effluvia" emanated from every situation even remotely connected with disease. Urged collection of data on diseases and environment to correlate their relationships.
Robert Hooke 1635–1703	English scientist	Developed a usable hygroscope. Improved the determination of the wind velocity and the measurement of precipitation.
G. W. Leibniz 1646–1716	German philosopher, lawyer, statesman, mathematician	Urged the state to support statistical measurements of weather-dependent health problems.

E. Halley 1656–1742	English astronomer	Explored the origin of tropical trade winds and monsoons.
G. Hardley 1682–1744	English lawyer	Theorized about the direction of trade winds.
C. de Montesquieu 1689–1755	French writer and politician	Saw weather and climate not only influencing individuals but also important for legislative and executive matters.
Voltaire 1694–1778	French philosopher	Weather-sensitive; classical self-description ("susceptible to east wind")
Richard Russel 1700–1771	English physician	Founder of the "sea therapeutics."
L. G. Monnier 1717–1799	French physician	Proved for the first time that the air is electrically charged even when the sky is totally clear.
Luigi Galvani 1737–1798	Italian scientist	Found during his frog-leg test that electrical discharges can have an effect on nerves and muscles.
J. G. von Herder 1744–1803	German philosopher, theologian, writer	His book *Ideas in the Philosophy of Mankind* discussed effects of the climate on human beings.
A. Volta 1745–1827	Italian physician	One of the first to explore natural and artificial electricity.

I. A. C. Charles 1746–1823	French physician	Charles's gas law, known now as the Gay-Lussac law.
J. W. Goethe 1752–1843	Writer	Distinctly weather-sensitive (according to his secretary Eckermann). Wrote *The Experiment of Meteorology*. First to notice differences of weather-sensitivity according to social level. Established network of meteorological observations. Corresponded extensively with Schiller about the influence of the weather on mental efficiency.
C. W. Hufeland 1762–1836	German physician	Found a connection between weather events and morbidity.
John Dalton 1766–1844	English physicist and chemist	Responsible for Dalton's law of the partial gas pressures.
A. von Humboldt 1769–1859	German scientist	First definition of the concept climate (in *cosmos*): "The climate comprises all changes of the atmosphere which our organs perceptibly register." Founded the Prussian Meteorological Institute in Berlin.
Sir F. Beaufort 1774–1857	English admiral	Developed the Beaufort Scale of wind intensities.
Benjamin Rush 1778	American Army physician	Book on military hygiene: "Sentries should always be provided with watch-coats, and they should be often relieved in very hot, cold, and rainy weather. It is a good custom for a sentry always to eat a hearty meal before he enters upon duty in cold weather. The gentle fever excited by digestion contributes to guard him in a degree against the effects of the cold."
J. P. Epsy 1785–1860	American meteorologist	Found the connection between convection (ascendance of warm air) and condensation of atmospheric vapors.
C. G. Carus 1789–1869	German physician and scientist	Described in his *Psyche* the influence of climate and weather on the organism.

Th. Forster 1790–1845	English physician	The first to draw attention to the "peculiarities of the electrical composition of the air."
G. G. Coriolis 1792–1843	French mathematician	Discovered that the rotation of the earth diverts winds eastward ("Coriolis force").
J. L. Schonlein 1793–1864	German clinician	Described in *General and Special Pathology and Therapy* the effect of atmospheric factors on the human being.
Luzius Ruedi 1804–1869	Swiss physician	The first to utilize the climate of high mountains and to establish an institute for tubercular diseased children (in Davos).
Harald Ackermann 1810–1873	German physician	Explained in *The Weather and Diseases* connection between certain weather conditions and pneumonia, liver diseases, and intestinal diseases.
K. A. Wunderlich 1815–1877	German clinician	Found the influence of atmospheric factors.
J. P. Joule 1818–1889	English physicist	Discovered Joule law: conservation of energy.
M. von Pettenkofer 1818–1901	German hygienist	Established the basics for today's hygiene. To investigate those factors useful or damaging for our health, he promoted scientific studies of the surroundings (air, water, soil, food, clothes, residence). Thus he made hygiene into a kind of applied physiology.
Hermann Brehmer 1826–1889	German physician	Started the modern therapy clinics for tuberculosis; rejected oxygen-poor mountain climates because of their lack of oxygen.
Paul Bert 1833–1886	French physician	Found that high-altitude sickness is largely a result of the diminished partial pressure of oxygen.
C. Lombroso 1836–1909	Italian psychiatrist and anthropologist	Observed that "psychic illnesses, especially psychotic anxieties, occur more frequently in spring, with great regularity, especially among nervous people."

Name	Profession	Description
Jakob Aall Bonnevie 1838–1904	Norwegian meteorologist	Developed the polar front theory.
F. Nietzsche 1844–1900	German philosopher	Distinctly weather-sensitive; classical self-observations, frequent change of location: "A weather that is unusual and unpredictable makes people distrust each other; they become obsessed with the new, because they have to give up their habits. That is why despots like all those areas where the weather is moral." He assumed air electricity was a co-trigger of his weather-dependent sensitivities.
Angelo Mosso 1846–1910	Italian physiologist	Bioclimatic research in high mountains and in high-mountain laboratories.
Nathan Zuntz 1847–1920	German physiologist	Led first German expedition into the high mountains for research.
Julius Elster 1854–1920 and	German teacher	
Hans Geitel 1855–1923	German physicist	Both were recognized for their research on atmospheric ions.
A. Haviland 1855	English physician	Coined the term "iatrometeorology" to describe those diseases caused by the atmospheric environment.
Oskar Bernhard 1861–1939 and	Swiss physician	
August Rollier 1874–1954	Swiss physician	Established heliotherapy schedules for extrapulmonary tuberculosis and for surgical treatment of bone and joint tuberculosis. Set up institute in Lausanne.

Name	Profession	Description
Wilhelm Bjerknes 1862–1951	Norwegian geophysicist and meteorologist	Pioneer of weather forecasting, meteorological observation stations, and the scheme of the low-pressure areas yielding to high-pressure areas.
Carl Dorno 1865–1942	Physicist and meteorologist	Cofounder of precise medical-meteorological research.
E. G. Dexter 1868–1938	American pedagogue	Conducted extensive statistical biometeorological tests on criminality, fluctuation of general conditions.
William F. Petersen 1887–1950	American pathologist	His monumental research, *The Patient and the Weather*, is all but unknown to contemporary medicine. Examining individuals case by case in great depth, he sought to understand how their symptoms varied, day by day, with the passage of weather fronts. Tested triplets for months, correlating and comparing their responses to weather change on a statistical basis. Developed explanatory interpretations similar to Selye's observations of stress. An American Hippocrates.
B. de Rudder 1935	German physician	Coined the term "meteorotropism," a tendency to change in response to weather conditions; an extreme version is "climatic disease" or "meteoropathology."
Manfred Curry 1946	American physician	Classified people into two types: a cold-front person (K), typically sensitive to cold, polar air fronts, inclined to have an overstimulated parasympathetic nervous system, likely to be pale, introverted personality with gastric ulcer; the warm-front person (W), particularly sensitive to warm-weather conditions, warms fronts, and influxes of warm tropical air, inclined to have overstimulated sympathetic nervous system, likely to be extroverted short-limbed, round-faced, and with gall bladder problems.

APPENDIX B: **Ranking of Weather Influence on "User" Groups in the United States**

User Group	(a) Weather Sensitivity	(b) Decision Latitude	Product of (a) and (b)	Rank	Projected 1972 National Income* ($ × 10⁹) in Billions of Dollars
General public	2.6	2.0	5.2	1	†
Fishing	2.3	2.3	5.3	2	$ 0.26
Agriculture	2.0	3.0	6.0	3	28.10
General science	2.7	2.3	6.2	4	†
Air transportation	2.0	3.3	6.6	5	2.30
Forestry	2.3	3.3	7.6	6	1.68
Construction	2.6	3.0	7.8	7	39.30
Land transportation	2.6	3.3	8.6	8	12.90
Water transportation	3.0	3.0	9.0	9	2.05
General welfare	3.6	2.6	9.4	10	†
Energy production and distribution	3.3	3.0	9.9	11	30.00
Health and safety	2.9	3.6	10.4	12	†
Resources utilization	3.0	3.6	10.8	13	†
Merchandising	3.3	3.3	10.9	14	145.30
Water supply and control	4.2	3.0	12.6	15	4.28
Communications	3.6	3.6	13.0	16	22.70
Recreation	4.0	3.3	13.2	17	3.35
Manufacturing	4.2	4.3	18.1	18	$262.40

Weather-Sensitivity	*Decision Latitude*
1 = Great—involves life, very large money values	1 = Very flexible
2 = Important—much money and/or direct health effects	2 = Quite flexible
3 = Significant—meaningful costs, secondary health effects	3 = Some flexibility
4 = Modest	4 = Little flexibility
5 = Small	5 = Rigid
6 = None	

*Adapted from information supplied by National Planning Association. All data are in terms of 1962 dollars.

† Not assessed.

APPENDIX C: **You and Your "Environment": A Self-Discovery Questionnaire**

This questionnaire will give you an opportunity to discover how various aspects of your body and mind respond to your "environment."

- Your personal ailments, disorders, or symptoms may be associated with one or more of the following conditions of stress:

Exercise	Financial Difficulties	Problems with Opposite Sex
Overwork	Weather Changes	Death of Relative or Friend

- Please choose the condition(s) of stress that seem to accentuate your symptoms, ailments, or disorders.
- In the appropriate column opposite to a symptom that occurs frequently, please place the following marks:

$\sqrt{}$ = once a month, $\sqrt{}\sqrt{}$ = twice a month, $\sqrt{}\sqrt{}\sqrt{}$ = three times a month or more.

- If a symptom is especially intense, please use these marks:

x = once a month, xx = twice a month, xxx = three times a month or more.

Your Symptoms, Ailments, or Disorders	*Conditions of Stress*					
	Exercise	Overwork	Financial	Weather	Opp. Sex	Death
I. How often do you have periods when you are suddenly quiet?						
periods when you seem endlessly busy, restless, overactive?						
periods when you have flights of ideas never pursued?						
periods of hypochondria?						
periods when you are facetious, sarcastic, abusive?						
periods when you feel boisterous?						
periods when you are sullen, inaccessible, meditative?						
periods of apathy or listlessness?						
thoughts of attempted suicide or homicide?						
increased tendency to have accidents?						

Your Symptoms, Ailments, or Disorders	Conditions of Stress					
	Exercise	Overwork	Financial	Weather	Opp. Sex	Death
II. How often are you susceptible to allergies?						
III. How often do you change color rapidly? are you quick to react or very "emotional"? do you feel depressed, "blue," in a bad mood? do you have periods of great energy, exuberance, buoyancy, or euphoria? do you feel explosive anger, high temper, or irritability? are your mood swings long and gentle? are your mood swings short and abrupt?						
IV. How often do you feel pains from arthritis? pains from gout or rheumatism? pains in your bone joints? pains from past surgical operations?						
V. How often do you have high blood pressure (hypertension)? low blood pressure (hypotension)? hemorrhages or bleeding?						
VI. How often do you have back pains or body pains? water retention, swelling, or edema in portions of your body?						
VII. How often are you disturbed by pains from scars? skin irritations, inflammations, lesions? slow-to-heal cuts or bruises?						

Your Symptoms, Ailments, or Disorders	Conditions of Stress					
	Exercise	Overwork	Financial	Weather	Opp. Sex	Death
VIII. How often do you experience diffuse pressure in your head? migraine headaches? regular headaches? dizziness or faintness?						
IX. How often do you have wheezy breathing or breathlessness? running nose? common cold or "flu"? asthma, bronchitis, or both? hoarseness or cough? sore throat or "tickle"? tightness or constriction in the throat? pain or tightness in the chest? feelings of suffocation?						
X. How often do you have periods of irritability? periods when you increasingly tend to make mistakes? periods of reduced concentration? periods of forgetfulness? periods of nervousness? periods of fatigue or exhaustion? periods when you feel confused? periods of absence from, distaste for, work? periods of poor sleep, insomnia, nightmares? periods of perspiration without cause? flickering visual images or twitching eyes?						

APPENDIX D: **Risk of Death by Cause**	*Approximate Deaths per 1,000 Persons exposed per Year*	
Voluntary Exposure		
Smoking (20 cigarettes per day)	5	
Car driving	0.17	
Motorcycling	20	
Involuntary Exposure		
Diseases* (U.S.: 1900)	28	
Diseases* (U.S.: 1977)	9	
Heart disease (U.S., Denmark, U.K.: 1953–7)	2.5	
Heart disease (Japan: 1952–6)	0.5–1.0	
Heart disease (Egypt: 1951–3)	0.2–0.3	
Cancer (U.K.: 1952–6)	2–2.5	
Cancer (U.S.: 1953–7, France: 1950–7)	1–1.5	
Cancer (Japan: 1952–6)	0.5–1	
Influenza (U.S., France, Japan, Denmark)	0.2	
Stroke or apoplexy (U.S.: 1952–6)	2–1.5	
Senility (U.S.: 1952–6)	0.1	
Senility (France: 1950–1)	2–2.5	
Senility (U.K., Denmark)	0.2	
Senility (Germany: 1956)	0.4–0.5	
Run over by a road vehicle (U.S.)	0.05	
Run over by a road vehicle (U.K.)	0.06	
Weather, prefrontal; approaching cold front* (Pittsburgh: January, 1962–5)	0.01	?
Extreme heat wave* (U.S.: 1963–6)	0.05	?
Normal heat and humidity (New York: 1962–5)	0.004	?
Tornadoes (Midwest U.S.)	0.0022	
Floods (U.S.)	0.0022	
Earthquakes (California)	0.0017	
Storms (U.S.)	0.0008	
Lightning (U.K.)	0.0001	
Cosmic rays from supernova explosion	10^{-5} to 10^{-8}	
Meteorite	6×10^{-8}	

* Note: Many uncounted deaths from disease are weather-induced. However, it is not clear how many; people usually die not of a single cause but of a number of causes, some of which may be triggered by the physical environment. The passage of a cold front does increase the death rate by some small amount, and a reduced death rate follows the frontal passage. The reason may be that people at risk, who may die, do so and thereby reduce the number of potential victims after frontal passage. Also, postfrontal weather may be salubrious. Everyday weather, because of the pre- and postfrontal compensatory effects, may not result in excess deaths. Over long periods of time, the weather causes fluctuations in the daily death rate but may not actually increase it. Brezowsky, correlating 43,347 deaths in a four-year period, found peak mortality in the warm-moist weather phase 4 and in the cold-dry weather phase 6, and minimum mortality in mild dry weather phases 1 and 2. The peak was some 17% above, and the trough some 11% below, the normally expected rates. (See Chapter 9.)

APPENDIX E: **Fabric Data and CLO Values for Individual Garments**

Description	Fabric Construction	Total Weight oz.	Fabric Weight oz./sq. yd.	CLO Value
Women's				
Cool dress	Knit	5.3	3.7 Dress	0.17
	Plain weave		2.2 Lining	
Warm dress	Plain weave	41.7	17.8	0.63
Warm long sleeve blouse	Plain weave	5.9	2.8	0.29
Warm skirt	Twill weave	14.9	15.5 Skirt	0.22
	Plain weave		2.8 Lining	
Cool long sleeve blouse	Plain weave	3.0	1.9	0.20
Cool slacks	Knit	5.7	3.7	0.26
Warm slacks	Twill	21.9	13.5	0.44
Warm jacket or blazer	Weave	25.0	—	0.43
Cool jacket or blazer	Weave	18.0	—	0.31
Cool sleeveless sweater	Knit	6.1	—	0.17
Warm long sleeve sweater	Knit	10.6	8.2	0.37
Cool vest	Weave	6.8	5.7	0.20
Warm vest	Weave	8.0	8.5	0.30
Warm shawl (over shoulders)	Knit	12.0	—	0.40
Cool shawl (over shoulders)	Knit	8.0	—	0.30
Cool short sleeve blouse	Plain weave	3.1	—	0.17
Pantihose	—	—	—	0.01
Warm "tights"	Knit	5.0	—	0.25
Warm knee-high socks	Knit	6.0	—	0.08
Cool knee-high socks	Knit	4.0	—	0.06
Bra & panties	—	—	—	0.04
Girdle	—	—	—	0.04
Full slip	—	—	—	0.19
Half slip	—	—	—	0.13
Long underwear-tops	Knit	5.0	—	0.25
Long underwear-bottom	Knit	7.0	—	0.25

Description	Fabric Construction	Total Weight oz.	Fabric Weight oz./sq. yd.	CLO Value
Long thermal underwear-tops	Waffle knit	6.0	—	0.35
Long thermal underwear-bottom	Waffle knit	8.0	—	0.35
Nylon-cotton coverall	50/50	16–18	—	0.55
Shoes	—	10.0	—	0.03
Knee-high fashion boots	—	16.0	—	0.25
Knee-boots, leather lined	—	32.0	—	0.30

Men's

Briefs	Knit	2.0	—	0.05
Sleeveless undershirt	Knit	3.0	—	0.08
Short sleeve undershirt	Knit	3.5	—	0.09
Long underwear-tops	Knit	5.0	—	0.25
Long underwear-bottom	Knit	7.0	—	0.25
Long thermal underwear-tops	Waffle knit	6.0	—	0.35
Long thermal underwear-bottom	Waffle knit	8.0	—	0.35
Shoes, low	—	16.2	—	0.04
High shoes and side-zips	—	20.0	—	0.15
Knee-high boots, leather lined	—	32.0	—	0.30
Cool socks	—	2.0	—	0.03
Warm socks	—	4.0	—	0.04
Cool knee-high socks	—	4.0	—	0.06
Warm knee-high socks	—	6.0	—	0.08
Short sleeve woven shirt	Plain weave	7.1	4.0	0.19
Long sleeve woven shirt	Plain weave	5.9	2.8	0.29
Cool trousers	Plain weave	11.7	5.4	0.26
Warm trousers	Twill weave	18.1	8.4	0.32

Description	Fabric Construction	Total Weight oz.	Febric Weight oz./sq. yd.	CLO Value
Short sleeve cool knit shirt	Knit	7.1	5.6	0.22
Short sleeve warm knit shirt	Knit	6.8	6.8	0.25
Long sleeve cool knit shirt	Knit	6.9	6.1	0.14
Long sleeve warm knit shirt	Knit	10.6	9.2	0.37
Warm sports jacket or suit coat	Twill weave	29.9	—	0.49
Cool sports jacket or suit coat	Twill weave	20.0	—	0.35
Nylon-cotton coverall	50/50	16–18	—	0.55
Vest, cool	Weave	7.1	5.7	0.20
Vest, warm	Weave	8.2	8.5	0.30

- Select the items of apparel that you or your children will wear. (Estimate values between cool and warm, etc. for your garments.)
- Add up the individual clo values for the ensemble you wish to consider.
- For men—Multiply that total clo by ¾ and add 1/10 to the result. For women—Multiply that total clo by 4/5 and add 1/20 to the result. This will give an approximate total clo value of the clothing ensemble.
- By trial and error, add a sweater or vest, until the result is what you want.

APPENDIX F: **Measures to Minimize the Effects of Weather on Drug Action** (Ask physician for guidance.)

Generic Name	Typical Brand	Drug Family	Meteorological Conditions	Apparent Sensitivity	Minimized if
Acenocoumarol	Sintrom	anticoagulant	Heat	increases blood-clotting time	decrease dosage in prolonged hot weather
Acetohexamide	Dymelor	oral antidiabetic	Sun	photosensitivity?	exercise caution until photosensitivity is known
Amitriptyline	Elavil	tricyclic antidepressant	Sun	photosensitivity?	exercise caution until photosensitivity is known
Amobarbital	Amytal	sedative, sleep inducer	Cold	severe drop in body temperature	dress warmly; diminish dosage in winter, especially the elderly
Anisindione	Miradon	anticoagulant	Heat	increases blood-clotting time	decrease dosage in prolonged hot weather
Anisotropine	Valpin	antispasmodic	Heat	may cause heat stroke	use extreme caution in warm environments
Aspirin	Bayer	mild analgesic	Cold	dilates blood vessels	retard heat loss
Atropine	Butibel	antispasmodic anticholinergic	Heat	may cause heat stroke impairs temperature regulation	avoid hot environment
Bendroflumethiazide	Naturetin	antihypertensive diuretic	Sun/Heat	photosensitivity? increases chances of stroke	check photosensitivity; avoid warm environments
Benztropine	Cogentin	anti-parkinsonism anticholinergic	Heat	reduces sweating; increases chance of stroke	avoid body temperature increases and exertion
Bethanidine	none	antihypertensive	Heat	reduces sweating; increases chance of stroke	avoid hot environments

Generic	Brand	Use	Sun/Heat	Effects	Precautions
Biperiden	Akineton	anti-parkinsonism	Heat	reduces sweating; increases chance of stroke	avoid hot weather, over-heated environments
Butabarbital	Buticaps	sedative, sleep inducer	Sun/Cold	photosensitivity? lowers body temperature	check photosensitivity; dress warmly; elderly should take lower dosage
Butalbital	Sandoptal	sedative barbiturate	Sun/Cold	photosensitivity? lowers body temperature	check photosensitivity; dress warmly; elderly should take lower dosage
Caffeine	Nodoz	stimulant, relieves drowsiness	Heat	constricts blood vessels	assist heat loss
Chlordiazepoxide	Librium	mild tranquilizer	Sun/Heat	photosensitivity? reduces urine volume; possible overdose	check photosensitivity; avoid excess sweating
Chlorothiazide	Diuril	antihypertensive diuretic	Sun/Heat	excessive loss of water and salt; photosensitivity	check photosensitivity; avoid excess sweating
Chlorpromazine	Thorazine	tranquilizer antipsychotic	Sun/Heat	photosensitivity? impairs temperature regulation; chance of a stroke	avoid excess sweating avoid hot environments; check photosensitivity
Chlorpropamide	Diabinese	antidiabetic hypoglycemic	Sun	photosensitivity?	exercise caution until photosensitivity is known
Chlortetracycline	Aureomycin	antibiotic	Sun	exaggerates sunburn	avoid exposure to sun
Chlorthalidone	Hygroton	antihypertensive diuretic	Sun/Heat	photosensitivity? excessive loss of water, salt	check photosensitivity; avoid excess sweating
Clidinium	Librax	antispasmodic anticholinergic	Heat	impairs heat regulation; risk of heat stroke	extreme caution in over-heated environments
Clindamycin	Cleocin	antibiotic anti-infective	Sun	photosensitivity?	check photosensitivity

Generic Name	Typical Brand	Drug Family	Meteorological Conditions	Apparent Sensitivity	Minimized if
Clonidine	Catapres	antihypertensive	Cold	blanching and numbness of hands and feet	avoid exposure to cold air or water
Clorazepate	Tranxene	tranquilizer anti-anxiety	Heat	reduced urine volume caused by sweat may cause an overdose	avoid perspiring, physical exertion
Cyclandelate	Cyclospasmol	vasodilator	Heat/Cold	may cause excessive perspiring; less effective in cold environments	avoid hot weather, exertion, cold environments, handling cold objects
Demeclocycline	Declomycin	antibiotic	Sun	photosensitivity	avoid sun exposure
Desipramine	Norpramin	antidepressant tricyclic	Sun	photosensitivity?	exercise caution until photosensitivity is known
Dextroamphetamine	Dexedrine	sympathemimetic, anorexiant, stimulant, appetite suppressant	Cold	accelerates mental activity	avoid heavy exercise
Diazepam	Valium	mild tranquilizer anti-anxiety	Heat	excess sweating may cause overdose	avoid hot temperatures, exercise
Dicumarol	Dicumarol	anticoagulent	Heat	increases blood-clotting time	decrease dosage in prolonged hot weather
Dicyclomine	Bentyl Triactin	antispasmodic	Heat	increases risk of heat stroke	extreme caution in hot weather
Diethylpropion	Tenuate Tepanil	appetite suppressant sympathomimetics	Heat	decreases heat regulation	avoid overstimulation, stress
Dihydroergotoxine	Hydergine	ergot preparation	Cold	impairs metabolism	avoid cold weather, low body temperatures

Diphenhydramine	Benadryl	antihistamine sleep inducer	Sun	photosensitivity?	exercise caution until photosensitivity is known
Doxepin	Adapin	antidepressant	Sun	photosensitivity?	exercise caution until photosensitivity is known
Doxycycline	Doxychel	antibiotic tetracycline	Sun	photosensitivity	avoid sun exposure
Ergotamine	Ergomar	migraine analgesic	Cold	restricts circulation in arms and legs	avoid cold environment, handling of cold objects
Erthrityl Tetranitrate	Angimar	anti-anginal vasodilator	Cold	reduces drug effectiveness	avoid cold environments
Estrogen	Estrogen	female sex hormone	Sun	photosensitivity?	exercise caution until photosensitivity is known
Fluphenazine	Prolixin	tranquilizer antipsychotic	Sun/Heat	photosensitivity; impairs heat regulation; chance of heat stroke	check photosensitivity; avoid heat, overexertion
Furosemide	Lasix	antihypertensive diuretic	Sun/Heat	photosensitivity; impairs regulation of heat; stroke possible	avoid sun exposure; avoid exertion in warm environments
Glyburide or Glibenclamide	Diabeta	antidiabetic	Sun	photosensitivity?	avoid sun exposure
Griseofulvin	Fulvicin U/F	antibiotic antifungal	Sun	photosensitivity?	exercise caution until photosensitivity is known
Guanethidine	Ismelin	antihypertensive	Heat	orthostatic hypotension	avoid hot weather, over-heated environments

299

Generic Name	Typical Brand	Drug Family	Meteorological Conditions	Apparent Sensitivity	Minimized if
Haloperidol	Haldol	tranquilizer	Sun	photosensitivity?	exercise caution until photosensitivity is known
Hydralazine	Apresoline	antihypertensive	Cold	possible increase in coronary angina	avoid cold environments, especially if susceptible to coronary insufficiency
Hydrochlorothiazide	Esidrix	antihypertensive diuretic	Sun/Heat	photosensitivity? excess water and salt loss	check photosensitivity; avoid perspiring, heat, exercise
Hydroflumethiazide	Diucardin	antihypertensive diuretic	Sun/Heat	photosensitivity? excessive water and salt loss	check photosensitivity; avoid perspiring, heat, exercise
Imipramine	Presamine	antidepressant tricyclic	Sun	photosensitivity?	exercise caution until photosensitivity is determined
Isopropamide Isosorbide Dinitrate	Darbid Angidil	antispasmodic anti-anginal	Heat Cold	increase risk of heat stroke reduces effectiveness	avoid hot environments avoid cold weather, handling of cold objects
Isoxsuprine	Vasodilan	vasodilator	Cold	reduces drug effectiveness	avoid cold environments, handling of cold objects
Lincomycin	Lincocin	antibiotic	Sun	photosensitivity?	exercise caution until photosensitivity is determined
Liothyronine	Cytomel	thyroid hormone	Heat/Cold	decreases tolerance for heat; increases tolerance for cold environments	avoid hot environments

Lithium	Eskalith	tranquilizer	Heat	excess sweating causes lithium toxicity	avoid hot environments, sweating, exertion
Mesoridazine	Serentil	tranquilizer	Sun/Heat	photosensitivity? excessive loss of salt and water	check photosensitivity; avoid excessive heat, perspiration
Methacycline	Rondomycin	antibiotic tetracyclines	Sun	photosensitivity	avoid excessive sun exposure
Methscopolamine	Pamine	antispasmodic	Heat	impairs heat loss; increases stroke risk	avoid heat, sweating, exertion
Methyclothiazide	Enduron	antihypertensive diuretic	Sun/Heat	photosensitivity? excessive water and salt loss	check photosensitivity; avoid exertion in warm environment, perspiring
Methysergide	Sansert	migraine preventive antiserotonin	Cold	may reduce circulation to extremities	dress warmly; avoid cold
Minocycline	Minocin	antibiotic tetracycline	Sun	photosensitivity	avoid excessive sun exposure
Nalidixic Acid	NegGram	antimicrobial	Sun	may cause severe, prolonged photosensitivity reduces effectiveness of drug	avoid sun exposure
Nitroglycerin	Nitrobid	anti-anginal vasodilator	Cold	photosensitivity?	avoid cold, see physician about increasing dosage
Nortriptyline	Aventyl	antidepressant tricyclic	Sun	photosensitivity?	exercise caution until photosensitivity is known
Oral Contraceptives	"The Pill"	female sex hormones (estrogen & progestin)	Sun	photosensitivity?	exercise caution until photosensitivity is determined
Oxazepam	Serax	mild tranquilizer benzodiazepine	Heat	may accumulate, cause overdose because of reduced urine volume	exercise caution until effect of excessive perspiration is known

Generic Name	Typical Brand	Drug Family	Meteorological Conditions	Apparent Sensitivity	Minimized if
Oxyphenbutazone	Oxalid	analgesic antipyretic	Sun	photosensitivity?	exercise caution until photosensitivity is determined
Oxytetracycline	Dalimycin	antibiotic tetracyclines	Sun	photosensitivity	avoid excessive sun exposure
Papaverine	Cerespam	vasodilator	Heat/Cold	may cause excessive sweating; cold environments reduce effectiveness	avoid extremes in temperatures
Pentaerythritol Tetranitrate	Perispan	anti-anginal vasodilator	Cold	may reduce drug effectiveness	avoid cold environments
Pentobarbital	Nembutal	sedative barbiturate	Sun/Cold	photosensitivity? elderly may experience excessive lowering of body temperature	check photosensitivity; keep dosage at a minimum when cold; dress warmly
Perphenazine	Trilafon	tranquilizer	Sun/Heat	photosensitivity? may increase risk of heat stroke	check photosensitivity; avoid hot environments, exertion
Phenobarbital or Phenobarbitone	Barbipil	barbiturate sedative	Sun/Cold	photosensitivity? lowering of body temperature	check photosensitivity; dress warmly; consult doctor about lower dosage
Phenoxybenzamine	Dibenzyline	vasodilator	Cold	reduces drug effectiveness	minimize exposure to cold
Phenylbutazone	Azolid, Butazolidin	analgesic antipyretic	Sun	photosensitivity?	exercise caution until photosensitivity is determined

Phenytoin	Diphenylan	anticonvulsant hydantoins	Sun	photosensitivity?	exercise caution until photosensitivity is determined
Prochlorperazine	Compazine	tranquilizer antinausea	Sun/Heat	photosensitivity? impairs heat regulation; risk of heat stroke	check photosensitivity; avoid excessive heat
Procyclidine	Kemadrin	anti-parkinsonism anticholinergics	Heat	sweat reduction increases risk of heat stroke	avoid hot environments, exertion in warm environments
Promazine	Sparine	antinausea tranquilizer	Sun/Heat	photosensitivity? impairs heat regulation; risk of heat stroke	check photosensitivity; avoid excessive heat exposure
Promethazine	Histamil	antihistamine antinausea	Sun	photosensitivity?	exercise caution until photosensitivity is known
Propantheline	Probital	antispasmodic	Heat	sweat reduction increases risk of heat stroke	avoid hot environments, exertion
Propranolol	Inderal	anti-anginal antihypertensive anti-arrhythmic	Cold	may further impair circulation in limbs	use caution in cold environment; dress warmly
Protriptyline	Vivactil	antidepressant tricyclic	Sun	photosensitivity?	exercise caution until photosensitivity is determined
Secobarbital	Seco-8	sedative barbiturate	Sun/Cold	photosensitivity? lowering of body temperature	check photosensitivity; dress warmly; check with physician about lower dose

Generic Name	Typical Brand	Drug Family	Meteorological Conditions	Apparent Sensitivity	Minimized if
Sulfamethoxazole	Gantanol	anti-infective	Sun	photosensitivity?	exercise caution until photosensitivity is determined
Sulfasalazine	Azulfidine	anti-infective	Sun	photosensitivity?	exercise caution until photosensitivity is determined
Sulfisoxazole	Barazole	anti-infective	Sun	photosensitivity?	exercise caution until photosensitivity is determined
Tetracycline	Tetracycline	antibiotic	Sun	photosensitivity	avoid excessive exposure to sun
Tetrahydrocannabinals	Marijuana	narcotic hallucinogen	Cold	potent hypothermic action	avoid cold weather
Thioridazine	Mellaril	tranquilizer phenothiazines	Sun/Heat	photosensitivity? impairs heat regulation; risk of heat stroke	check photosensitivity; avoid hot environments
Thiothixene	Navane	tranquilizer thioxanthines	Sun/Heat	photosensitivity? impairs heat regulation; risk of heat stroke	check photosensitivity; avoid hot environments, exertion
Thyroid preparations	Thyrobrom	thyroid hormone	Heat/Cold	decreases tolerance for heat; increases tolerance for cold	avoid temperature extremes; avoid exertion in heat; dress warmly when cold
Thyroxine	T-4	thyroid hormone	Heat/Cold	decreases tolerance for heat; increases tolerance for cold	avoid temperature extremes; avoid exertion in heat; dress warmly when cold
Tolazamide	Tolinase	antidiabetic hypoglycemic	Sun	photosensitivity?	exercise caution until photosensitivity is determined

Tolbutamide	Orinase	antidiabetic hypoglycemic	Sun	photosensitivity?	exercise caution until photosensitivity is determined
Triamterene	Dyrenium	antihypertensive diuretic	Sun	photosensitivity?	exercise caution until photosensitivity is determined
Tridihexethyl	Pathilon	antispasmodic anticholinergics	Heat	may significantly increase risk of heat stroke	avoid sweating, exertion, hot environments
Trifluoperazine	Stelazine	tranquilizer	Sun/Heat	photosensitivity? impairs heat regulation; increases risk of heat stroke	check photosensitivity; avoid hot environments
Triheyphenidyl	Artane	anti-parkinsonism anticholinergics	Heat	reduced sweating increases risk of heat stroke	avoid exertion, hot environments
Trimeprazine	Temaril	anti-itching antipruritic	Sun	photosensitivity?	exercise caution until photosensitivity is determined
Triprolidine	Actidil	antihistamines	Sun	photosensitivity?	exercise caution until photosensitivity is determined
Trisulfapyrimidines	Trisulfazine	anti-infective	Sun	photosensitivity?	exercise caution until photosensitivity is determined
Warfarin	Panwarfin	anticoagulant	Heat	prolonged hot weather may increase prothrombin time	ask physician about reducing dosage

appendix G: **Systemic Classification of Symptoms and Signs of Tropical Neurasthenia**

Emotional

1. Inability to concentrate; impaired or reduced powers of concentration; inability to sit quietly thinking or reading; deterioration in capacity and speed of thought; slowness of mental processes; mental retardation; mental lassitude; limited capacity to concentrate; mental fatigue.
2. Loss of memory; low-grade amnesia; deterioration in memory; forgetfulness.
3. Irritability; irritability with temper outbursts; increase in irritability or loss of temper; general lack of control.
4. Indecision; procrastination; reduction in power of making decisions; bibulousness.
5. Lack or loss of interest.
6. Inertia; deterioration in drive; loss of initiative; increasing deliberate effort to complete routine work; diurnal somnolence.
7. Depression; acute and severe depression with suicide or attempted suicide.
8. Worry over trifles or inconsequential matters.
9. Emotional disturbance; loss of emotional stability; emotional imbalance (weeping at least provocation); flood of tears when referring to health; emotional fluctuations; irritable; uncontrollable fits of weeping.
10. Insomnia; sleeplessness.
11. Reduced alertness and keenness.
12. Tendency to paranoid feeling of resentment.
13. Obsession of persecution.
14. Excessive smoking.
15. Mental confusion.
16. Restlessness.
17. Excitability altering with depression and general discouragement.
18. Fear of insanity and loss of job.
19. Reduced sense of responsibility.
20. Personality changes.
21. Slovenliness of dress.
22. Alcoholic indulgence.
23. Anxiety state.
24. Hypochondriasis; hypochondriacal tendency.
25. Hysteria.
26. Attacks of terror with sensation of dying.
27. Oppressive dreams.

Neuromuscular system
1. Feeling of exhaustion; lassitude; physical lassitude; tiredness; fatigue disproportionate to exertion; loss of energy; constant feeling of tiredness; inability to produce customary amount of work; lethargy.
2. Headache; headache in temperal or parietal region; occipital headache; migraneous headache.
3. Sense of increased intracranial pressure.
4. Exaggerated reflexes; hyperreflexia; hyporeflexia.
5. False ankle clonus.
6. High degree of tremor; motor restlessness; trembling of hands, feet, head.
7. Dilated pupils; constricted pupils.
8. Epileptiform convulsions followed by transient hemiplegia.
9. Parasthesias.
10. Cloudiness of vision; scotomata.
11. Difficulties of hearing; tinnitus.
12. Zones of hyp- or anaesthesia unrelated to dermatomes.

Gastro-intestinal system
1. Ill-defined digestive disorders.
2. Flatulent dyspepsia; atonic dyspepsia.
3. Anorexia; feeling of hunger; craving for salt.
4. Weight loss; emaciation.
5. Sinking feeling in abdomen; empty weak feeling.
6. Indefinite abdominal pain; pyloric spasms; colonic spasms; biliary spasms.
7. Hyperconsciousness of bowel function.
8. Chronic obstipation; constipation alternating with diarrhoea; diarrhoea without cramps.
9. Nausea and vomiting.
10. Eructation; dilated stomach with aerophagia.
11. Profuse salivation in children; dry mouth in others.
12. Visceroptosis.

Cardiovascular system
1. Dizziness on standing ('black-out' spells); fainting.
2. Tachycardia after light work or at rest; tachycardia with mental effort, bradycardia otherwise.
3. Low blood pressure; rise in blood pressure; reduced systolic but normal diastolic pressure; reduced systolic but elevated diastolic pressure.
4. Vasomotor instability; facial pallor; flushing; pale skin; dermographia; urticaria; wide sinuous retinal arteries and pink white discs; narrowed retinal vessels.

5. Palpitations; heart tremulous; extra-systoles.
6. Vascular murmurs over large arteries.
7. Accentuated P_2.
8. Pains in chest, over heart, and between shoulder blades.
9. Cutaneous oedema over tibia.
10. Right enlargement of heart.

Respiratory system
1. Rhinitis vasomotorica; uncontrollable fits of sneezing at night.
2. Asthma.
3. Dyspnoea; dyspnoea on effort.

Urogenital system
1. Nocturia.
2. Oliguria.
3. Bladder cramps.
4. Oligomenorrhoea; amenorrhoea.
5. Reduced libido; sexual impotency.

Disturbances of heat-regulating mechanism
1. Subnormal or unstable temperature (permanently elevated about 1° F in hot seasons); moderate pyrexia.
2. Excessive sweating; hyperhidrosis; bouts of severe sweating.
3. Sweating on palms; hyperhidrosis on palms and soles.

Other symptoms
1. Increase in ill-health.
2. General malaise.

APPENDIX H: **Sheldon's Three Components of Temperament**

I Viscerotonia	II Somatotonia	III Cerebrotonia
*1. Relaxation in posture and movement	*1. Assertiveness of posture and movement	*1. Restraint in posture and movement, tightness
*2. Love of physical comfort	*2. Love of physical adventure	2. Physiological over-response
*3. Slow reaction	*3. The energetic characteristic	*3. Overly fast reactions
4. Love of eating	*4. Need and enjoyment of exercise	*4. Love of privacy
5. Socialization of eating	5. Love of dominating, lust for power	*5. Mental overintensity, hyperattentionality, apprehensiveness
6. Pleasure in digestion	*6. Love of risk and chance	*6. Secretiveness of feeling, emotional restraint
*7. Love of polite ceremony	*7. Bold directness of manner	*7. Self-conscious motility of the eyes and face
*8. Sociophilia	*8. Physical courage for combat	*8. Sociophobia
9. Indiscriminate amiability	*9. Competitive aggressiveness	*9. Inhibited social address
10. Greed for affection and approval	10. Psychological callousness	10. Resistance to habit, and poor routinizing
11. Orientation to people	11. Claustrophobia	11. Agoraphobia
*12. Evenness of emotional flow	12. Ruthlessness, freedom from squeamishness	12. Unpredictability of attitude
*13. Tolerance	*13. The unrestrained voice	*13. Vocal restraint, and general restraint of noise
*14. Complacency	14. Spartan indifference to pain	14. Hypersensitivity to pain
15. Deep sleep	15. General noisiness	15. Poor sleep habits, chronic fatigue
*16. The untempered characteristic	*16. Overmaturity of appearance	*16. Youthful intentness of manner and appearance

I Viscerotonia	II Somatotonia	III Cerebrotonia
*17. *Smooth, easy communication of feeling, extraversion of viscerotonia*	17. *Self-distant (horizontal cleavage)*	17. *Environs-distant (vertical cleavage), introversion*
18. *Relaxation* and sociophilia under alcohol	18. *Assertiveness* and aggression under alcohol	18. *Resistance* to alcohol, and to other depressant drugs
19. *Need of people* when troubled	19. *Need of action* when troubled	19. *Need of solitude* when troubled
20. Orientation toward *childhood* and family relationships	20. Orientation toward goals and activities of *youth*	20. Orientation toward the *later periods of life*

Note: The thirty traits with asterisks constitute collectively the short form of the scale. The italicized traits are tripolar; they comprise trichotomies.

APPENDIX I: **Weather Events: Their Favorable and Unfavorable Influence on Health and Disease**

	Weather High/Low		Transition Stable	Transition Un-stable	Transition Sub-tropical	Unstable Ground	Unstable High	Fronts Warm	Fronts Cold	Fronts Mixed	Falling Air Sink	Falling Air Glide	Falling Air Inversions
concentration ability	+.	⊘					⊘		⊘		+		
reaction time	+.	●				O	O	●	●	●	+.	●	●
traffic accidents	+.	●	+	⊘	⊘	+.	+.	⊘	⊘	⊘	+.	●	
accidents at work	+.	●			⊘		⊘	⊘	⊘	⊘	+.	●	
sensations of pain	+	⊘		⊘	⊘	⊘	⊘	⊘	⊘		+		
need to sleep	+	⊘		⊘	●		⊘	⊘+	⊘	●	O	+	+
depth of sleep	+	⊘	+	●	⊘	O	+	●	O	O	+	●	
bronchial asthma	+	●	O	O	●	O	●	⊘	●	●	+	+	●
heart attacks	+	⊘			●			⊘	●	O			
angina pectoris	+.	●	+	●	●	+	●	●	●	●	+.	+	
heart infarcts	+.	●		●	●	⊘	⊘	●	●	●	+.	⊘	O
heart deaths	+.	●	O	●				●	●		+.	⊘	
incidence of deaths	+.	●	⊘	●	●	+.		●	●	●	+.	⊘	⊘
embolisms	+	⊘	+	⊘	⊘	O	⊘	⊘	⊘	O	+	O	⊘
kidney colic	+	⊘			●				●		+.	+	
gall bladder colic	+	⊘			●				●		+	+	
stomach perforations	+	⊘	⊘	⊘	●	+	+	⊘	●	⊘	+.	+.	O
appendicitis	+	⊘			●		●				+.	+.	O
bleeding after eye operation	⊘											⊘	
glaucoma	+	⊘						⊘	⊘	⊘		⊘	
headache	+	⊘			⊘			⊘	⊘				
suicides	+	⊘			⊘					⊘			
weather condition % time	54.5	45.5	9.4	2.3	21.2	1.3	4.3	2.0	3.9	1.1	23.4	31.1	
degree of biotropy		•											
degree of biotropy			mod. to weak	strong	very strong	weak	mod.	strong to mod.	strong to mod.	strong	in-diff.	weak to indiff.	strong low lvl.

Symbols:
+ favorable influence
+. statistically favorable influence (above chance)
O influence not established
⊘ unfavorable influence
● statistically unfavorable influence (above chance)

APPENDIX J: **The Approach and Passage of Warm and Cold Fronts**

Phenomenon	Warm Front		Cold Front		Occluded Front		Observer North of Frontal System
	Approach	Passage	Approach	Passage	Approach	Passage	
Pressure	Falls steadily	Levels off, or falls unsteadily	Falls slowly; or rapidly if storm intensifying	Sharp rise	Falls steadily	Rises, often not as sharply as cold front	Falls slowly; then rises slowly as system passes
Wind	SE quadrant; speed increases	Veers to S quadrant	S quadrant; may be squally at times	Sharp veer to SW quadrant; speed increases; gusty	E quadrant; may veer slowly to SE quadrant; speed increases	Veers to SW quadrant; speed decreases	NE quadrant; backs through N to NW quadrant
Clouds	Cirrus; cirrostratus; altostratus; nimbostratus; thickening	Stratocumulus; sometimes cumulonimbus; clearing trend	Cumulus or altocumulus; cumulonimbus in squall line	Cumulonimbus; sometimes few clouds; clearing trend	Cirrus; cirrostratus; altostratus; nimbostratus	Slow clearing; stratocumulus; altocumulus	Cirrus; cirrostratus; altostratus; nimbostratus; stratocumulus; cumulus
Precipitation	Steady rain or snow starts as clouds thicken; intensifies as front approaches	Precipitation tapers off; may be showery	None or showery; intense showers or hail in pre-front squall line	Showery; perhaps thunderstorms; rapid clearing	Steady rain or snow starts as clouds thicken; intensifies as front approaches	Precipitation tapers off slowly	Rain or snow starting as clouds thicken and lower; slow clearing
Temperature	Increases slowly	Slight rise	Little change or slow rise	Sharp drop	Slow rise	Slow fall	Steady or slow decrease
Humidity	Increases	Increases; may level off	Steady; or slight increase	Sharp drop	Slow increase	Slow decrease	Increase; slow decrease as storm passes
Visibility	Becomes poorer	Becomes better	Fair; may become poor in squalls	Sharp rise; becomes excellent	Becomes poorer	Becomes better	Becomes poor; slow improvement

ARS Phase (Anabolism, Reduction, Spasm) of Petersen; "Pressor Crisis"

- body's blood volume *shrinks* to the central organs, torso
- shuts off periphery of the body against the outer world
- blood pressure increases; accelerators dominate depressors
- blood sugar increases
- protein concentration of blood decreases
- oxidation rate decreases
- vasoconstriction involves the pelvis, cerebral cortex, the spinal cord, smooth muscles
- relative air hunger
- carbon dioxide content in blood decreases
- synthesis of new substance in body increases (anabolism)
- relative blood alkalosis
- generally a period of relative sympathicotonia, or *adrenal* phase

COD Phase (Catabolism, Oxidation, Dilation) of Petersen; Vagotonia

- body's blood volume *expands* to the extremities
- compensatory mechanisms begin; depressors dominate accelerators
- blood pressure declines
- blood sugar declines
- cholesterol increases
- oxidation rate increases
- vasodilation to accommodate demand for increased oxygen
- air hunger disappears
- carbon dioxide content of blood increases
- breakdown of body substances increases (catabolism)
- relative blood acidosis
- approximately a parasympathetic, or *acetylcholine* phase

Characteristic "Exhaustion" Stage of Selye

- may appear immediately after massive "alarm" and "resistance"
- or only after many swings between alarm and resistance
- result of general "wear and tear" aggravates existing dysfunctions
- energy of "adaptation" is consumed
- diverse diseases and ailments a function of genetic constitution, predispositions, organ weaknesses
- mood changes, a function of body type, personality
- nevertheless, many symptoms are shared in common: the "syndrome of just being sick"
- damage to body under attack: adrenal enlargement, thymus and lymph structures contract, gastrointestinal ulcers

APPENDIX L: **Air, Waters, and Places—Updated: Weather and Climate Spas Around the World**

United States

Arkansas:	Hot Springs National Park (Hot Springs)
California:	Murrieta Hot Springs (Murrieta)
	Hidden Valley Health Ranch (Escondido)
Colorado:	El Dorado Springs (25 minutes from Denver)
	Glenwood Springs (70 miles west of Denver)
	Radium Hot Springs Spa (Idaho Springs)
	Manitou Springs (Manitou)
	Ouray Swimming Pool (Ouray)
Florida:	The Palm Beach Spa (Palm Beach)
	Warm Mineral Springs (Venice)
Georgia:	Warm Springs Foundation (Warm Springs)
Hawaii:	The Royal Door Health and Beauty Spa (Honolulu)
Idaho:	Lava Hot Springs
Illinois:	St. Joseph's Health Resort (Wedron)
	Original Mineral Springs Hotel and Bath House (Oakville)
Indiana:	French Lick-Sheraton Hotel and Country Club (French Lick)
Louisiana:	Hot Wells Resort Center (Boyce)
Massachusetts:	The New England Conservatory of Health at Magnolia Manor (Magnolia)
Montana:	Fairmont Hot Springs Resort (Anaconda)
New Mexico:	Ojo Caliente Mineral Springs (Jemez Mountains)
	Radium Hot Springs (near Las Cruces)
	Truth and Consequences (southeast of the state)
New York:	Saratoga Spa (Saratoga Springs)
Oregon:	Kah/Nee/Ta Vacation Resort (Warm Springs)
South Dakota:	Evan's Plunge (Pierre)
Virginia:	The Homestead (Hot Springs)
	Warm Springs Inn (Warm Springs)
Washington:	Soap Lake (Soap Lake)
West Virginia:	The Greenbriar (White Sulpher Springs)
Wyoming:	Thermopolis (Thermopolis)

Canada

Banff Hot Springs (Alberta's Banff National Park)
Miette Hot Springs (Jasper National Park)

South America and the Caribbean
   Argentina: Rio Hondo (northern Argentina)
   Brazil: Araxa
   Bermuda: Deepdene

Mexico
   Ixtapan (90 miles from Mexico City, near Taxco)
   Rio Caliente (12 miles north of Guadalajara)

Europe
   Austria: Baden bei Wien (Vienna Woods)
   Bad Hofgastein (Bad Gastein, Austrian Alps)
   Warmbad Villach
   Belgium: Spa
   Ostend
   Chaudfontaine (5 miles from Liège)
   Bulgaria: Bankya (11 miles from Sofia)
   Velingrad (Rhodope Mountains' Chepino Valley)
   Czechoslovakia: Marienbad
   Carlsbad
   Frantiskovy
   Piestany
   Denmark: Silkeborg Bad
   Finland: Savonlinna
   France: Vichy
   Evian-les-Bains
   Germany: Baden-Baden
   Wiesbaden
   Sylt
   Great Britain: Forest Mere (Liphook, Hampshire)
   Bath (Somerset)
   Droitwich (Worcestershire)
   Greece: Loutraki (on the Gulf of Corinth)
   Kammena Vourla (on the Gulf of Euboea)
   Hungary: Budapest
   Heviz Spa
   Hajduszoboszlo Spa
   Iceland: Hveragerdi (30 miles from Reykjavik)
   Ireland: Lisdoonvarna
   Italy: Montecatini Terme (Montecatini)
   Ischia (island in the bay of Naples)
   Merano
   Fiuggi
   Bagni de Bormio (Lombardy region)

Luxembourg:	Mondorf-les-Bains
Norway:	Sandefjord
Poland:	Krynica (valley in the Carpathian Mountains)
Portugal:	Moncao (northern border)
	Melgaco (northern border)
Romania:	Eforie Nord
	Felix (northwest Romania)
Spain:	La Toja (Iberian peninsula)
Sweden:	Ramlosa Brunn
	Mossebergs Sanatorium (Mossebergs)
Switzerland:	Baden (Near Zurich)
	Bex-les-Bains
	Bad Ragaz
Yugoslavia:	Rogaska Slatina (north of Zagreb)
	Niska Banja (eastern Serbia)

Middle East

Israel:	Hamei Zohar (southern Dead Sea)
	Tiberias
	Ein Noit (Ein Bokek)
Turkey:	Cagaloglu (Istanbul)
	Asclepium
	Pamukkale

Asia

India:	Bakreswar Spring (Calcutta)
Japan:	Noboribetsu (island of Hokkaido)
	Beppu (island of Kyushu)
USSR:	Sochi-Matsesta (90-mile stretch of Caucasian shore)
Australia:	Hopewood Health Center (37 miles from Sydney)
	Warburton Sanitarium

Notes

Chapter 1 Notes: The Weather Experience

The advice to "Beat This Weather" is Hesiod's to his brother Perses, in *Hesiod's Works and Days and Theogony*, translation by Richard Lattimore (1959). University of Michigan Press, Ann Arbor.

The half-dozen or so definitions of the word "weathering" may be found in *The Oxford English Dictionary*, Compact Edition. Oxford University Press, New York, 1971.

The quotation is from "Weather or Not," by Richard L. Tobin, *Saturday Review* (Nov. 12, 1966), pp. 95–6. He cites a reader's survey (by the North American Newspaper Alliance) of what TV viewers think about weather broadcasting. Nine out of ten want "the fullest possible presentation of meteorological information in preference to a brief official bulletin from the local weather bureau." He says these "Americans want more weather news, not less. To follow the average temperatures, the accumulated rainfall (or lack of it), the winds and preparation of summer, fall, winter and spring; to see how hot or cold it was yesterday in the home-town we come from or are going to; to read the all-time lows and highs and means; to watch a great meteorological news story develop on the weather map is far too intriguing and important to brush off as if it didn't exist or had no effect on us all."

For an uninformed view of the same subject, consider Clive Barnes (dance and drama critic formerly for *The New York Times*), writing in *Punch*, as quoted in *Television Quarterly*, Vol. XIV, No. II and III, Summer/Fall, 1977: ". . . there is that strange phenomenon of the American weatherman. If anyone thinks the British are obsessed with weather, they should consider the Americans. The weather is constantly being given, and at length. In the late news broadcasts something like a sixth of the program is devoted to a discussion of weather past, weather present and weather future.

"The meteorologists providing this—I must say—largely erroneous information are all characters. They are funny. They make jokes. They are kidded by the other anchormen and they josh the other reporters. So you can have up to a sixth of your news program devoted to a quirky account of weather conditions. It is as if a 24-page newspaper gave over 4 pages to weather reports. Hardly makes sense, does it? But it does make ratings. And ratings are what make the world go round."

The renowned meteorologist is Charles L. Hosler, Dean, College of Earth and Mineral Sciences, Pennsylvania State University, in private correspondence.

The middle-aged physician is Lloyd H. Ziegler, writing in *Jour. Amer. Med. Assoc.* (1940), *115*, 19, 1590.

The psychiatrist is Hans H. Reese, writing in *Jour. Amer. Med. Assoc.* (1940), *115*, 19, 1587–91.

The recent study by two cardiologists is Burch, G. E., and Giles, T. D. "Influence of Weather and Climate on Cardiovascular Disease," in *Progress in Biometeorology*, edited by S. W. Tromp (1977). Swets and Zeitlinger, Amsterdam and Lisse, 52–60.

Chapter 2 Notes: Sensitivity to Weather . . . Sensitivity to Life

The meteorological idioms are found in Neuberger, Hans. "Meteorological Imagery in Language, Music and Art." *Mineral Industries* (January, 1961), *29*, 4. Pennsylvania State University.

McLuhan, Marshall, in *Subliminal Seduction* (1972). Key, Wilson Bryan, Prentice Hall, Englewood Cliffs, N.J.

Faust, Volker. *Biometeorologie* (1976). Hippokrates Verlag, Stuttgart.

Reese, Hans H. "The Significance of the Meteorological Environment in the Etiology of Psychotic Episodes." *Jour. of Mt. Sinai Hosp.* (1942), *9*, 717–33.

The results on women's reactivity to heat stress comes from Morimoto, T., Slabochova, Z., Naiman, R. K., Sargent, II, F. "Sex Differences in Physiological Reactions to Thermal Stress." *Jour. Appl. Physiology* (1967), *22*, 3, 526–32; and Weinman, K. P., Slabochova, Z., Bernouer, E. M., Morimoto, T., and Sargent, II, F. "Reactions of Men and Women to Repeated Exposures to Humid Heat." *Jour. Appl. Physiology* (1967), *22*, 3, 533–8.

Data on age- and sex-dependent, subjective weather-sensitivity came from Faust (*op. cit.*); the figure is his data reworked by Dirnagl, K., "Neure Untersuchungsergebnisse zur Beeinflussung des menschlichen Befindens durch des Wetter." *Therapiewoche* (1977), *27*, 6, 858–70.

The changes in organ function with age come from Bafitis, H., and Sargent, II, F. "Human Physiological Adaptability Through the Life Sequence." *Jour. Gerontology* (1977), *32*, 402–10.

The age demographics come from *Monthly Economic Letter* (December, 1977), Citibank, and the Bureau of the Census.

Class-dependent weather-sensitivity data is found in Faust, Volker. *Die Med Welt* (1975), *26*, 2074–80; and *op. cit.*

Change in Organ Function with Age

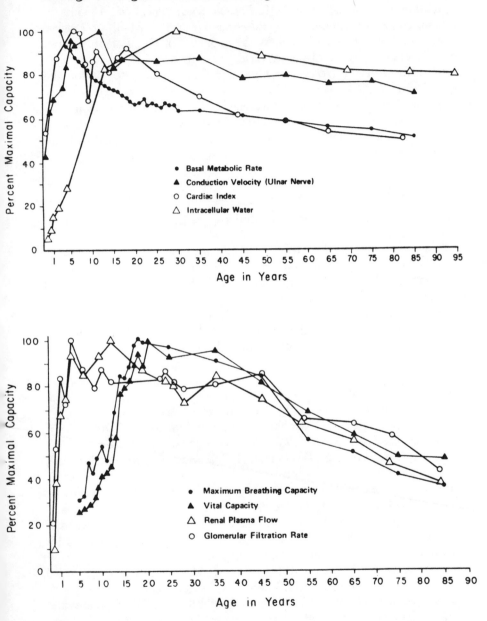

The three tables on weather and dysfunction are adapted from Faust, V., Harlfinger, O., and Neuwirth, R. *Fortsch. Med.* (1977), *95*, 4, 331.

Tromp, Solco W. "Influences on Infectious Diseases in Man," in *Progress in Biometeorology*, edited by S. W. Tromp. (1977), Vol. *1*, Part II. Swets and Zeitlinger, Amsterdam and Lisse.

Selye, Hans. *Stress in Health and Disease* (1976). Butterworths, Boston and London.

Both tables on stress from Arnold Mitchell. "The Effects of Stress on Individuals and Society." (February, 1977), SRI Project 4676, Assessment of Future National and International Problem Areas, National Science Foundation, Washington.

Chapter 3 Notes: Weather-Beaten . . . or Weather-Proof?

Rabkin, Judith G., and Streuning, Elmer L. "Life Events, Stress and Illness." *Science* (Dec. 3, 1976), *194*, 1013–20.

Sulman, Felix G. *Health, Weather and Climate* (1977). S. Karger, Basel.

Jokl, E. "Effects of Altitude on Sports Performance," in *Progress in Biometeorology*, edited by S. W. Tromp. (1977), Vol. *1*, Part II. Swets and Zeitlinger, Amsterdam and Lisse.

The table of sports performance under thermal stress comes from Egan, C. J., "Effects of Thermal Stress on Sports Performance," in *Progress in Biometerology*, edited by S. W. Tromp. (1977), Vol. *1*, Part II. Swets and Zeitlinger, Amsterdam and Lisse (see opposite page).

The estimates of energy output come from Auliciems, A., deFreitas, C., Hare, F. K. "Winter Clothing Requirements for Canada," Climatological Studies Toronto (1973). Information Canada.

Cooper, Kenneth H. *The Aerobics Way: New Data on the World's Most Popular Exercise Program* (1977). M. Evans, New York.

Ried, Jozsef. *Kornyezet Es Tevekenyses* (1972). Akademici Krado, Budapest, 423–8.

The Polish research on sportsmen is described in Grzedzinski, E., Posynski, J., and Izdebska, M. "Influence of Meteorological Factors on the Physiological Functions of Sportsmen." Proceedings of the Seventh International Biometeorological Congress, August, 1975 in College Park, Md. Swets and Zeitlinger, Amsterdam and Lisse.

Hentschel, Gerhard. "Sports & Climate," in *Medical Climatology*, edited by S. Licht. (1964). E. Licht, Publishers, New Haven.

Heat-wave mortality information comes from Ellis, F. P., "Mortality and Morbidity Associated with Heat Exposure." *Int. Jour. Biomet. Suppl.* (1976), *20*, II, 6, edited by S. W. Tromp and J. J. Bouma, 36–40.

Acclimatization to heat and cold, and the heat-acclimatization experiment mentioned come from Hardy, James D., and Bard, Phillip. *Body Temperature Regulation* (in press).

Sports Performance Under Thermal Stress

High-Temperature Stress

Location of Stress Response	Incidence	Cause	Effect
core of body	*Common* distance running	heat production exceeds heat loss	
	jogging tennis summer	prolonged: high metabolic rate ambient temperature humidity	elevated body temperature
peripheral body tissues	*Rare* summer water sports water skiing	solar radiation	sunburn

Low-Temperature Stress

Location of Stress Response	Incidence	Cause	Effect
core of body		heat loss exceeds heat production	
	Uncommon boating accidents	prolonged: low metabolic rate ambient temperature	depressed body temperature shock exposure

peripheral
body tissues
	Occasional
	skiing
	accidental
	  exposure
		heat loss exceeds
		heat restored
			depressed
			  skin temperature
			frostbite

The diagrams of *clo* units and weather symbols comes from Auliciems, A., and Hare, F. K. "Visual Presentation of Weather Forecasting for Personal Comfort." *Weather* (1973), Royal Meteorological Society, 28, 478–80.

The table of clothing insulation required for comfort comes from Nevins, R. G., McCall, Jr., P. E. , Stolwijk, J. A. J., "How to Be Comfortable at 65 to 68 Degrees." *ASHRAE Jour.* (April, 1974), 16, 4, 41–3.

Hesiod's advice is found in *Hesiod's Works and Days and Theogony* translated by Richard Lattimore. (1959). University of Michigan Press, Ann Arbor.

Auliciems, Andris, and Hare, F. K. "Weather Forecasting for Personal Comfort." *Weather* (1973), Royal Meteorological Society, 28, 118–21.

The studies showing that people want *more* weather information are found in Maunder, W. J. *The Value of the Weather* (1970). Methuen and Company, London, p. 283, and Tobin's article cited in the first chapter.

The "orange-red underwear" caper is soberly related by Sargent, II, Frederick. "An Experiment in Orange-Red Underwear." *Texas Reports on Biology and Medicine* (1974), 32, 1, 157–71.

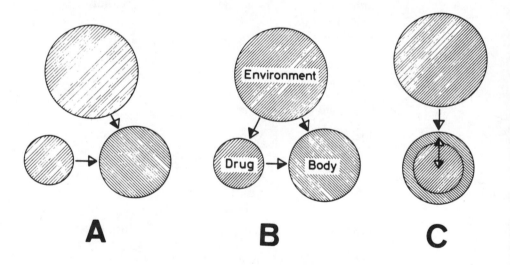

You and the Drug and the Atmosphere

In situation A, the thermal environment (upper, large circle) and the drug (small circle, left) act upon the body independently. In situation B, the thermal environment acts on the drug (before application) and both act upon the body. This is important in the production and storage of drugs, especially organic drugs. In situation C, once the drug enters the body, both adjust to the thermal environment together, which may increase the drug's potency or provoke other serious side effects.

Weihe, Wolf H. "The Effects of Temperature on the Action of Drugs." *Ann Arbor Rev. Pharmacol.* (1973), *13*, 409–25. (see opposite page)

The discussion and interaction diagram of drugs, body, and environment come from Weihe, Wolf H. "Effects of Drugs in Adaptation to Heat and Cold." *Int. Jour. Biomet. Suppl.* (1976), *20*, 125–36.

Fuhrman, Frederick. "Modification of the Action of Drugs by Heat." *Env. Phys. and Psych. in Arid Conditions* (1963), UNESCO, *22*, 223–37.

Diagram of drug toxicity types from Fuhrman, G. J., and Fuhrman, F. A. "'Effects of Temperature on the Action of Drugs." *Ann Arbor Rev. Pharmacol.* (1961), *1*, 65–78; also Weihe, W. *Int. Jour. Biomet. Suppl.* (1976), *20*, 125–36.

Marijuana temperature effects come from Haavik, C. O., Collins, F. G., and Hardman, H. F. "Studies in the Mechanism of Hypothermic Action of Tetrahydrocannabinols," in *Temperature Regulation and Drug Action Proc. Symp. Paris 1973.* Karger, Basel 1974, 293–309.

Petersen, W. F. "Drug Sensitivity and the Meteorologic Environment." *New Int. Clinics* (1942), *1*, 255–69.

Ellis, John M., et al. "Survey and New Data on Treatment with Pyridoxine." *Research in Chemical Pathology and Pharmacology* (May, 1977), *17*, 1, 165–77.

Announcement of some early results of Richard J. Wortman's work will be found in "Diet Material Found to Affect the Brain," *The New York Times* (Jan. 25, 1978), A22.

The experiments on diets in hot and cold are in Mitchell, H. H., and Edman, M. *Nutrition and Climate Stress.* (1951). C. C. Thomas, Springfield, Ill.; and Edman, M. "Effects of Nutrition on Bodily Resistance," in *Progress in Biometeorology*, edited by S. W. Tromp (1977). Swets and Zeitlinger, Amsterdam and Lisse.

Sargent, II, F. "Season and the Metabolism of Fat and Carbohydrates: A Study of Vestigial Physiology." *Meteorological Monographs* (1954), *2*, 8, 68–80.

Jarvis, D. C. *Folk Medicine* (1958). Holt, Rinehart and Winston, New York.

The airline food director is Bruce Axler, Pan American Airlines.

Mayer, K. E. "The Physiology of Violence, Allergy and Aggression." *Psychology Today* (July, 1975), 77–8; and see *Clinical Ecology* edited by L. D. Dickey (1976). C. C. Thomas, Springfield, Ill.

Harlfinger, Otmar. "Bioklimatologie des Mittelmeerraumes." *Notabene Medici* (1975), 5 Jahrgang 6, 47–50; and "Bioklimatologie der Vereinigten Staaten von Amerika." *Notabene Medici* (1977), 7 Jahrgang 5, 46–52.

Tromp, S. W. "General Biometeorological Effects of Sea, Air and Car Travel," in *Progress in Biometeorology*, edited by S. W. Tromp (1977). Swets and Zeitlinger, Amsterdam and Lisse, 218–23.

The Marburg work is reported by Hildebrandt, G., Besterhorn, H. P., and Strempel, O. "Significance of Biological Rhythms for Sea, Air and Car Travel," in *Progress in Biometeorology*, edited by S. W. Tromp (1977). Swets and Zeitlinger, Amsterdam and Lisse, 223–32.

Marmor, M. "Heat Wave Mortality in New York City, 1949–1970." *Arch. Env. Health* (1974), *30*, 130.

Silver, Francis. "The Breath of Life," in *Clinical Ecology*, edited by L. D. Dickey (1976). C. C. Thomas, Springfield, Ill.

Auliciems, Andris. "Weather Perception: A Subtropical Study." *Weather* (1976), Royal Meteorological Society, *31*, 312–6. This was done in Australia in May to September, the subtropical winter.

Auliciems, Andris. "Classroom Performance as a Function of Thermal Comfort." *Int. Jour. Biomet.* (1972), *16*, 3, 233–46.

Mood Depends on Minor Atmospheric Changes

	Endurance	Play	Liking of School	Aggression
For Increasing:				
Temperature outdoors	decreases	decreases	decreases	decreases
Humidity (before precipitation)	increases	increases	increases	—
Cloudiness	—	—	increases	—
Windiness	—	increases	—	increases
Sunlight intensity	—	decreases	—	—
Thermal discomfort indoors	decreases	decreases	decreases	increases

Rabkin, J., and Streuning, E. "Life Events, Stress and Illness." *Science* (Dec. 3, 1976), *194*, 1013–20.

Kinsey, Alfred. Attributed by Houck, C., in "Exercise: The True Aphrodisiac." *Forum* (1977), 14–7.

Kostrubala, Thaddeus. *The Joy of Running* (1976). MacMillan, New York.

Udry, J., and Morris, N. "Seasonality of Coitus and Seasonality of Birth." *Demography* (1967), *4*, 2, 673–9.

von Mayersbach, H. "Time—A Key in Experimental and Practical Medicine." *Arch. of Toxicology* (1976), 36, 185–216.

Reiter, R. J. "The Pineal Gland and Seasonal Reproductive Adjustment." *Int. Jour. Biomet.* (1975), 19, 282–8.

Winkless, III, Nels, and Browning, Iben. *Climate and the Affairs of Men* (1975). Harper & Row, New York.

Chapter 4 Notes: The Elegant Science of Racism

Data on land masses and climate accommodation are from Harrison, G. A., Weiner, J. S., Tanner, J. M., and Barnicot, W. A., eds. *Human Biology: An Introduction to Human Evolution, Variation, and Growth* (1964). Oxford University Press, New York and Oxford.

Tropical neurasthenia symptoms are from Sargent, II, Frederick A. "Tropical Neurasthenia: Giant or Windmill?" in *Env. Physiol. and Psych. in Arid Conditions* (1963). UNESCO, Paris.

Wheeler, Raymond H. "The Effects of Climate on Human Behavior in History." *Cycles* (December, 1962), 342–52; "The History of Music in Relation to Climate and Cultural Fluctuations." *Proc. Mus. Teach Assoc.* (1940) 35, 432–8.

McClelland, David C. *The Achieving Society* (1961). The Free Press, New York.

Huntington, Ellsworth, *Civilization and Climate* (1915). Yale University Press, New Haven; *Main Springs of Civilization* (1945). Harper & Row, New York.

The maps come from Woytinsky, W. S., and Woytinsky, E. S. *World Population and Production* (1953). The Twentieth Century Fund, New York.

Roberts, D. F. "Body Weight, Race and Climate." *Amer. Jour. Phys. Anthrop.* (1933), 11, 533–5.

Beller, Anne Scott. *Fat and Thin: A Natural History of Obesity* (1977). Farrar, Straus & Giroux, New York.

Newman, Russell, and Munro, Ella. "The Relation of Climate and Body Size in U.S. Males." *Amer. Jour. Phys. Anthrop.* (1955), 13, 1–15. (The correlations are respectively: -0.587, -0.384, and -0.535.)

The arctic explorer is quoted in Harrison, Wiener, et al., *op. cit.*

Mills, Clarence. *Medical Climatology* (1939). C. C. Thomas, Springfield, Ill.

Gilfillan, R. "The Coldward Course of Progress." *Pol. Sci. Quart.* (1920), 35, 393.

Neuberger, Hans. "Climate in Art." *Weather* (1970), *Royal Meteorological Society*, 25, 46–56. The ratios of frequencies of pale-blue to deep-blue painted skies are: Britain, 3.1; North America, 2.0; The Low Countries, 1.6; France, 1.4; Germany, 0.8; Italy, 0.2; and Spain, 0.1.

Lamb, David. "The Unseen Ruler of West Africa Is 'Wawa'." *The International Herald Tribune* (Sept. 9, 1977).

Lewis, Flora. "Rich and Poor: Shifting Ties." *The New York Times* (June 3, 1977).

Prinsky, Robert. "Next Week's North-South Dialogue Is Expected to Be Long Commitments, Short on Specifics." *The Wall Street Journal* (May 27, 1977).

Safire, William. "Christmas in July." *The New York Times* (July 18, 1977).

McFadden, Robert D. "Sutton Says Looting Was Criminal, Not Racial." *The New York Times* (July 30, 1977).

Maunder, W. J. *The Value of Weather* (1970). Methuen & Co., London.

Chapter 5 Notes: Air—Our Ancestral Home and Master

Many of these meteorological figures of speech were kindly furnished by Hans Neuberger in "Meteorological Imagery in Language, Music and Art." *Mineral Industries* (January, 1961), 29, 4, Pennsylvania State University.

Stephen Sondheim's lyrics come from "A Funny Thing Happened on the Way to the Forum." (1962), Chappell and Co., New York.

Petersen, William F., *The Patient and the Weather* (1934–8). Edwards Brothers, Ann Arbor.

Petersen, William F. *Man-Weather-Sun* (1947). C. C. Thomas, Springfield, Ill.

Wilder, Joseph. *Stimulus and Response: The Law of Initial Value* (1967). John Wright & Co., Bristol.

Petersen's detailed observations may seem of interest to physicians only but nevertheless provide important conclusions:

1. Each individual has to be examined in relation to the *totality* of heredity and environment.
2. All biochemical and biophysical processes participate in a continuously varying rhythmic pattern for normal individuals and for patients.
3. No single biological component or symptom is altered without corresponding effects on all other components. Indeed, demonstrable changes in any one major component or symptom may frequently serve as an indicator for all. (For example, if carbon dioxide content of the blood is altered, then coagulation of the blood is altered because calcium ionization is altered. Simultaneously, the irritability of nervous tissue or sensory perception threshold is altered, and so is cellular permeability changed. If cell permeability changes, so does the blood pressure, and consequently heart rate changes.)
4. Cerebral functions or mental reactions participate in the integrated coordination and weather conditioning of the whole organism.
5. Genetically identical individuals react alike to the weather environment.
6. In the totality of muscles and glands that respond to a stimulus or nerve impulse, the change in air mass surrounding an organism (above all elements out of its entire environment) is probably of major significance.

7. Our entire metabolism is built upon an adequate supply of oxygen. The mechanism by which muscles and glands respond to a stimulus or nerve impulse primarily involves a tide of oxygen inadequacy (anoxia), followed by a physiological correction or overcorrection. Oxygen inadequacy may stimulate: (a) return to normalcy, (b) depression of activity, (c) temporary or permanent inhibition or atrophy of various parts of the anatomy, (d) irritability, (e) instability, (f) states of fatigue, (g) death.

8. Awareness of any clinical symptoms or disturbances is merely a person's conscious recognition that the normal organic pattern—a rhythm of oxygen inadequacy, correction, and overcorrection—has been unduly disturbed. Consequently, treatment to be effective must be governed by the internal organic responses to the external forces of weather. The patient has to be regarded not only from a static and anatomical aspect but also as a whole entity within a whole environment.

9. The population at large follows a pattern that is identical to the reaction seen in a normal individual. (For example, psychotic admissions, births, the sex ratio of infants conceived, death, the sex ratio of the dead, the ratio of daily deaths to daily conceptions, and twinning are statistically and significantly related to the basic biochemical rhythms seen in the genetically similar triplets.)

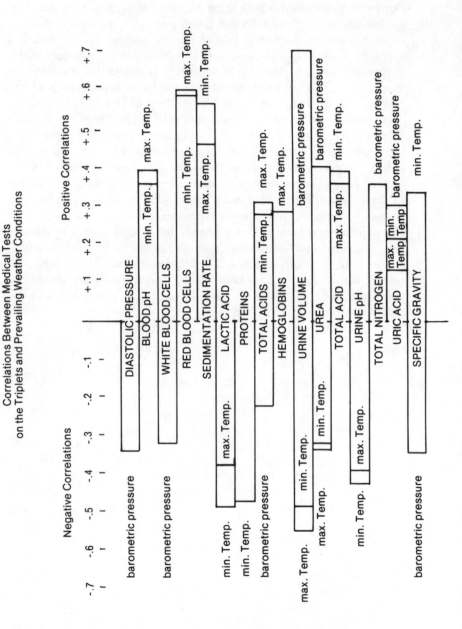

Correlations Between Medical Tests
on the Triplets and Prevailing Weather Conditions

The chart shows that the medical tests changed with daily temperature (maxima and minima) and barometric pressure. The length of each bar indicates the *strength* of the correlation; to the right they tend to co-vary in the same direction, to the left in opposite directions.

Chapter 6 Notes: World Winds

David E. Scherman has kindly furnished notes on the chinook and foehn.

The wind idioms are courtesy of Hans Neuberger in "Meteorological Imagery in Language, Music and Art," *Mineral Industries*, Pennsylvania State University. (January, 1961), 29, 4.

Hippocrates quotes come from *The Genuine Works of Hippocrates*, translated by Francis Adams (1939). Bolt, Williams and Wilkins Co.; and *Hippocrates*, translated by W. H. S. Jones (1931). Heinemann Ltd., London. Aristotle quotes are from Shaw, Sir Napier, *Manual of Meteorology* (1926). Cambridge; and *The Drama of Weather* (1939). Cambridge University Press, Cambridge and New York.

The table of wind-related ailments come from Faust, V., Harlfinger, O., and Neuwirth, R. "Wetter und Krankheit." *Fortschritte der Medizin* (1977), 95, 268.

Hesiod's description comes from *Hesiod's Works and Days and Theogony*, translated by Richard Lattimore (1959). University of Michigan Press, Ann Arbor.

The direct effects of wind are found in Jankowiak, Jozef, "Effects of Wind on Man," in *Medical Climatology*, edited by S. Licht (1964). E. Licht, Publisher, New Haven.

Carson, Stella L. "Human Energy (Physical and Emotional) Under Varying Weather Conditions," Doctoral Dissertation (1947). University of Washington, Seattle.

Sulman, F. G., Donano, A., Pfeifer, Y., Tal, E., and Weller, C. P. "Urinalyses of Patients Suffering from Climatic Heat Stress (Sharav)." *Int. Jour. Biomet.* (1970), 14, 45–53; and Sulman, F. G. *Health, Weather and Climate* (1976). S. Karger, Basel.

Several of Sulman's recent utterances have earned him criticisms from other scientists who have done similar studies. After his respectable findings, Sulman made two statements that he has not truly proven to the satisfaction of the scientific community, the biometeorologists, physiologists, and pharmacologists.

First, he argued that the Israeli sharav and the Alpine foehn, both being hot, dry winds, should induce identical clinical symptoms among those exposed. The two winds are different in many respects: They originate from different meteorological factors and they spend different amounts of time harassing their victims, who live in widely different climates and who have different social and thermal conditioning.

Second, Sulman claimed that positive air ionization always accompanies or even precedes the arrival of both the sharav and the foehn. Then, using this unproven assertion, he cited recent accepted research showing that inhaled air ions reduce your respiratory capacity (by lowering oxygen consumption and raising carbon dioxide levels). The diminished respiratory capacity decreases mental abilities, diminishes resistance to stress, and produces or overproduces the stress-hormone serotonin. He says the "positive air ionization always precedes the weather front by one or two days because electricity moves faster than air," and this accounts for the pre-sensitivity to weather changes of many people who, he says, justifiably claim to be weather prophets. Finally, his line of reasoning concludes that negative ions alleviate the conditions by neutralizing the detrimental positive air ions. He says, "negative ionization applied to the air conditioning of a modern high rise . . . actually represents a social step forward." Consequently Sulman is urging the sale of ion generators (in which he may have a financial stake). One reputable scientist said of him, "He has lost his scientific objectivity and become a huckster."

It may be true, as some experiments demonstrate, that positive ions have deleterious biological and psychological effects. However, the situation is not clear and unequivocal. The final word has not been written. In brief, the status of Sulman's ion controversy is the following:

- On the purported connection between positive ions and forthcoming weather changes, it has not been demonstrated that the sharav or foehn are always heralded by positive ions or by net positive ion concentrations.
- On the purported connection between desert winds, positive air ions, and human performance, the air ions do not eradicate the loss of performance on sharav days.
- On the purported connection between air ions and physiology, Sulman later found that sharav-sensitive people excreted larger amounts of serotonin on days with high positive-ion levels in the atmosphere, and small amounts of serotonin on nonionized days. Nonsensitive persons did not change their serotonin production during high ion–level days. However, independently, Peter Krölling has shown that motor activity of mice was essentially uninfluenced by the presence of positive air ions.
- On the purported connection between air ions and air conditioning, research shows that minor changes in air humidity, temperature, smoke content of the air, and nearby metal objects, alter the ratio of negative and positive ions in the air, and that the ions often cannot reach the trachea in humans. The fluctuations in both directions, positive and negative, are often random, and cannot be predicted.
- On the purported connection between air ions, performance, and moods, positively ionized air had, Jonathan Charry found, a clearly dampening effect on the psychological and physical state of almost everyone.
- On the purported similarities between the effects of the sharav and the effects of the foehn, Posse has demonstrated that a definite increase in

serotonin due to the foehn cannot be proven, and that the foehn and sharav are meteorologically very different winds.

Krölling, Peter. "Modellversuche zu elektrischen Komponenten des Klimas," *Zeitschrift Für angewandte und Klimaheilkunde* (1977), 24, 137–141 and personal communications.

Charry, Jonathan, and Hawkinshire, F. B. W. "Biologically Mediated Behavior in Response to Meteorological Conditions" (in press), and personal communications. (Presented at 84th Annual Convention of the American Psychological Association.)

Posse, P., et al. "Langsschnittuntersuchungen zur Wetterwirkung auf die Ausscheidung von Serotonin und 5-HIES im Urin." *Zeitschrift für Physikalische Medizin* (1977), 2, 67–71.

The foehnologist is Jurgen von Hollander in *Föhn und anderer Wetterschreck* (1962). Ehrenwirth Verlag, Munich.

Chapter 7 Notes: The Vortex of History: Weather, Temperament, and Physique

The material on Lincoln and Douglas leans heavily on Petersen, William F. *Lincoln-Douglas: The Weather as Destiny* (1943). C. C. Thomas, Springfield, Ill., which is also the source of the quotations.

Sheldon, William H. *The Varieties of Human Physique* (1940). Harper & Row, New York; and *The Varieties of Temperament* (1942), Harper & Row, New York; and *Atlas of Men* (1952), Harper & Row, New York.

Beller, Anne Scott. *Fat and Thin: A Natural History of Obesity* (1977). Farrar, Straus & Giroux, New York.

Child, Irvin L. "The Relation of Somatotype to Self-Ratings on Sheldon's Temperamental Traits." *Jou. Personality* (1950), 18, 444–53.

Chapter 8 Notes: The Touch of Zeus

Many idioms and religious motifs come from Neuberger, Hans, *op. cit.*

Browne, Lewis. *This Believing World* (1925). Macmillan, New York.

Semple, Ellen Churchill. *Influences of Geographic Environment* (1941). Henry Holt & Co., New York.

Sheldon, William H. *The Varieties of Temperament* (1942). Harper & Row, New York.

Michanowsky, George. *The Once and Future Star* (1977). Hawthorn Books, New York.

Petersen, William F. *The Patient and the Weather* (1934–8). Edwards Brothers, Ann Arbor.

Greek lore comes from *Harper's Dictionary of Classical Literature and An-*

Clustering of good and bad responses to weather

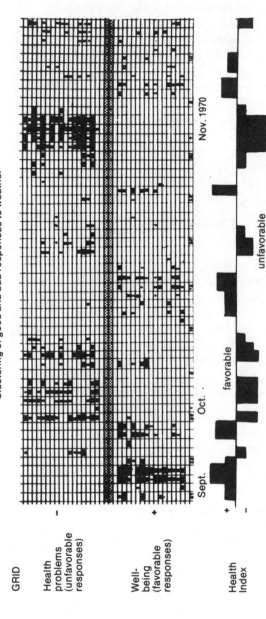

Each vertical column on the grid represents a calendar day. The vertical lines characterize the state of health; *unfavorable* responses (−) are indicated by tiny black marks placed *above* the grid's mid-line, *favorable* responses (+) by black marks *below*. A small black mark above horizontal line 2 means that a few respondents slept worse than normal; above line 11, they had more headaches, and so on. Each line indicates a health problem or sign of well-being.

Heavy black bulges below the grid are the *overall* health index. Excessively frequent *favorable* states of health, when added up on a given day, will show an *upward* black bulge; excessively *unfavorable* responses show a *downward* black bulge. Upward bulges show a distinct clustering of positive responses, or well-being; the downward bulges show a clustering of health problems, or negative responses. The percentage of all persons denoting a day as favorable was called the "index of indisposition."

332

tiquities (1897), edited by Harry Thornton Peck. Harper & Row, New York.

Bettelheim, Bruno. *The Uses of Enchantment: The Meaning and Importance of Fairy Tales* (1977). Random House, New York.

Hesiod's Works and Days and Theogony, translated by Richard Lattimore (1959). University of Michigan Press, Ann Arbor.

The Iliad of Homer, translated by Richard Lattimore (1965). University of Chicago Press, Chicago.

Cook, Arthur Bernard. *Zeus, A Study in Ancient Religion* (1914). Cambridge University Press, Cambridge.

Aristophane's The Clouds, translated by B. B. Rogers (1919). Heinemann, London.

Jaynes, Julian. *The Origin of Consciousness in the Breakdown of the Bicameral Mind* (1976). Houghton Mifflin, Boston.

Watzlawick, Paul. *How Real Is Real? An Anecdotal Introduction to Communications Theory* (1976). Random House, New York.

Chapter 9 Notes: "Objective" Weather-Sensitivity

Persinger, M. A. "Lag Responses in Mood Reports to Changes in the Weather Matrix." *Int. Jour. Biomet.* (1975), *19*, 2, 108–14.

Dirnagl, Karl. "Neuere Untersuchungsergbnisse zur Beeinflussung des menschlichen Befindens durch das Wetter." *Therapiewoche* (1977), *27*, 6, 858–70.

The equation is $S = 0.77\,T - 0.13\,RH - 0.11\,p$, where T is the seven-day weighted temperature, RH is the relative humidity, and p is barometric pressure.

Harlfinger, Otmar, and Jendritzky, G. "Betriebunsfalle und Wetter." *Münch. med. Wschr.* (1976), *118*, 3, 69–72.

Posse, P. "Einfluss des Wetters auf die Morbidatsdynamik einer Grosstadt." *Münch. med. Wschr.* (1975), *117*, 11, 425–30.

Becker, Friederich. *Verein Deutscher Ingenieure* (1974), *116*, 1367–454.

Brezowsky, H. "Die Abhängigkeit des Herzinfarkts von Klima, Wetter und Jahreszeit." *Ark. f. Kreislfrshg.* (1965), *47*, 159–88; and Brezowsky, H. "Morbidity and Weather," in *Medical Climatology*, edited by S. Licht (1964). E. Licht Publishers, New Haven.

Rapid pressure changes of 0.040 pounds per square inch are the likely human threshold for detection, according to Williams, D. H., and Cohen, E. "Human Threshold for Perceiving Sudden Changes in Atmospheric Pressure." *Perceptual and Motor Skills* (1972), *35*, 2, 437–8.

Dordick, I. "The Influence of Variations in Atmospheric Pressure upon Human Beings." *Weather* (1958), Royal Meteorological Society, *13*, 359–64.

Richner, Hans. "Wetterlagen und korperliche Beschwerden—Das Problem der Wetterfuhligkeit." *Universitas* (1975), *30*, 5, 501–7.

The Cycle of Weathering: Tolzer Weather Phases

	1	2	3A	3	3F	4	5	6Z	6
Weather phase	1	2	3A	3	3F	4	5	6Z	6
A Clouds	*(cloud symbols)*	*(cloud symbols)*	*(cloud symbol)*	*(cloud symbol)*	*(cloud symbol)*	*(cloud symbols)*	*(cloud symbols)*	*(cloud symbols)*	*(cloud symbols)*
B Character	Mod'y Good weather	Improving weather	Extremely good weather	Exceptional weather		Forth-coming precip'n	Beginning precip'n	Complete precip'n	Clearing calm weather
C Barometer	*(curve)*								
D Temperature	*(curve)*								
E Relative humidity	*(curve)*								
Weather phase	1	2	3A	3	3F	4	5	6Z	6
F 24-hour change in Temp.-Humid Env.	*(curves — dry-bulb temp. ——, wet-bulb temp. ----)*								
G Increasingly: T / H	cool-mild / dry	mild-warm / dry	mild-warm / extremely dry	mild-warm extremely dry		mild-warm / moist	cool-cold / humid	cold / humid	cool-cold / dry
H Wind speed	*(curve)*								
I Air-mass motion	none		vertical			horizontal			none
J 24-hour period	mod'y manifested	strongly manifested		disturbed or suppressed					returning

The Cycle of Weathering: Tolzer Weather Phases
(See page 336 for further information)

	minimal	small	moderate	strong	very strong	strong	strong	small
K Biotropic irritant								
L Intensity of arousal; Demand for organic adjustment								
M Biological effect	biologically favorable			biologically unfavorable				biologol'y favorable
Weather phase	1	2	3A 3 3F		4	5	6 Z	6

Morbidity (median deviation from expected value of nine ailments: emboli, hemorrhages, migraine and asthma attacks, myocardial infarcts, colic, angina, osteoarthritis)

Scale: +10%, +5%, -5%, -10%

Mortality (deviation from expected value of death rate in Munich, 1954-1957)

Scale: +10%, -10%

In his *Manual of Meteorology*, Sir Napier Shaw (see page 336) wrote that trying to explain the course of meteorological events in nature "is necessarily based on some process of simplification that is to some extent, therefore, a fairy tale." Consider the complexity of these Tolzer Weather Phases.

The vertical columns show properties of weather phases (numbered 1 to 6) as indicated by the horizontal rows (lettered A to M). Row A gives an idea of how the clouds appear in each phase, and row B short verbal descriptions of the "character" of each weather phase. Row C is the barometric pressure, D the temperature, and E the relative humidity of the air mass; note the sharp changes at the onset of precipitation in weather phase 5. The very important rows F and G are the *change* in the Temperature-Humidity Environment during the past twenty-four hours (the diurnal T.H.E. change), as measured by a normal dry-bulb thermometer and by a wet-bulb thermometer (its readings depend on the humidity and rapidity of evaporation). Row G has short descriptions of each diurnal T.H.E. change corresponding to table on pages 208–211. The wind speed, shown in row H, rises in weather phases 5 and 6Z. The kind of air-mass motions (advection) are vertical, horizontal, smooth (laminar) flow, or turbulent flow (eddies, whorls, and vortexes), shown in row I. The twenty-four-hour meteorological periodicity, row J, gives the likelihood that the normal daily weather rhythms (minimum temperature at sunrise, barometric pressure maximum at 4 A.M. and 4 P.M., maximum temperature two to three hours after local noon) will be disturbed or apparent in each phase.

The overall effects on people are shown in the next three rows: along row K is the level of biological irritation ranging from minimal to very strong; row L is the intensity of arousal and consequent demand upon the organism to adjust and readjust to each phase; and row M shows the biologically favorable or unfavorable weather phases.

The table on page 335 shows the deviations from the normal, expected values of mortality (for 43,347 deaths in Munich during 1954 to 1957), and of morbidity (nine clinical illnesses).

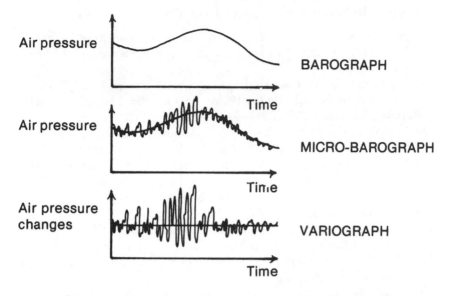

Atmospheric pressure measurements by three instruments

A *micro*barograph records both the long-term trend of Highs and Lows, and the rapid-but-minute pressure fluctuations as in the middle illustration. The bottom curve depicts the atmosphere's rapid pressure fluctuations alone, with the long-term trends in the barograph removed. This is done by means of a special measuring device designed by Zurich physicist Hans Richner, called a *variograph*.

With the variograph, Richner has analyzed these small rapid-pressure fluctuations. He finds that they are of two kinds: those whose periodic changes are between one and four minutes long—"acoustic" pressure waves—and those that take from four to thirty minutes—slow-moving "gravity" waves. The acoustic waves oscillate and travel faster than the gravity waves.

Richner looked at how these two kinds of micropressure waves change their pressure amplitude (or intensity) during the course of a day. The slow gravity waves maintain constant intensity during a day. But the fast acoustic waves change, so that around 4 P.M. their intensity is maximum, perhaps three times their minimum intensity at about 4 A.M. The intensity of air turbulence throughout a day shows a similar distribution, suggesting that *acoustic waves accompany or signal turbulent atmospheric conditions*. These conditions are often present at interfaces of cold fronts, warm fronts, Highs, Lows, and at occlusions. Strong or moderate cold fronts or warm fronts will register acoustic waves. *Strong occlusions and cold fronts seem to generate gravity waves.*

Chapter 10 Notes: Fire, Ice, and Inner Weather

The similarities of exercise and emotional stress are from Bove, Alfred A. "The Cardiovascular Response to Stress." *Psychosomatics* (October, 1977), 13–7.

Cyclone frequency data from Hosler, C. A., and Gamage, L. A. "Cyclone Frequencies in the U.S. for the Period 1905 to 1954." *Monthly Weather Review* (November, 1956), 388–90.

The analysis of the "pendulation" of our involuntary nervous system leans heavily on Petersen, William F. *The Patient and the Weather* (1934–8). Edwards Brothers, Ann Arbor, and his other works. Neuropsychiatrist Hans M. Reese explains mental illness in "The Significance of the Meteorological Environment in the Etiology of Psychotic Episodes." *Jour. of Mt. Sinai Hosp.* (1942), 9, 717–33.

The drug actions and nervous-system function come from Wingate, Peter. *The Penguin Medical Encyclopedia* (1976). Penguin Books, London.

Selye, Hans. *Stress in Health and Sickness* (1976). Penguin Books, London; Butterworths, London and Boston.

The data on hierarchy of variation is found in Sargent, II., F. "Biological Variability in Man." *Medical Bulletin, Rush–Presbyterian–St. Lukes* (October, 1971), 10, 4, 106–24; and Wechsler, D. *The Range of Human Capability* (1935). Williams & Williams, London.

Diagram of environmental temperature and zone of human temperature regulation from Stolwijk, J. A. J., and Hardy, James D. "Control of Body Temperature," in *Handbook of Physiology*, 45–68 (preprint).

Anatomy of thermal regulation from Hardy, James D. "Biometeorology: Physiological and Behavioral Perspectives." *Int. Jour. Biomet. Suppl.* 20 (1976), Vol. 6, Part II, 29–34.

Neural interconnection chart from Hardy, James D. "Brain Sensors of Temperature," Brady Memorial Lecture VIII, University of Missouri–Columbia Special Report 103 (May, 1969), p. 13.

Graph of subjective estimates of pleasantness, comfort, and temperature from Gagge, A. P., Stolwijk, J. A. J., and Hardy, James D. "Comfort and Thermal Sensation and Associated Physiological Responses at Various Ambient Temperatures." *Env. Res.* (June, 1967), 1, 1–2.

Auliciems, Andris. "Effects of Weather on Indoor Thermal Comfort." *Int. Jour. Biomet.* (1969), 13, 3, 147–62.

Hale, Edward T. *The Hidden Dimension* (1966). Doubleday, New York.

Luchterhand, Elmer. "Sociological Approach to Massive Stress in Natural and Man-Made Disasters." *Int. Psychiatric Clinics* (1971), 8, 1, 29–53.

Neuberger, Hans. "Meteorological Imagery in Language, Music and Art." *Mineral Industries* (January, 1961), 29, 4. Pennsylvania State University.

Geniuses and weather-sensitivity is discussed by Petersen, W. F., in "An Expanded Formulation of Environment," and "Some Neglected Factors in the Personality-Cultural Complex: 'Genius' and 'Fatigue' 11, Second

American Congress on General Semantics, 1941, Chicago, Institute of General Semantics (1943), 139–44; and in *The Patient and the Weather* (1934–8), Vol. II, p. 3. Edwards Brothers, Ann Arbor.

The split brain is discussed in Dimond, S. J. *The Double Brain* (1972). Churchill and Livingstone, Edinburgh.

MacRae, Donald G. "Sinister Notes on Left and Right." *Encounter* (April, 1977), 37.

Epley, David, and Ricks, David F. "Foresight and Hindsight in the TAT." *Jour. Proj. Tech.* (1963), 27, 1, 51–9; also Rosen, Stephen. "The Future of Hindsight and Foresight." *The Wall Street Journal* (Feb. 10, 1972), editorial page.

Chapter 11 Notes: Beat This Weather!

Petersen's advice is found in Petersen, William F., *The Patient and the Weather*, 1934–8. Edwards Brothers, Ann Arbor.

Faust, Volker, *Biometeorologie* (1977). Hippokrates Verlag, Stuttgart.

Rauscht-Froemsdorf, Werner, "Diagnostik von Wetterfuhligkrit und Wetterschmerz." *Zeitschrift fur Allgemeinmidizin* (Feb. 20, 1976), 52, 5, 228–36.

Tromp, Solco W. "The Relationship of Weather and Climate to Health and Disease," in *Scientific Foundations of Environmental Medicine*, edited by Howe, Melvyn G., and Loraine, John A. (1974). William Heinemann Medical Books Ltd., London; and personal communication.

The quotes on medical self-care come from Yeager, Robert C. "Doctoring Isn't Just for Doctors." *Medical World News* (Oct. 3, 1977), 271–8. Condensed in *Reader's Digest* (February, 1978), 237–42.

Thomas, Lewis, "Notes of a Biology Watcher: The World's Biggest Membrane." *New England Journal of Medicine* (1973), 289: 576–7.

APPENDIX A: **How Weather Affects People Directly: A Short Chronological History of Human Biometeorology Since Civilization Began**

Cassedy, F. "Meteorology and Medicine in Colonial America." *Jour. Hist. Med.* (1969), 24, 2, 193–204.

Faust, Volker. *Biometeorologie* (1977). Hippokrates Verlag, Stuttgart.

Petersen, William F. *The Patient and the Weather* (1934–8). Edwards Brothers, Ann Arbor.

Sargent, II, Frederick. "Changes in Ideas on the Climatic Origin of Disease." *Bulletin American Meteorological Society* (May, 1960), 41, 5, 238–43.

Snorrason, Egill. "Early History of Medical Climatology," in *Medical Climatology*, edited by S. Licht. (1964). E. Licht, Publisher, New Haven.

APPENDIX B: **Ranking of Weather Influence of "User" Groups in the United States**

Maunder, W. J. *The Value of the Weather* (1970). Methuen & Co., London.

APPENDIX C: **You and Your "Environment":**
A Self-Discovery Questionnaire

The author designed this questionnaire, and administered it to groups in the United States. Preliminary factor- and item-analysis corroborates that the weather is a critical aspect of our environment, and that certain clusters of body organs are particularly susceptible; the questionnaire seems to promote awareness of both. The results, from analysis of subjects tested in various parts of the United States, are given in the following table:

Symptom Cluster	*Conditions of Stress*	
Disturbances of the:	In Females associate with:	In Males associate with:
Allergies (II)	Weather	Weather
Bones and joints (IV)	Weather	Weather
	Exercise	Exercise
Cardiovascular system (V)	Exercise	Exercise
	Overwork	Overwork
Central nervous system (IX)	Overwork	Overwork*
	Opposite sex	Exercise
	Weather	
Cerebral system (VII)	Overwork	Overwork
	Weather	Exercise
	Exercise	Weather
Disposition (I)	Opposite sex*	Overwork*
	Overwork	Sex
	Weather	Weather
Emotions, moods (III)	Opposite sex	Overwork*
	Weather	Weather
	Overwork/Exercise	Opposite sex
Respiratory system (VIII)	Weather	Weather
	Exercise	Exercise
Skin (X)	Weather	Weather
	Exercise	Exercise

* Especially strong connection

Note: You may go back over the questionnaire, for those symptoms which are weather-induced, and indicate specifically if hot, cold, wet, or dry weather aggravates the symptom.

APPENDIX D: **Risk of Death by Cause**

Kletz, Trevor. "The Risk Equation." *New Scientist* (May 12, 1977), 320–2.
Cassell, Erich. *The Healer's Art* (1976). Lippincott, Philadelphia.
Momiyama, M. "Biometeorological Study of Seasonal Variation of Mortality in Japan and Other Countries." *Int. Jour. Biomet.* (1968), 12, 4, 377–93.
Driscoll, Dennis M. "Base Lines for Measuring Adverse Effects of Air Pollution: Some Evidence for Weather Effects on Mortality." *Env. Res.* (1971), 4, 233–42.
Ellis, F. D. "Mortality and Morbidity Associated with Heat Exposure." *Int. Jour. Biomet. Suppl.* (1976), 6:II, 36–40.

APPENDIX E: **Fabric Data and CLO Values for Individual Garments**

Nevins, R. G., McCall, Jr., P. E., Stolwijk, J. A. J., "How to Be Comfortable at 65 to 68 Degrees." *ASHRAE Jour.* (April, 1974), 16, 4, 41–3.

APPENDIX F: **Measures to Minimize the Effects of Weather on Drug Action**

Long, James W. *The Essential Guide to Prescription Drugs* (1977). Harper & Row, New York.
Weihe, Wolf H. "The Effects of Temperature on the Action of Drugs." *Ann Arbor Rev. Pharmacol.* (1973), 13, 409–25.
Weihe, Wolf H. "Effects of Drugs in Adaptation to Heat and Cold." *Int. Jour. Biomet. Suppl.* (1976), 20, 126–36.
Fuhrman, Frederick. "Modification of the Action of Drugs by Heat." *Env. Physiol. and Psych. in Arid Conditions* (1963). UNESCO, Paris.
Fuhrman, G. J., and Fuhrman, F. A. "Effects of Temperature on the Action of Drugs." *Ann Arbor Rev. Pharmacol.* (1961), 1, 65–78.
Haavik, C. O., Collins, F. G., and Hardman, H. F. "Studies in the Mechanism of Hypothermic Action of Tetrahydrocannabinols," in *Temperature Regulation and Drug Action*, Proc. Symp. Paris 1973. Karger, Basel 1974, 293–309.
Petersen, William F. "Drug Sensitivity and the Meteorologic Environment." *New Int. Clinics* (1942), 1, 255–69.

APPENDIX G: **Systemic Classification of Symptoms and Signs of Tropical Neurasthenia**

Sargent, II, Frederick. "Tropical Neurasthenia: Giant or Windmill?" in *Env. Physiol. and Psych. in Arid Conditions* (1963). UNESCO, Paris.

APPENDIX H: Sheldon's Scale of Temperament

Sheldon, William. *The Varieties of Temperament* (1942). Harper & Row, New York.

APPENDIX I: Weather Events: Their Favorable and Unfavorable Influences on Health and Disease

Becker, Frederick. *Verein Deutscher Ingenieure* (1974), 116, 1367–454.

APPENDIX J: The Approach and Passage of Warm and Cold Fronts

Reifsnyder, William E. "What Is Weather?" in *Medical Climatology*, edited by S. Licht (1964). E. Licht, Publisher, New Haven.

APPENDIX K: Comparison of Body States and Phases

Petersen, William F. *The Patient and the Weather* (1934–8). Edwards Brothers, Ann Arobor.

APPENDIX L: Airs, Waters, and Places—Updated: Weather and Climate Spas Around the World

Wilkens, Emily. *Super Spas* (1976). Grosset & Dunlop, New York.

A Glossary of Human Biometeorology

Acclimatization: A form of physiological conditioning to specific atmospheric circumstances: hot or cold, warm or cool, dry or wet, high or low altitude. The body adapts to a new climate or weather circumstance (in days or weeks) by adjustments in blood composition and other thermoregulatory maneuvers, by changes in diet, speed of return to normal functioning.

Acetylcholine: A transmitter substance released by nerve endings of neurons in the parasympathetic nervous system to trigger impulses in adjacent nerve cells. Many of its effects (short-lived because it is quickly destroyed) resemble the effects of stimulating the vagus nerve (or vagotonia) slowing heartbeat, dilating the capillary bed, and other (cholinergic) symptoms often present in warm weather or climates.

Acidosis: A relative accumulation of acid, or loss of base or alkalines in the body (decreased pH or increased hydrogen ion concentration).

Adrenal Gland: Hormone-producing organ situated above the kidneys; produces adrenaline and noradrenaline in its core (medulla) and the corticosteroids in its shell (cortex). The latter are excreted in the urine as 17-KS and 17-OH (*ad* = beside, *ren* = kidney).

Adrenaline = Epinephrine: Hormone secreted by the adrenal medulla; the most powerful vasopressor substance known, increasing blood pressure, stimulating the heart muscle, accelerating the heart rate, and increasing cardiac output (*ad* = beside, *ren* = kidney).

Aerobics: Exercises and activities which force the consumption of oxygen.

Alkalosis: Relative accumulation of base or alkalines, or loss of acid in the body (increased pH, increased hydrogen ion concentration).

343

Allen's Rule: Long arms and legs, having a heat-loss advantage, are generally found in hot climates; short arms and legs, having a heat-retention advantage, are generally found in cold climates.

Altocumulus: Middle altitude; 8,000-feet high, fleecy cloud, with rounded masses or rolls in sharp outline, varying from white to nearly black. May produce showers or snow (*alto* = height, *cumulus* = heap).

Anabolism: The biological processes whereby more complex substances are built up as reserves (fats, carbohydrates, proteins) from the simpler components.

Anaerobic: Without air or oxygen.

Angina: Chest pains.

Anorexia: Severe lack of appetite for food.

Anoxia (Hypoxia): The result of any interference with the air (oxygen) supply to the tissues (literally, without oxygen).

Anticyclone (High): A closed atmospheric circulation of high pressure, rotating clockwise in the Northern Hemisphere (counterclockwise in the Southern Hemisphere). The air mass extends hundreds of thousands of miles, and migrates eastward and southward in the northern latitudes of the United States. From the north, they bring cold waves in winter and cool clear weather other seasons. From the south, they bring mild weather in winter and hot dry spells in summer.

ARS Phase: Anabolism, Reduction, and Spasm—characterizes the human body state in a cold environment, like shutting down the guest rooms and attic of a large house to conserve energy.

Atmosphere: An ocean or blanket of gases, clasped by gravitational force to the earth surface. Some three-fourths of the total atmospheric mass (estimated at one-millionth of the earth's mass) lies below 35,000 feet (10,700 meters, or 7 miles), consisting of 20.9 percent of oxygen gas and 79.1 percent nitrogen gas, by volume (*atmos* = vapor).

Autonomic: The self-regulatory or involuntary mechanisms of organic control, including chemical, physical, endocrine, nervous systems.

Barometric Pressure: The weight per unit area of a column of atmosphere resting on the earth's surface. Usually reported as the height of a mercury column the air pressure can support, or approximately 750 millimeters mercury (mm Hg), 14.7 pounds per square inch, 10^6 dynes per square centimeter, or 1,000 millibars. Air pressure generally is maximum at about 4 A.M. and 4 P.M. (This rhythm is pronounced in the tropics.) No known human organ (apart from eardrums and general membranes) detects barometric pressure specifically or exclusively.

Bergmann's Rule: Low body weights are found in high-temperature habitats, generally; and high body weights in low-temperature habitats, among warm-blooded animals, including man.

Bilious: The constitutional type that is hot and dry; irritable; choleric.

Biometeorology (Human): The study of direct and total effects of weather on the human organism, diseased or healthy.

Bioprognosis: System used in Germany to alert physicians of forthcoming weather changes and medical consequences to their patients.

Blue: A background color, as in the blue sky, favored by assertive northern-climate peoples, or cold-dwellers.

Buffers: The chemical substances that can neutralize and balance any excess, as, for instance, an excess of hydrogen ions.

Catabolism: The biological processes involved in the breakdown of more complex substances (reserves) with resulting freeing of energy for the use of the organism. It involves the process of oxidation.

Cerebrotonia: A temperament characterized by inhibition, restraint, hyperattentionality, mental overintensity. Tends to be dominated by central nervous system and its major sense organ, the skin. Statistically associated with ectomorphy.

Chinook: A warm, dry wind on the eastern side of the Rockies, in Colorado, Montana, British Columbia, called the "snow-eater" since it may send below-zero winter temperatures soaring.

Choleric: Hot; fiery; impetuous; irascible; bilious (liver bile).

Cirrus: High altitude (20,000 feet) ice-crystal cloud in form of white, delicate filaments or narrow banks, usually thin, wispy, in streaks (cirrus = hair lock).

Climate-Leap: A rapid change in climate due to travel, usually in a north-south direction.

Climatic Regression: Reacclimatization to one's old climate, following an extended period of acclimatization to a new climate.

"CLO" Unit: A standardized unit of clothing which has an insulation value of one vested, American, winter business suit.

CO_2: Carbon dioxide, the gaseous end product of carbon metabolism in the body, eliminated through the respiratory system.

COD Phase: Catabolism, Oxidation, Dilation. Characterizes the human body state in a warm environment, like opening the doors and windows of a large house to dissipate heat.

Cold, Cool: Subjective sensations of vasoconstriction, or shivering, objectively corresponding to environmental temperatures below thermal neutrality.

Cold Front: A cold air mass replacing a warm air mass is called a cold front. During its approach, passage, and recession, the weather usually unfolds in this order: increasing cloudiness, overcast with showers, clearing; altocumulus, cumulus cumulonimbus, few clouds; southerly or westerly winds, shifting, with gusts, from southwesterly to northwesterly (Northern Hemisphere), fresh wind; temperature steady or rising slightly, then dropping steadily or sharply; barometric pressure falls slowly before wind shift, then rises rapidly; humidity is steady, then drops sharply. Biotropic effects (strong to moderate): increased bronchial asthma, heart attacks, embolisms, kidney and gall bladder pains, stomach perforations.

Correlation, Co-relation: In statistics, the degree of departure of two quantities from independence, or the extent of their dependency upon one another. A correlation coefficient, when "zero" implies independence; when "plus one" implies strict dependence in the same directions; and when "minus one" the two quantities co-vary in opposite directions. The probability of two quantities varying in the same (or opposite) directions by chance is described by high significance (low chance-probability), or low significance (high chance-probability).

Cos: Famous Greek health resort and medical center; one of the small islands in the Dodecanesian group off the coast of Asia Minor; halfway station to Egypt and Crete.

Creatinine: A basic substance produce by protein metabolism; indicates daily protein turnover and appears nearly always in variable quantities in the urine (*creas* = meat).

Cumulonimbus: Thunderstorm cloud, exceptionally dense, tall, billowy, with great contrasts from inky black to brilliant white. Appears in vertical development (bases at 500 to 15,000 feet, tops at 10,000 to 50,000 feet) as huge towers or mountains. May be responsible for the formation of almost all other clouds (*cumulo* = heaped, *nimbus* = violent rain).

Cumulus: Low-altitude clouds in the form of billowed heaps of vertical development, with about horizontal bases at 1,000 feet and dome-shaped tops at 20,000 feet. May evolve into severe thunderstorm cloud (*cumulus* = heap).

Cyclone: A *low* central pressure region, relative to its surroundings, circulating counterclockwise in the Northern Hemisphere. Usually accompanied by inclement, often destructive, weather, hence sometimes called "storms" (*cycle* = circle).

Diastolic Blood Pressure: Roughly the resistance against which the heart pumps; the blood vessels exert a back pressure on the heart, elevated by their constriction in cold weather.

Disaster Episodes: Massive snowstorms or tornados will follow a general pattern (*warning, threat, impact, inventory, rescue, remedy,* and *recovery*) that is a population-wide analogy to an individual's response to stress (alarm, resistance, fatigue, exhaustion, recuperation) from emotion, exercise, or weather.

Diurnal: Pertaining to the day.

Dyspnea: Difficulty in breathing.

Dysuria: Painful urination.

Ecoclimate: The artificial weather indoors.

Ecology: The study of the integration of organic form, involving time and place; the mutual interrelation of organisms and environment.

Ectomorphy: A linear, vertical, fragile physique, dominated by maximal skin-surface area in proportion to body mass, and thus greatest sensory exposure to the elements. (Compare with **endomorphy** and **mesomorphy**.) Susceptible to abrupt swings and sharp peaks in weather; likely to be sensitive early in life, cold-sensitive, particularly symptomatic in the spring; females are likely to be weather-sensitive *pre*-menstrually (see **cerebrotonia**).

Edema: Excessive fluid in the tissues and cavities of the body; dropsy.

Effective Temperature: A comfort-health index of the thermal-humidity-wind environment. It indicates the objective combinations of air temperature, air moisture, and air movement that will evoke subjective sensations of comfort or discomfort. An effective temperature of 78°F (25°C) will evoke thermal neutrality.

Endocrines: The specific products of the glands of internal secretion, such as the thyroid and adrenal, important in the autonomic of involuntary regulation of the organism (*endo* = internal, *crine* = secreting).

Endomorphy: A rounded physique in which the digestive organs and viscera tend to dominate the body economy (compare **mesomorphy** and **ectomorphy**). Usually susceptible to long and gentle swings in weather changes, generally in the fall, later in life, especially vulnerable to the heat; and females likely to be weather-sensitive *post*-menstrually (see **viscerotonia**).

Epinephrine: Adrenaline (*epi* = above, *nephros* = kidney).

Focus: The localized area of tissue dysfunction or disease.

Foehn: A warm, dry alpine wind that causes discomfort among the inhabitants of Bavaria and Switzerland.

Front: The foremost border or interface between two air masses of different character, for instance, tropical or polar air. (First used by Hippocrates.)

Genius: Characterized by "disinhibition," a relative absence of the screen (or superego) between the organism and the environment. The involuntary nervous system and the unconscious may be so closely interwoven with the inorganic world and so pronounced that the genius is exquisitely weather-sensitive.

Geoclimate: The thermal-humidity environment of the atmospheric air mass.

Habitus: Body form or proportion; the kind of person; the constitution.

Heat: Energy in transit from a high-temperature region or object to a low-temperature region or object.

Heat Exhaustion: Failure of circulatory system; symptoms include loss of consciousness or strength, breathlessness, moist and cool skin. Victim requires salt, water and stimulants.

Heat Stroke: Failure of the sweating mechanism, extremely dangerous. The skin is hot and dry. The victim's entire body must be cooled with ice promptly.

Hemoglobin: The iron-containing pigment of the red blood corpuscles which carries oxygen from the lungs to the tissues.

5-HIAA (5—Hydroxyindole Acetic Acid): a chemical constituent of the urine created by metabolic destruction of serotonin, indicating its production and turnover (*indole* = indigo derivative).

High: See **anticyclone.**

Histamine: A physiologically active, nitrogen-containing product of cellular metabolism, powerfully effective in dilating small blood vessels (*histos* = tissue, *amine* = ammonia-like).

Homeostasis: A tendendy to uniformity or stability in the normal body states, internal environment, or fluid matrix of the organism.

Hormone: The specific product of certain tissues (glands of internal secretion) effective in coordinating bodily activities (*hormo* = stimulate).

Humours: The fluid constituents of the body, symbolized by blood, bile (yellow and black), and phlegm.

Humidity: The water-vapor content of air. *Absolute* humidity is the mass of water per unit volume of air. *Relative* humidity is the fraction or percentage concentration necessary to render the vapor saturated at a given temperature (ratio of air's actual vapor pressure to maximum saturation pressure at the same temperature). A rise of temperature reduces the relative (but not absolute) humidity; a fall increases it. High and low humidity have strong biotropic effects, especially cold-moist, and warm-dry. Relative humidity tends to be maximum at dawn (when fogs prevail) and minimum in the afternoons (when fogs disappear). Evaporation and cloudiness increase by day; condensation and cloudlessness, by night.

Hydration: Fluid excess. The fluid balance between the vascular beds (blood, lymph, etc.) and the cellular elements is maintained by constant exchange of water, both free and bound. Hydration and dehydration are opposite poles of this balance.

17-Hydroxysteroids (17 OH): The compounds formed by cortisone and similar adrenal cortex hormones which are secreted in the urine and indicate cortisone production and turnover (*hydroxy* = chemical configuration containing hydrogen = H and oxygen = O).

Hyperpyrexia: Highly elevated body temperature.

Hypothalamus: The central master gland of the brain. Secretes hormones called "releasing factors," which stimulate secondary hormone production in the pituitary gland ("tropins") and regulate growth, sex, thyroid, adrenal and visceral activity, emotions, sleep, pain, water balance—and temperature (*hypo* = below, *thalamus* = brain center or inner chamber).

Ions: Electrically charged atoms or molecules that populate the atmosphere. Their degree of biotropic effect are a matter of unsettled scientific controversy.

17-Ketosteroids (17 KS): Steroids which possess ketone groups on functional carbon atoms. The 17-Ketosteroids have a ketone group on the 17th carbon atom. They are found in the urine of normal men and women in excess in certain adrenal cortex and ovarian tumors (*keton* = chemical configuration containing an O = oxygen, *steato* = fat, *oid* = shaped).

Lability: Instability, sensitivity, usually of the involuntary (*autonomic*) nervous system.

Lightning: Charged ice particles, coated with water, may fall or ascend at different rates, delivering positive charge to clouds that act as vast static machines. When the charge buildup is too great to sustain, discharge (from one cloud to another or from cloud to earth) appears as lightning. Perhaps 100 such flashes per second (4 billion kilowatts of continuous power) occur over the entire earth.

Low: See **cyclone.**

Melancholic: The person stigmatized by "black bile."

Mesomorphy: A hard, dense, firm physique, relatively prominent in muscle. (Compare with **endomorphy** and **ectomorphy**); relatively insensitive to weather (see **somatotonia**).

Metabolism: The biochemical processes of the body, involving both the constructive as well as the destructive mechanisms incidental to life.

Meteorology: The science of weather and atmospheric phenomena. (First used by Hippocrates.) (*meteor* = things in the air.)

Meteorotropism: Any change in the organism (*trope* = turning; tendency) due to atmospheric agents (*meteor* = things in the air).

Miasma: Noxious influence of the atmosphere.

Microclimate: The thermal-humidity environment of a thin layer of air clinging to your body's skin.

Migraine: Serious unilateral headache, with associated symptoms in other organs.

Milieu: Environment; setting; the medium.

Morphological: Pertaining to structure, shape.

Neurohormones: Hormones stimulating neural mechanisms (*neuron* = nerve, *hormo* = stimulate).

Nimbostratus: Large, low- or middle-altitude, thick water cloud, grey-colored, dark, dull with ragged edges from which steady rain or snow falls. Its great density and thickness often obscures sunlight and makes it appear as if it is dimly lighted from within. Low-flying *scud*—black, patchy streaks—often accompany nimbostratus. (*nimbo* = violent rain, *stratus* = spread).

Noradrenaline = Norepinephrine: A hormone secreted by the adrenal medulla in response to visceral stimulation and stored in the chromaffin granules, being released predominantly in response to hypotension (*nor* = a chemical formulation of nitrogen: N,o: *ohne* = without, *r: radical* = chemical substituent).

Occlusion, Occluded Front: A composite formed as cold air overtakes and undercuts warm air, the steep wedge of cold air replacing the warm air at the earth's surface. A wedge of advancing warm air can displace surface cold air aloft, called a warm occlusion. Biotropic effects are strong and include increased reaction times, bronchial asthmas, heart infarcts, and incidence of deaths.

Paraphrase: A change, recondition or modification of the organism by environmental forces.

Parasympathetic: See **vagotonia, endomorphy, viscerotonia.**

Pendulation: Body swings from or to adrenaline and acetylcholine phases.

Peripheral: Marginal; outside, as, for instance, the extremities and skin.

pH: The symbol used to express the relative balance of hydrogen (acid) and hydroxyl (basic) ions. Lowering of pH means relative acidity; increase of pH, relative alkalinity.

Phlegmatic: Cold; moist, slow. Typified by mucus or phlegm.

Physiological: The normal, organic processes of the body (biochemical, biophysical).

Physiometeorology: The study of physiological consequences (blood chemistry and urine changes) of weather conditions or weather changes.

Pineal Gland: A cerebral body which may be sensitive to light and heat; may regulate the timing of our hormonal functions (*pineal* = pine-cone shaped).

Pituitary: The endocrine headquarters, situated underneath and obeying the hypothalamus, protruding from the brain and producing special hormones, the tropins, which regulate the activity of our endocrine glands (*pituita* = mucus).

Prognosis: Foretelling the outcome.

Psychometeorology: The study of psychological, emotional, or mental consequences (ability to concentrate, desire to work, pain sensitivity) of weather conditions or weather changes.

Psychopathic: Mentally disturbed.

Rainbow: A sheet of fog or spray illuminated from behind by strong white light will create one, sometimes two, concentric spectrum-colored rings, called rainbows. The inner ring is narrower and brighter, red inside and violet outside; the outer ring reverses these colors. White light entering spherical water droplets is reflected and refracted (color components traveling at different speeds) until, upon exiting, the colors are spread.

Range Ratio: The ratio of maximum to minimum range of variability in measurable human traits. The most closely guarded trait, with the smallest range ratio, is body temperature.

Red: Along with yellow or orange, an intrusive color, favored by gentle, tropical-climate peoples, or warm-dwellers.

Sanguine: Flushes, reddish.

Scotoma: Visual impression of flashing geometric figures, due to vascular disturbance.

Serotonin: A hormone serving as neurotransmitter of the brain. It is also produced in the enterochromaffin cells of the intestines and transported from there into the whole body where—when released—it may produce manifold irritant reactions (*serum* = blood fluid, *tonus* = pressure).

Skin: The sensory apparatus of the involuntary (**autonomic**) nervous system; relays sensations of hot or cold, touch, pressure, and pain from some ten million perceptor cells to the brain for appropriate action, which includes instructing the two million sweat glands and 44,000 feet of blood vessels to equilibrate temperature.

Sky Color: Clear blue skies come about from the scattering of sunlight by air molecules. The short wavelength (high frequency) blue component of sunlight is preferentially deviated. The presence of foreign particles in the atmosphere (aerosols, smog, haze, pollutants) will reduce the blueness.

Somatotonia: A temperament characterized by love of action, power, assertiveness, and push. Tends to be dominated by musculature. Statistically associated with **mesomorphy**.

Splanchnoperipheral: Abdominal versus peripheral organs, i.e., the balanced interplay of the functional state between the internal and external organs and vascular beds.

Splenetic: The constitutional type conditioned by too much "spleen"; malicious; peevish; fretful.

Stratocumulus: Low-altitude, light grey, rounded clouds, arranged in orderly groups, casting shadows, rarely producing snow or rain: blue occasionally shows through (*strato* = spread; *cumulus* = heaped).

Stress: The non-specific response of the body to any demand made upon it, whether emotional, physical, or atmospheric. The response may be generalized (the General Adaptation Syndrome) or localized (the Local Adaptation Syndrome).

Sympathicotonia: A state of the human organism in high gear, with a preponderant arousal of the sympathetic nervous system: adrenaline and noradrenaline stimulate sweat glands, dilate pupils and muscular arteries; heartbeat and respiration are stimulated, and digestive-organ activity is depressed. Normally these conditions occur during stress but may become pathologically chronic. See *ectomorphy, cerebrotonia*.

Syncope: Sudden loss of strength or temporary suspension of consciousness due to cerebral anemia.

Syndrome: A group of symptoms or disease-signs that occur together.

Systolic Blood Pressure: The pressure level at which heart pumps blood *out* of its cavities.

Temperature: A property that determines whether two systems are in energy equilibrium, their temperatures (measured on the same scale) are equal when neither system transfers energy or heat to the other. Human mouth temperatures, normally 98.6°F or 37°C (rectal temperature is 1°F higher), fluctuates during the course of a day by some 2°F. Air temperatures tend to reach maximum two to three hours after (local) noon, minimum at sunrise.

Thermal Neutrality: A subjective feeling of "comfort" or "pleasant," neither too warm nor too cold; corresponds objectively to absence of blood vessel constriction or dilation, sweating or shivering, or any other thermoregulatory effort.

Thermal Stress: When heat production exceeds loss at high air temperature and humidity, heat stress can provoke heat stroke or heat exhaustion. At low temperatures, heat loss exceeds production; cold stress may culminate in shock, exposure, or frostbite.

Thermoregulation (Temperature Regulation): *Conscious* regulation of body temperature by clothing or artificial external measures can adapt to wide temperature range ($-100°F$ to $+250°F$). *Involuntary* thermal regulation, shunting blood between the body core and periphery, can equilibrate in a narrow range ($82°F$ to $110°F$).

Thunder: The sound emitted by rapidly expanding gases along a lightning discharge channel. Most electrical energy of the discharge heats the atmospheric gases precipitously, generating a pressure wave, followed by rarefactions and compressions heard in thunder. Rarely heard further than fifteen miles away, typically ten miles distant. Timing the lag between lightning flash and first onset of thunder, in seconds, gives its distance in one-fifths of a mile.

Thyroid: The gland which covers our throat and neck like a shield. It produces hormones which regulate metabolism, heart action, and mental acuity (*thyreos* = shield, *eidos* = shape). (See Appendix G)

Tropical Neurasthenia: Nervous debility among European settlers in the tropics. The warning symptoms include difficulty in concentration, speed and capacity for thought; forgetfulness; lassitude, irritability, indecision, boredom, and many others.

Vagotonia: A state of the human organism in low gear, preponderantly sluggish, relaxed and vegetative, governed by the vagus nerve, the primary component of the parasympathetic nervous system. Compare **viscerotonia, endomorphy.**

Variograph: A recording device that measures rapid-but-minute fluctuations in the atmospheric pressure. These are found at the interfaces of cold fronts, warm fronts, and at occlusions, and appear to be associated with our subjective sense of well-being, and ailments.

Vasoconstriction: Peripheral blood vessels in the capillary bed (vasomotor system) contract their caliber in response to a cold environment (or other stressors). This conserves body heat by centralizing the warm-blood mass. In warm environments or upon relaxation of vasoconstriction, the vessels expand, allowing the blood to return in vasodilation.

Viscerotonia: A temperament characterized by love of comfort, food, people, and affection. Tends to be dominated by viscera. Statistically associated with *endomorphy*. See **vagotonia.**

Vortex: A whirling mass of fluid (gas or liquid); a circulatory air mass, cyclonal (low pressure) or anticyclonal (high pressure).

Warm, Hot: Subjective sensations of vasodilation or sweating, objectively corresponding to environmental temperatures above thermal neutrality.

Warm Front: Occurs when a warm air mass advances, replacing a cold air mass and overriding it. During approach and passage, the following weather sequence usually unfolds: increased wide cloudiness, first cirrus, then cirrostratus, altostratus, stratus, clearing to cumulus; rain, snow, fog for considerable periods over a wide area, tapering off; easterly winds, speed increasing, shifting to southerly (in Northern Hemisphere); temperature increasing slowly or considerably; barometric pressure falling with wind shifts, then remaining steady or falling slightly; humidity increasing and then stabilizing. Biotropic effects (strong to moderate) include disturbed sleep, heart infarcts, heart deaths, death rate increases.

Weathering: The action of the atmosphere or the elements on objects or persons exposed to its influences; wearing away or disintegrating due to the weather; adapting and accommodating to weather changes; good or bad weather conditions.

Weather Phases (Classification Schemes): Of some seventy-five classification-schemes for weather or climate, few have considered comfort or discomfort as the organizing principle. The Bad Tölzer weather phase system is based on man's temperature-humidity environment and its evolving favorable or unfavorable biologic effects. Other systems consider the changes in air mass, the effects on agriculture, or dynamic circulations of the atmosphere.

Weather-sensitivity (Objective): Symptoms or ailments associated statistically with specific phases of weather. Heart attacks tend to occur in cold fronts; bronchial asthma in cyclonal weather, reaction time and traffic accidents in low-pressure, downgliding air masses.

Weather-sensitivity (Subjective): A set of symptoms, or syndrome, that one-third to two-thirds of humanity subjectively ascribes to weather conditions. The remainder, at lower intensity, report the same syndrome. Out of thirty-seven symptoms the leading symptoms are "tiredness," "bad moods," "disinclination to work," "head pressure," "restless sleep."

Wilder's Law of Initial Value: Antecedent conditions determine response. The higher the physiological level of arousal, or involuntary (*autonomic*) nervous system, the less the tendency for the process once begun to increase further. This principle, related to the phenomenon of "accommodation" during electrical excitations of nerves, explains how a certain biometeorological effect created by an influx of cold air (a cold front) may differ in the same person at different times or different people at the same time, depending upon whether the cold air mass was preceded by a warm front or a number of cold fronts passed at short intervals. Beyond a medium range of initial values, there is a tendency to paradoxic or reversed response.

Wind: Air movements relative to the earth's surface, or circulations of the atmosphere due to thermal convections driven by the sun's heat. Winds may be permanent (trade winds, if tropics), seasonal (monsoons, mountain or valley winds), and local (storm interruptions). Winds increase and veer by day, decrease and back by night.

Zeus: Literally "bright sky" or "day." In ancient Greece, the sky god, father of all the gods, governed weather, good and evil, future and past.

Credits

Endpapers courtesy of The Library of Congress, Washington, D.C. Chapter openings reproduced by permission of the Bibliothèque Nationale, Paris. "Cold Weather," from *One Man's Meat* by E. B. White. Copyright 1943 by E. B. White. Renewed 1971 by E. B. White. Reprinted by permission of Harper and Row Publishers, Inc. Newspaper cartoon, "A Difference of Opinion," courtesy of the New York Public Library Picture Collection. Illustration, Wilder's Law of Initial Value, from *Annals of New York Academy of Sciences* (1962) 98, 1222, Helmut Selbach, reprinted by permission of the publisher. Table, Wilder's Law of Initial Value from *Stimulus and Response* (1967), Joseph Wilder (John Wright & Sons: Bristol) reprinted by permission of the publisher. Stephen Sondheim's lyric, "Love Is In The Air," from *A Funny Thing Happened On The Way To The Forum*, copyright © 1962 Chappell & Co., reprinted courtesy of Mr. Sondheim. The tables, Psychometeorology, and Favorable And Unfavorable Weather Influences, from *Fortschritte Medizin* (1977) 95, 268, Volker Faust, et al. adapted and reprinted by permission of the author and publisher. The table, Symptoms of Weather Sensitivity, from *Biometeorologie* (1976), Volker Faust, Hippokrates Verlag: Stuttgart, reprinted by courtesy of the author and publisher. The illustration, Percentage of Weather-Sensitives by Age and Sex, from *Therapiewoch* (1977) 27 6, 858, Karl Dirnagl, reprinted courtesy of the author and the publisher. The "clo" men and weather forecast symbols, from *Weather Roy. Met. Soc.* (1973) 28, 478, Andris Auliciems, reprinted courtesy of the author. "Clo" Units Appropriate for Comfort, from *ASHRAE Journal* (April 1976) 16, 4, 41, R. G. Nevins, et al., reprinted by permission of the publisher. The maps of Temperature Zones In The World, Industrial Production, Climatic Energy, and Diseases of the World, from *World Population and Production* W. S. Woytinsky, and E. S. Woytinsky, copyright © 1953 The Twentieth Century Fund, New York, reprinted by permission of the publisher. The graphs, Religious Dominance of Countries by Temperature, and The Latitude of Coups, from *Climate and the Affairs of Men* (1975) Nels Winkless III, and Iben Browning (Harper & Row: New York) reprinted courtesy of Dr. Browning. The Robert Frost poems from *The Poetry of Robert Frost*, edited by Edward Connery Latham. Copyright 1923, 1928, © 1969 by Holt, Rinehart and Winston. Copyright 1951, © 1956 by Robert Frost. Reprinted by permission of Holt, Rinehart and Winston, Publishers. The table, Health Consequences of Winds, adapted from *Fortschritte Medizin* (1977) 95, 268, Volker Faust, Otto Harlfinger, R. Neuwirth, reprinted by permission of the publisher and authors.

The quotations on Lincoln and Douglas and the weather, from *Lincoln-Douglas: The Weather As Destiny* (1943), William F. Petersen (C. C. Thomas: Springfield, Ill.) reprinted by permission of the publisher. The tables, Deities and the Weather, and Sacred Texts Refer to Weather Motifs, adapted from *Weather and Man*, Hans Neuberger, Television Lecture Notes, Copyright © 1977 University of South Florida, reprinted courtesy of Dr. Neuberger. The quote on Greek gods as hallucinations, from *The Origin of Consciousness in the Breakdown of the Bicameral Mind*, Copyright © 1976 by Julian Jaynes (Houghton Mifflin: Boston) reprinted by permission of the publisher. Illustrations of Semele, Prometheus, and Jupiter Destroying the Titans, reprinted by permission of Bibliothèque Nationale, Paris. The graph, Weather And Personality, from *Therapiewoch* (1977), 27, 6, 858, Karl Dirnagl, reprinted courtesy of the author and the publisher. The table, Weather Phases and T.H.E., adapted from materials kindly furnished by Hans Schirmer (German Weather Service: Offenbach/Main) reprinted with permission of Dr. Schirmer. Bioprognosis samples (health-weather forecasts) reprinted courtesy of German Weather Service. Illustrations of The Human Thermal Response, Computer Analog to Human Thermoregulation, and Our Response to Temperature, from *Handbook of Physiology* (in press), and Brady Memorial Lecture, University of Missouri (1969) and *Environmental Research* (1967) 1, 1–20, James D. Hardy, et al., reprinted by courtesy of the author. The attributes of right and left, from *Encounter* (1977) Donald G. MacRae, reprinted by permission of the publisher. The graphs, Change In Organ Function With Age, from the *Journal of Gerontology* (1977) 32, 402, Harold Baftis and Frederick Sargent, II, reprinted by permission of Dr. Sargent. Stephen Sondheim's lyric, "I Remember Sky," from *Evening Primrose*, copyright © 1966 Burthen Music Co., Chappell & Co., reprinted courtesy of Mr. Sondheim. The quote by Dennis Driscoll about belief in human-weather response from *Environmental Research* (1971) 4 233–42, reprinted by kind permission of Dr. Driscoll. The history of human biometeorology (Appendix A) adapted in part from *Biometeorologie* (1977) Volker Faust (Hippokrates Verlag: Stuttgart) reprinted by permission of the author and the publisher. Ranking of Weather Influences (Appendix B) reprinted from *The Value of the Weather* (1970), W. J. Maunder (Methuen & Co.: London) reprinted by permission of the publisher. Fabric Data and "Clo" Values (Appendix E), from *ASHRAE Journal* (April 1974) 16 4, 41–3, by R. G. Nevins, et al., reprinted by permission of the publisher. Systemic Classification of Tropical Neurasthenia (Appendix G), from "Tropical Neurasthenia: Giant Or Windmill?," in *Environmental Physiology and Psychology in Arid Conditions* (1963), by Frederick Sargent, II, UNESCO: Paris, reprinted by permission of Dr. Sargent. Weather Events (Appendix I), and Tolzer Weather Phases (Chapter 9 Notes), from *Verein Deutscher Ingenieure* (1974) 16, 1367, Frederick Becker, reprinted by permission of the author. Approach and passage of Fronts (Appendix J), from "What Is Weather?,"

William Reifsnyder, in *Medical Climatology* (1964), edited by S. Licht (E. Licht, Publisher: New Haven) reprinted by permission of the author. The illustration, You And The Drug And The Atmosphere, from *International Journal of Biometeorology* (1976) 20, 125, by Wolf H. Weihe, reprinted courtesy of Dr. Weihe. The illustration, Clustering of Good And Bad Reactions To Weather, from *Therapiewoch* (1977) 27 6, 858, by Karl Dirnagl, reprinted courtesy of the publisher and Dr. Dirnagl. The variograph illustration, (Chapter 9 Notes), from *Universitas* (1975) 30 5, 501, by Hans Richner, reprinted courtesy of Dr. Richner.

Acknowledgments

The hospitality of many European scientists, and their generosity in discussing biometeorological research, made this American comfortable there and grateful. Many of these physicians and meteorologists have also read portions or all of this manuscript, and offered valuable suggestions. It is a pleasure to thank Karl Dirnagl and Peter Krölling of the Institute of Medical Balneology and Climatology, University of Munich; Volker Faust of the Psychiatric and Nerve Clinic, University of Freiburg; Otmar Harlfinger, Medical Meteorology Department of the German Weather Service in Freiburg; Bernard Primault of the International Society of Biometeorology and the Swiss Meteorological Institute in Zurich; Hans Richner, Atmospheric Physics at the ETH in Zurich; Hans Schirmer and his colleagues at the German Weather Service in Offenbach/Main; Solco W. Tromp, Biometeorological Research Centre in Leiden; Wolf H. Weihe, Biological Central Laboratory at the Kantonsspital and University of Zurich; and Ingrid Weiss of the German Military Command's Geophysics Office in Traben-Trarbach.

I have also been fortunate to receive encouragement and perceptive comments about the ideas in this book from American scientists who have taken time from their busy schedules to read the manuscript, or to impart the benefit of their clinical and research experiences. I thank Dennis M. Driscoll, Department of Meteorology, Texas A&M University; Frederick Sargent, II, School of Public Health, University of Texas at Houston; Jonathan Charry, Rockefeller University; Ana Glick, Psychiatric Institute, Columbia University College of Physicians and Surgeons; James D. Hardy, John B. Pierce Foundation Laboratory, Yale University; Dick Hallgren, National Oceanic and Atmospheric Administration, Department of Commerce, Rockville, Maryland; William T. Hodge, National Climatic Center, Environmental Data Service, National Oceanic and Atmospheric Administration, Asheville, North Carolina; Charles L. Hosler, College of Earth and Mineral Sciences, Pennsylvania State University; Helmut Landsberg, University of Maryland; Hans Neuberger, formerly of Pennsylvania State University; Thomas D. Potter, Environmental Data Service, National Oceanic and Atmospheric

Administration, Washington; and Harry Wiener of Pfizer and Company.

Others have graced this book: Elizabeth Hubbard and Jeremy Bennett, Lenore Migdal, Kiki Nelson, Louis K. Nelson, Marion Neustadter, William Peisachowitsch, Richard Bader, Dora Wechsler, Ted Scher; Neale Ward, Allen D. Tanney, Jeannie Pfeiffer, and Paul J. Rosch. Stephanie Vendetti converted my illegible scrawl into a typed manuscript with great efficiency and kindness. Capri Fillmore, my research assistant, helped in the library, and Dietlinde Nitta did some difficult translations.

George C. de Kay, my editor at Evans, urged me to simplify the complex ideas; any clarity, brevity and perhaps a few short words are due to him. Diane Gedymin's patience and tact were admirable. This is not quite the book that Peter Matson asked me to write, but I would not have begun this fascinating topic without him.

About the Author

STEPHEN ROSEN is the author of *Future Facts: The Way Things Are Going to Work in the Future in Technology, Science, Medicine, and Life*. Popular articles by him about human behavior, science, and the future have appeared in *The Wall Street Journal, Penthouse, Forum, Innovation, New Scientist, The New York Times, Television Quarterly*, and in over 150 papers of the Field Newspaper Syndicate.

His book on astrophysics, and his research papers in *Nature, The Physical Review, Il Nuovo Cimento, La Recherche*, and other international scientific journals, deal with the origins of cosmic radiation and its influence in the earth's atmosphere. He has taught at the University of Pennsylvania, Bryn Mawr College, the State University of New York, and Fairleigh Dickinson University.

Dr. Rosen is a veteran of the Hudson Institute, a consultant to several corporations, and has held joint appointments at the Centre d'Etudes Nuclèaires in Saclay and the Institut d'Astrophysique in Paris. He lives in New York City.

Index

Weather sensitivity symptoms, 21-27
Weather Sensitivity Risk Factor
  profile, 4-5, 206-207
Weather stress, xiii, 32, 51, 52-54, 56-58,
  119, 120-121, 129, 222-223, 227,
  228, 230, 244, 250, 321, 340
Weihe, Wolf, 64-65, 275
"Well-being," 215-216, 332
West Africa, 108
Wheeler, Raymond, 91-92
Wilder's Law of Initial Value, 14-17, 44,
  200, 226, 227, 228, 244
Wind Tower of Athens, 2, 17
Wind turbulence, 145

Winds, 312
  and diseases, 140-141, 147-150
  and elderly, 7-8
  and emotions, 145
  and physical fitness, 145
  world winds, 146
Woodruf, Charles Edward, 61, 63
Wurtman, Richard J., 69

Yogi, 258

Zephyrus, 134
Zeus, 176, 180, 185-196, 269
  cults, 193-194
Zone of contentment, 75-76